Sport and Tourism: Globalization, Mobility and Identity

Sport and Tourism: Globalization, Mobility and Identity

James Higham and Tom Hinch

AMSTERDAM · BOSTON · HEIDELBERG · LONDON · NEW YORK · OXFORD
PARIS · SAN DIEGO · SAN FRANCISCO · SINGAPORE ·SYDNEY · TOKYO
Butterworth-Heinemann is an imprint of Elsevier

Butterworth-Heinemann is an imprint of Elsevier
Linacre House, Jordan Hill, Oxford OX2 8DP, UK
30 Corporate Drive, Suite 400, Burlington, MA 01803, USA

First edition 2009

British Library Cataloguing in Publication Data

A catalogue record for this book is available from the British Library

Library of Congress Cataloging-in-Publication Data

Higham, James E. S.
  Sport and tourism: globalization, mobility and identity/James Higham and Tom Hinch.–
1st ed.
    p. cm.
Includes bibliographical references and index.
ISBN: 978-0-7506-8610-5
1. Sports and tourism. I. Hinch, Tom. II. Title.
G156.5.S66H54 2009
338.4'791–dc22

                                        2008053611

ISBN: 978-0-7506-8610-5

Printed and bound in Great Britain

09 10 11 12 10 9 8 7 6 5 4 3 2 1

For information on all Butterworth-Heinemann
publications visit our website at elsevierdirect.com

Contents

List of Tables

List of Figures

List of Case Studies

Acknowledgements

This book, like those that we have worked on previously, represents a combined effort involving a number of people who must be acknowledged. Francesca Ford and Eleanor Blow (Oxford) provided friendly and effective publisher support. The planning of this book was made possible by a grant from the University of Alberta, which allowed the authors to work together in Edmonton, Canada, in November 2006. We are grateful to Professor George Benwell (Dean, School of Business, University of Otago) and Professor Mike Mahon (Dean, Faculty of Physical Education and Recreation, University of Alberta) who supported our respective study leave applications in 2007, and continue to support our research collaborations. The William Evans Fellowship (University of Otago) is acknowledged for providing the funding that supported Tom's visit to the University of Otago in February–April 2008.

The research assistance provided initially by Sarah Fredric (University of Otago) and latterly by Layla Carruthers (University of Otago) and Cory Kulczycki (University of Alberta) was instrumental to the completion of this book. We are also indebted to our case study contributors whose works add critical dimensions to this book; Scarlett Cornelissen (Stellenbosch University), Tara Duncan (University of Otago), Mark Falcous (University of Otago), Ken Hodge (University of Otago), Ian Jones (Bournemouth University), Chris Lonsdale (Chinese University of Hong Kong), Dan Mason (Alberta, Canada), Dieter Müller (University of Umeå), Anton Oliver (All Black), Jay Scherer (University of Alberta) and Bob Stebbins (University of Calgary). Colleagues at the School of Physical Education (University of Otago), including Mark Falcous, Ken Hodge, Doug Booth and Steve Jackson have provided stimulating discussions that have informed our thinking considerably.

Our deliberations on the subjects of sport and tourism have been influenced by the writings of, and discussions with, a number of scholars who are cited throughout this book. An invitation from the European Association of Sport Management (EASM) to present a paper on sport and tourism authenticity (Newcastle, September 2005) greatly informed our thoughts presented in Chapter 8 (*Authentic experiences*). Professor Mike Weed's (Canterbury Christ Church University) organization of the sport tourism session at the 2005 EASM conference and subsequent editing of a special issue of the *European Sport Management Quarterly* provided valuable opportunities for us to develop our thoughts on the subject of sport and authentic experiences.

Our colleagues continue to provide the stimulation of a collegial academic and wider working environment. They include, at the University of Otago, Julia Albrecht, Charlene Bowden, Neil Carr, Tara Duncan, Helen Dunn, David Duval, Diana Evans, Donna Keen, Teresa Leopold, Brent Lovelock, Richard Mitchell, Jan Mosedale, Caroline Orchiston, Arianne Reis, David Scott, Eric Shelton, Anna Thompson, Hazel Tucker and Richard Wright; and at the University of Alberta, Suzanne de la Barre, Karen Fox, Suzanne French, Liz Halpenny, Cory Kulczycki, Dan Mason, Carol McNeil, David Mitsui, PearlAnn Reichwein, Greg Ramshaw, Jay Scherer, Gordon Walker and Aggie Weighill.

This book has been written during extended periods away from home during which time the authors have received the great support of family and friends: Polly and Charles Higham, Liz and Fergus Moynihan, Tim and Claire Moynihan, Martin and Sarah Talks, Richard and Jill Spearman, Tom Higham and Katerina Douka, John and Jo Higham, Shelagh Hinch, Wayne and Elaine Jefcoate, and Jane and Richard Higham.

Finally, the support of our immediate families; Linda, Alexandra, Katie and George, and Lorraine, Lindsay and Gillian, has been critical to this book and everything else besides.

James Higham
Dunedin, New Zealand

Thomas Hinch
Edmonton, Canada

PART 1

Introduction

CHAPTER 1

Sport and Tourism: Globalization, Mobility and Identity

It has been widely stated that heightened personal mobility (Hall, 2004; Burns & Novelli, 2008) and increasing interest in both passive and active engagements in physical activities (Glytpis, 1991) are two defining features of late twentieth century and early twenty-first century societies. Unexplained, such claims risk accusations of gross generalization. In many societies, the higher reaches of personal mobility remain the exclusive domain of the privileged (Hall, 2004). Similarly, participation in many sport and recreational pursuits is rigidly defined by social class, race and gender (Gibson, 2005). 'Irrespective of culture or historical period, people use sport to distinguish themselves and to reflect their status and prestige' (Booth & Loy, 1999:1). Booth and Loy (1999) state that similar status groups generally share lifestyle and consumption patterns. This is a claim that relates equally to the consumption of sport and the consumption of tourism. Participation in physical activities remains beset with concerns surrounding increasingly sedentary and unhealthy lifestyles and obesity in some societies (Coakley, 2007).

However, interests in contemporary mobility and increasingly diverse engagements in sport are such that the intersection of the two has become an area of considerable research scholarship (Glyptis, 1982; Maguire, 1993, 1994; Standeven & De Knop, 1999; Weed & Bull, 2004; Gibson, 2004). There has been a relatively longstanding tradition of sport-related tourism research with a focus on sports mega-events (Hinch & Higham, 2004). Situated initially from the 1980s within the events management literature, sports mega-events have featured prominently in discourses on events management and tourism (Ritchie, 1984; Getz, 1997). This focus has moved beyond often flawed economic impact analyses of mega-events (Crompton, 1995; Mules & Faulkner, 1996) to more fine-grained and critical analyses of sports mega-events (Hall & Hodges, 1996; Hiller, 2000; Olds, 2000; Cornelissen, 2004; Preuss, 2005; Weed, 2008). However, as Cornelissen

CONTENTS

(2004:40) notes, 'since the vast majority of mega-events are hosted by industrialized states, discourse and research on the processes and impacts of these events tend to be framed around the economic and political circumstances characteristic to the developed world'. It is evident that much critical scholarly work addressing the growing diversity of sports events remains outstanding.

WIDER AND CRITICAL PERSPECTIVES

Cornelissen's (2004) observation that discourse and research on the processes and impacts of sports events are situated firmly in the circumstances of the developed world bears considerable influence over the discussions presented in the following chapters. This bias has also occurred at the expense, at least in relative terms, of more critical and nuanced considerations of the wider manifestations of sport-related tourism. Bull and Weed (1999:143) noted ten years ago that 'sport tourism is really a collection of separate niches but while tourism associated with mega-sporting events … in major urban locations is clearly evident, the potential of sport as a tourism niche elsewhere is perhaps less well appreciated'. This criticism remains as applicable today as it was a decade ago. The focus of much research serving the field remains largely concentrated on high profile, mainstream and often professional or semi-professional sports, and global or international sports events that typically take place in major cities in the Western developed world.

One response to Weed and Bull (1999) and Cornelissen (2004) is to critically explore the wider manifestations of sport-related tourism and mobility. There are some notable contributions that have followed this approach. In terms of sports events, research into bundling (Chalip & McGuirty, 2004) and leverage (Chalip, 2006; Chalip & Leyns, 2002) signal a move away from descriptive event evaluation, to a more strategic and analytical approach. Such studies represent a paradigmatic shift from *ex post* to *ex ante* analyses of events (Chalip, 2008). Hiller (2000) and Olds (2000) present critical analyses of the lower socio-economic community impacts felt by the residents of cities bidding for and hosting sports mega-events. Cornelissen and Solberg (2007) examine South Africa's hosting of the 2010 football world cup in terms of the migration of athletic talent, observing South Africa as an alternative to Western Europe which, in terms of the migration of African footballers, is '… mostly viewed as exploitative and an extension of neo-imperialist relations between the continent and its former colonial powers' (Cornilessen & Solberg, 2007:674). Gratton, Shibli and Coleman (2005:233) have addressed the growing competition between second tier cities to host 'less globally recognized sports events in a wide range of other sports where spectator interest is less assured and where the economic benefits are not so clear cut'. Others have contributed empirical insights into elements of production, consumption and experience associated with non-elite (Carmichael & Murphy, 1996; Ryan & Lockyer, 2002) and non-competitive sports events (Nogawa et al., 1996). These works are indicative of a move towards move critical and nuanced insights into sports events.

However, beyond events comparatively little recognition has been given to the wider relationships that may exist between sport and tourism. Recognition of this intersection of interests was established with a platform of work in the 1980s and 1990s (Glyptis, 1982; Gibson, 1998; Standeven & De Knop, 1999). Standeven and De Knop (1999), for example, describe sport tourism as the sum of the cultural experiences of activity and place. Efforts to build upon this platform with more critical (Weed & Bull, 2004; Hinch & Higham, 2004) and theoretical (Gibson, 2005) contributions have followed. Weed and Bull (2004) call for a move beyond defining sport tourism phenomena and the development of classifications and typologies of sport tourists (e.g., Hall, 1992; Gammon & Robinson, 1997; Standeven & De Knop, 1999; Reeves, 2000). They present a compelling argument that an understanding of the unique manifestations of sport-related tourism may be well served by conceptualizing sport tourism as a composite of activity, people and place. Alternatively, Higham and Hinch (2006) adopt a geographical approach to raise questions that are situated within the concepts of space, place and environment. They do so to highlight research questions relating to the spatio-temporal travel flows associated with sport (e.g., as it relates to tourism seasonality), place attachment and meanings, and the manifestations of environmental change associated with sport and tourism at various (local, regional, national or global) scales of analysis.

Alongside these conceptual contributions, the theoretical platform that serves the study of sport tourism has been initiated (Gibson, 2005). The adoption of concepts and theories from related fields has provided theoretically informed insights into the study of sport and tourism. The use of leisure constraints theory (Hinch, Jackson, Hudson & Walker, 2005), destination branding theory (Chalip & Costa, 2005), role theory (Gibson, 2005) and concepts such as authenticity (Hinch & Higham, 2006) and serious leisure (Jones & Green, 2005) are recent examples. To these conceptual and theoretical foundations have been added an expanding and diverse range of empirical contributions that address specific elements of the relationship between sport and tourism. The aforementioned study of sports event leverage (Chalip, 2006; Chalip & Leyns, 2002), for example, has progressed from the study of events into the wider field of elite sport (Sparvero & Chalip,

2007). This work builds upon a body of work that critically explores sport as it relates to destination branding (Chalip & Costa, 2005; Xing & Chalip, 2006), sports media and destination image (Chalip, Green & Hill, 2003) and destination marketing (Harrison-Hill & Chalip, 2005). These are notable contributions, at the very least for providing theoretically informed empirical insights into the potential diversity of sport tourism phenomena and the unique challenges and complexities with which they may be associated. But many relevant questions remain largely or entirely unanswered.

Hitherto, the relationship between sport and tourism in regional and peripheral economies has been generally limited to high profile winter (e.g., skiing and snowboarding) and other nature-based adventure sports (e.g., Hudson, 1999, 2003). Exceptions include studies on sport and tourism in regional economies (Chalip & Costa, 2005) and peripheral areas (however, peripherality may be defined in a spatial, economic or political sense) such as rural Europe (e.g., Wales, *see* Weed & Bull, 2004; Portugal, *see* Costa & Chalip, 2005) and Malta (Weed & Bull, 2004). Little focus has fallen upon environmental impacts, either local/regional (e.g., environmental/ecological impacts) or wider national or global environmental change (e.g., climate change), despite calls to this effect (Gössling & Hall, 2005). The unique manifestations and challenges associated with sport and tourism in developing world countries have been poorly served by researchers (Cornelissen, 2004). The roles played by sport and tourism in indigenous and non-Western religious communities have also been largely neglected (Hinch & de la Barre, 2005). Beyond the considerable research effort that has been directed towards mega-events and the interests of cities that host them, relatively little attention has been paid to sport and tourism interests in the wider context. Less apparent are critical considerations of sport-related tourism in terms of globalization, patterns of personal mobility (and other contemporary mobilities) and manifestations of personal and collective identity, all of which bear considerable relevance to tourism places.

BEYOND DEFINING PHENOMENA

Andrews (2006) observes that the definition of terms is a common starting point in the academic discussion of any phenomenon (e.g., sport or tourism) or, in this case, phenomena (i.e., sport *and* tourism). Indeed, this is true to the point that the definition of terms by academics has become an obligatory and in many cases burdensome element of many scholarly discussions. While well intended, the proliferation of definitions that seek to specifically delineate socially constructed phenomena is bound to prove to be an exercise in futility. A proliferation of definitions, many of which are used barely beyond those who propose them, can counter the advance of scholarship. However, what is necessary from the outset of this book is the establishment of parameters around which to understand the phenomena of sport and tourism as they are addressed in the pages that follow.

The defining parameters of sport are well established (Coakley, 2007). McPherson, Curtis and Loy (1989:15) consider sport as 'a structured, goal-oriented, competitive, contest-based, ludic physical activity'. Sport is structured by rules that may be manifested in the form of defined playing areas, duration of play and rules of engagement. Rules vary from the strictly enforced (often associated with higher levels of competition) to the unwritten or unspoken. Sport is goal-oriented insofar as participants may seek to attain certain levels of achievement or competence. Goal orientation may be directed towards some form of inter-personal competition as expressed in terms of winning and losing. Duda and Nicholls' (1992) ego ('being the best') and task ('doing my best') competitive orientations aptly describe this distinction. That said, competition may be interpreted more widely in terms of competing against personal standards (e.g., time), degrees of difficulty (e.g., course design) or the forces of nature (e.g., challenges of terrain, climate or other more or less natural phenomena). Closely associated with competition is the contest-based nature of sport in which uncertain outcomes are determined by a combination of physical prowess, strategy, skill, composure under pressure and, to a greater or lesser degree, chance. Physical prowess consists of physical speed, stamina, strength, and skill and, within the context of competition, is one of the most consistent criterion used to define sport (Gibson, 1998). In this book we adopt a deliberately broad and inclusive approach to define sport so as to accommodate recreational as well as competitive pursuits.

These criteria give some meaning to the term 'sport' as used in this book. However, they fail to adequately express the diverse and dynamic nature of sport phenomena. Thus, while sports are as old as civilizations, and while many of the criteria outlined in the previous paragraph have defined sports since the dawn of civilization, these criteria do not capture the changing place of sports in societies over time. Coakley (2007:7) notes that 'some scholars reject the idea that sports can be defined once and for all time and decide to use an alternative approach to identifying and studying sports in society'. As Andrews (2006:1) observes, 'although physically-based competitive activities are a feature of virtually all human civilisations, the popular myth of sport as a fixed and immutable category is little more than a pervasive, if compelling, fiction'. Thus Andrews (2006) gives priority to an interpretive strategy in which sports, different forms of sport and sport experiences are situated within their socio-historical context. Sports, then, are a reflection of their historical and social circumstances. This point is imbedded in Bale's (1989) simple but useful suggestion that sport may be defined by what features in the sports section of local newspapers. The content of any daily newspaper will be a reflection of the historical and social context of the day. If nothing else, scrutiny of the sports pages of local newspapers confirms the vast diversity of sports relative to their situation in place and time (Hinch & Higham, 2004).

The socio-historical construction of sport that is advocated by Coakley (2007) and Andrews (2006) serves our purposes in this book well. This approach allows due recognition of the fact that sports are dynamic. Sports and sports events are constantly being adapted to reflect the changing face of the societies within which they are set (Keller, 2001). These dynamics have been illustrated in recent years by the changing fortunes of highly structured team sports relative to individualized and unstructured sports (de Villiers, 2001; Murray & Dixon, 2000; Thomson, 2000). Keller (2001) notes that organised sports are in decline relative to the uptake of new generation freestyle sports. In many such cases (e.g., snowboarding and surfing) these sports are built upon strong subcultural associations, which provide participants with a sense of personal and/or collective identity. Performance and rankings have become secondary to aesthetics and style. As such, in this book we use a broad and inclusive approach to understand sports that may vary dramatically between places, and evolve – sometimes very rapidly – in different societies over time.

We adopt a similar approach to define tourism. In doing so we seek to move beyond traditional reductionist definitions of tourism to embrace alternative conceptions that acknowledge the wider interdependencies that are influenced by and influence tourism phenomena. This approach is informed by the writing of Coles, Duval and Hall (2004) who argue the need for any understanding of tourism to be set within the wider context of the social science of mobility, particularly leisure-oriented mobility (Hall, 2005). Their critique of traditional definitions of tourism notes that reductionist approaches to tourism offer 'little statistical or intellectual overlap with other fields concerned with mobility such as transport, retailing, migration or the realms of diaspora and global networks' (Hall, 2004:2). Within one temporal dimension, they note the folly of excluding day-trippers from definitions of tourism, given the time-space compression that has resulted from rapid recent advances in transport technology and infrastructure. On another, tourism phenomena such as visiting friends and relatives (VFR), repeat travel and heritage tourism (to name a few) are commonly set within the context of mobility, migration and/or diaspora. Hall (2004) suggests, therefore, that tourism 'constitutes just one form of leisure oriented temporary mobility, and it constitutes part of that mobility, being both shaped by and shaping contemporary practices of consumption, production and lifestyle' (Hall et al., 2004:2). In light of this, it is of convenience on one hand, and no surprise on the other, that the concept of mobility and manifestations of migration are as applicable to the study of sport as they are to tourism (Maguire et al., 2002; Cornelissen & Solberg, 2007).

Sport labour migration, for example, which exists on a range of spatial and temporal scales, is an established feature of sport at a range of competitive and, indeed, non-competitive levels. Professional sports including ice hockey, football, baseball, cricket and rugby are at the forefront of this phenomenon (Maguire, 1996, 1999; Maguire & Stead, 1996; Lanfranchi, 1998), both in terms of public awareness and academic attention. Driven largely, but not solely, by economic forces, Maguire and Pearton (2000:175) note that 'a complex and shifting set of interdependencies contours the migrant trails of world sport. These interdependencies are multi-faceted and incorporate not only economic, but also political, historical, geographical, social and cultural factors'. Less well recognized, however, are the elements of mobility, lifestyle choice and migration that arise directly from the values, experiences and aspects of identity that everyday individuals derive from their associations, active or otherwise, with particular sports. Reflecting the position of Hall et al. (2004) on the study of tourism and contemporary mobility, Maguire and Pearton (2000) advocate a broad approach, incorporating where possible wider societal processes to the study of sport. These points only serve to further justify the approach that we adopt here, which is free of limiting definitional parameters.

In this book, then, we move away from criteria-based definitions of sport and tourism. Instead we treat sport and tourism as complex and dynamic phenomena that have in recent decades been engaged in an expanding interplay of mutual interests at a range of spatial and temporal scales. Sport is constantly in a state of change, subject to socio-economic forces, innovation and experimentation. Within the mainstream of professional team sports, cricket is a good case in point. Few thought that traditional five-day test cricket would survive the one-day cricket phenomenon that arose in the late 1970s. Today it is not test cricket but one-day cricket that is at risk of being cannibalized itself by the new Twenty–20 version of the sport. Alternative sports, including extreme sports, evolved initially in part as an escape from rules and regulations (Thomson, 2000). But these sports too are part of an evolutionary process as sports institutions, media, equipment and clothing manufacturers and the tourism industry itself play a part in the shift from the alternative to the mainstream (Hoffer, 1995; Heino, 2000; Hinch & Higham, 2004). In recent decades tourism has for some become a search for serious leisure (Stebbins,

1982), authentic experiences of place (MacCannell, 1973; Wang, 1999), a means of building personal or collective identity (Green, 2001) or a search for self (Giddens, 1991). Within the context of tourism it has been argued that sport may feature prominently in such terms (Hinch & Higham, 2004).

THE BROAD CONTEXT: GLOBALIZATION, MOBILITY AND IDENTITY

Within these broad parameters, it is our view that sport tourism may be productively considered in a way that is integrated with an understanding of three key themes: globalization, mobility and identity. Globalization has received significant attention from a broad range of academics including those focused on sport (e.g., Maguire, 1994, 1999; Silk & Andrews, 2001) and tourism (e.g., Mowforth & Munt, 2001). For example, Cornelissen (2004:40) notes that 'scholars have also started to view mega-events as contingents of globalization and to analyse how events are used as instruments of government policy to, for instance, attract foreign investment'. Sport and tourism have figured prominently in the development of new relationships between cities, regions and states in terms of international trade, business development, capital investment and job growth (Roche, 2000). A central element of sport (Silk & Andrews, 2001) and tourism (Hall, 1998; Page & Hall, 2003) discourses as they relate to globalization is whether globalization is leading to increasing standardization or whether local resistance and negotiation will retain or even foster greater differences between places (Bale, 2000; Silk, 2004). Perhaps the reality is that there are coexistent forces for homogeneity and diversification at play (Markel et al., 1998; Washington & Karen, 2001; Harvey & Houle, 1994). Discussion and critical consideration of these coexistent forces in Chapter 2 (*Sport and tourism in a global world*) are engaged to provide an important part of the context for the discussions of sport and tourism that follow.

Contemporary mobility, the second key theme underpinning the discussions presented in this book, is both a driving force and consequence of globalization. The economic, socio-cultural, political and technological processes that have given momentum to the processes of globalization have, in turn, given rise to diverse manifestations of contemporary mobility. Harvey (2000) identifies four recent shifts in the dynamics of globalization that include deregulation, technological change and innovation, media and communications and reductions in the cost and time involved in moving commodities. These dynamics have had significant consequences for sport

(Maguire, 1999) and tourism (Hall, 2005). Chapter 3 (*Sport and contemporary mobility*) is founded on the premise that contemporary sport-related tourism has developed in close association with diverse forms of mobility, including personal, professional, financial, environmental, political and, among others, sporting mobilities. An understanding of sport tourism, therefore, is (like any other tourism phenomenon) incomplete without a consideration of phenomena such as recreational mobility, leisure tourism, seasonal workforce mobility, long-term travel and migration (Lundmark, 2006).

Globalization and contemporary mobility have brought enormous change to the values and reference points that once framed peoples' lives. Heightened levels of exposure to new ideas, educational and employment opportunities, different people and unfamiliar places have heralded new forms of consumption. It has also challenged many aspects of personal and collective identity. Maguire (1993) refers to the 'crisis of identity' that has resulted from globalization and increased mobility, one consequence of which has been an erosion of collective identity through national citizenship. Alternatively, personal values and identity may be forged and expressed through distinctive lifestyle and consumption patterns (Mowforth & Munt, 1998). Aspects of national identity have been further compromised by the mediation of identities that blend local and global cultures (Melnick & Jackson, 2002). As elements of personal identity have become more malleable and pluralistic (Milne & Ateljevic, 2001), sport and tourism have emerged as important drivers of identity. Chapter 4 (*Culture and identity*) explores the 'crisis of identity' that has followed on the coat tails of globalization and contemporary mobility. It also explores the notion that sport and tourism are playing significant roles in the development of personal identity and, furthermore, that sport and tourism cultures have become important elements in the construction of new identities.

In this book we consider sport tourism within the context of discourses on globalization processes, the study of contemporary mobility and the various manifestations of identity; personal, collective, place-specific and national identities among them. Following this introduction (Part 1), these three overarching themes are addressed in Chapters 2–4 (Part 2). It is within these themes that we then seek to situate our discussions of sport and tourism phenomena in the chapters that follow (Chapters 5–13).

SPORT AND TOURISM: ACTIVITY, PEOPLE AND PLACE

Within this general context we organize Chapters 5–13 into three parts (each of three chapters), which consider sport and tourism in terms of activity, people and place (respectively). This conceptualization is principally derived from the writing of Weed and Bull (2004), as elaborated by Weed (2005) in his editorial for a special issue of *European Sports Management Quarterly* on sports tourism method and theory. In his editorial Weed (2005) is critical of definitions of sport tourism, and particularly classifications of sport tourism which categorize sports participants as 'hard' and 'soft' (e.g., Gammon & Robinson, 1997; Standeven & De Knop, 1999), which may be seen to effectively subordinate sport to tourism, or vice versa, in order to understand the sport tourism experience. Rather, sport tourism might be understood as '... a synergistic phenomenon that is more than the simple combination of sport and tourism' (Weed, 2005:233). This requires that the unique features of sport and tourism, as they exist in combination, are understood and considered in an integrated manner so as to allow an exploration of the heterogeneity of sport tourism phenomena.

This conceptualization may in part be derived from Standeven and De Knop (1999:58) who see 'sport and tourism as cultural experiences—sport as a cultural experience of physical activity; tourism as a cultural experience of place'. Thus sport involves some form of physical activity, be it competitive or recreational, structured or unstructured, goal orientated or participatory (Hinch & Higham, 2004). In all of its diversity, sport involves engagements with people as competitors, co-participants, spectators, officials and hosts/guests. Indeed even individual sports, some of which take place in extreme isolation (e.g., mountain running, ultra-marathon and solo yachting), involve interactions with other people given that 'participants may reference their participation in terms of the subculture of the activity' (Weed, 2005:233). This can give rise to the experience of inter-personal authenticity in sport (Hinch & Higham, 2005:253) through feelings of tourist 'communitas' (Turner, 1974; Weed, 2005).

By the same token, tourism involves interactions with other people most obviously through contact with fellow travellers. Even the most independent forms of lifestyle travel involve the development of backpacker 'trails' that are inadvertently established among those who, ironically, seek to escape any notion of an established trail. Similarly, all forms of tourism involve interactions with local communities in some form or another, be they with tourism industry service staff or local residents who have little or no association with the tourism sector *per se*. In the absence of common interests (e.g., sports competition) beyond the service encounter, many such interactions are problematically fleeting, contrived or standardized. Of course the interplay between hosts and guests occurs in places that are beyond the tourists' usual environment of work and/or other routine domestic activities. Tourism inevitably involves a spatial travel dimension (Dietvorst &

Ashworth, 1995) which takes the tourist to other places. The appeal of such places may in part lie in the fact that they are unusual or unfamiliar. Equally, in a globalized world of high mobility, travel may take people to places of regular visit, where inter-personal interactions are different but familiar nonetheless (Müller, 2005).

Thus sport tourism may be viewed, according to Weed and Bull's (2004) conceptualization, as the amalgam of specific sporting activities, being undertaken by people in various forms of competitive interplay or other interaction, that occur in places (of high or low familiarity) that may be instrumental to the sport and/or tourist experience. This conceptualization sits most comfortably with the foregoing discussion given that it allows a shift '... away from a dependence on either sport or tourism as the primary defining factor' (Weed & Bull, 2004:234). Weed (2005) has called for dedicated and critical consideration of sport tourism as it relates to the interaction of activity, people and place. We set out in this book to contribute to addressing this call. So, set within the broader context of globalization, mobility and identity (Part 2), the themes of activity (Part 3), people (Part 4) and place (Part 5) give this book its structure (Figure 1.1).

In Part 3 (Activity) we consider elite competition (Chapter 5), sport spectatorship (Chapter 6) and the pursuit of serious leisure through recreational sports (Chapter 7) – three distinct activities – as they relate specifically

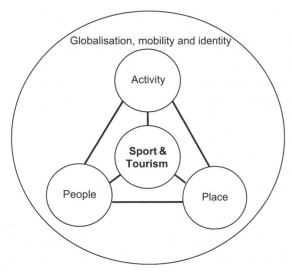

FIGURE 1.1   *Sport tourism as a composite of activity, people and place set within the contextual themes of globalization, mobility and identity.*

to sport and tourism experiences, within the context of the themes established in Chapters 2–4. Then, in Part 4 (People), those who engage in sport-related tourism are discussed with specific attention paid to the search for authenticity through sport-related travel (Chapter 8), transient migrants – those who adopt mobile lifestyles entirely or in part to pursue their sporting passions (Chapter 9) and migrants and diasporic communities (Chapter 10). Finally, in Part 5 (Place), we discuss place in terms of modern landscapes and retro parks (Chapter 11), place attachments and meanings (Chapter 12) and place competition (Chapter 13). These chapters include invited case studies written by scholars in a range of disciplines whose works provide critical insights into the complex interplay of sport and tourism as it is addressed in this book.

The subjects of discussion presented in Chapters 5–13 are indicative as opposed to representative of the three themes activity, people and place. For example, in terms of People (Part 4), we consider elite athletes as tourists, people who for all intents and purposes have always been treated as producers of sport rather than consumers of the places in which they engage in their sporting endeavours (Higham, 2005). Obviously the destination needs of elite athletes differ fundamentally from the needs of spectators and others who travel to a specific place to experience a particular sport or competition. Disregarding the destination needs of elite athletes continues by and large, despite clear signs that sports organizations, managers, support personnel, funding agencies and sports people themselves are thinking ever more critically about the experiences of elite athletes at places of training, preparation (e.g., acclimatization) and competition (Francis & Murphy, 2005), but also as places of leisure, rest, stimulation (e.g., from the routines of training) and pressure relief as no less important elements of preparation and competitive performance.

In Part 4 (People) we could alternatively have focused the spotlight of our discussions on sports media celebrities, business travellers, football hooligans, university/college athletes, professional or amateur athletes, individual or team competitors, members of particular sports subcultures, representatives of professional sports organizations, event bid groups, casual participants in sports, or competitive sports people ranging from age group (child/youth) to Masters competitors (among countless others). Here we seek not to justify the subject matter that we have chosen to include in this book, but only to highlight the diversity of sport and tourism phenomena. Notwithstanding this point, integration of our discussions of activity, people and place within the overarching themes of globalization, mobility and identity is attempted in Chapter 14, the concluding chapter, so as to draw coherent conclusions on the subject of sport tourism as it currently stands, and to provide insights into the future, and future research serving, the study of sport and tourism.

PART 2

Globalization, Mobility and Identity

CHAPTER 2

Sport and Tourism in a Global World

Globalization, in all its complexity, has emerged over the past two decades as the major socio-economic force. In many ways, sport and tourism have been at the forefront of globalization both in exhibiting its manifestations and as agents of its processes. Although there are substantial bodies of literature that examine this phenomenon in the separate realms of sport (Maguire, 1999; Miller, Lawrence, McKay & Rowe, 2001) and tourism (Cooper & Wahab, 2001; Mowforth & Munt, 1998), there have been few attempts to study globalization at the confluence of these fields. In this chapter we redress this omission by articulating an understanding of globalization in the context of sport tourism. This chapter examines the processes of globalization, the role of culture and consumption and the key globalization issues that have emerged in the realm of sport and tourism.

CONTENTS

GLOBALIZATION PROCESSES

The process of globalization is complex and powerful. While it is difficult and perhaps dangerous to try to simplify, an overview of this phenomenon is a necessary starting point for more in-depth examinations. The following section articulates the basic concept of globalization as it is used in this book, discusses the place of sport tourism in relation to globalization and highlights the contested nature of the concept.

The concept and phenomenon of globalization

As in the case of both sport and tourism as discussed in Chapter 1 (*Sport and tourism: Globalization, mobility and identity*), there is no single, widely accepted definition of globalization. There are, however, key characteristics of the concept that are consistently raised by a variety of commentators (e.g., Maguire, 1999). These include 1) the accelerated compression of time and space; 2) a growing interdependence that crosses traditional spatial and non-spatial boundaries 3) an uneven distribution of impacts; and 4) increasing flexibility of production.

The first general characteristic of globalization is the accelerated compression of time and space. While history is full of examples of time and space compression such as that which occurred during the Roman Empire or the European colonial period, a distinguishing feature of the current phase of globalization is the accelerated pace at which it has been occurring (Maguire, 1999; Mowforth & Munt, 1998). Interactions are happening faster and faster whether it is in the realm of communications, transport, business or other areas of endeavour. Activities and processes that used to take weeks now take days; those that took days now take hours, minutes, seconds or nanoseconds. A similar development has occurred in terms of space and mobility (see Chapter 3, *Sport and contemporary mobility*). Geographic locations that were considered distant and perhaps isolated are now often seen as being close and accessible. For example, twenty-five years ago an overseas trip to participate in sport was a major expedition reserved for elite athletes. Today, it is a routine occurrence, even for many recreational athletes.

As time and space have been compressed, a second common characteristic of globalization has emerged in the growing interdependence of territories and societies. In very tangible terms, this interdependence is manifest in the formation and development of the European Community and the various trade agreements and associations, such as the North American Free Trade Agreement (NAFTA) and the Asia Pacific Economic Cooperation (APEC) coalition. Figure 2.1 illustrates this spatial interdependence. Under Milne and Ateljevic's (2004) articulation of this model, the global has replaced what was formerly described as the international level. This change highlights the perspective that the global level signifies interactions that are initiated from a global perspective rather than the interaction of two or more nation states, in which the interests of the participating states serve as the point of reference (Miller, Lawrence, McKay & Rowe, 2001). Under globalization, interdependence goes beyond these international linkages; it reflects a global orientation that crosses traditional spatial boundaries and is characterized by a global–local nexus. This interdependence also crosses over non-spatial boundaries traditionally found in the areas of economics, culture and society in general.

A third common characteristic of globalization is that its impacts are increasingly recognized as being unevenly distributed given interdependencies that are asymmetric in nature (Amin & Thrift, 1997). Some areas and actors are advantaged while others are disadvantaged even though they

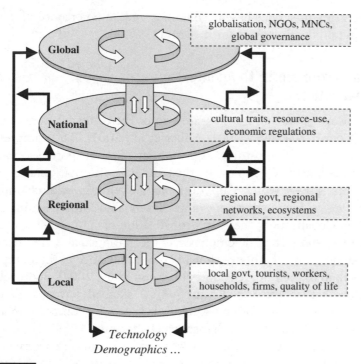

Technology
Demographics ...

FIGURE 2.1   *Tourism and the global–local nexus (Source: Milne & Ateljevic, 2004).*

are all part of the same web of globalization. The suggestion that globalization is like a rising tide that will lift all boats (nations) to the same level is
simply not accurate (Reid, 2003). Different starting points and substantial
power differentials have contributed to uneven benefits and uneven costs.
While globalization processes

> ... *have not occurred evenly across all areas of the globe, the more*
> *recent history of these processes would suggest that the rate of change*
> *is gathering momentum, and despite the unevenness of these*
> *processes, it is more difficult to understand local or national*
> *experiences without reference to these global flows.* (Maguire,
> 1994:400)

Finally, globalization is characterized by flexible modes of production
(Cooper & Wahab, 2001). Rather than production being anchored in time
and space as it was viewed under the Fordist process of mass production,
different parts of the production process have migrated to different
regions based on the supply of labour, capital and resources. This flexibility
is consistent with a post-modern world. There has been a shift from

manufacturing to service-based economies and an emergence of 'footloose' capital and production (Mowforth & Munt, 1998).

Sport and tourism in the context of globalization

In many ways sport and tourism are two of the principal fronts of globalization (Cooper & Wahab, 2001; Miller et al., 2001). The compression of time and space is manifest in the spectacularizaton of sport associated with global events like the Olympics and the Fédération Internationale de Football Association (FIFA) World Cup of football. While world championship competitions in many sports are more closely associated with internationalism than globalization, the professionalization of an increasing number of achievement sports has de-emphasized the national and has resulted in a cosmopolitan mix of athletes showing more allegiance to their employer or sponsors than to their home country or region (Jutel, 2002). Sport celebrities like Michael Jordan and Kobe Bryant (NBA Basketball) have also emerged as global stars even though for non-Americans they have competed in a distant land and in a more or less familiar sport (Halberstam, 1999). Similarly, time and space compression in tourism is a fundamental characteristic of the industry that aggressively promotes new destinations. For example, the popularity of short break vacations is due in no small part to the development of fast and economical transportation options that have dramatically extended the feasible travel range per unit of vacation time (Coles et al., 2004).

Interdependence networks in sport have also grown more prominent as illustrated by commodity chains in ice hockey. Donnelly (1991) describes one such intricate chain in which hockey equipment is designed in Sweden, manufactured in Europe, Asia and the United States and distributed to major hockey markets in North America and Europe. Similar interdependencies have emerged in tourism, as networks are consciously developed and refined in order to connect the multitude of service providers found in the disparate geographies of the tourist's home and the destination. Multinational and transnational tourism corporations have grown as the result of vertical and horizontal expansion through numerous mergers and takeovers (Go, 2004; Reid, 2003) and the development of less formal networks (Milne & Ateljevic, 2004).

Despite emerging global sporting and tourism cultures, the distribution of the impacts of globalization has been uneven. For example, notwithstanding increasing involvement in a broad range of sporting activities, the 2010 FIFA World Cup will be one of the few major global sporting events ever hosted in Africa. In a tourism context, Mowforth and Munt (1998) make the point that a lesser developed country like Gambia is impacted far more by changing international travel flows and constraints than are individual tourists who have a multitude of destination options. Similarly, while the distribution of tourist arrivals is widespread, it varies substantially by country, with the developed world reaping most of the benefits (Reid, 2003).

Both sport and tourism have proven to be very adaptable in this climate of globalization. Sporting teams and their players are more mobile than they have ever been, with professional teams being uprooted in the search for new stadiums and the revenue streams that go along with them. Player movements have increased as legal precedents such as the Bosman labour mobility decision in Europe have enabled professional athletes to pursue more lucrative opportunities elsewhere (Miller et al., 2001). Greater flexibility has also materialized in tourism with the increasing presence of customized travel products for niche markets. While large transnational companies still enjoy the advantages of economies of scale, innovations such as the Internet have allowed small operators to address unique market needs and to bypass many of the traditional travel trade intermediaries (Cooper & Wahab, 2001).

In addition to being manifestations of globalization, sport and tourism are also its agents. Milne and Ateljevic (2001) hint at this role by raising the metaphor of the 'coal face', which is the point of production and consumption.

> *Tourism, in simple terms, must be viewed as a transaction process which is at once driven by the global priorities of multi-national corporations, geo-political forces and broader forces of economic change, and the complexities of the local – where residents, visitors, workers, governments and entrepreneurs interact at the industry 'coal face'.* (Milne & Ateljevic, 2001:84)

This 'coal face' not only serves as the point of production and consumption but also as a point of acceleration of globalization.

Sport and tourism globalization as a contested concept

Globalization is a contested concept in general and in the context of sport and tourism in particular. Short, Breitbach, Buckman and Essex (2000) have identified four main globalization discourses. The first is the discourse found in the popular press, which essentially argues that the world is becoming more alike – that a common global culture is emerging. A second discourse is the business mantra that suggests that businesses can either take advantage of the opportunities offered by globalization or be consumed by them. Under this discourse, businesses must chase global markets as their local market is at risk to competitors from across the globe. A third discourse positions globalization as a term of criticism. Accordingly, globalization is seen as bringing unwanted change, typically through the exploitation of labour and resources in less powerful regions of the world. The fourth discourse is found in academia. As can be expected in academia, a variety of perspectives of globalization are being explored. While many of these are discipline based, it is apparent that given the complexity of globalization, a multidisciplinary or trans-disciplinary perspective has proven to be the most insightful. Hall (2001a:22) underscores this perspective stating that globalization

> ... *should be seen as an emergent, evolutionary phenomenon which results from economic, political, socio-cultural and technological processes on many scales rather than a distinctive causal mechanism in its own right.*

While the disciplinary focus of scholars examining the globalization of sport has been dominated by sport sociologists (e.g., Donnelly, 1996; Maguire 1994, 1999; Miller et al., 2001), the globalization of tourism tends to have attracted more attention from researchers with business (e.g., Go, 2004), geographical (e.g., Hall, 2001; Milne & Ateljevic, 2001) and socio-economic (e.g., Mowforth & Munt, 1998) perspectives. In spite of the varied disciplinary perspectives, four dominant interpretations of globalization in the realm of sport and tourism are evident: 1) modernization; 2) cultural imperialism often in the form of Americanization 3) figurational hegemony; and 4) cultural hegemony.

Modern interpretations of globalization suggest that the changes occurring in sport and tourism are manifestations of normal development (Donnelly, 1996). This perspective highlights the fact that social transformation has been occurring since the origins of humankind. Initially, realms of contact were local in nature but as advances were made in transportation, communication and technology these realms began to expand to regional, provincial and national levels. Transformations at a global level are seen as natural extensions of the preceding national level.

The *cultural imperialism* hypothesis warns of the imposition of a dominant American culture over other world cultures as manifest through the global spread of US-created fast food chains like McDonalds and products like Coca Cola. It is commonly seen as 'a one-way process in which American cultural form, products, and meanings are imposed on other cultures at the expense of the domestic culture' (Donnelly, 1996:242). In a sporting context, the relatively limited uptake of American sports like gridiron football and baseball, and conversely, the popularity of football outside of the United States seem to undermine claims of the Americanization of sport. However, as Donnelly has argued, at the level of the commercialization, administration and the values that underlie sport, the Americanization argument is much stronger. A variety of scholars have used this perspective to study the globalization of sports such as the Americanization of Israeli Basketball (Galily & Sheard, 2002) and the way that the National Basketball League has been presented and mediated by locals in New Zealand (Jackson & Andrews, 1999).

Maguire (1999) has positioned his analysis on the globalization of sport firmly within a *figurational/process-sociological approach*. This analysis is heavily influenced by the work of Elias (1991) who argued that a global frame of reference is now needed to understand social relations. From this perspective, Maguire argues that '... the present global sport formation has arisen out of an interweaving between the intentional acts of individuals and social groups that are grounded in the relatively unplanned features of inter-civilizational processes' (Maguire, 1999:4–5). An important aspect of this approach is that social identity can be strongly influenced by sport as it is played out at the local, national and increasingly global levels.

Finally, the *hegemony* perspective probably enjoys the broadest range of support among commentators on the globalization of sport and tourism (Donnelly, 1996; Hargreaves, 1982). Hegemony is the ability of the dominant group to persuade less powerful groups to adopt its position. This perspective recognizes that there is an element of negotiation in this process, but there are limits to this negotiation. Cultural hegemony is seen as a 'two-way but imbalanced process of cultural exchange, interpenetration, and interpretation' (Donnelly, 1996:243). In the context of sport tourism, this perspective suggests that the political and business elites associated with sport and tourism exert considerable influence over globalization processes. The involvement of media interests in sport and tourism provides a very strong platform for hegemonic influence in this field (Morley & Robins, 1995).

A CULTURE OF CONSUMPTION AND THE CONSUMPTION OF CULTURE

Among the many interdependencies that characterize the compression of time and space under globalization, one of the most significant is that found between economics and culture. In *The Condition of Postmodernity*, Harvey

(1989) points out the growing link between culture and economic restructuring throughout the globe:

While simultaneity in the shifting dimensions of time and space is no proof of necessary or causal connection, strong a priori grounds can be adduced for the proposition that there is some kind of necessary relation between the rise of postmodernist cultural forms, the emergence of more flexible models of capital accumulation, and a new round of 'time-space compression' in the organization of capitalism. (Harvey, 1989:vii)

This section of the chapter explores the emergence of a culture of consumption under globalization followed by a discussion of the consumption of culture, particularly in terms of sport tourism.

A culture of consumption

Globalization is characterized by consumption, and increasingly, it is culture that is being consumed. Mowforth and Munt (1998) have explored this relationship in the context of tourism and it is useful to revisit their explanation. Figure 2.2 highlights the changing relationship between economic processes and culture under globalization. Prior to the current period of globalization, the regime of accumulation can be characterized as Fordism. This term is derived from the process of production exemplified by Henry Ford's assembly line innovations and 'centred around mass production and mass consumption, with an appropriate "mode of regulation"' (Morley & Robins, 1995:27). Harvey (1989) contends that the rigidity of this system created a 'crisis of accumulation' as time and space were compressed. In order to achieve satisfactory increases in productivity and in the face of increased global competition, capitalists were forced to become more flexible, which has become a defining element of Post-Fordism. This flexibility was manifest in production through greater sensitivity to consumer wants, decentralized manufacturing, new product development with shorter product lifecycles and more attention to form or aesthetics (Lash & Urry, 1994). It has also been characterized by a shift from goods to services, with a resulting interest in consumables such as sport tourism experiences.

The mode of representation or cultural environment that predated the recent acceleration of globalization is characterized as late modernism. At this point, a crisis of representation occurred as globalization brought more and more changes to the everyday lives of individuals (Harvey, 1989). Given the degree of time and space compression, and given the growth in the middle class, the traditional ways in which people derived their identities were

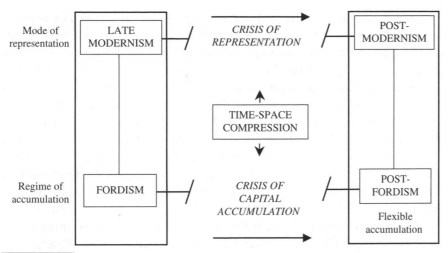

FIGURE 2.2   *Relationship between economics and culture under globalization (Source: Adapted from Gregory, 1994; Mowforth & Munt, 1998).*

eroded. 'Very broadly, postmodernism refers to the emergence of new cultural styles (in art, architecture, music and the objects and experiences we buy and consume), and post modernity is the idea that we now live in a new social epoch that has superseded modernity' (Mowforth & Munt, 1998:31). The key link between the regime of the new economic realm and the new cultural realm is that people are increasingly constructing their identities through consumption (see Chapter 4, *Culture and identity*).

Milne and Ateljevic (2001:92) have described this situation as a 'culture of consumption' in which 'you are what you buy' and 'where you go' (also see Featherstone, 1995). The consumption of travel and sport experiences can form a significant part of one's personal identity. For example, sport tourism is influenced by fashion, as consumers modify travel practices, sport activities and sporting allegiances in response to local and global trends. The relatively short shelf life of these new travel and sport products is consistent with time and space compression and the need for capitalists to accelerate the return of capital under Post-Fordism (Harvey, 1989).

The consumption of culture

The flip side of a 'culture of consumption' is the 'consumption of culture'. Culture, in all of its various forms, is being commodified and consumed as part of the processes of globalization. It is important to understand the nature of this consumption, the ways in which sport is a form of culture, how sport is being commodified and the role of tourism in this process of sport commodification.

One of the major trends of globalization has been the growth of 'popular' or 'global culture'. While there is considerable debate on whether or not a single global culture is emerging, there are clear indications that people now share more common cultural interests, particularly in the realms of music, cinema and increasingly, sport. Morley and Robins (1995) note that often culture-based products presented at the global level have their roots at the local level. They suggest that global firms consciously seek out cultural differences at a local level, including those related to tourism and sport. 'The local and "exotic" are torn out of place and time to be repackaged for the world bazaar. So-called world culture may reflect a new valuation of difference and particularity, but it is very much about making a profit from it' (Robins, 1995:113).

Local heritage represents a particular aspect of culture that is important in terms of the establishment of place identity and place image. It therefore has a vital role to play in a tourism context in a post-modern world where consumers are looking for reference points from which they can establish their own identities.

> In this process, local, regional or national cultures and heritage will be exploited to enhance the distinctive qualities of a city or locality. Tradition and heritage are factors that enhance the 'quality of life' of particular spaces and make them attractive locations for investment. An emphasis on tradition and heritage is also, of course, important in the development of tourism as a major industry. Here, too, there is a premium on difference and particularity. In a world where differences are being erased, the commodification of place is about creating distinct place-identities in the eyes of global tourists. Even the most disadvantaged places, heritage, or the simulacrum of heritage, can be mobilized to gain competitive advantage in the race between places. (Morley & Robins, 1995:119–120)

Sport is ubiquitous as a form of popular culture while maintaining its significance as a form of place-based local culture. This claim is addressed in more detail in Chapters 4 (*Culture and identity*) and 12 (*Place attachment*), but it is helpful to introduce the argument at this point. According to Miller et al. (2001:np) '[s]port is the most ubiquitous feature of popular culture. It crosses language barriers and slices through national boundaries, attracting both spectators and participants to a common lingua franca of passions, obsessions and desires'.

While similar claims may be made in the other realms of the arts and entertainment industry, there is little doubt that sport does cross boundaries and that large portions of the world population share a passion for sport, albeit one that may find its expression in a variety of different forms. Increasingly, however, athletes throughout the world are not only competing against each other in a variety of patriot games like the Olympics but are often competing in very cosmopolitan settings with team mates and competitors from across the globe (Wong & Trumper, 2002). Professional football is the classic example. The fandoms for these sporting competitions are becoming more cosmopolitan even in the context of 'patriot games' as flows of immigrants spill out beyond the traditional nation state (see Chapter 6, *Spectatorship and spectator experiences*).

Notwithstanding the prominent place of sport as a form of popular culture, it remains a touchstone of the modern in an increasingly postmodern world.

Societies and individuals rely on some stability in visions of the past construed for the purposes of present tasks, and sport has been seen as an important technical and metaphorical container for such cultural ballast. (Wieting & Polumbaum, 2001:237)

This concept of cultural ballast appears to have played a role in the resistance to English Rugby League initiatives in Northern England (Denham, 2004). When faced by an attempt to spectacularize and globalize the sport, local resistance led to modifications in the way that Rugby League was being transformed. It exemplified the power of the local to negotiate the cultural meaning of sport in a global world.

While sport has been an expression of local culture since its inception and remains so, its growth as an expression of global culture is closely tied to processes of commodification. There are three main faces of this commodification of sport: 1) professionalization and commercialization of elite sporting competitions; 2) the growth of a global sport apparel and equipment industry and 3) the embracement of sport as a form of relatively inexpensive entertainment programming on national and global broadcast networks.

The trend towards the privatization and commercialization of elite sport since 1990 is exemplified by developments in football. Crolley, Levermore and Pearson (2002:277) argue that football in England '... has been transformed, particularly at its highest levels, from a loss-making social institution, with clubs usually privately-owned by local benefactors, into a multi-million dollar industry'. Ben-Porat and Ben-Porat (2004) outline a similar process in terms of football in Israel where the adoption of an economic model has transformed the game into a commodity. Aspects of this commodification have included professionalization, floating sport clubs on stock exchange markets and court rulings that recognize clubs and leagues as business operations that are subject to normal corporate legal regulations. Similar commodification processes are increasingly evident in other sports across the globe (Miller et al., 2001).

The evolution of a sport industry with global commodity chains represents a second major type of commodification in sport. Maguire (1999) describes three kinds of sport commodity chains in the areas of clothing, footwear and equipment. While all three types of commodity chains provide popular lines of sport-related products in the global market, Nike, which was initially a footwear company, provides one of the best examples of a company engaged in this type of sport commodification. Nike promotions convey a sense that it is the real thing, but the company is essentially focused on managing, promoting and distributing products produced by others. Its aggressive marketing activities have not only served to sell the world on its products but to sell the world on sport (Miller et al., 2001).

The third type of sport commodification that has been a popular focus of sport sociologists is the media–sport complex (Maguire, 1999). This is very evident in the fierce competition to buy the rights to broadcast global sporting spectacles like the Olympic Games and the FIFA World Cup. The driving forces behind this competition include the global market both in terms of viewers and interested sponsors and the relatively inexpensive production costs of this type of broadcast. Rupert Murdoch has consciously used sport as a growth strategy for his media empire. An interesting aspect of Murdoch's approach has been direct involvement in the production of sport – not just the broadcasting of it. While it is true that all sport broadcasts are mediated to some degree, Murdoch has actively been involved in the restructuring of sporting codes – such as English Rugby League. This involvement has included the altering of team ownership, team locations and the fundamental rules of the game (e.g., Denham, 2004; Miller et al., 2001). Sport tourism is another form of sport commodification (Hinch & Higham, 2004). Just as the study of the commodification of sport in terms of commercialization, industrial commodity chains and the media can provide insight into the globalization process, so too can the study of the commodification of sport by the tourism industry. It is this topic that we now address.

GLOBALIZATION ISSUES FACING SPORT TOURISM

Globalization has been and will continue to be a powerful force in the development of sport tourism. The way this force will play out over the next decade will be an important focus of researchers studying this phenomenon for the foreseeable future. Two issues of the globalization of sport tourism are particularly relevant: 1) whether or not globalization is leading to homogenization and 2) whether globalization brings with it an inextricable force for (de)territorialization whereby the bonds between sport and place are eroded.

The issue of homogenization

The homogenization thesis suggests that globalization is leading to a single global culture that will overshadow and eventually smother local differences. Go (2005:52) describes the convergence argument as the belief 'that whole societies are steadily moving together so that the similarities between cultures will eventually become greater than the differences'.

While even Maguire (2002:20) has conceded that globalization forces have created 'a tendency towards the emergence of a global achievement sport monoculture', he sees this monoculture being concentrated in the realms of values, ideologies and organizational structure. More generally, however, Maguire (1994:402) and most other sport sociologists have rejected the homogenization thesis. Maguire articulates this perspective by arguing:

> There is no single *global flow; in the interweaving of global scapes, disjunctures develop and cause a series of diverse, fluid, and unpredictable global conditions and flows. Competing and distinctive cultures are thus involved in an infinitely varied, mutual contest of* sameness *and* difference *across different figurational fields. Rejecting the idea of some global cultural homogeneity does not, however, mean accepting the idea of some haphazard, unstructured growth in global cultural diversity. In highlighting issues of homogeneity, and in the mutual contest of sameness and difference in global cultural flows, the analysis can be developed with reference to the twin figurational concepts of diminishing contrasts and increasing varieties.*

Evidence of increasing varieties in a non-sporting context includes the proliferation of cable television stations rather than the emergence of one global network (Miller et al., 2001). Similarly, Morley and Robins (1995:113) have pointed out that 'globalization does not mean the end of segments. It means, instead their expansion to worldwide proportions'. While Donnelley (1996:248) recognizes that the globalization of sport has lead to sameness at the corporate levels of sport, he suggests that it also has created '… vast areas of cultural space in which new sporting activities may emerge and traditional sports may thrive'. Evidence of these increasing differences can be found in the emergence of the Gay Games, the Paralympics, extreme sports, the rejuvenation of certain folk cultural sports and the growth in non-western sports such as various forms of martial arts. This line of argument, of heterogeneity rather than homogeneity, is consistent with theoretical views on post-modernity (Harvey, 1989).

Three consistent criticisms of the homogenization argument dominate the sport sociology literature. The first is that it fails to recognize the unevenness of the power relationships that underlie globalization as discussed earlier in this chapter. Secondly, it fails to recognize that even where global power outweighs local power, negotiation is inescapable. A variety of examples have been presented in the literature to support this argument, including Denham's (2004) study of Rupert Murdoch's unsuccessful initial attempt to popularize the English Rugby League at a global level due to local resistance in Northern England and indifference in the regions in which the League was being introduced. A broad range of other studies have resulted in similar conclusions about the power of locals in this negotiation process (e.g., Melnic & Jackson, 2002). The third criticism of the homogenization thesis is its failure to recognize points of disjuncture that are found in these global–local negotiations (e.g., Maguire, 1999). Jackson and Andrews (1999:32) have described these points as 'the diverse set of consequences that result when global forces and local contexts meet'. They emphasize the unpredictability of these disjunctures as they can 'provoke conflict, incongruence, and resistance' but can also result in 'accommodation, acceptance, and even ambivalence'. These disjunctures are found on Figure 2.1 at points of contact between the global and the local across all spatial scales. The unpredictability of these interactions ensures a dynamic environment and serves to mitigate homogeneity in sport.

Mowforth and Munt (1998) echo this view in the context of tourism. They feel that the homogenization argument is simplistic and fails to recognize the inequalities in power and the negotiation that occurs between the global and the local. Their position is strongly influenced by Harvey's (1989:33) view that 'postmodernism helps capture the high degree of difference and "fragmentation" that lies at the heart of contemporary cultural change'. Despite their compelling argument, Mowforth and Munt represent a minority view, with the bulk of tourism commentators on globalization expressing significant, if tempered, concerns about the tendency of homogenization trends found in tourism landscapes and systems.

Morrow's (1995) comments exemplify the more alarmist views with his reference to tourism as a '… radio-active cloud of banalizing sameness' which, '… threatens the earth; the sacred and beautiful places, all the uniquenesses, have been invaded, desacralized, franchised for the masses, dissolved into the

United Colors of Beneton' (Morrow in Mowforth & Munt, 1998:32). This refrain, while not always as passionate, is a common one in tourism literature. For example, Cooper and Wahab (2001:322), in the concluding chapter of their book *Tourism in the Age of Globalization*, note that

> *the consumption and adoption of global culture is significant for tourism, with criticism of many resorts as consisting of a uniform landscape of fast food restaurants, international hotels and chain resorts. The homogenization of tourism products is a problem for tourism as tourism places are increasingly commodified to reflect a global culture of consumption and it becomes difficult to differentiate them from the visitor's home surroundings...*

While the tourism industry has long been populated by small to medium-sized tourism operations, it has also been subject to a growing number of corporate mergers and buyouts, which have led to the emergence of several major transnational corporations that feature a high degree of vertical and horizontal integration (Coles & Hall, 2008). Like other types of transnational corporations, those found in tourism actively dismantle national boundaries in their pursuit of global markets although they are somewhat constrained by the fact that many tourists are seeking 'difference' – at least on the surface (Cooper & Wahab, 2001). Go (2004:70–71) argues that the competitive conditions of a global travel market require travel firms to '... build a market edge by simultaneously capturing global scale efficiency, responding to local market needs, and developing worldwide learning capacity that drive continuous innovation'.

Achieving all three of Go's (2004) recommended objectives is not easy. One increasingly popular strategy for doing so is through the affiliation of small and medium-sized firms with the larger ones. While many of these affiliations have taken the form of corporate mergers and buyouts, there has also been a growth in voluntary and mutually beneficial but non-binding associations. Such associations not only have the advantage of flexibility in a Post-Fordist economy, they also make it possible to stay connected at a local level. In contrast to this trend towards an intensification of industry networks and associations, the other significant strategy has been the pursuit of niche travel markets by small operators as made increasingly feasible by Internet technology. Notwithstanding the emergence of small-scale operators in response to niche markets, mass tourism experiences are still in high demand and this dimension of the industry continues to thrive (Go, 2004).

In summary, there is no general consensus that globalization processes are leading to the homogenization of tourism landscapes and experiences. While there is implicit, if not explicit, recognition of a touristic equivalent of

Maguire's (1994) argument of 'increasing varieties' in sport, the question remains as to whether recognized increases in niche tourism markets and independent travel are being overshadowed by the 'diminishing contrasts' associated with the continued growth of mass tourism and the 'smoothing' effects of increased networking throughout the tourism industry.

The issue of (de)territorialization

Another important issue in the globalization literature is that of (de)territorialization. The discourse associated with (de)territorialization argues that the processes of political economic restructuring and transformation have resulted in changes to the historical system of accumulation and social organization (Morley & Robins, 1995). Such changes have in turn spurred spatial restructuring and reconfiguration. In fact, Miller et al. (2001:126) argue that under the processes of globalization '[s]pace is torn asunder as traditional social bonds are compromised by ownership based on profit rather than township'.

The (de)territorialization discourse suggests that the processes of globalization result in a disconnect between space and people at the level of the nation state. The rapid growth of transnational corporations which owe their allegiance to unbounded shareholders rather than to the state is cited as a key factor in this (de)territorialization phenomenon (Cooper & Wahab, 2001; Miller et al., 2001). Along with the growth of transnational corporations, there has been an increase in 'offshore' economic spaces and macro regional blocks – 'all largely beyond the control of states', and all of 'which challenge the territoriality of the nation state' (Ben-Porat & Ben-Porat, 2004:423).

Under the impact of transnational migration and other aspects of globalization,

> … the nation-state is being 'unpacked'. Community, polity, and territory are becoming, rather than coextensive, discrete if overlapping spheres. Regional and transnational political institutions, transnational, subnational, and diasporic communities, and the state itself, now more an administrative entity that is increasingly being stripped of a primordial quality, occupy different (if linked and partly shared) spaces. Identities are being deterritorialized. (Jacobson, 1997:123)

From a sport perspective, this discourse suggests that despite vestiges of sporting identities at the nation state level, there is a trend towards the (de)territorialization of sport as indicated by the following: 1) the emergence of professional leagues made up of players from across the globe; 2) professional competitions in sports such as downhill skiing, golf, tennis and automobile racing that feature global circuits of competition; 3) global broadcasts of competitions; and 4) the emergence of multinational sport equipment corporations. The (de)territorialization of sport could have profound implications for sport tourism where space and place are at the core.

Despite the popular notion that globalization has eroded the relevance of the nation-state, Short, Breitbach, Buckman and Essex (2000:322) have noted that '... the nation-state has not wilted in the sun of globalization'. Increasingly, globalization is seen as being characterized by (re)territorialization rather than (de)territorialization. There are a variety of reasons for the continued importance of territory. At a nation-state level these include resistance to globalization, the uneven nature of globalization processes and a need for membership in territorial communities between the impersonal (global) and the personal (family) (Milne & Ateljevic, 2001). Amin and Thrift (1997) argue that globalization does not mean the end of geography in terms of the (de)territorialization of the economy. They also disagree with the view that under globalization the world has shifted from a 'space of places' to a 'space of flows'. Their logic lies in the realm of socio-economics, which suggests that economic activity is rooted in the geography of 'the centrality of innovation, learning and information to network building and path dependency' (Amin & Thrift, 1997:153). A global economy makes it more important than ever to foster place connections that provide access to local environments of trust, forbearance and reciprocity. The key point is that while globalization has changed the way people relate to spaces, this relationship still has meaning.

While Hall (2001a:42) recognizes the dynamic and complex nature of global processes across spatial hierarchies, he notes that these spatial hierarchies 'will continue to act as the spatial setting within which economic globalization will be negotiated within the foreseeable future'. Such views are consistent with those of Ben-Porat and Ben-Porat (2004:423) who state that

> *Globalization implies, ..., on the one hand, a rise of supra-territoriality or deterritorialization, but on the other hand, because of the uneven nature of the process, territory and territorial identity still matter... Thus, not only do local identities persist in spite of global flows, the resistance to globalization may even reinforce them.*

CONCLUSION

Globalization has been a major force for the last two decades with its attendant compression of time and space, growing interdependencies across spatial and a-spatial boundaries, uneven distribution of impacts and flexible forms of production. Sport and tourism have been directly impacted by globalization and in many ways the growth of sport tourism is an outcome of these processes. At the same time, sport and tourism have acted as forces for globalization in their own right. In fact, the confluence of sport and tourism represents a focal point in this dynamic, with sport tourism acting both as an agent for globalization as well as being an artefact of it. Travellers engaging in sport away from their home environments engage in a broad range of interrelationships across time and space. As such, they are significant agents for globalization and form an important part of the dynamic between the global and the local.

Globalization has fostered a culture of consumption with sport and tourism taking on increasing significance as products within this market place. A central feature of this dynamic is the commodification of sport by the tourism industry. While sport is commercialized in many different ways, its commodification through tourism is especially interesting because of its potential to accelerate globalization processes and the direct association between the local and the global inherent in this activity. Similarly, globalization has been accompanied by a growing appetite to consume culture. To the extent that sport is culture at both a global and a local level, the market for sport tourism experiences is likely to grow.

One of the key points of divergence between the sport and tourism literatures is the contrasting response to the question of whether globalization leads to homogenization. There is a consensus among sport scholars that this is not the case, that is, globalization has not erased local differences in sport. In contrast, there are significant concerns raised about the threat of homogenization by tourism scholars. This is an issue that merits further investigation at the confluence of sport and tourism. (De)territorialization is also an issue of interest. For sport, the emergence of professional competitions that result in cosmopolitan groupings of elite athletes is a recognized outcome of globalization. As such it has implications in the way that sport is used to construct identity. From a tourism perspective, the issue of (de)territorialization is particularly challenging. On one hand the travel industry has actively sought to break down spatial barriers while on the other, place difference is one of the key reasons that people travel. The confluence of sport and tourism is, therefore, a volatile realm in the context of issues of homogenization and (de)territorialization, which merits the attention of scholars in this area. These studies are clear that the outcomes of globalization are mediated and the processes of mediation are important to understand. Chapter 3 (*Sport and contemporary mobility*) provides further insight into this topic by focusing on the nature of mobility as a central characteristic of the globalization of sport and tourism.

Sport and Contemporary Mobility

CONTENTS

Hall (2004:229) notes that in an increasingly mobile world 'improvements in transport and communication technologies, population growth, deregulation and internationalisation of the world economic system, and moves towards free trade have all encouraged greater mobility of goods, services, ideas, businesses and people'. Contemporary mobility is, simultaneously, a cause and a consequence of globalization. Various forms of mobility have emerged in association with the economic, socio-cultural, political and technological processes that have given rise to globalization. Harvey (2000) identifies four recent shifts in the dynamics of globalization that include deregulation, technological change and innovation, media and communications and reductions in the cost and time involved in moving commodities. These dynamics have had significant consequences for sport (Maguire, 1999) and tourism (Hall, 2005).

Discussions of contemporary sport and tourism require as a starting point an understanding of diverse forms of mobility (see Chapter 1, Figure 1.1), including personal, professional, financial, environmental, political and, among others, sporting mobilities. This chapter addresses the need to understand these manifestations of globalization, as such an understanding affords insights into phenomena such as recreational mobility, leisure tourism, seasonal workforces, long-term travel and migration as they specifically relate to sport. To begin, this chapter explores the various forms of contemporary mobility that are an integral part of the process of globalization; personal and professional, commercial and political, and environmental and amenity mobility. This discussion serves as a basis for considering manifestations of contemporary mobility that specifically inform the study of sport and tourism.

GLOBALIZATION AND MOBILITY

Personal and professional mobility

Increased freedom to travel for both work and leisure purposes is a hall-mark of globalization (Mowforth & Munt, 2001). The forces driving this process have included the development of new transport technologies, expanded and less constrained information flows, raised awareness of other places, reduced costs of leisure travel in both actual and real terms and the dismantling of political barriers that previously rendered the movement of people seeking to engage in work or leisure either less straightforward or utterly impossible (Williams & Hall, 2000; Williams & Hall, 2002; Hall, 2004). Counter forces include political unrest, security concerns and military action, such as the continuing conflict in the Middle East as well as the related rise in crude oil prices. Concerns for climate change and the contribution of aviation to carbon emissions are also growing in prominence (Becken, 2007; Gössling & Hall, 2005). Yet the major travel markets of the west continue their love affair with foreign holidays. Figures released by the Official Airline Guide (OAG) show that more than 2.5 million aircraft movements took place worldwide in the month on May 2007, an increase of 400,000 flights on the same month in 2003 (*The Daily Telegraph*, 2007).

The manifestations of personal and professional mobility are manifold. The rise of leisure travel as a global phenomenon (albeit a discretionary activity that is highly sensitive to regional security and other factors at the destination level) is the most obvious manifestation of personal mobility. Hall (2004) argues the case that contemporary mobility extends to the study of second-home ownership, while Coles et al. (2004) draw specific attention to the multiple social networks that are established and maintained by transnational labour markets and the consequences of these multiple social relationships for tourism. Similarly, Duval (2004) highlights the rise of return visitation travel associated with diasporic communities. McHugh and Mings' (2006) study of personal mobility centres on the movements of retirees including seasonal travel to escape harsh winters and cyclical movements between multiple 'homes'. Both, they argue, have implications for the identities and well-being of aging people. Williams, King and Warnes (1997) chart the development and consequences of international retirement migration (IRM) in Europe, particularly between the United Kingdom and southern Europe (e.g., Italy, Malta, Portugal and Spain) highlighting the social, cultural and economic implications for both emigrants and their adopted communities.

In this vein, McHugh, Hogan and Happel (1995) call attention to the phenomena of multiple residences and cyclical patterns of mobility, highlighting the dynamics that emerge from life course perspectives of analysis (Figure 3.1). They use the term 'life course' rather than 'life cycle' arguing that the latter implies a predetermined set of life stages through which all individuals pass (e.g., childhood, marriage, child rearing, empty-nest, retirement). The assumption of a single fixed place of permanent residence no longer describes the living circumstances of many. In recognition of this, the term 'life course' captures the reality that not all individuals follow the same normative stages of the life cycle. Rather, they argue, 'individuals may exhibit diverse histories and paths relating to events such as schooling, cohabitation and living arrangements, marriage, childbearing, separation, divorce, remarriage, employment and career changes, children leaving and returning to the parental home, and retirement' (McHugh et al., 1995:253). Under this approach, contemporary mobility can be understood in many dimensions of production and consumption, such as commuting to work (daytime production), shopping (daytime consumption), migrant labour (medium–long-term production) and seasonal migration (temporary consumption). The study of contemporary mobility, therefore, should accommodate daily and weekly mobility (e.g., to second homes) and seasonal migrations (e.g., inter-semester travel and snowbirds) and less frequent circulations (e.g., return visits to natal homes).

These avenues of discussion serve to illustrate two important points. One is the diversification of the study of tourism beyond leisure travel *per se*, to

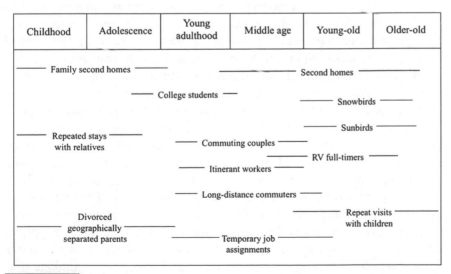

FIGURE 3.1   *Examples of multiple residences by life-course phase (Source: McHugh, Hogan & Happel, 1995).*

incorporate diverse manifestations of contemporary mobility (Burns & Novelli, 2008; Hall, 2008). The other, largely by implication, is the erosion of the dividing line between leisure travel and the mobilities associated with seasonal workforces, transnational labour migrations and emigration (Coles et al., 2004), which is often inspired by the search for improved or more desirable lifestyles, employment opportunities and/or economic circumstances (Duval, 2004). While the dividing line between personal and professional mobility may have been clear in the past, one consequence of globalization would appear to have been the blurring of that division (Hall et al., 2004).

Labour mobility, historically driven by the search for better economic and employment circumstances, is not a new phenomenon. In the late 1840s labour migrants converged on the gold fields of California to seek their fortune. As the San Francisco gold fields waned, some remained. Many others moved on to the gold fields of Victoria (Australia) and Coromandel, Westland and Central Otago (New Zealand) during the 1850s and 1860s. These places remain connected by a shared gold rush heritage as well as the common diasporic roots of Chinese and European migrants who worked the gold fields. Personal and professional mobility has increased dramatically in recent decades, due in large part to the adoption of liberal attitudes towards foreign labour immigration. Indeed some countries have actively encouraged labour immigration to ease skill shortages that would otherwise hinder innovation and economic growth in targeted sectors (Salt & Clarke, 2001).

Restrictions on foreign workers entering the United Kingdom date to 1919 when a system of work permits was introduced to manage the movement of non-Commonwealth nationals seeking to work in the United Kingdom (labour immigration from Commonwealth countries was not brought under control until the Commonwealth Immigrants Act of 1962). Labour immigration into the United Kingdom has vacillated since 1919, reaching a peak following 1945 as the rebuilding of Europe's shattered postwar economies required that labour shortages were addressed with urgency. The issuing of permits, particularly to those outside the European Economic Community (EEC), declined during the 1970s and 1980s but has risen sharply, once again, over the last two decades to post-2000 levels which exceed the peak of the post-war years (Clarke & Salt, 2003). The work permit system in the United Kingdom now functions as a mechanism to enable economic migration that will 'meet the shortfall in the domestic supply of certain skills … to increase the competitiveness of the UK economy' (Clarke & Salt, 2003:564). Advances in information and transport technologies, as well as the liberalization of social, economic and political barriers, have also greatly influenced the mobility of sport and tourism labour markets.

Indeed this sequence coincides with the upward mobility of sport labour migrants (Maguire, 1999). Maguire and Bale (1994:1) note that the 'migration of sports talent as athletic labour is a pronounced feature of sports development in the late twentieth century'. They highlight their deliberate use of the term *sport labour migration* so as to emphasize the nature of sport development as intimately integrated with the commodification processes of the capitalist world economy. It is apparent, therefore, that the processes driving labour migration outlined in the previous paragraphs have acted also upon the increasing mobility of athletic talent as a labour workforce. Indeed transnational mobility has also become a feature of professional sports administration and voluntary labour. The movement of international volunteer staff to support the human resource needs of staging and hosting sports events such as the Olympic Games highlights yet another increasingly prominent dimension of sport labour mobility.

Similarly, one of the most critical elements of tourism development has historically been the supply of labour (Szivas, Riley & Airey, 2003). Given that much tourism development takes place in rural, regional, peripheral or remote areas, tourism labour has typically been highly mobile. Indeed Szivas et al. (2003) point out that two forms of labour mobility are particularly relevant to tourism employment. One is spatial mobility, as much tourism employment requires movement on a range of spatial scales; from one country to another, between regions or cities, from urban to rural settings or from populous cities to small towns or villages that are remotely located. It is also noteworthy that much tourism labour lies at the extreme of high mobility. Those employed on both domestic and international airline carriers, including charter carriers, as well as cruise ships and package tours, are the nomads of tourism labour. The other notable feature of mobility in tourism labour is inter-sector labour mobility. Szivas, Riley and Airey (2003) highlight that tourism labour is typically drawn from other employment sectors, particularly at times of organizational and economic change (e.g., redundancy and forced changes in career direction), which has historically placed considerable emphasis on job adaptability, adaptation to new working environments and socialization processes (Szivas et al., 2003). This in many ways reflects the challenges faced by sport labour migrants (see Chapter 10, *Transnationalism, migration and diaspora*), albeit for very different reasons and under quite contrasting circumstances.

Commercial and political mobility

Recent shifts in the dynamics of globalization have signified important changes for sport. One consequence has been the rapid development of new forms of sports mobilities motivated by economic and political goals. In 1969 Montreal became the first non-US Major League Baseball (MLB) franchise to compete in the US professional baseball league. This was a move that received aggressive support from Canadian political and business leaders seeking economic and trade objectives to counter the diminution of traditional trade links at a time when Britain sought to build EEC links. Such developments inevitably create tradeoffs between local integrity and global expansion (Wieting & Polumbaum, 2001). In recent years commercial mobility has resulted in a trend towards foreign ownership of sports clubs. In the case of English Premier League football, seven of twenty clubs – Aston Villa, Chelsea, Fulham, Liverpool, Manchester United, Portsmouth and West Ham United – are now owned by companies or individuals who are not English or British. In June 2007 the British Sports Minister Richard Caborn announced his intention to hold talks with senior English football administrators to discuss concerns over the increase in foreign owners at top English football clubs. This followed a £81.6 million bid from former Thai Premier Thaksin Shinawatra to buy Manchester City FC after an unsuccessful bid to buy Liverpool FC in 2006. The Minister also announced his intention to lobby the European Commission to develop strict rules on foreign owners in sports management reforms covering the twenty-seven-nation European Union (EU).

Since the 1960s, sport has increasingly become a vehicle for promoting commercial and financial objectives. The 'leveraging' of events to maximize financial and commercial gains has, for example, become established in the events lexicon (Chalip, 2006; Chalip & Leyns, 2002). However, despite an extensive literature on event impacts, few studies address the strategic and long-term business interests that may be fostered through the leveraging of events (O'Brien, 2006). Chalip (2001) claims that the focus on short-term event impacts fails to justify the public investment required to stage large-scale events. The leveraging of sports events has grown through the development of public–private sector linkages to harness the potential long-term benefits associated with mega-events. These according to Dwyer, Mellor, Mistilis and Mules (2000) include the exchange of intellectual capacity and human resources, business development, fostering business relationships and technology transfer.

O'Brien (2006) reviews the business leveraging undertakings of the Australian Federal government in association with the Sydney 2000 Olympic Games. This extended to the creation of Business Club Australia, an initiative launched in advance of the Olympic Games to foster and provide opportunities for business networking and the facilitation of international trade (Brown et al., 2002). They argue that this event marks a paradigmatic shift in the strategic use of events vis-à-vis maximizing the commercial, business and investment opportunities that they may afford. O'Brien's (2006) work examines the efforts that were invested in institutionalizing accumulated knowledge in such a way that it might be applied recurrently in a range of different sport and non-sport event contexts.

The processes of globalization, as they apply to the fields of business, employment and investment, are closely linked to political processes and the relatively unconstrained movement of labour, investment, knowledge, goods and services across international borders. Thus, political decision-making across geopolitical boundaries represents a critical element in globalization processes. Such developments are typified by international agreements that facilitate business links, international trade, military cooperation and humanitarian efforts, among many other things. In terms of commercial and political mobility, various bodies that span international borders in different parts of the world have influenced regional trade and politics in recent decades. Prominent examples include the EU, the North American Free Trade Agreement (NAFTA), Asia-Pacific Economic Community (APEC) and the Association of South East Asian Nations (ASEAN). In terms of sport and tourism, the United Nations World Tourism Organisation (UNWTO), the International Olympic Committee (IOC) and a plethora of international sports organizations, functioning at the global (International Rugby Board, IRB; swimmings Fédération Internationale de Natation, FINA; Fédération Internationale de Football Association, FIFA and the International Amateur Athletics Federation, IAAF) or regional levels (e.g., Union of European Football Assoications, UEFA; South Africa, New Zealand, Australia Rugby, SANZAR) vividly illustrate the globalization of commercial and political forces in sport and tourism at play.

Of course national, international and global forces in the commercial and political world exist as they relate to sport and tourism in complex interactions. Hall (2003) highlights the links between tourism and trade by arguing that leisure travel is often a precursor to the development of business links between places, although such links are no doubt mediated by conducive commercial and political relations. Furthermore, while international sports associations and federations oversee sports competitions that take place on a range of national and international stages, they remain subject to national and international law. The EU, which typifies the reduction or removal of commercial and political barriers through such things as the adoption of common currency and common labour market laws, is a case in point. European law protects the free movement of workers and self-employed professionals in the European Community as this freedom is seen as critical to the integration of a single market (McCutcheon, 2002; Crolley, Levermore & Pearson, 2002). The European Court of Justice has played a leading role in eliminating restrictive practices in all sectors of the European economy, and professional sport is no exception. As McCutcheon (2002:308) notes, 'the court has confirmed that EC law applies to the commercial aspects of sport. It has examined employment practices that have curtailed the ability of sports professionals to move freely in the EU'.

Environmental and amenity mobility

The processes of globalization have had significant implications for global environmental change with widespread consequences for sport and tourism. As such a prominent manifestation of personal mobility, it is little surprise that tourism has been implicated in issues of global environmental change (Hall, 2004). This has taken place in a myriad of different ways as it relates to tourism. One has been the trend towards increasing standardization of tourist places (see Chapter 2, *Sport and tourism in a global world*). The development of standardized resources and facilities (e.g., hotel chains, restaurants, retail and shopping malls) including international brands and retail outlets, such as Vodafone, Apple Mac, McDonalds, Pizza Hut and Ikea, are obvious examples. Another example of standardization is the creation of facsimiles or replicas of iconic landmarks. The Americanization of tourist attractions, including the creation of EuroDisney and other themed parks, are also examples of creeping standardization.

Within the context of natural rather than urban environments, mobility has also had consequences, many detrimental, for natural ecologies. The development of infrastructure including the construction of transport systems, air, land and sea transport ports and hubs and tourist services directly consume terrestrial, coastal and marine environments, natural areas and biodiversity resources. This applies regardless of the scale of development (Gössling, 2007), be it a new airport in Hong Kong or an extended runway serving remote islands such as the Maldives or the Seychelles. The development of tourism infrastructure contributes to the destruction of environments (Krippendorf, 1987) and the reduction of biodiversity, which is globally cumulative (Hall, 2004). In a similar vein, tourist demand for nature-based sports has driven the standardization of environments to provide resorts for skiers and snowboarders and golf courses for leisure and competition. Priestley (1995) warns that despite green appearances, golf courses are highly modified cultural sportscapes that are intensively maintained and manicured, high in pesticide and herbicide use and low in biodiversity.

The forces of globalization have also influenced the standardization of policy, planning and management approaches for terrestrial and marine parks in distant parts of the globe. One might argue that the application of the North American template for the creation and management of national parks is evidence of global standardization. So too is the standardization of policy and planning guiding visitor management practices and interpretation, among other things. International agreements and accords such as the UNESCO world heritage programme have no doubt contributed to standardization of many aspects of natural and cultural heritage management. Tourism may also be implicated in the imposition of western environmental values upon non-western and indigenous peoples who may feel pressured by alien viewpoints on issues such as the indigenous harvesting of marine mammals (Hinch, 1998).

Tourism is also implicated in the translocation of super-species, diseases pathogens and infections (Gössling, 2007). The destruction of indigenous and endemic birdlife in the small Pacific Island of Guam is traced to the introduction of a single snake in the wheel well of a jet aircraft arriving from Asia. Super-species such as insect pests, rats, wasps and gulls commonly accompany human movements and migrations, both historically and in contemporary times. Tourists are not the sole agent of such processes of environmental change. Returned servicemen introduced Giardia into Australia and New Zealand following the Second World War. Migratory birds that travel vast distances across the continents and oceans of the world may carry avian diseases. However, expanded transport networks and tourism flows have become significant vectors for the translocation of plant and animal species, insect pests and diseases. It is also noteworthy that where tourism has pushed into remote and peripheral environments, the consequences of introductions such as these may be catastrophic. The translocation of disease pathogens, potentially via faecal matter relocated on the soles of footwear, between remote Antarctica and sub-Antarctica areas could have ruinous consequences for large and isolated penguin breeding colonies (International Association of Antarctica Tour Operators, 2002).

The early years of the twenty-first century have provided numerous examples of global environmental biosecurity concerns, including foot and mouth disease in the United Kingdom (2001 and 2007) and SARS (Severe Acute Respiratory Syndrome) in the Asia-Pacific region (2003). The rapid transmission of diseases and infections through international transport hubs raises heightened concerns in cases where diseases are able to move between species and mutate into strains that can infect humans. The outbreak of bird flu, initially in China and parts of southeast Asia in 2004, and Creutzfeldt-Jakob disease (CJD) in the United Kingdom are two examples of diseases that must be contained as a first measure. While tourism is a prominent agent of global environmental change, it also bears the consequences of such processes. According to Sharpley and Craven (2001) the foot and mouth outbreak cost the tourism industry in England an estimated £5 billion.

Alongside these processes, recent decades have witnessed accelerating advances in the reproducibility and transportability of sports resources and amenities (Bale, 1989). With this has come increasing standardization in design, an outcome no doubt influenced by the international mobility of workforces specializing in the design, costing and construction of sports facilities, arenas and stadiums. Hinch and Higham (2004) have argued the case that increasing standardization and the creation of sportscapes (Bale, 1989) have eroded the cultural fabric that makes places unique, with potentially deleterious consequences for tourism.

Both sport and tourism resources can be classified in terms of the extent to which they can be reproduced or transported (Boniface & Cooper, 1994; Hinch & Higham, 2004). Resorts, theme parks and stadiums are readily reproduced and relocated while, in contrast, natural landscapes and cultural heritage are less so. Nature-based sports such as downhill skiing and rock climbing tend to be dependent on certain types of landscapes or specific landscape features. Artificial sports resources (e.g., climbing walls and artificial ski slopes) generally serve introductory levels of participation, primarily in large urban centres. Green sports are those that are dependant on the integration of a physical activity with specific environmental attributes (Bale, 1989). These are sports that are built around specific features of the natural environment as sources of pleasure, challenge, competition or mastery (Hinch & Higham, 2004). Examples of such sports include surfing, sailing, mountain climbing and orienteering. The resources for these sports are inherently non-transportable.

In contrast, other sports are readily transported. Sports such as ice skating have been successfully transported from the high- to mid- and equatorial latitudes with the development of improved ice-making technology and expanding markets. Many sports, such as competitive swimming, diving, squash and racket ball, are performed in indoor sports centres, which can be readily relocated with the temporary or permanent development of facilities. Other sports that are traditionally played in outdoor settings can also be transported and performed in indoor sports centres and arenas. Examples include tennis, netball, athletics and hockey. More recently, with the advent of retractable and fixed roofing on stadiums, even football, rugby and cricket may be played in enclosed facilities. These sports have been subjected to a process that Bale (1989:171) refers to as the 'industrialisation of the sport environment'.

Other examples exist in outdoor sports. Snow can also be transported or created artificially. This has created opportunities for some resorts to develop and host winter sports events in temporary facilities developed in civic areas or on city streets. Artificial reefs and wave machines allow surfing events to take place in places where formerly it was not possible. Climbing walls, bridges, antennae, helicopters and submerged ship hulks have been used strategically to allow rock climbing, bungy and BASE jumping, and diving to take place in new locations. These developments highlight the contemporary mobility of many sports. The hosting of the FIVB (Fédération Internationale de Volleyball) World Tour beach volleyball championships in Stavanger (Norway) is an excellent illustration of sport mobility. This event has taken place in June/July each year since 1999. Temporary courts and arenas are constructed in the inner city harbour basin adjacent to the historical waterfront and the cafés, restaurants and bars of the sentrum (town centre). This picturesque and pedestrianized inner city location provides a vibrant setting for competition based on high levels of casual spectatorship. Over 200,000 spectators and teams from 50 countries attend this five-day event, which seeks to position the city of Stavanger as the 'Wimbledon of beach volleyball' (Stavanger Travel, 2007)

A recent counter trend against standardization in sport has been the retention or development of distinctive features of stadium design. So too has been the incorporation of distinctive features in architectural design. The redevelopment of Wembley Stadium (London) encountered heated debate surrounding the demolition of the distinctive 'twin towers'. The search for new elements of design has, in the case of Wembley, resulted in the creation of a stadium arch as well as the retention of Empire Way and, overlooking Empire Way, a bronze statue of England's victorious 1966 World Cup team. While far more sophisticated aspects of architectural design were incorporated into the new stadiums built in Korea for the 2002 Football World Cup (Hinch & Higham, 2004), these are nonetheless attempts to build elements of uniqueness and counter the detrimental effects of standardization. These discussions highlight the prominent roles performed by sport and tourism in terms of environmental mobilities, both as part of globalization processes and as a counter trend.

TOURISM AND MOBILITY

Hall (2005:21) notes that '... in addition to being defined in relation to its production and consumption, tourism is increasingly being interpreted as one, albeit highly significant, dimension of temporary mobility and circulation'. Clearly, tourism is an important manifestation of contemporary mobility. However, an understanding of tourism is incomplete in the absence of insights into the relationship between tourism and other forms of temporary mobility. These include travel for career advancement or work experience, international study, health and fitness, long-term travel and visits to places of personal significance. Forms of temporary mobility extend to phenomena such as travel to second homes, labour migration, the movement of seasonal workforces, immigration and return migration (Hall, 2005; Duval, 2003).

The geography of tourism considers the 'spatial expression of tourism as a physical activity, focusing on both tourist-generating and tourist-receiving areas as well as the links between' (Boniface & Cooper, 1994). The time–space relationship that prevails in the study of tourism dictates that the number of trips or movements from the point of origin declines the further one travels in both time and space. Central place theory and concepts such as distance decay and location hierarchy lend themselves conveniently to the spatial analysis of tourism. However, in times of unprecedented personal mobility there are other ways beyond linear expressions of mobility to explain the movements and circulations of people. McHugh and Mings (2006), for example, counter the view of migration as a one-way or permanent movement of residence. Their study of retired migrants concludes that 'rather than view migration in linear, origin-destination terms, we suggest a circle as a more illuminating metaphor' (McHugh & Mings, 2006:530). Thus, the lives of seasonal migrants reflect a cycle of movements and experiences that contrast between multiple home places, perhaps giving rise to multiple personal and social identities.

Figure 3.2 attempts to illustrate the cyclical movement of people in space and time as it relates to sport. Thus short-term movements predominantly take place from a point of origin to local sports venues in order to engage in recreational sport or local/regional sports competitions. In the more extended temporal timeframe, temporary mobility takes people to different seasonal sports venues at different times of the year. Season ski passes generate significant seasonal mobility over a period of some months, which might encompass the use of second homes or short-term rental accommodation in proximity to a chosen ski resort or groups of affiliated resorts (Müller, 2006). Similar cycles of mobility also apply in the long-term temporal dimension, which can extend to years or decades in cases where athletes take up tertiary scholarships or engage in sport labour migration (Maguire, 1999). These too should be viewed in cyclical terms, as students and athletes take breaks in semesters or competition seasons to return to their place of origin. Migration and return migration are also associated with ancillary travel flows as friends

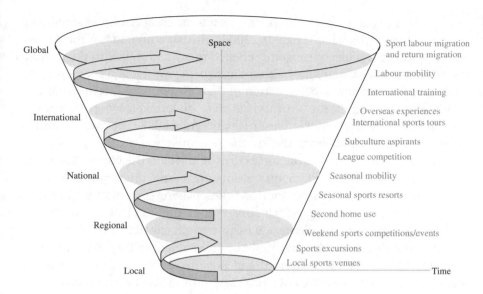

FIGURE 3.2

Manifestations of temporary mobility and circulation in sport.

and family become increasingly mobile in order to visit sports people at their new place of temporary or permanent residence or at single or multiple places of competition.

SPORT AND MOBILITY

Sport has long been an agent of personal and professional mobility. Since ancient times, sports people have travelled in search of competition. The ancient Olympic Games is commonly cited as one of the earliest forms of sporting competition that stimulated considerable travel flows (Crowther, 2001). These regional and national flows of people included competitors but extended to merchant traders, politicians and other notable dignitaries, for many of whom competition spectatorship was of minor importance (Crowther, 2001). Macdonald (1996:4) describes sport as an 'enemy of distance and separation'. It is a fundamental element of sport that competitors find themselves increasingly on the move as they progress through the established hierarchies of competition. With each successive level of the competitive sport hierarchy come increasing levels of competitor mobility.

Throughout competitive sport seasons, a multitude of athletes set out to travel locally or nationally, across their home country or abroad, to compete against their rivals. In many ways, the search for competition is a defining element of sport (Hinch & Higham, 2004). British emigrants to the Antipodes brought sports like horseracing, cricket, rugby and golf, with the earliest visitors to Britain's Commonwealth colonies being royalty and sports people. Following the systematic colonization of New Zealand by Britain from the 1830s, the first significant return visits were undertaken by sports teams, initially the New Zealand 'Natives' rugby team in 1888. For over a century before long haul travel from the southern hemisphere to Europe became commonplace in the 1970s, the forces driving travel to the United Kingdom were trade, war and sport. Sports teams travelling internationally were commonly referred to being on 'tour' and their playing personnel as 'tourists'. The labels of 'home' team and 'visitors' that commonly featured on scoreboards and changing room doors add further emphasis, if it is needed, to the essential travel component that underlies all competitive sports (Hinch & Higham, 2004). Indeed Giulianotti and Robertson (2007) identify sport as one of the early driving forces of globalization from the 1870s onwards.

More recently, this scenario has changed dramatically. The forces of accelerating globalization and heightened mobility have resulted in new forms of sports mobility. In recent years reductions in fuel and noise emissions have been the focus of transport development. However, historically the reduction of time/distance/cost barriers has been the key to new developments in transport technology (Hall, 2005). The major technological advances in reducing the cost and time of movement were achieved in the 1960s and 1970s. The advent of the wide-bodied jet aircraft, initially the Boeing 707 in the 1960s, shattered existing barriers to personal mobility. Since that time the mobility of sports people, not just competitors but also spectators and fans, has increased spectacularly (Morgan, 2007). Thus, the 2005 British and Irish Lions rugby tour of Aotearoa/New Zealand was associated with the movement of over 20,000 travelling supporters (Wright, Higham & Mitchell, 2007).

Increasing mobility of sports phenomena is not restricted to players and their supporters. Sports mobility has also been facilitated by technological advances, such as satellite television broadcasting (Halberstam, 1999), that have influenced the 'sportification of society' (Standeven & De Knop, 1999). As Maguire notes, 'this interchange … also involves the flow of sporting goods, clothing and equipment, media images, ideologies and capital' (Maguire, 1999:97) with significant implications for personal, regional and national identities. One consequence has been the formulation of multiple fan identities. Stewart and Smith (2000) identify that singular and parochial fan loyalties have been largely replaced by multiple fan loyalties at all spatial scales. Thus in the suburban streets of cities in South America, Australasia,

Europe and Asia, it is not uncommon to see young sports fans wearing the shirts and other regalia of sports clubs and teams such as Manchester United FC, Boca Juniors, the Los Angeles Lakers, the All Blacks or the San Francisco 49ers.

SPORT AND CONTEMPORARY MOBILITY

Sport exerts considerable influence over patterns and flows of contemporary mobility. Hall (2005:23) explains that 'tourism may therefore be interpreted as an expression of leisure or recreational lifestyle identified either through voluntary travel or a voluntary temporary short-term change of residence'. This applies comfortably to the context of sport-related travel mobility, although it should be noted that voluntary changes in residence in both the amateur and professional sports context may be short, medium or long term. The movement of seasonal workforces that are associated with sports such as skiing, snowboarding, sailing and mountain biking and the high long-term mobility of sport labour markets are good cases in point (see Chapter 9, *Temporary sport migrants*). The component parts of the subject of tourism are diverse and include health, business, education and leisure (across all temporal scales), none of which should be differentiated from the study of tourism and mobility relating specifically to sport.

In presenting this argument, Hall (2005) places deliberate emphasis on the notion that those who engage in some of these forms of temporary mobility may best be described as 'partial tourists'. This is a point of importance to the study of tourism and mobility as it relates to sport. Thus, football fans who travel to support their team in 'away' fixtures are likely to describe themselves as, for example, Liverpool fans, rather than tourists. Similarly, a young athlete who takes up a US college scholarship, or a professional athlete from Africa or South America who plays football in the English premiership, are unlikely to view themselves as tourists. Yet the term 'partial tourist' may be apt in these instances. As these people adopt mobile lives their travel behaviours are bound to incorporate departure from their place of origin, travel to and occasional return travel from their new place of residence, exploration of their new city, region and/or country of residence and of course domestic and/or international travel as part of their programmes of training and competition.

Figure 3.3 applies Hall's (2005) conceptualization of temporary mobility in space and time to the field of sport-related tourism and mobility. It incorporates classic leisure tourism (e.g., annual/seasonal vacations) that may include singular or multiple sporting elements. It also accommodates

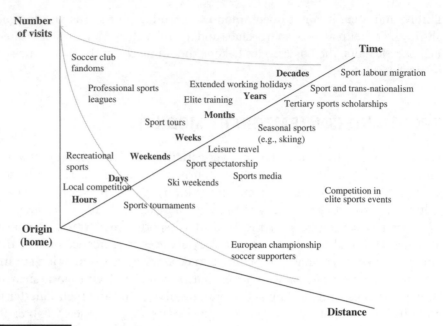

FIGURE 3.3   *The extent of sport-related mobility in space and time (Source: Adapted from Hall, 2005).*

'partial tourism' as it relates to sport-motivated mobility (e.g., football fandoms and other forms of sport spectatorship). Furthermore, Figure 3.3 incorporates classic elements of sport-driven mobility, which apply to all levels of competitive sport, from social competition through to elite and/or professional sport. These range from engagement in recreational sports and local/regional sports competitions (e.g., those commonly associated with school teams, young sports club members and their families) through to the production line of elite athletes, which includes training programmes, university scholarships, travel to participate in sports competitions and the migrations of professional sports people.

The spatial and temporal dimensions of sport tourism illustrated in Figure 3.3 are important given Hall's (2005) emphasis that tourism must be viewed within the wider social context of a range of mobilities and the factors that facilitate and/or constrain personal mobility at different life stages. Therefore, the spatial dimension in Figure 3.3 recognizes that sport-related mobility may involve regular local visits (e.g., to local sport facilities and competition venues) or typically less frequent visits to more distant destinations (e.g., to engage in sport spectatorship or to take up professional contracts). Equally, the temporal dimension ranges from trips that take hours (e.g., school teams travelling to compete in interschool sports) or days (e.g., sport tournaments) through seasonal sport-motivated mobility to years or decades in the case of the migration of elite athletes. Hall (2005) notes that migrations are rarely permanent as people commonly return to their place of origin either permanently or temporarily. This is certainly the case in sport labour migrations, which usually involve return trips to the athlete's place of origin (e.g., to visit friends and family during off seasons or simply to return 'home') and/or permanent return at the end of an athletic playing career or professional term.

THE EXTENT OF SPORT-RELATED MOBILITY

Clearly, sport and tourism phenomena can be viewed and analysed through a narrow or broad lens. A narrow approach may focus on discretionary leisure tourism as it relates to sports and may incorporate engagement in recreational sport while on holiday (e.g., skiing, kayaking, windsurfing) as well as participation and spectatorship at competitive and elite sports. Viewing sport through a wider lens, the approach adopted in this book, allows for a broader conceptualization of tourism, which includes leisure travel and business travel as well as various manifestations of long-term travel, circulation, migration and other forms of contemporary mobility. Such an approach incorporates patterns of circulation, tourism and mobility on a range of spatial scales including local, regional, domestic, international and global scales as well as various temporal scales, ranging from hours and days to years and decades.

In adopting a broad lens approach to the definition of tourism and mobility, this book also advocates an inclusive approach to the definition of sport (see Chapter 1, *Sport and tourism: Globalization, mobility and identity*). In an increasingly globalized world, patterns of sport-related mobility have rapidly diversified and now extend far beyond the long-established tradition of international representation involving outbound and return travel on competitive tours. Sport-related mobility spans a broad range of spatial and temporal scales as well as an ever diversifying range of competitive motivations, business and media interests and tourist/spectator experiences (Weed & Bull, 2004; Hinch & Higham, 2004). In terms of its spatial dimension, sport-related mobility incorporates the local, often daily or weekly, movements involving all age ranges. It extends through regional, domestic and national mobility in pursuit of interests in sport to transnational mobility relating to spectatorship, competition or the business of sports. Similarly within the temporal dimension, engagements in sport-related mobility range from several hours (to engage in or support local sports participation) through to the patterns of repeat travel, circulation and tourism associated with migrants and diasporic communities. Thus, participation in school sports now ranges from weekend local competition through to club representation at world events. Domestic competitions have become one level of aspiration as national competitions have merged into new scales of transnational and continent-wide leagues (e.g., UEFA, SANZAR). These now commonly occupy a new strata of competition between national and world championships. Professional competitions have expanded into minor leagues, college leagues, qualification tours and professional circuits (international and regional), all of which are associated with new mobilities in sport.

Contemporaneously, the phenomenon of sport labour migration has emerged as a significant consequence of the forces of globalization. The phenomenon of sports people migrating to take up professional player contracts is not new. Williams (1994), for example, describes the outward migration of Welsh rugby players to rugby league clubs in the north of England, noting that of 227 home union internationals who changed codes from rugby union to rugby league between 1895 and 1990, 156 were Welsh. Williams estimates that non-international players changing codes out-numbered internationals at the rate of 12–1, suggesting that over 2000 Welsh rugby players migrated to the North of England to play rugby league in the post-1895 period. This outward migration was symptomatic of economic trends in Wales where, particularly during the 1920s and 1930s, unem-ployment was consistently 10% above the national average (Williams, 1994). Interestingly, the revival of the post-war Welsh economy, leading to increased capital investment and employment in the 1960s, resulted in a reversal of this outward migration and the 'second golden era' of Welsh rugby in the 1970s. The historically close relationship between economy and sports labour migration is reconfirmed, however, by the fact that during the Thatcher years (1978–1990) and with the decline of coal mining, steel working and manufacturing since 1979, the outward migration of the interwar years was re-established and the 'second golden era' came to an end.

While sport labour migration is clearly not new, the transitory and highly mobile nature of sports talent as athletic labour is a relatively recent phenomenon (Maguire, 1999). As business professionals have become increasingly mobile (Jamieson, 1999), so is the case in sport. Maguire (1999:97) notes that 'today, the migration of sports talent as athletic labour is a major feature of the "new global cultural economy" '. Bale and Maguire (1994:1) note that 'athletes are on the move'; a statement that applies to professional athletes (e.g., football, baseball, basketball and ice hockey players) as well as coaches (e.g., ski instructors), managers, fitness trainers, dieticians and sports administrators. When Arsenal played Crystal Palace in an English Premier League fixture on 14 February 2005, it was notable for the fact that for the first time in the club's long history it fielded a team that did not include a single English-born player.

Sports labour migrations have become a common feature of the 'new global cultural economy'. The migration of athletic talent between countries and continents is most evident in professional sports such as American football, baseball, basketball and football (Maguire, 1999). Some small island states have long-standing traditions as nurseries for star athletes in specific sports. Examples of such links between professional sports and athletic talent include Cuba and baseball, Samoa and Rugby Union and Tonga and Rugby League. Reference is made to the term 'brawn drain' to describe the loss of outstanding athletes from these countries as they migrate in search of professional sports careers. For many these migrations extend throughout their competitive careers and may continue into retirement from competition.

At other temporal scales, sports such a cricket and skiing involve movements and migrations that are determined by sports seasons. Maguire (1999) refers to the natural rhythms of sporting seasons which, although increasingly subject to interference through the development of sports-capes, continue to dictate the seasonal context of many sport mobilities. Athletes who compete in other sports may experience even more transient forms of migration as they search for competition. Bale and Maguire (1994) describe the interweaving of seasonal and transitory migration patterns in sports such as golf and tennis. Those who compete professionally in these sports are subject to a constantly shifting workplace as determined by competition seasons and tournament schedules. Maguire (1999) explains that in 1996, while in search of a world ranking, Tim Henman played in 25 ATP tournaments in fifteen countries requiring over 65,000 miles of travel. Such short-term movements of athletes led Maguire (1999:98) to describe tennis and golf professionals as 'the nomads of the sports labour migration process with constantly shifting workplaces and places of residence'.

CONCLUSION

Contemporary mobility is the second of three overarching themes that provide a general context for the discussions presented in Chapters 5–13 (see Chapter 1, Figure 1.1). McCutcheon (2002) notes that some restrictive practices in sport that would be intolerable in other sectors of the market economy do still exist. These include non-recognition of coaching qualifications, national quotas and transfer deadlines. However, the reality for many is that the processes of globalization have reduced travel barriers and advanced various manifestations of mobility, including personal and professional mobilities (Hall, 2004). Viewing sport and tourism through the lenses of globalization and mobility provides rich veins of analysis and inquiry. For instance, the evolution of new sports offers opportunities to create strong ties between emergent sports and specific places (Hinch & Higham, 2004). The transportability of sports and sports resources allows destinations to 'adopt' sports and events, temporarily or permanently (Bale, 1989). The reproducibility of the sportscape facilitates the transportation of sports resources, some more so than others. This may represent a threat to specific destinations (Hinch & Higham, 2004). Yet, that threat can perhaps be countered with consideration given to unique, place specific and, therefore, non-transferable sport/tourism experiences (Morgan, 2007).

Place competition has become a central element of the globally competitive events bidding process (Cornelissen, 2006). In association with successful bids, it is not uncommon for second tier locations to feverishly develop their sports resource base to meet the criteria to host teams and/or competition events. They seek to host competitors or entire teams as they prepare for competition or acclimatize (Chalip, 2002) (see Chapter 5, *Globalization and the mobility of elite competitors*). Others may alternatively seek to attract the interests of tourists who visit destinations to experience large-scale sports events (Wright et al., 2007). Clearly, the mobility of sports resources, as well as the mobility of people who want to have a first-hand experience of their chosen sports, creates opportunities for the development of sports, the hosting of events and the pursuit of interests in tourism and hospitality (Higham, 2005).

The high mobility of sports, environments, amenities and resources, as well as sports people and tourists, has challenged the historical links between sports and places. Retaining and enhancing the idiosyncrasies and elements of uniqueness associated with a tourism site are important strategies to mitigate this threat (Bale, 1989:171). Many major sports are increasingly embedded within their historical contexts, with emphasis given to auras of tradition, perhaps as a strategy to counter the threat of athletic (individual), team and amenity mobilities. This has been successfully achieved at major events such as grand slam tennis tournaments, the golf majors (where little mobility between venues exists) and equestrian and horse racing events. Thus, place names like Wimbledon, St. Andrews, Aintree and Flemington have become synonymous with specific and iconic sports. The opposite is the case in Formula 1 (F1) motor racing where commercial rather than traditional values reign. Consequently, cities hosting F1 live under the constant threat of relocation. These manifestations of high contemporary mobility in sport and tourism provide an important overarching context for the discussions presented in the chapters that follow.

Culture and Identity

Globalization and increased mobility have changed us. We are no longer who we once were. Traditional reference points have disappeared. Our personal and collective worlds have expanded through exposure to new ideas, new activities, new people, new places and new forms of consumption. These changes have shaken the foundations of our personal and collective identities and in some cases have destroyed them. But as old foundations fall, new foundations are constructed. In this chapter we argue that globalization has resulted in a 'crisis of identity'. Sport and tourism represent important strategies that are being used to address this crisis. They represent manifestations of culture in a global world that are actively being used to build personal and collective narratives, which can ultimately provide the basis for the (re)construction of identity.

Prior to the 1991 World Cup rugby union semi-final match between Scotland and England, a Scottish player was quoted as saying that the match was not 'so much to do with rugby but nationhood' (Maguire, 1993:293). While the statement was apparently uttered in jest, Maguire suggests that it rang true in that it captured an important undercurrent of the competition. He used this issue of British/English culture and identity to raise questions about the 'crisis of identity' as it has emerged in the 1990s world of sport. It is this crisis of identity to which we now turn, with an examination of its roots in terms of the erosion of traditional reference points for identity formation. Typical responses to the crisis are then considered in terms of the emergence of fragmented and pluralistic identities. Finally, it is argued that a culture of leisure-based consumption has emerged as an important strategic response to this crisis.

THE CRISIS OF IDENTITY

Identity is typically determined in relation to difference. However, as boundaries are eroded through globalization and as worldwide popular cultures have grown, these traditional reference points have become less distinct. The 'great social categories which used to stabilize our collective identities, such as class, gender, race, and nation, have been deeply undermined by social, political, economic, and technological developments' (Jackson, 1998a:21). Globalization has caused us to rethink our views of these reference points, and while there have been many positive outcomes as old prejudices have been challenged, there have also been costs as the personal and collective narratives that helped us to articulate who we are and where we fit have become much more complex (Palmer, 1999). Since its inception, tourism has allowed privileged travellers to gaze on exotic 'others' thereby helping travellers to define themselves in a comparative sense. With the increased mobility described in Chapter 3 (*Sport and contemporary mobility*), contact with others has become more common. The exotic nature of this contact is, therefore, fading. Morley and Robins (1995:25) note that '[g]lobalization means that those we consider as Other or alien – the "new barbarians" – will be increasingly in our midst'. The divide between us and others is narrowing. Despite these changes to our social landscape, tourism remains a significant realm for the formation of identity. For example, the popularity of heritage tourism has grown as the crisis of identity has emerged. 'Rapid modernization and the concomitant destruction of the past have deepened nostalgia for the simpler and safer life of former times' (McLean & Cooke, 2003:156). Such nostalgia has increasingly taken the form of a search for roots and historical identity, as people try to make sense of their place in the world. Heritage tourism, including the veneration of sport-based heritage, represents one of the most direct manifestations of this search (Gammon & Ramshaw, 2007). Spectatorship and active participation in sporting activities also provide the opportunity for the development of personal and collective identities. For example, the 1991 rugby World Cup match between Scotland and England presented the spectators, as well as the players, with an opportunity to demonstrate their individual and collective identities through a high-profile sporting competition.

One of the major challenges of globalization in terms of identity formation is decreasing or at least changing relevance of the nation state or (de)territorialization as it was described in Chapter 2 (*Sport and tourism in a global world*). During the first seventy-five years of the twentieth century, nation states served as major sources of collective identity, but since then, their role in this process has been dramatically modified. Crolley et al.'s

(2002) examination of the commercialization of football in Europe suggested that like other traditional markers, sport is losing its strength as a symbol of national identity, at least in terms of professional competition. While Maguire's (1999) concept of international competitions as 'patriot games' continues to flourish in contests like the FIFA (Fédération Internationale de Football Association) World Cup and the Olympic Games, professional sport has grown less attached to the nation state. The cosmopolitan nature of professional team rosters along with cross-border leagues has eroded the status of many professional teams as national icons. Miller et al. (2001:37) capture this sentiment in their view that '[i]n rendering problematic both space and time, globalization confuses identity – one effect of which is to question the meaning and efficacy of nationalism'.

Responses to this identity crisis have taken a variety of forms. For example, rather than seeking identity through citizenship in a nation state, Mowforth and Munt (1998) have suggested that members of the growing middle class are constructing identities by adopting distinctive lifestyles such as those found in sport subcultures (see Chapter 7, *Recreational sport and serious leisure*). Other strategies include the conscious retrenchment of traditional nation-state identities, mediated identities that blend local and global cultures (Ben-Porat & Ben-Porat 2004; Melnick & Jackson, 2002) and recognition that identity is fluid and pluralistic (Milne & Ateljevic, 2004). This fluidity is exemplified in Wong and Trumper's (2002) example of the apparent contradiction of expatriate celebrity athletes like Ivan Zamoranon (formerly of Chile) and Wayne Gretzky (formerly of Canada) being held up as symbols of national identity in their countries of origin despite that fact that they have immigrated to other nation states.

Individuals and collectives have been forced to construct new identities as traditional ones have been eroded. Viken (2006:10) suggested that to 'survive, the post-modern individual is obliged to create a personal identity that is distinct and flexible'. These identities require the individual to develop and continually adjust narratives of the self. The rapid pace of change accompanying globalization means that identity evolves much faster than it has in the past. Similarly, the complexity of a globalized world means that identity has become much more pluralistic than it ever has been. Individuals and collectives have multiple identities, which, on some levels, resemble a form of schizophrenia with many of its associated challenges. On other levels, these multiple identities simply reflect the reality of the complex global society in which we live.

One of the responses to the crisis has been a retrenchment of the local. In some instances, globalization processes have

... prompted resistance by those within a national culture who still cling to more intense versions of the invented traditions that underpin their habitus and sense of identity. This may take various forms. Resistance both to pluralization processes and to the integrative tendencies associated with globalization reflects the ability of national cultures to be responsive to global flows. (Maguire, 1994:422)

As outlined in Chapter 2 (*Sport and tourism in a global world*), globalization is characterized by the 'consumption of culture' and by a 'culture of consumption'. Globalization has created economies based on the symbolic value of culture (Robinson & Smith, 2006) with tourism and sport being important elements in these economies. Urry (1995) has argued that while work is losing its influence as a determinant of identity, consumption, including leisure-based consumption, is becoming more influential. The choices that people make in terms of their consumption of sport and their consumption of tourism experiences form an important part of their identity narrative. It is not an accident that sports paraphernalia such as team jerseys are found in the souvenir kiosks in the departure lounges of international airports. Wearing a sport jersey that was purchased on an international trip is a personal statement. It is symbolic of an active global lifestyle balanced by an interest in local sporting cultures. Similarly, purchasing a sport tourism package such as a scuba diving expedition or a golf vacation contributes to the construction of an identity narrative for the individual, which reflects the collective to which he/she belongs or aspires. At the root of these behaviors is the cultural meaning attached to sport and tourism.

CULTURE, SPORT AND TOURISM

Culture is closely aligned with identity. It is a malleable concept that readily changes shape to suit the purposes of a broad range of users. Yet, culture is central to the way we construct our identities and in the way we discuss this construction. This section of the chapter positions sport and tourism as important cultural phenomena in the process of globalization.

The essence of culture

Culture is a nebulous term. While it generates serious debate both in the realms of academia and policy, there is no single definition that is universally accepted or, for that matter, acceptable. In their study of tourism in Scotland, Jack and Phipps (2005:11) expressed their frustration with this state of affairs by stating:

*... we are skeptical of the benefits of a continued overuse of the term
culture or the essentialising and intercultural modeling of so-called
cultural behaviours and national stereotypes. The idea of culture as
a concept has indeed become so overweening and overwritten as to
have become a problematic term in analytical contexts.*

Despite their concerns, Jack and Phipps go on to grudgingly argue the
utility of the term due to its common usage and acceptance as a reference to
the lives of peoples and the way of life found in nations. Part of their frustration might be attributable to the fact that culture is often used to refer to
the visual and performing arts. This 'high culture' interpretation is common
in Europe and is used more broadly in political and public debates on 'cultural
policy'. In this sense, sport is often seen in opposition to culture because of its
physical nature, although the boundaries blur in the context of sports such as
figure skating and rhythmic gymnastics with their emphasis on the
aesthetics of human movement.

For the purposes of this book, culture is seen as a 'way of life'. It is the
system of values, beliefs and behaviors found in the practice of living (Allison,
1982; John Hargreaves, 1982; Henderson, 2003; Robinson & Smith, 2006).
Culture is shared and exchanged in a wide range of forms inclusive of
institutional elements that characterize a place and its history but more
profoundly, it is found in day-to-day activities including the sporting activities of the people who live there.

Culture and tourism

Cultural tourism encompasses 'both the cultural nature of, and the role of,
tourism as a process and set of practices that revolve around the behavioural
pragmatics of societies, and the learning and transmission of meanings
through symbols and embodied through objects' (Robinson & Smith,
2006:1). It includes a broad range of cultural products but is increasingly
anchored in perceived differences between the home culture of the visitor and
the everyday culture found in the destination.

The Grand Tour which saw English privileged classes travelling to centres
of high society throughout continental Europe in the sixteenth century serves
as a good example of an early form of cultural tourism, albeit with a 'high
cultural' flavour. More generally, however, a significant portion of today's
tourists has an interest in different ways of life or different cultures. One
reason for this interest was articulated by McCannell (1973, 1976) who
suggested that the pressures of modernity were responsible for the emergence
of a search for authenticity by tourists. As work and home-based alienation
grew, tourists became increasingly interested in finding meaning through

their travels. By gaining insight into different ways of life or culture, travellers captured a sense of the authenticity they were searching for (see Chapter 8, *Authentic experiences*).

We do not mean to imply, however, that this search for authenticity is universal. In fact, much of mass tourism is dominated by a hedonistic search for pleasure. Craik (1997) used the term 'culture-proof' in reference to tourists who have no interest in cultural differences. A good example of this type of tourists is one who frequents seaside resorts with a focus on the sea, sand, and sun. Such tourists tend to consciously avoid contact with people from the surrounding communities and to remain oblivious to the cultural nuances that may have infiltrated the resort.

Notwithstanding the existence of indifference in some quarters, it is clear that culture is an important dimension of tourism. High culture attractions such as Broadway plays in New York, opera performances in the Sydney Opera House or art exhibits in galleries throughout the world are in great demand. Heritage tourists flock to museums and interpretive centres (Timothy & Boyd, 2003). Indigenous cultures have been the focus of many tourism developments in core and peripheral areas (Butler & Hinch, 2007). Festivals of all types continue to be promoted as cultural tourism products (Sofield & Sivan, 2003). Cultural icons like the British monarchy and the pyramids of Egypt are prominently featured in tourism promotions. All of these aspects of culture and countless others have been commodified for tourism. They are commonly referred to as 'products' in the tourism industry, and while critics of cultural tourism have high-lighted a range of negative impacts associated with their commodification (Greenwood, 1989), they continue to be in demand. For many visitors, they have provided genuine insight into the culture of a destination. While the tourism industry has been guilty of distorting place-based culture in its pursuit of profit, destination communities attempt to highlight the things they find positive about their identities by the way they produce these cultural tourism attractions. Urry (1995) has suggested that tourism is, in fact, an extension of normative culture in that it represents those aspects of the community that tourism producers choose to display to others.

More and more tourists are looking for more than the 'cultural icons' and are seeking 'everyday culture'. Rather than seeing the changing of the guard at Buckingham Palace, it is the purchase of fish and chips at a local shop that often defines an authentic cultural experience for today's visitor to England. Robinson and Smith (2006) argue that it is these 'popular' everyday expressions of culture that are of growing interest to tourists. Sport is one of the most prominent manifestations of this everyday culture.

Culture and sport

Huizinga (1938) was one of the first scholars to highlight the connection between sport and culture with his suggestion that culture is rooted in play. Contemporary scholars continue to see sport as a manifestation of local and global culture. For example, notwithstanding the issue of (de)territorialization, Jackson (1998b:236) argues that '[a]s a popular cultural form and practice, sport has been at the forefront of many nations' search for a national identity'. Sport features prominently in news and entertainment media including print, traditional broadcast and emerging forms of electronic media. It is at the heart of the culture of consumption given its broad-based appeal and the relative ease with which it can be packaged for consumption. Sport's appeal as a form of popular culture is manifold, but important elements include 1) the passion that is engendered by sport competition and active sport pursuits; 2) tensions that accompany uncertain outcomes; 3) sport's ability to generate vicarious excitement as spectators align themselves with their favorite athletes and teams; 4) the collective experience of sport that goes beyond the confines of the spectators at the competition site to what is usually a much larger broadcast audience and, 5) its unique rituals, drama and symbolism (Hargreaves, 1982).

In addition to being a form of popular culture, sport is a form of deep culture (Galtung, 1982). Given this characteristic of sport, scholars such as Allison (1982:14) have called for further academic enquiry in this realm.

> Beyond the immediately recognizable content of the game such as of rules, styles, strategies, and materials which make up the raw data which the social scientist must understand, analyses must try to discern, beyond such content, the implicit pattern, design or deep structure which form the cultural foundation of such behaviour.

Sport serves as an agent for socialization between generations (e.g., Piaget, 1965) and between other types of social groups. For example, Bourdieu (1978) used the term 'class habitus' to describe class socialization process. He suggested that working classes tend to have an instrumental orientation. Their preferred sports were characterized by strength, endurance and aggression. In contrast, privileged classes preferred sporting activities that were aimed at maintaining and enhancing one's own health. Interaction between these groups not only provides each with insight into the other's culture but also results in socialization as each group adopts some of the traits of the other or modifies their own sporting culture.

Sport also serves as a medium for socialization between visitors and hosts in the case of sport tourism. Allison (1982:33) studied a similar dynamic in the context of native American Indians in the United States with the conclusion that

> … *play, games, and sport become one of the media within which cultural messages are communicated and transferred from one individual to another, and in this case from one culture to another. Thus, play, games, and sport forms are simultaneously the content of culture which is to be transferred, and too, are the media with which such transfer occurs. They are products of culture, yet part of the process of culture transmission as well.*

Sport as a cultural tourist attraction

The culture dimension of sport makes it a powerful tourist attraction. Its appeal is found in both the 'deep cultural' differences imbedded in local practices and in the more subtle differences associated with the ways that popular global sports are produced and consumed in other places. The physicality of sport is one of its defining characteristics as a tourist attraction.

> *Regardless of the form (professional/amateur, athletic/gymnastic, cosmopolitan/nationalistic), sporting movements articulated explicit reflexive practices that enabled participants and spectators to learn about themselves individually and collectively. At the core of these reflexive practices were the physical, sensual and ephemeral bodies of athletes and spectators.* (Brown, 2001:78–79)

Hargreaves (1982) pointed out that the relationship of the individual to his or her body is a central feature of sport and that it forms a fundamental aspect of the habitus. More recently, Hockey and Collinson (2007) have argued along a similar line in terms of embodiment and sport. This fundamental relationship between the body and sporting activity is relatively easy to illustrate in the case of active participation whether it is the sensual feel of the water, sun and sand when participating in water sports at a beach or the physical exertion that is required of a cycle tour in the mountains (see Chapter 8, *Authentic experiences*). It is less explicit in the case of spectator activity but even though the actual physical performance may be vicarious in nature, it encourages reflexive practices that provide unique opportunities to gain insight into the physical culture indigenous to a place, and in turn, it serves to construct the personal narrative of the sport tourist.

Leiper's (1990) definition of a tourist attraction as the empirical relationship between tourists (people), a nucleus (the site of the tourist experience) and the markers that inform the visitors about the nucleus provides a good framework for understanding sport as a cultural attraction

(Hinch & Higham, 2004). In their search for identity, tourists are able to develop personal narratives based on their cultural experiences of sport and place as played out at the nucleus. A wide array of markers, inclusive of tourism promotions and sport commentaries are available to help the individual to articulate the relevance of these sport tourism experiences as determinants of personal and collective identity.

NEGOTIATING IDENTITY

Sport and tourism cultures can be important factors in the way we see ourselves and how others see us. These cultures often form core elements of the personal narratives that are used to construct individual and group identities. In challenging identity, globalization has forced us to articulate new personal narratives or to actively protect and reinforce our existing identities. In essence, we have been required to (re)negotiate our identities within the volatile landscape of globalization, with sport and tourism offering attractive forums for this negotiation.

Nature of identity

There are two dominant perspectives on the nature of identity. The first and more traditional perspective suggests that there is one underlying identity at the core of an individual and collective. While identities are seen to change as individuals or collectives progress through their lifecycle, these changes are viewed as being incremental and predictable. The alternative view is that individual and collective identities are closely related to the environment in which they exist. Given the complexities and dynamic nature of the global environment, this view implies that personal and collective identities are pluralistic and dynamic.

Jackson (1998b) has suggested that the singular perspective 'emphasizes the search for an authentic identity' or what Grossberg (1996:89) referred to as a 'common origin or common structure of experience or both'.

> *Within this model, where struggles occur with respect to the politics of media representation, there is a tendency to define collective identities, including national ones, as distinct, fully constituted entities. Hence, sport is assumed to act as a vehicle for confirming a sense of citizenship, fostering a sense of social bonds and serving as an unashamed celebration of nationalism and patriotism.* (Jackson, 1998b:229)

Viken (2006:10) described this ethos view of identity as being 'primordial, immanent and primarily inner-driven'.

The alternative view suggests 'that identities are unstable, continually in process, incomplete, and relational' (Jackson, 1998b:230). Despite lingering longings about some underlying unitary sense of being, this view sees identity as being multi-faceted and in constant flux. Viken (2006:10) expands on this pluralistic perspective by suggesting that contemporary western society is 'characterized by cultural hybridity, float and fluidity'. He suggests that while some elements of identity appear to be fixed, more generally they are a matter of reflection, choice and change. He goes on to suggest that there are 'layers of identities, some being more profound and stable than others, but that these identities can be of different types and have different origins' (Viken, 2006:11).

This pluralistic view of identity dominates current academic views on the topic, with the relational nature of identity being the most common. Identities are formed through comparisons to other individuals or groups. One of the challenges of identity formation in a global world is that there are countless identities that can be used for comparison and most of these are transitory in nature. Tourism can be seen as a search to establish identity through contact with the 'other'. By implication, tourism marketing and destination development are processes of identity construction for both the hosts and the guests.

Tourism and identity

Tourism is a form of consumption that helps individuals and collectives construct their identities in an increasingly complex world. Tourists are consumers of places. Consumption occurs as tourists search for reference points that help them (re)construct their personal identity. In contrast, the tourism industry and destination hosts are the producers. Through their tourism activities, producers articulate place-based identity, which influences both hosts and guests. In this vein, Milne and Ateljevic (2004:97) suggest that

> *The creation of meaning and experiences is becoming a key avenue for capital accumulation, with leisure and tourism at the forefront of this trend. The identities of geographically defined places, namely tourist destinations, are endlessly (re-)invented, (re-)produced, (re-)captured and (re-)created by the simultaneous coexistence of global and local forces. Tourism activity not only gives shape to the land, and provides jobs and income to local peoples, but also produces meanings and representations. Tourism promotional material creates and projects powerful social, cultural and psychological meanings of place, in turn increasing and reproducing its value. For their part, consumers collect, read, interpret, compare and communicate these meanings (re-)producing processes of place (re-)construction.*

While many, if not all, forms of tourism play important roles in the formation of individual and collective identities, heritage tourism is one of the most consciously produced and consumed forms of tourism in this regard. Typically, heritage tourism is offered as a peaceful retreat from the bustle and confusion of globalization. Palmer (1999:315) suggests that its main aim is 'the packaging of an identity for sale to tourists'. As such, it goes 'to the heart of a people because it serves to define their cultural identity and to make this visible, both to themselves, and to "others"' (Palmer, 1999:316).

A good example of the role of heritage tourism in identity formation can be found in contemporary national museums. While the primary purpose of these museums is to serve as a repository of artefacts of national significance, in doing so, they become public statements of national identity. In their role as tangible manifestations of identity, museums are increasingly positioned as domestic and international tourist attractions. McLean and Cooke (2003:154) argue that the 'national museum … represents the nation in time and place, embodying the legitimacy of the heritage of the nation for both citizens and the "other"'. It, therefore, serves a formative as well as reflective role in terms of identity. This is particularly true of sport halls of fame and museums (Gammon & Ramshaw, 2007).

Sport and identity

Sport also plays a prominent role in the formation of identity in the western world and increasingly across the entire globe. Bale (1986:18) argues that

> [w]hether at local, regional or national level, sport is, after war, probably the principle means of collective identification in modern life. It provides one of the few occasions when large, complex, impersonal and functionally bonded units such as cities or countries can unite as a whole. Identification with a sports team binds people to a place simply through ascription, an unfamiliar way of obtaining pride and status in a meritocracy.

Evidence to support this claim abounds in the form of the partisan support given to a nation's sport teams during international competitions or to local competitions between neighbouring communities. This perspective is illustrated by the Bedouin saying, 'I against my brother; I and my brother against my cousin; I and my brother and my cousin against the world' (Fougere, 1989:116).

Not only does sport play an important role in terms of the formation of collective identities, it also serves a similar function for individuals. To be involved in particular sports as a participant or a supporter is part of a personal narrative that is used to articulate one's identity. Such involvement can become a 'badge of identity' in combination with other cultural markers such as religion and nationality (Boyle & Haynes, 2000). As these badges of identity are aggregated at various levels, collective identities emerge.

Sport has been pursued and used as an 'anchor of meaning' in a world characterized by the turbulence of globalization. Maguire (1999) has suggested that events like the Wimbledon Tennis Championships serve as counterpoints to change given their long history and relatively stable focus. Another example of the use of sport to recapture what may, in fact, have been an imagined past of simpler times and clearer collective identities is what Maguire (1999) has referred to as 'patriot games'. These games take the form of international competitions 'in which the "special charisma" embodied in the view which nations have of themselves can be nurtured, refined and further developed' (Maguire, 1999:182). Tuck (2003) expressed a similar view by arguing that '[s]porting competition arguably provides the primary expression of imagined communities; the nation becoming (at least temporarily) more "real" in the domain of sport. As such, sport becomes an important expression of collective identity for the consumption of internal as well as external audiences'.

In a related argument, Devine and Devine (2004) suggest that sport is politicized in Northern Ireland, with Protestants more likely to engage in games like football, rugby, hockey and cricket while Catholics are more likely to engage in Gaelic games. As such, the activities of the Gaelic Athletics Association (GAA) of Ireland offer an interesting variation of the 'patriot games' approach to promoting traditional collective identities. Devine and Devine (2004:178) argue:

> [t]he GAA was set up to nurture a sense of Irish identity and throughout Northern Ireland the local GAA club is at the heart of the community. It is not just a form of recreation but an expression of the people and their culture. The commitment and the passion of the GAA members is (sic) not just confined to sport - they also promote Irish language, music and dance.

Jutel (2002:195) may perhaps overstate the case by suggesting that sport 'is a perfect forum for identity construction, as the nature of competition, with the mandatory opponents, circumscribes teams (or individuals into the team) and their adversaries: us and them, self and other'. She goes on, however, to highlight emerging notions of identity that reflect the complexities of a globalized world. She uses the example of conflicting strategies used by cyclists in international races when they compete against individuals who are their teammates on professional circuits. This conflict demonstrates that cyclists have difficulty in separating their traditional national identities from their professional identities in today's global world. Identity confusion is likely to increase. Maguire (1994) postulates that identity has become multilayered and can be thought of as a flexible lattice of interconnections.

Clearly, sport is an arena where processes of personal habitus/identity testing and formation are conducted. Sport plays an important role in embodying multiple notions of identity. Different sports represent individuals, communities, regions and nations, and a key feature of the sports process is that it is used by different groups, established as well as emergent or outsider groups, to represent, maintain and/or challenge identities (Maguire, 1994:410)

CONCLUSION

The tourism industry actively responds to the crisis of identity that has accompanied globalization because it is good for business. Tourists are consciously and unconsciously building their personal narratives based on the travel experiences that they accumulate, and the industry reacts willingly to these demands. Sport is also a fertile realm for the development of personal narratives that help individuals and collectives to (re)negotiate identity given its identity discourses and its physical and experiential nature. The confluence of sport and tourism is, therefore, a very potent area for identity formation. It is the combination of the tourism industry's economic incentive to respond to the need for tourists to develop personal narratives with sport's unique ability to function as a culturally based attraction that makes sport tourism particularly significant in terms of identity formation.

The cultural discourses of sport form an important discursive practice that emphasizes sport's role in the formation of individual and collective identities (Tuck, 2003). Hargreaves (1982) described the hegemony of the dominant class as being perhaps the most pervading form of influence in the (re)negotiation of identity. She described it as a form of class domination embedded in 'commonsense'. It is a form of influence that is not coercive in nature but nonetheless reflects the interests of the dominant class. Hegemonic practices become the norm that defines acceptable ranges of behavior and debate. In the context of sport, the parameters of identity formation are set by those in positions of power such as the sport governing bodies. Sporting identities are, therefore, strongly influenced by the rules of behavior and the overriding cultures that characterize a given sport in a given place.

While the emergence of the Gay Games, Paralympics and counter cultural oriented extreme sports suggests that hegemonic control is not absolute in sport, it remains a dominating force. Under globalization, this hegemonic force is being shaped by parties with major financial interests in sport. Beyond the central role of professional sport owners, media and major event hosts, there are a broad range of groups such as sport equipment manufacturers like Nike who consciously commodify sporting images and identities in pursuit of financial gain. The tourism industry is one of the cultural industries that constantly search for 'new varieties of ethnic wares' (Maguire, 1994:409). In promoting sport tourism, it is actively influencing identity formation by articulating a sport-based discourse that plays an increasingly important role in the formation of individual and collective identities.

While these powerful discourses go a long way in explaining how sport tourism helps or perhaps constrains the (re)negotiation of individual and collective identities, they do not provide much insight into the popularity of sport tourism in this search for identity. It is clear that more research is needed into 'the corporeal realities of the lived sporting body' (Hockey & Collinson, 2007:115). The physical and sensory nature of sport provides very concrete but often overlooked aspects of culture that are used in the development of personal narratives. While academics have tended to examine intellectual discourses on sport, these are not the only discourses at play in identity formation. Physical practices and physical ways of knowing are also important parts of identity narratives. To a large extent, it is the physical culture of sport that is responsible for its passion, tension, excitement and drama. The sensory dimensions of sport as a physical practice provide unique links between the sport tourists and the sites that they visit. Negotiating a mountain pass by motor coach is a dramatically different experience to negotiating an alpine trail by mountain bike. The physical dimension of the latter is likely to have a much more profound impact on the tourist's sense of place and sense of self than the former. This difference lies in the practical consciousness gained through the physical nature of sport tourism.

PART 3

Activity

CHAPTER 5

Globalization and the Mobility of Elite Competitors

The globalization of sports, sport leagues and competitions and the high contemporary mobility of elite competitors provide a new and intriguing domain of sport-related tourism research. This chapter explores the sport and tourism interests associated with elite competition. It may be argued that for most athletes travel is both an unavoidable requirement of the search for competition and a constraint, perceived or otherwise, acting against optimum performance. An emerging discourse now addresses the relationship between travel, competition in unfamiliar environments and elite sports performance, although little detailed attention has been paid to the travel and destination needs of elite athletes *per se*. This chapter seeks to redress this imbalance by considering issues that arise from the high mobility of elite athletes. It also raises questions about the functions that tourism places perform for competitive athletes, both in terms of places of performance as well as leisure and tourism spaces serving interests in escape from the pressures of competition.

These considerations differ with the context of competition. Tennis was one of the first international sports in the 1870s. The Davis Cup was truly global by the 1960s by which time it was contested by fifty nations (Smart, 2007). Prior to this major global sports events were essentially limited to a small number of four-yearly events such as the Summer (1896) and Winter (1924) Olympic Games, Winter Olympics and FIFA World Cup. A small number of biennial events, such as the world athletics championships (held exclusively in Europe prior to 2002), attracted athletes mainly from Europe and North America. In recent years this situation has changed completely as various annual and biennial world championships serving genuinely intercontinental and global athletic coverage have been established for a myriad of mainstream and alternative sports. Indeed club competitions, formerly

CONTENTS

domestic, have expanded with the establishment of transnational and pan-continental competitions and champions leagues. Thus, high mobility and trans-meridian travel now extends to athletes involved in daily or weekly league competitions and seasonal tournament schedules as well as annual or biennial world championship events or four-yearly mega events (Table 5.1). These aside, athletic mobility includes travel undertaken by individual or groups of individual competitors and team sport personnel, for the purposes of training, acclimatization and competition. This chapter, then, considers contemporary manifestations of mobility and tourism within the sphere of elite sport as an activity.

THE GLOBALIZATION OF INTERNATIONAL SPORT

Until recently, the Olympic Games were one of the very few truly worldwide sporting events. Few other sports were contested at regularly recurring global championship competitions. The forces of globalization, including high contemporary mobility and global media coverage, have dramatically changed this scenario (Maguire et al., 2002). In recent years countless sporting codes, from the mainstream to the alternative and the obscure, have developed their own forms of national, international and global competitions, many of which require athletes to travel in order to compete on the domestic, national and global stages of elite competition (Manfredini et al., 2000).

This changing competitive environment throws up manifold issues and challenges. Gratton et al. (2005), for example, note that since the mid-1980s cities have competed to host global events such as the Olympic Games. However, as international and world championship competitions have developed to serve the plethora of less globally recognized sports, many have identified opportunities to develop sports event programmes in second-tier or regional cities, which may never aspire to hosting global sports mega events. In many respects this is a less certain event development strategy given that the world championships serving many sports, such a badminton, judo and equestrian, are subject to less assured levels of spectator interest and less dependable economic benefits (Gratton et al., 2005).

Manifold issues and challenges must also be addressed by elite athletes themselves and those supporting their competitive endeavours directly or indirectly. One consequence is that elite athletes travel great distances, usually by air, to international competitions, and their periods of travel and competition may extend over days, weeks, months or years. Many elite athletes may be required to travel almost continuously through the years of their competitive careers. Some individual athletes (e.g., golf and tennis professionals)

Table 5.1	Examples of Elite Domestic and International Sports Competitions that Require Trans-Meridian Travel		
Domestic and International Competitions	**Sports Leagues and Events**	**Spatial Range**	**Time Zones**
Daily, weekly league seasonal competitions	UEFA Cup football	Trans-Europe	4
	Champions League football	Trans-Europe	4
	European Basketball	Trans-Europe	4
	European Ice Hockey	Trans-Europe	4
	NBA Basketball	Trans-USA	6
	NFL American Football	Trans-USA	6
	US College Sports	Trans-USA	6
	NHL Ice Hockey	North America	6
	Major League Baseball	North America	6
	Super 14 Rugby	South Africa, Australia, New Zealand	12
	AFL Football	Trans-Australia	4
	ANBL Basketball	Australia, New Zealand, Singapore	6
	Netball	Australia, New Zealand	7
Seasonal tournament schedules	PGA European Golf tour	Trans-North America	12
	PGA North American Golf tour	Trans-Asia	6
	PGA Asian Golf tour	Global	4
	ATP Tennis tour	Trans-USA	12
	Nascar motor racing	Global	6
	Formula One Grand Prix	Global	12
	A1GP	Global	12
	IRB Sevens	Global	12
	World Surfing championship tour		12
Annual events	European Short Course Swimming	Trans-European	4
	Grand slam tennis tournaments	Global	12
	British Open Squash	Global	12
	National horse racing events	Global	12
	US National Track and Field champs	Trans-USA	6
	Hong Kong Sevens	Global	12
	World Squash Championship	Global	12
	Davis Cup/Federation Cup tennis	Global	12
	World Badminton Championship	Global	12

Table 5.1	Examples of Elite Domestic and International Sports Competitions that Require Trans-Meridian Travel—*continued*		
Domestic and International Competitions	**Sports Leagues and Events**	**Spatial Range**	**Time Zones**
Biennial events	FINA World Swimming Champs	Global	12
	FISA World Rowing Champs	Global	12
	FIFA World Track and Field Champs	Global	12
	Asian Games	Trans-Asia	4
	European Football Champion	Trans-Europe	4
Four-yearly events	Olympic Games	Global	12
	Winter Olympic Games	Global	12
	Para Olympic Games	Global	12
	FIFA World Cup	Global	12
	IRB Rugby World Cup	Global	12
	ICC Cricket World Cup	Global	12

purchase multiple places of residence to allow themselves to feel more at home in places of training and regions of seasonal competition. All are required to develop strategies to minimize the stresses of travel, strike appropriate balances between stimulation and boredom and achieve a temporary living environment from which they are most likely to achieve their highest possible level of competitive performance. Some, such as those competing at international equestrian (e.g., Badminton Horse Trials) or international horse racing events (e.g., Japan Cup, Kentucky Derby, Melbourne Cup or Dubai Classic), also need to contend with the travel arrangements, quarantine, health and fitness of the animals with which they compete.

SPORT, GLOBALIZATION AND IDENTITY

The globalization of elite sport has had implications for sport performance as it relates to national identity (see chapter 4, *Culture and identity*). Sport is one of the main ways in which people develop personal and collective identities. National identity may be thought of as ways in which nations differ from one another in terms of stereotypes, symbols and practices, including those associated with sport (Jackson, 1994; McConnell & Edwards, 2000). Nauright (1996:69) notes that sport 'is one of the most significant shapers of collective or group identity in the contemporary world. In many cases, sporting events and people's reaction to them are the clearest public manifestations of culture and collective identities in a given society'. Certainly international sporting success provides a sense of common identity (Bale, 1989; 1993; McGuirk & Rowe, 2001). The performances of sport heroes and heroines may generate a great sense of personal esteem, emotional wellbeing and national pride (Nauright, 1996; Dauncey & Hare, 2000). As Beardsley (1987:111) noted in the late 1980s '… Wayne Gretzky is the latest in a long line of hockey heroes who personify the hopes, wishes, and dreams of the Canadian people'.

It is perhaps for these reasons, among others, that elite sport development systems have been created in a number of countries to promote elite international sports performance. From 1955–1988 the former German Democratic Republic (GDR) and Soviet Bloc countries were at the vanguard of national elite sport systems. Their development systems were built on systemic youth talent identification, a professional system of talent development and support for sporting excellence (Green & Oakley, 2001). Despite contrasting western ideologies of the role of sport in society, western countries have increasingly taken the development of elite sport seriously (Green & Oakley, 2001). Thus, it is increasingly common for national sport policies to

1. Identify and monitor the development of athletic talent;

2. Create and fund institutes of sport to foster the development of athletic talent;

3. Support competitive programmes that focus on high levels of international exposure;

4. Develop training and science facilities to specifically serve elite athletes;

5. Target resources at a limited number of sports or individual athletes based on an analysis of real prospects of success on the world stage;

6. Undertake comprehensive planning for the specific needs of individual sports/athletes; and

7. Invest in lifestyle support and preparation for life after sport.

Following the Soviet model, and through the development of similar policies in countries such as Australia, USA, Canada, the United Kingdom, France and Spain (Green & Oakley, 2001), there is some evidence of a trend towards uniformity in elite sport development systems. The evolution of close athletic management systems in many countries, in pursuit of athletic identification, development and elite international sport performance, is one manifestation of globalization in sport. Bosscher, De Knop, Van Bottenbury and Shibli (2006) observe that 'medal counting' has become an indicator of international success, which is commonly used by media and politicians. They also provide some interesting perspectives on factors leading to international success in elite competition. They classify these factors into three levels:

1. Micro level: Individual athletes (genetic qualities) and their immediate environment (e.g., parents, friends, competitors, coaches). At the micro level some factors such as training regimes and tactics can be controlled, while others such as genetic make-up (as yet) cannot;

2. Meso level: Sport policies and politics. Carefully considered sports policies can influence long-term sporting success; and

3. Macro level: The social and cultural context, including economic welfare, population, urbanization, geographic and climatic factors, political and cultural systems.

In terms of sport development and elite sport performance systems, Bosscher et al. (2006) note that macro-level factors lie entirely or largely beyond the influence of sport policies, at least in the short term. On the other hand, meso-level sports policies and politics can, if carefully considered, bear influence over the identification of youth talent and the nurturing of that talent with the aim of fulfilling elite international competition ambitions. That said, Bosscher et al. (2006:186) also note that 'although many attempts have been made to explain why certain countries are more successful than others, the relationship between policies and success is not clear'. However, while macro and meso-level factors influence many aspects of sport development, such as sports that people choose to pursue, talent identification, training and coaching and support for elite competitors, it is ultimately micro-level factors, particularly those immediately surrounding the competition environments, that assert direct influence over performance in the days, hours, minutes or seconds of concentrated competition. With this in mind, and given the need for most elite athletes to travel considerable distances in search of the highest levels of international competition, it is remarkable that so little attention has been paid to the interface between athlete mobility and elite performance.

THE ATHLETIC MOBILITY CONTEXT: CHANGING PERSPECTIVES

Different competition contexts provide quite unique travel and performance challenges (see Chapter 3, *Sport and contemporary mobility*). Not only have sporting competitions been globalized, but competition contexts have diversified with implications of travel demands placed on elite and non-elite sport participants. Table 5.2 relates specifically to elite sports, highlighting four manifestations of elite competition (annual league competitions, seasonal sports, regularly recurring sports events and annual tournament schedules) that raise specific travel demands and challenges for those who travel in search of competition.

Table 5.2	The Competition and Travel Context for Mobile Elite Sports	
Competition Context	**Manifestations of Mobility**	**Travel Considerations**
Annual league competitions	Frequent (daily/weekly) Generally intercity, short–medium haul	Travel schedules Team living arrangements Location of accommodation Accommodation facilities Security
Seasonal sports	Regular (seasonal) Long haul (N–S hemisphere)	Trans-meridian travel Travel stress and jet lag Individual and/or team living arrangements
Events	Regular (e.g., annual) Medium–long haul	Trans-meridian travel Travel stress and jet lag Travel schedules Pre-event training Protecting routines Balancing novelty and routine Acclimatization Immunization Individual and/or team living arrangements Location of accommodation Accommodation facilities
Tournament schedules	Frequent	Travel weariness Training and living bases Mental fatigue Dietary concerns Training facilities Protecting routines Mental stimulation Accommodation facilities

The perspectives of both sports organizations and tourism destination managers have changed dramatically in recent years in response to this changing context. Professional sports organizations (PSOs) and teams have little or no say in where competition games take place, unless safety and security concerns arise. Sports governing bodies, competition owners, sports associations and/or media rights holders possess negotiated influence over places of competition. However, Francis and Murphy (2005:76) note that 'while team management does not determine the choice of venue, it does have direct influence on the choice of destination selected and revenue spent for "away match" preparation. The decision process concerning where sports teams are based in preparation for, and immediately in advance of, competition is poorly understood. There is no doubt that facility availability and service quality are two important factors'.

The destination management perspective has changed in response to the evolving demands of professional sports organizations and team management. In the amateur era of sport, athletes had little influence over choice of destination and were seen as low-budget and potentially unruly visitors who were prone to compromising the goodwill of other guests (Francis & Murphy, 2004). As Francis and Murphy (2005) note, aside from on field performance, the success of PSOs is now determined in large part by public image, positive media attention and uncomplicated and enduring sponsorship arrangements. As a consequence, professional athletes and administrators are now subject to strict codes of conduct in terms of behaviour. Professional sports teams are also lucrative clients in terms of the resourcing of team preparation prior to competition. These priorities have made sports teams a much more attractive proposition for destination managers and accommodation providers. The fact that many travelling supporters like to base themselves close to their team may mean that destinations that are successful in hosting sports teams also attract the benefits (and perhaps costs) associated with volumes of travelling supporters. Unlike in the recent past, lodging establishments are increasingly aware of and responsive to the needs of elite athletes and are prepared to customize both the physical environment and service delivery to cater specifically to the needs of PSOs (Francis & Murphy, 2005).

ATHLETIC MOBILITY AND COMPETITIVE PERFORMANCE

Home ground advantage

The importance of the travel factor in elite sport is perhaps best captured by Bale (1989) who notes a discernable pattern between the home or away status of sports contests and the probability of winning. This is no doubt due in part to the advantages of home ground support and of playing and competing in familiar surroundings (e.g., training facilities, stadium facilities, familiar weather conditions). However, this is a partial picture. Again, Bale (1989) notes that not only is winning away less probable than at home, but 'the probability of winning forms a clear gradient according to distance from home' (Bale, 1989:31). The further a team travels from its home venue, the less likely it is to win. So home ground advantage and home support is important, but apparently so too are the stresses of long haul travel, which brings with it disturbances of physical and mental routines.

Manfredini et al. (2000:182) note that 'rapid air travel across time zones exposes the traveller to a shift in the internal biological clock and to a transient desynchronization of their rhythms which lasts until rhythms adjust to the new environmental conditions'. The symptoms of jet lag, again according to Manfredini et al. (2000), may include sleep disorders, difficulties with concentration, depression, irritability, distorted estimation of time, space and distance, light-headedness, loss of appetite and gastrointestinal disturbance. Furthermore, the further one travels, the more likely it is that the traveller encounters new climates and weather conditions as well as possibly new atmospheric conditions associated with the altitude and air quality of the destination, which may complicate or prolong the readjustment period. Clearly, travelling to new and unfamiliar places of competition brings with it a range of physiological, psychological, immunological, bacterial and environmental challenges, which also serve to explain why winning is much more straightforward when competition takes place close to, or preferably at, home (Table 5.2).

A number of studies addressing a range of sports have sought to quantify home advantage scientifically (Hugh Morten, 2006). These include studies of such varied sports as cricket (Clarke & Allsopp, 2001), ice hockey (Gayton, Matthews & Nickless, 1987), alpine skiing (Bray & Carron, 1993), football (Clark & Norman, 1995) and Australian Rules Football (Stefani & Clarke, 1992) as well as events such as the winter and summer Olympic Games (Balmer, Nevill & Williams, 2001). All of these studies, and others, have 'almost invariably demonstrated the existence of a high positive home advantage, either on average or to most of the competitors (individuals or teams) taking part in sports events or sports league competitions' (Hugh Morten, 2006:495).

Hugh Morten's (2006) study of home advantage in the Super 12 (now Super 14) and Tri-nations rugby competitions (2000–2004) confirms that home ground advantage exists when analysed on the basis of both results (win/loss) and points scored. The Super 12 recorded 345 matches in the five seasons between 2000 and 2004, of which 217 (63.0%) were won by the home team (five-year range, 58–72%). During the same period the three teams involved in the Tri-nations (Australia, South Africa and New Zealand) recorded 22 home wins from 30 test matches played (73.3%) (Hugh Morten, 2006). However, it is also noted that home advantage tends to vary considerably from one year to the next in both competitions, and no teams established a consistent home advantage record from one season to the next during the period under analysis.

These results occurred consistently despite the fact that one is a balanced league and the other is an imbalanced league. In the former case, the Tri-nations was played between three national teams, each playing the others once at home and once away from home. In the case of the latter, the Super 12 involves 5/6 home and 6/5 away games for each team, and it is possible, and indeed not uncommon, that in a given year any team may face weak opposing teams at home and strong opposition teams away, or vice versa. One of the few constants in Hugh Morten's (2006) study, and Pretorius, Pierce and Litvine's (2000) study of South Africa's domestic Currie Cup (rugby) competition, is that the highest home advantage in both cases lay with the Cats (Super 12) and Lions (Currie Cup), and indeed the Springboks (Tri-nations) when they play in Pretoria and Johannesburg, pointing clearly to the home advantage associated with playing at high altitude. As a result, Hugh Morten (2006:498) notes that sports scientists have recognized the potential to 'improve performance in a competition if causal factors behind the size and variability of home advantage can be identified and then, if possible, minimised or exploited as appropriate'. Indeed, as such travel demands have become increasingly routine, so responses to mitigate the consequences of travel for competitive performance have emerged.

Randall Smith et al.'s (2000) study of the Major League Baseball (MLB) competition in North America is particularly relevant to this discussion simply because it seeks to isolate travel as a variable influencing success in 'away' competition games. They note that 'travel is one of a constellation of factors that have been used to account for teams winning a greater percentage of home contests' (Randall Smith et al., 2000:365). Of course the influence of travel is difficult to isolate from other factors such as crowd support, the peculiarities of the home field and, according to Nevill and Hodder (1999), the tendency for officials to demonstrate a decision making bias in favour of home teams. The lack of travel effects found by Randall Smith et al. (2000:365) is explained as a *perception* of travel effects on the part of players, coaches and journalists, which 'arises from the mundane routine of the everyday life of the professional athlete'. This, too, might suggest that in the case of very frequent intercity and short haul travel maintaining levels of stimulation and novelty, in an appropriate balance with the security and familiarity of the team environment, is an important aspect of team management.

These studies of course relate to financially well-supported professional sports franchises. It is interesting to note that, with the expansion of second and third tier as well as qualification competition schedules, many athletes travelling to engage in international competition are unable to meet their playing and travelling expenses from tournament winnings alone. Woodman and Hardy (2001) highlight that financial concerns are a major cause of organizational stress in elite sport. In some sports, such as European football, American professional leagues in basketball and baseball and the Indian Premier League (IPL cricket), the earnings of many players have skyrocketed due to the combined influence of television media, sponsorship and endorsement (Halberstam, 1999). The reality for most athletes in the majority of sports (e.g., athletics, rowing, squash, netball) is that all but the absolute elite are semi-professional, poorly remunerated or amateur, to the point that travel to competition is compromised due to lack of funding and, in some cases, competitive careers are compromised or curtailed due to financial pressures. Thus while some travel to compete in private jets and limousines, the majority undertake travel to international competition under varying degrees of financial hardship.

Long haul travel, elite athletes and travel medicine

It is a common misconception that travel and positive health outcomes go hand in hand. Many destination marketers and researchers espouse the positive physical and mental health consequences of travelling abroad (Schmidhauser 1996; Urry 1990; May 1989; Vellas & Becherel 1995). However, the reality is that upward of 50% of tourists are affected by some form of physiological or psychological health problems while travelling (Dawood, 1989; May, 1989; Musa, Higham & Hall, 2004). World Health Organisation (WHO) statistics reveal that for every 100,000 people who travel internationally 50,000 have health problems; 30,000 suffer from diarrhoea; 3,000–4,000 contract malaria and eight will die abroad (Musa et al., 2004).

Air travel is commonly associated with the stresses of flight delays, and environmental factors such as climatic contrasts and changes in time zones, diet and altitude may also compromise the immune system of the traveller, rendering travellers more susceptible to local public health concerns and communicable diseases (Ryan 1996). Travel may also expose individuals to endemic diseases (Cartwright 1996; Rudkin & Hall 1996; Cossar 1996; Petty 1989; Musa et al. 2004), reduced levels of sun safety (Carter 1997; Weston 1996), sexually transmitted diseases and infections (Ford & Eiser 1996; Gillies & Slack 1996) as well as crime and terrorism (Pizam & Mansfield 1996). Those who travel to remote and/or developing regions and countries may be isolated from modern medical facilities and place additional pressures on local health care facilities. Thus, travel medicine is an emerging and important area in tourism research, and it has become a priority focus, serving the interests of mobile elite athletes who travel to diverse and distant destinations in search of international competition.

Young, Fricker, Maughan and MacAuley (1998) address the medical issues associated with travellers and elite competition. Such is the mobility of international athletes as global travellers that medical support and comfort at places of competition have become significant issues. These, according to Young et al. (1998), include immunization, vaccinations, jet lag and acclimatization. Like studies addressing the tourist experience (see Clawson and Knetch, 1966), research and practice serving the study of travel medicine typically arrange concerns into distinct travel phases.

Pre-travel phase

The pre-travel phase includes general health screening, immunization, vaccinations and preparations to ease acclimatization concerns. Two concerns arise in the pre-travel phase as it relates to elite athletes. These include, first, the need to remain healthy given the susceptibility of those travelling by aircraft to respiratory tract infections, tiredness and dietary irregularity. Remaining healthy is obviously a precondition if athletes are to be able to compete at the optimum level (Young et al., 1998). The second relates to being able to continue training efficiently and effectively in new and (possibly) unfamiliar environments. Team selection timeframes should accommodate the specifics of places of competition if, for example, immunizations (e.g., malaria prophylaxis) are required. Many athletes are prone to viral infections due to travelling conditions, close living conditions in training accommodation and competition facilities and rigorous training regimes (Young et al., 1998) and should therefore have the influenza vaccine before departure. Athletes who use medications that require the notification of drug testing authorities must undertake notification in the pre-travel phase.

Travel phase

Assumptions, often false, about the ease and efficiency of international travel have significant implications for the travel demands of elite athletes. Few enjoy the luxuries of advance travel and acclimatization due to training and competition schedules or because of insufficient funding support. The problematic aspects of the travel phase relate to the disruption of normal bodily processes due to rapid travel. 'Jet leg refers to the effects of rapid trans-meridian travel and included bowel disturbance, fatigue and poor sleep' (Young et al., 1998:78). Jet lag is not readily distinguished from jet stress, which relates to the dehydrating effect of pressurized cabins as well as unfamiliar diet and crowded seating conditions. Young et al. (1998) note that circadian rhythms take seven days to normalize if more than five time zones have been crossed but that this varies with direction of travel (eastbound air travel results in shortened days, which is more onerous physiologically) as well as age, travel stress (including anxieties associated with air travel that are felt by some) and the consumption of alcohol.

Some athletics authorities will plan travel phase sleep strategies for individual athletes based on preferences for 'cat napping' or re-establishing sleep–wake cycles (Young et al., 1998). Such strategies may include the use of hypnotics or sleep Medication (e.g., Melatonin) during and in the nights immediately following long haul travel. While many trans-meridian travellers including elite athletes use Melatonin to counter the effects of jetlag, Manfredini, Manfredini and Conconi (2000) warn of the importance of individually tailored rather than standard doses, particularly as they differ based on gender. Some athletes may be provided with guidance on in-flight relaxation techniques, preferential seat booking and priority terminal services to ease transit arrangements and reduce total travel time. Arranging appropriate meals and carrying supplementary foods and drinks in hand baggage may be necessary for some. These initiatives, as well as a range of specific transit, seating and medication requirements, also apply to disabled athletes (Darcy, 2003).

At the place of competition

All athletes, but particularly those who travel to compete in developing countries, are inevitably brought into contact with unfamiliar organisms and therefore face the possibility of intestinal infection. Most cases of traveller diarrhoea are the result of non-viral causes, including pathogens such as *Salmonella*, *Giardia* and *Campylobacter*, and as such can be guarded against with simple food hygiene initiatives (Young et al., 1998). Meeting familiar, calculated and safe dietary regimes has become a necessary part of elite performance away from home, at least in advance of and perhaps during competition. Young et al. (1998) note that '… exercise performance is impaired in the heat, but repeated exposures bring about adaptive changes that serve to minimize negative effects on performance' (Young et al., 1998:79).

While *acclimatization programmes* remain the subject of ongoing research, it is generally agreed that training (and preferably living) in the heat (32–35 °C, with humidity greater than 70% being the optimum range) for 7–14 days before competition is important and that training intensity should be reduced and performed in the coolest part of the day initially (Young et al., 1998). Acclimatization should take place alongside a planned strategy to prevent dehydration because as acclimatization to a hot climate takes place, sweating increases. Sweating results in the loss of body fluid and electrolytes, which without compensation will impair both physical and mental performance (Young et al., 1998). The *rehydration regime* and carbohydrate and sodium content of replacement fluids will vary with the nature of training programmes, the nature of a given sport (e.g., timing and duration, amount of standing and waiting between periods of competition) and whether or not the sport takes place at indoor or outdoor venues. *Lifestyle issues*, at least prior to competition, are also critical to elite athletes who compete in unfamiliar geographical, climatic and weather conditions. Sunburn can cause heat stress and compromise sweating responses long after the obvious symptoms of skin damage have faded (Young et al., 1998).

While this dialogue relates to long haul air travel from temperate to equatorial climates, the same principles may be applied to all forms of travel for elite competition. Thus, in the case of US college competitions bus journeys can be planned to minimize disruption of daily routines as well as travel times on days of competition (Newell, 2003). Access to training facilities in close proximity to accommodation at the destination may be given priority, and actions to minimize distractions (e.g., incoming telephone calls) may also be taken in advance (Newell, 2003). Pace and Carron's (1992) quantitative study of the National Hockey League (NHL) provides two interesting insights into regular and recurring road trips. First, the longer the team road trip, the more likely that the visiting team will win away games. Secondly, where teams travel across multiple time zones, the greater the number of rest days before competition, the lower the chances of winning the game. The first of these two results is explained by suggesting that teams become accustomed to the rigors of long road journeys if time on the road can be effectively used to create a special team bond and generate team cohesion. This clearly needs to be balanced against a tour schedule that limits time off between games to get used to unfamiliar environments and new time zones, because this may contribute to a loss of focus and concentration (Pace & Carron, 1992).

SPECIFIC INDIVIDUAL AND/OR TEAM NEEDS AT THE PLACE OF COMPETITION

Training and service needs

Aside from interests in travel medicine, elite athletes may have more private and emotional needs as they seek the right mental state in which to achieve the highest levels of competitive performance. Woodman and Hardy (2001) highlight a range of causes of organizational or work-related social psychological stress in elite sport, many of which bear upon or relate directly to the circumstances that athletes face at places of competition. They organize these causes into environmental, personal, leadership and team issues (see Table 5.3). These causes of organizational stress highlight the need for

Table 5.3	Causes of Organizational Stress in Elite Sport	
Factors	**Causes**	**Examples**
Environment	Selection	Late selection
		Length of selection process
	Finances	Lack of financial support
		Differential financial support
	Training environment	Boredom and isolation
		Unfamiliar kit at competition
		Tense training environment
	Accommodation	Noisy hotel at competition site
Personal	Nutrition	Poor provision of food
		Disordered eating
	Injury	Training despite injury
		Lack of structure regarding injury treatment
	Goals and expectations	Lack of direction with goals
		Tension because of personal goals within a team
Leadership	Coaches	Coach acting differently in international arena
		Coach not practising psychological skills
		No female coaches
	Coaching styles	Inconsistent coaching styles
Team	Team atmosphere	Lack of social cohesion
		Separate groups within the team
		Athletes not training together
	Support network	General lack of support
		Inappropriate psychological support
		Unapproachable team director
	Roles	Lack of role structure
		Individual roles within a team
	Communication	Lack of communication regarding training
		Confusion regarding team meetings
		Lack of access to information
		Feeling of no one to talk to

(Source: Woodman & Hardy, 2001)

consistency, predictability, support and in some cases control over the social and physical environment prior to competition. Many relate directly to the sports context. Protracted or late selection confirmation, financial hardship, loss of form, injury and rehabilitation and unfamiliar training facilities or medical support services may all contribute to organizational stress. Stress may also be managed through consideration of specific destination, training and competition needs of athletes (e.g., disabled athletes; see Darcy, 2003).

It is noteworthy, however, that other causes of organizational stress highlighted by Woodman and Hardy (2001) may be mitigated or eliminated with careful consideration given to locational and living arrangements when athletes are based in foreign countries while preparing for competition. Accommodation and nutritional arrangements can be closely managed at places of training and/or competition. Boredom and isolation in the training environment may be mitigated or eliminated through strategies such as integration into local communities of competitors as well as through the tourist experiences achieved in novel and stimulating places in an attempt to establish a balance between the business of sport and escape from the pressures of competition (see Case study 5.1). It is also likely that team atmosphere may be enhanced through the shared experiences of new places, although an understanding of such experiences in building team culture is anecdotal rather than empirical.

Case Study 5.1

The Elite Athlete as a 'Business traveller/tourist'
Ken Hodge (University of Otago), Chris Lonsdale (Chinese University of Hong Kong) and Anton Oliver (Professional athlete)

One could argue that the elite athlete is also a 'business traveller/tourist' (cf. Murphy, 1985); the main purpose of global travel is for business (playing and/or training), not pleasure. Historically, athletes in many sports have gone 'on tour' to compete. For example, the 1894–1895 'Ashes' Cricket Tour to Australia by England (24 matches over 4 months), the 1888–1889 New Zealand Natives Rugby Tour to the United Kingdom (107 matches over 6 months), the 1948 Cricket Tour to England by Australia (31 matches over 5 months) and the 1978 New Zealand Rugby Tour to the United Kingdom and Ireland (18 matches over 2 months) all involved considerable travel. In some sports these

extended tours are still commonplace (e.g., the 2006–2007 'Ashes' Cricket Tour to Australia by England; the 2005 British and Irish Lions Rugby Tour to New Zealand), although the length of these tours has typically been truncated (i.e., 1–1.5 months).

Other examples include the modern Olympics (summer and winter) and the Commonwealth Games, for which 5,000–10,000 athletes travel to a different host country/city every four years for a global 14–16-day multisport festival (Hodge & Hermansson, 2007). Similarly, a number of sports have a four-year cycle of World Cups (e.g., football, rugby, netball, cricket, softball), and a World Masters Games multisport festival is held very four years in a different host country/city. Furthermore, with the development of professional sport 'tour-naments' during the twentieth century many sports were created or evolved into a series of annual international, global competitions (e.g., Professional Golfers' Association (PGA) and European Golf 'Tours'; the Association of Tennis Players (ATP) Tennis Tour; the Fédération Internationale de Ski (FIS) Skiing World Cup Series; Formula 1 Car Racing; European Cup in Football Six Nations Rugby Championship; Super 14 Rugby competition).

Moreover, within national borders many countries now sustain full-scale nationwide competitions (e.g., the National Football League (NFL) American Football; UK Premier League Football; Australian Rules Football) and some national-level competitions cross borders (e.g., MLB and NHL Ice Hockey in USA and Canada; the National Rugby League NRL Rugby League in Australia and New Zealand). Finally, many athletes also travel internationally to specific locations for training purposes – altitude training (e.g., European triathletes training in Boulder, USA), heat/cold acclimation, equipment/facility availability (e.g., New Zealand snowboarders/skiers training in Aspen, USA and Banff, Canada, during the southern hemisphere summer) and for the use of purpose-built facilities (e.g., bobsleigh track in Calgary, Canada).

Given these examples of the sustained need for extensive national and international travel by elite athletes, combined with the ever-increasing demand for better trained and better performing athletes (i.e., athletes must train as well as compete whilst they are travelling), it is clear that elite athletes can be easily characterized as business travellers/tourists. Their main purpose for travel is utilitarian – they travel to train, play, compete and perform in their respective sports (Hodge & Hermansson, 2007). Just like business travellers their main purpose for travel is work, not leisure. Nevertheless, like business travellers, athletes' travel to various international locations affords an opportunity for tourism activities in their downtime. Indeed, during the amateur era of cricket and rugby tours mentioned here, tourism activities were viewed as a necessary means of achieving some recreation time away from the world of work (i.e., training and playing sport) (Mourie & Palenski, 1982).

Training and performing away from home and family over an extended period of time generate additional pressures and

frustrations for athletes beyond the ubiquitous performance pressure and stress on 'game/race day' (Cresswell & Eklund, 2006; Hodge & Hermansson, 2007). For example, an elite rugby player who is a member of the New Zealand national team as well as a Super 14 team will be away from home for half the year (approximately 180 nights) (Donaldson, 2008). Combined with the impact of jetlag and travel fatigue which often accompanies international travel (Waterhouse, Reilly, & Edwards, 2004), these additional pressures and frustrations can increase the potential for athlete 'burnout' and may have a significant negative impact on the athlete's enjoyment and performance. These pressures and frustrations may be more insidious and less obvious to the 'outsider', but their effect on the athlete can be just as serious as performance stress. The risk of burnout for elite athletes is a very real and increasingly common occurrence (Cresswell & Eklund, 2006). For example:

> I didn't really want to play - no desire to play whatsoever, I didn't want to turn up. [I would be] sitting there going 'What am I doing here? It's a beautiful sunny day, I could be out'. I started thinking about other things I could be doing, thinking about [travelling] overseas .... I found I was getting quite tired in games. I was rooted, physically knackered [i.e., exhausted]. I'd turn up to play and be rooted in the warm up .... Your mental attitude ... it can cause a lot of lethargy and tiredness. (Anton Oliver, All Black 1995–2007, personal communication July 7, 2004).

This quotation illustrates that for some elite athletes sport is a less than fulfilling experience as they struggle to find the desire and energy to continue their participation. Burnout in elite sport has been the focus of considerable media attention in recent years, with athletes (e.g., BBC Sport, 2002; Majendie, 2005), coaches (e.g., Otago Daily Times, 2005) and administrators (e.g., Donaldson, 2006; BBC Sport, 2002; Majendie, 2005) expressing concern about the issue. Sport scientists have also viewed burnout as a potentially serious problem (e.g., Cresswell & Eklund, 2005; Hodge,

Lonsdale, & Ng, 2008), and while there is limited empirical evidence on the topic, burnout has been hypothesized to result in concentration problems, mood swings, poor performance and potential dropout from sport (Cresswell & Eklund, 2006). Burnout may be especially relevant for elite athletes who must invest extraordinary amounts of time and effort in order to be successful (Baker, Cote, & Abernethy, 2003) and who travel extensively.

Raedeke (1997) suggests that athlete burnout should be viewed as a syndrome characterized by (a) emotional and physical exhaustion, (b) sport devaluation and (c) a reduced sense of accomplishment. This definition allows for cases in which athletes are suffering from burnout symptoms but have *not* discontinued their sport participation. One could argue that there is a need for elite athletes to focus on attaining a degree of balance in their lives whilst on tour (e.g., via tourism activities) in order to reduce perceptions of exhaustion, devaluation and reduced accomplishment. Clearly, tourism activities could be viewed as one prevention measure regarding burnout. In this vein, the coach of the Lions Super 14 rugby team from South Africa (Eugene Eloff) observed while on tour in New Zealand:

> *People make travelling a mental block. I get our players to focus on the game rather than the time difference [time zones & jetlag]. My philosophy is not to focus on the negatives of travelling. I see it as a positive because playing in another country gives players the chance to meet new cultures and see what's going on in the world* (McMurran, 2008:19).

Furthermore, Graham Mourie (All Black captain 1977–1982) offered the following advice about attaining a 'tour balance' in order to succeed as an elite athlete on tour (e.g., the 1978 New Zealand Rugby Tour to the UK and Ireland; 18 matches over 2 months):

> *The major part of a [rugby] tour is concerned not with rugby, but with 'touring'. … I always promoted the philosophy that the most important aspect on a tour was the personal achievement of a balance between rugby and touring life, the sweet life. The finding of a tour rhythm which enabled the player to gain the most enjoyment from the tour while enabling him to produce the best rugby of which he was capable. Each found his balance in different ways … [Players needed to be wary of] an insidious syndrome that afflicts new [players]: the 'gee wizz' disease, the desire of first-time travellers to spend so much time trying to absorb the sights of a world much bigger than them that they don't notice the world of rugby passing them by … Balance is the key. 'Have you got your balance?' That was the question* (Mourie & Palenski, 1982:87–88).

Elite athletes typically lead a regimented, structured, routine-driven life of training, preparing and performing their sport whilst away from home. Unless the athlete makes an effort to engage in some non-sport activities whilst on tour he/she can end up living a life devoid of spontaneity, stimulation and novelty – the potential for burnout in such a situation is considerable. Consequently, engaging with the local culture and participating in some forms of tourist behaviour, such as leisure activities, visiting local attractions and/or sightseeing, can be viewed as a proactive and positive step for preventing burnout and maintaining the elite athlete's motivation and enjoyment. Finally, whilst expanding on the concept of 'tour balance' mentioned above, Mourie drew the following conclusion about the potential for *positive* touring/travelling experiences for the elite athlete/business traveller:

> *The life of an [elite athlete] … is a strange one, a celebrity without base, dependent on the whims of selectors and public fancy for the artificial recognition of your worth. It is a lifestyle that leads to many changes in individual personalities … In my experience, the players who have been on a few overseas trips soon develop tastes and knowledge of culture which far exceeds their more educated*

brethren who have stayed at home to climb the economic ladder (Mourie & Palenski, 1982:256).

Selected references

Hodge, K., and Hermansson, G. (2007). Psychological preparation of athletes for the Olympic context: The New Zealand Summer and Winter Olympic Teams. *Athletic*

Insight: The Online Journal of Sport Psychology, 9 (4). http://www.athleticinsight.com/

Hodge, K., Lonsdale, C., and Ng, J. (2008). Burnout in elite rugby: Relationships with basic psychological needs fulfilment. *Journal of Sports Sciences.*, vol. 26, pp. 835-844

Raedeke, T. D. (1997). Is athlete burnout more than just stress? A sport commitmentperspective. *Journal of Sport & Exercise Psychology*, 19, 396–417.

Sports psychology

Motivational and psychological interests during the build-up to competition may be either individual or collective. Sports psychology addresses mental preparation and the motivation to perform either as an individual athlete or a member of a team (Hodge & Hermansson, 2007). The systematic integration of mental preparation into training and competition, on par with physiological and biomechanical parameters, has become well recognized. In this respect Vikander and Solbakken (1996) provide an intriguing study into the psychological profiles of elite Russian and Norwegian female cross-country skiers. Their study highlights sharply contrasting psychological profiles between the nationalities of study participants, noting among other things that for Norwegian women Olympic and World Championship medallists, 'travelling out of town to competitions is not one of the great satisfactions from skiing'. Russian athletes, by contrast, reported the desire to 'always perform their very best effort even if the odds are really against them'. Vikander and Solbakken (1996) provide a raft of characteristics that differentiate Russian female athletes from their Norwegian counterparts, all of which may bear influence over the way in which travel for competition should be managed to accommodate individual and collective norms and values as they relate to important aspects of sport psychology and mental preparation.

Klausner and Hoch (1997) consider the importance of team chemistry in determining levels of team performance. They highlight the various factors that strongly influence the capacity of teams to perform at their best. These include, among other things, the ability of players to coexist in a team environment and work effectively with teammates and coaching staff, the development of mutual feelings of loyalty and the development and maintenance of a strong sense of team identity. It is interesting to note that team travel and time spent together away from home is seen as an important element of shared experiences that may contribute to team chemistry (Klausner & Hoch, 1997).

However, it is also true that travel away from home can cause stress and uncertainty among team members. Stress may arise when members of a squad are brought into competition for team selection. Eroding elements of routine and familiarity that may be used under normal home ground conditions to build or maintain team chemistry may cause stress to some. Responses to unusual settings and circumstances vary between athletes based on experience. While new players may feel the stress of uncertainty and unfamiliarity, veterans may suffer boredom. Thus, creating an environment of familiarity and predictability in alien settings has become an important aspect of elite team competition when it takes place in distant or foreign settings (Francis & Murphy, 2005).

There are also gender issues in preparations for competition. Gore (2004) provides an interesting thesis that considers elite female athletic development. She notes that women's involvement in elite sport is a dominant feature of the development of international sport in recent decades. Her study of elite female track and field athletes competing at collegiate level in the USA highlights two critical factors that relate closely to performance in national competition. The first is access to services and facilities before and during competition. Secondly, the roles performed by teammates when travelling to competition may, despite simultaneously being competitors and teammates, include trainer partner, motivator and supporter (Gore, 2004). Gore's (2004) research points towards the need to establish appropriate living and training conditions for teammates and individuals within a team, highlighting the likelihood of differences in preference based on gender.

THE SUPPLY-SIDE OF ELITE ATHLETIC MOBILITY

The foregoing discussions imply that elite athletes have specific destination preferences and requirements that relate to important aspects of preparation for competition and competition itself. These preferences and demands will vary considerably between individuals, sports, purpose of travel (e.g., training, acclimatization, competition), places of origin and competition. They will also vary between those travelling and competing either as individuals (e.g., golf players), individuals within a national team (e.g., national track and field team representatives) or as team members (e.g., football and cricket teams). Studies in the fields of sports science, sports management, sport and travel medicine and sport psychology have all started to address the issues faced by elite athletes travelling to foreign places for international competition (Hodge &

Hermansson, 2007). The literature serving the fields of tourism and destination management has, by comparison, been very slow to respond to the needs of this discrete and highly specialized travel market (Francis & Murphy, 2005).

The relative lack of attention paid to the actual places where, following months, years or entire careers of training and preparation, athletes actually engage in international competition is perplexing. Many of the important causes of organizational stress felt by elite athletes, such as those highlighted by Woodman and Hardy (2001), relate directly to the conditions and circumstances encountered at places of competition. It has been noted that part of the failure of the British and Irish Lions tour to New Zealand in 2005 was because the team was cloistered and lacked meaningful interactions with local communities. Historically, a feature of Lions tours has been close interactions with host communities in local/regional places of competition (Wright, Higham & Mitchell, 2007; Morgan, 2007). A single-minded focus on training, competing and winning, it has been argued, contributed to the failure to produce the desired results.

Despite high stakes relating to career achievement, sponsorship, the survival of sports clubs and professional sports franchises and the success or failure or professional sports organizations (Roberts et al., 2001), remarkably little attention has been committed to understanding the destination needs of athletes. One exception is the work of Francis and Murphy (2005:75) who note that 'a notable gap in the literature pertaining to the optimization of planned or existing sports facilities is the perspective of sports teams and athletes'. Both active (competitor) and passive (spectator) sport tourists have different priorities and perspectives when considering their choice of destination and destination needs as they relate to accommodation facilities, transportation, food and beverage services, retail business and attractions (Francis & Murphy, 2005; Morgan, 2007). 'Both however, have a higher level of needs that they wish to satisfy and these needs differ' (Francis & Murphy, 2005:76). The needs of the former are entirely aimed at achieving optimal competitive performance, although it has been noted that high performance requires the establishment of a balance between preparation and focus on one hand and diversion and escape from pressure on the other.

Location, accommodation and service

Elite athletes and professional sports teams are likely to have clear preferences for specific locations where they may feel most at home training and preparing in the days or week immediately before competition. This may extend to groups or entire teams of athletes for whom travelling, living and training together is an essential part of preparation for competition. Chalip

(2004) notes that the entire British Olympic team was based on the Gold Coast (Queensland) in advance of the 2000 Sydney Olympic Games. While Olympic teams were identified as a specific Olympic target market by Gold Coast marketers, and with considerable success, the choice of destination on the part of the British Olympic team was due to considerations such as climate and quality and capacity of training facilities as well as the lifestyle values of the Gold Coast which allow athletes to relax and escape from the pressures that build in advance of competition (Chalip, 2004).

Lifestyle, leisure and recreation opportunities should not be under-estimated in these considerations. Francis and Murphy (2005) note that the Crusaders (Christchurch, New Zealand) Super 14 professional Rugby Union franchise established in 2002 new priorities centred on creating the right environment to win 'away' games as a strategy to achieve competition success. This strategy extended to creating bases in Australia and South Africa, where the team could be accommodated in familiar and desirable surroundings. The choice of resort on the coastal outskirts of Cape Town (South Africa) was based on team preference, distance from media intrusion and links to team culture. Subsequently, South African teams such as the Sharks (Durban, South Africa) have established team bases in Queenstown (New Zealand) on similar grounds, although the choice of this location centres largely on opportunities to engage in leisure activities to relieve the monotony of training and escape the pressures of competition.

It is intriguing to contemplate the myriad factors that may influence the choice of destination prior to competition. No doubt climate, training facilities, air travel connections, lifestyle and ambiance, removal from media attention and access to leisure facilities, recreation opportunities and tourism attractions are important factors. But so too, perhaps, are factors such as previous visitor experiences, success at previous competitions (e.g., personal best times, winning important matches) or even the heritage and history of the destination. Interestingly, the Scottish national rugby team, when on tour in New Zealand, is commonly based for extended periods of time in the southern city of Dunedin (the old Gaelic name for Edinburgh). This city was systematically settled in the late-1840s by Scottish immigrants, the first arriving on two ships, the *John Wickliffe* and the *Phillip Laing*, in 1848 (see Chapter 10, *Transnationalism, migration and diaspora*). The city is marketed as the 'Edinburgh of the South' and bears many of the names of streets and suburbs (e.g., George Street, Princes Street and Corstorphine) in Edinburgh, Scotland, as well as a statue of Robert Burns in the inner city Octagon. The descendants of Scottish immigrants go to great lengths to make the Scots welcome in their southern city; some even admit to supporting the Scots when they play the All Blacks in Dunedin. No doubt these factors explain the contemporary preference for Scottish touring teams to base themselves in Dunedin prior to test matches. The settlement heritage associated with the Scottish diaspora also provides the opportunity to create unique sport experiences for visitors and local residents alike (see Chapter 6, *Spectatorship and spectator experiences*).

Destination service quality, athlete preference and the desired level of service are critical elements of athletic performance. Shilbury et al. (1999) notes the importance of understanding expectations and perceptions of service quality in terms of strategic sports marketing. In response to this Francis and Murphy (2005) review destination service quality variables that are likely to bear heavy influence over the destinations of preference for elite athletes and professional teams (Table 5.4). In terms of accommodation, for example, they highlight the importance of such variables as exclusive access to lodging facilities, security and noise control, controlling unwanted incoming telephone calls, priority check-in and advance checkout. Through all of these considerations, perhaps the key variable is flexibility to accommodate the specific needs of professional sports organizations and the athletes or teams that they serve. Willingness to customize settings and services is most apparent in Table 5.4. The former includes customizing room specifications and layout, sleeping arrangements, in-room services and business centre facilities, among others. The latter may extend to providing flexible twenty-four-hour food and beverage service, exclusive access to kitchen facilities for team chefs and dieticians and customized security arrangements.

Transport and infrastructure

Transport and infrastructure demands relate to accessing key points within the destination efficiently as well as transport between the pre-competition base and the place of competition. One of the key considerations for PSOs assessing the suitability of destinations is high-quality sporting facilities for training purposes and the potential for exclusive access to facilities when required (Francis & Murphy, 2005). Maier and Weber (1993) highlight the importance of coordinating the development of sport and tourism resources in regional planning if sports teams are to be a realistic target market for training and/or competition purposes. The sports event portfolios of many destinations are compromised by world class sports facilities existing in combination with inadequate tourist infrastructure (often insufficient high-quality hotel accommodation and limited transport infrastructure) or vice versa.

A recent development in some city sport and tourism development strategies has been a focus on the development of dedicated and specialized

Table 5.4 Destination Service Requirements of Elite Athletes and Professional Sports Teams

| | Accommodation and Lodging | | | |
Public areas	Room specifications	Communications	Accessibility	Management/staff
Privacy from external influences (e.g., public and media)	Door and room size	In-room Internet	Bus access	Professionalism
Noise from road	Bedding style	Wireless availability	Coach parking	Willingness to customize environment
Noise from public areas	Bed configuration	Telephone ports	Access to airport	Capacity to accommodate team dietary needs
Security	Bed size	Business centre	Training facilities	Accommodate the needs of team chef/s
On-site parking	In-room facilities	Meeting facilities	Playing venue	
Porter service	Suite availability	In-room cable/pay television	Medical facilities	
Information service	Suite availability for medical staff	Video analysis facilities	Business precinct	
Informal food and beverage service	Floor layout		Parks	
Lifts	Floor security		Entertainment precinct	
Door sizes	Room key security		Tourist attractions	
			Public transport	
			Proximity to training facilities (e.g., see below)	

Training facilities

Gymnasium	Aquatic facilities	Athletic track facilities	Training ground/medical facilities	Management/staff
Equipment and layout	Layout	Surface conditions	Training facilities	Professionalism of staff
Availability for exclusive use	Availability for exclusive use	All-weather facilities	Specialized equipment	Willingness to customize environment
		Availability for exclusive use	Physiotherapy facilities	
			Medical facilities	
			Surface conditions	
			All weather facilities	
			Able to guarantee complete privacy for closed training sessions	
			Post-training warm down facilities (e.g., plunge pools)	
			Availability for exclusive use	

(Source: Adapted from Francis & Murphy, 2004: 86–87)

infrastructures to serve elite athletes. Following the Rugby World Cup held in Australia in 2003, the city of Melbourne has witnessed the development of accommodation places dedicated to serving the destination-specific needs of elite athletes (Francis & Murphy, 2005). The Melbourne Sports and Aquatic Centre, a multiple sport/multi-user complex, has the capacity to provide for exclusive use for world championship events, as well as exclusive elite training facilities, in a range of sports. A willingness to create temporary facilities to accommodate elite sports events is also evident. The Melbourne Cricket Ground (MCG), an iconic sport stadium with a seating capacity of 90,000, was temporarily transformed into an athletics stadium to host the Commonwealth Games in 2006. Track and field facilities that were constructed specifically for the event were removed within two weeks of the closing ceremony and the cricket oval restored. These emerging directions in sport and event management have cemented the status of Melbourne as one of the great sport cities.

Creating the right environment

For both individual athletes and team members, optimum competitive performance is often a function of creating the right environment for preparation and competition (Roberts et al., 2001). Sports managers refer to 'team culture' as an essential element of a successful team. In seeking to establish a culture for team success, team management will consider all aspects of the team environment that may influence competitive team performance. It has been noted previously in this chapter that home ground advantage is seen as a product of familiarity with living and playing conditions, home crowd support and uncompromised normal daily routines in advance of competition as well as relief from the rigours of trans-meridian travel. 'To counter the perceived disadvantages of away games, professional sports teams have invested heavily in addressing these factors in their quest to win away games' (Francis & Murphy, 2005:78).

A major focus of this effort has been to create the desired team environment, which may be achieved in a number of ways. One strategy aimed at creating a familiar and homey team environment is to surround athletes with symbols of home. At one level this strategy may be used to instil or enhance a sense of national pride in international competition, reminding athletes of the people and place they represent when they compete. It may also be used to mitigate feelings of isolation, particularly among athletes who may be away from their homes and families for extended periods of time in advance of and during competition. This is a strategy that has been adopted with some success by the New Zealand Olympic Committee during the Olympic Games in Sydney (2000), Athens (2004) and Beijing (2008) as well as during Winter Olympic Games. Iconic images and a Māori pounamu (greenstone) carving were installed in the Olympic village accommodation used by the New Zealand team in Beijing before the arrival of the athletes. Furthermore, all arriving athletes were welcomed by a traditional Māori haka (challenge) upon arrival at the Olympic village (Hodge, 2008 personal communication).

Achieving a strategic fit between the destination where the team is based and team culture is a second strategy. Sports teams are not necessarily located in geographical proximity to the place of competition, but in instances where this is not the case, transportation links become an important consideration. Indeed the location of preference, in instances where preference may be accommodated, is increasingly determined by where athletes may be allowed to feel most comfortable and 'at home'. Creating the right environment is likely to require meeting a balance between familiarity and novelty. Many sports teams seek an 'environmental bubble' in which to prepare for competition in a setting that is low in stress and high in familiarity. However, athletes may also describe the monotony of training and the mental stresses of public expectation and preparing for important, perhaps, career defining contests. Under these circumstances an insular, familiar and routine team environment can become suffocating for athletes. Therefore, creating the right environment may extend to locating the team at a destination that offers opportunities to engage in tourist and leisure activities, which can serve the function of bringing the desired level of novelty to the competition preparation phase. Distinctive and interesting tourist and heritage attractions may also serve to either provide distraction from the building pressures of imminent competition or to provide mental focus for players.

The All Blacks annual autumn tour of Europe takes place in October/November each year. In recent years, as part of a now established tradition, the All Blacks team has been based in northern France and, on Armistice Day (11 November), the team undertakes a remembrance visit to the Commonwealth War Graves Commission (CWGC) Nine Elms cemetery located west of Poperinge (Belgium) to specifically visit the grave of David Gallaher. Gallaher was the captain and tactical mastermind of the 'Original' All Blacks team that toured Europe in 1905. He died in October 1917 serving the Auckland Regiment of the New Zealand Expeditionary Force (NZEF) as a Company Sergeant at Passchendaele. His grave has become a shrine for All Black teams touring Europe. Gallaher's birthplace (Ramelton, County Donegal) and school in Ireland have also become places of pilgrimage for touring All Black teams, and the homecoming reception that they receive from members of the Ramelton community has become an established part of the team's heritage. The links between contemporary sports teams, heritage and diaspora on one hand (see Chapter 10, *Transnationalism, migration and diaspora*) and travel patterns, team culture and preparation for competition on the other are evident in this case.

CONCLUSION

Growing investment and heightened interest in maximizing individual and team performances in elite international competition have been at the general neglect of the visitor experience and, to a less degree, travel demands of elite sports people. Francis and Murphy (2005) place emphasis on the importance of understanding how individuals and teams may be able to best perform in international competition. No doubt such an understanding varies between sports, travel circumstances and on the basis of individual preference. Therefore, while some Olympians thrive on atmosphere, team unity and sense of occasion in the games village, others prefer to distance themselves from the hype and expectation through individual location, accommodation and training arrangements of preference.

One important point to emerge from these discussions is the importance of creating environments and routines in unfamiliar destinations, which allows elite athletes to maximize preparations for competition. The concept of 'tour balance' (Hodge, Lonsdale & Oliver, see Case study 5.1) aptly describes an important part of this challenge. It applies equally to various competition contexts. One, for example, is the balance required to be in peak physical and mental form for career defining moments of competition. Another relates to countering the potential for player 'burnout' during long tours or competition seasons that place considerable international travel demands on competitors. It is ironic that the activity of elite competition has been so neglected in terms of managing the travel demands, destination preferences and unique needs of athletes preparing for and engaging in international competition. Such a focus raises interesting questions, some of which are addressed in this chapter, although many others remain largely unanswered. How do athletic fortunes in elite performance relate to evaluation of the destination, recollection and return travel, perhaps, in post-competition careers? What role can destinations and host communities play in terms of mitigating boredom and isolation in the training environment? To what extent and in what ways can unique elements of place (e.g., settlement histories, cultural heritage) and tourist experiences play a part in the experiences of elite athletes? How and in what ways can these be related to the unique experiences of spectators and supporters? What role may unique places and visitor attractions play in creating a team culture through shared experiences of new places and the establishment of 'tour balance'? There exists much scope for collaboration between sport and tourism researchers to better understand the specialized needs of elite athletes as they relate to travel for competition, the search for optimum athletic performances and unique sport/tourist experiences.

CHAPTER 6

Spectatorship and Spectator Experiences

The globalization of sports, in combination with the diverse manifestations of contemporary mobility, have significant implications for tourism and the search for authentic experiences. With globalization (see Chapter 2, *Sport and tourism in a global world)*, multiple fandoms and identities have emerged as new manifestations of spectatorship and team support. Simultaneously, team fandoms have become entrenched as team heritage and nostalgia provide social and cultural meanings that are to be safeguarded in an increasingly transitory modern life. This chapter is also set within the theoretical context of authentic experiences of sport and place (see Chapter 8, *Authentic experiences)* as a means of building a sense of collective or personal identity. It explores how spectatorship and multiple fandoms relate to tourist behaviour and the search for authentic experiences. The unique identities of, and experiences sought by, discrete groups of spectators and fans (Morgan, 2007) are the central focus of this chapter.

Within the sport tourism activity that is the subject of this chapter – spectatorship and spectator experiences – there is a diverse range of motivations and desired experiences that may be sought by groups or individuals who exist within globalized, highly mobile multi-media western societies. Table 6.1 outlines a categorization of sport spectators and discrete groups of spectators within each category. Memberships of these categories and groups are not mutually exclusive (Hinch & Higham, 2004). Single sports or events may appeal to multiple categories of spectators. Moreover, individual sport spectators may comply with multiple spectatorship categories and groups in different dimensions of time (e.g., life-course phase) and space (e.g., when at home, living away from home or when travelling abroad).

Table 6.1 presents the diversity of different manifestations of sport spectatorship and support as an activity set. The first category presented in

CONTENTS

Sport spectatorship and the search for authentic experiences

Live and mediated spectator interests

Theorizing live sport spectatorship in a globalized multi-media society

Conclusion

Table 6.1   Classification of Sport Spectators

Spectatorship Categories	Discrete Groups	Description
Event goers	Elite competition	Seek to observe history in the making (e.g., Olympic games spectatorship).
	Identifiers	Seek to support their country of residence or origin. Build a sense of national or personal identity.
	Sport as carnival	International party atmosphere, cultural events, post-match/competition celebrations.
	Emergent competition	Spectators with personal or professional interests in the development of athletic talent (e.g., Minor leagues, youth competitions).
	Supporters of elite athletes	Support those competing in elite competition (e.g., Wimbledon tennis) including junior sport competitors.
	Supporters of friends and relatives (SFR)	Attend to watch and support those competing in sports at all non-elite levels (e.g., Masters games, social sports events).
Sports fans	Passionate partisans[a]	Football supporters club members. Hardcore supporters who attend games regularly.
	Champion followers	Less fanatical but actively support their team when it performs well. Cup final spectators.
	Reclusive partisans	Interested in team but attend games infrequently. Selective spectators.
	Theatregoers	Enjoy the spectacle and entertainment of live sport. Spectators at important games. More interested in sport rather than a particular team.
	Aficionados	Historically significant games. Seek to watch legendary or star players. More interested in the demonstration of skill, tactical complexity and aesthetic pleasure rather than the outcome of the game.

Passive consumers	Connoisseur observer	Tourists who seek authentic experiences of sport. Spectators at iconic and prestigious sports events (e.g., Wimbledon tennis, F1 Grand Prix).
	Casual observers	Tourists who seek authentic experiences of place. Spectators who seek out sports that are locally or nationally unique (e.g., Thai boxing, Hurling, Sumo).
Subculture aspirants	Watch and emulate	Those who seek to build subculture membership through association and emulation (e.g., sports competition).
	Subculture associates	Seek subculture membership through association (e.g., spectators at surf championships).
Business travellers	Passive/non-holiday[b]	Business travellers watching sports
	Passive/business	VIPs, PSOs, sponsors.
	Media broadcasting	Television, commentators, print and electronic media.
Virtual spectators	Private television	Global television spectator audiences.
	Public gatherings	Spectators at pubs, club, public gatherings to watch on big screens.
	Online spectatorship	Video streaming, play-by-play online updates.
	Sports betting	Online, television and tabulated betting agency spectators.

[a] Fandom classification adopted from Stewart (2001)
[b] Adopted from Standeven & De Knop (1999).

Table 6.1 relates to those who travel to attend elite sports events. As in the ancient past (Crowther, 2001) spectator attendance at events such as world and Olympic championship competitions is rich in motivational diversity (Pyo, Uysal & Howell, 1998). For some, the primary motivation associated with this activity is to experience first-hand the very highest levels of elite competition. Perhaps related to this is the desire to capture rare and fleeting sports spectatorship opportunities, which consequently may deliver defining moments in history (Delpy-Neirotti, Bosetti & Teed, 2001). They may represent moments of sporting greatness and those of controversy or infamy. They may also include moments of social, cultural or political significance. Moments of national significance may inspire spectators as 'identifiers' (Table 6.1) from different countries or states of origin who seek to witness world class performances by their compatriots. In doing so, sports events may function for some as builders of national or personal identity.

Increasingly, major world championship sports events are being delivered as global sports fan, media and tourist events. Thus, the experiences of sport spectators may extend to those who seek to engage in a carnival atmosphere at places where sports fans from around the world congregate at a moment in time to experience intense sport competition. Manifestations of the national carnivalesque, such as Irish celebrations at the USA 1994 Fédération Internationale de Football Association (FIFA) World Cup, may emerge in these settings (Giulianotti, 1996). Sport then becomes a cultural experience, not only in terms of sport as a manifestation of culture (Bale, 1989) but also in the collective behaviour of fans from different regions, countries and continents (Giulianotti, 1995; Morgan, 2007). These expressions of individual and collective identity coalesce within the context of the destination where competition takes place. So visitors to a given place, at a given time, are also subject to the cultural experience of a specific place. Indeed for some sports fans, the experiences of place (perhaps through visiting tourist attractions or iconic local places and historical sites) may be a prominent motivation for attending a particular sports event. This again highlights sport tourism as the integration of activity (sport), people (sports fans) and place (the place of competition).

It has been argued that the uncertainties of sports performances, circumstances and outcomes, particularly when combined with the unique atmosphere of world championship events (arising from infrequency and the pressures of one-off performances) may function as very powerful tourist attractions (Hinch & Higham, 2004). However, these uncertainties and other elements of intrigue may attract different spectator types to quite contrasting sports events. Removed somewhat from elite international competition is the observation of emerging sports talent. Spectators may have personal or professional interests in the development of athletic talent (e.g., minor leagues, youth competitions). Conversely, identifying the dominant athletes of new and yet to emerge eras of competition may be a motivation to experience emergent competition, such as college sports, junior championships or minor leagues. For some, watching sporting greats in the twilight of their competitive careers may attract significant spectator interest, perhaps inspired by feelings of nostalgia associated with the passing of a dominant era in sport (Gammon & Ramshaw, 2007). The defeat of seven times winner Pete Sampras at the hands of Roger Federer in the 2002 Wimbledon quarterfinal was seen by some at the time as a significant moment in the sport of tennis as the flame was passed from a departing to an emerging great of the sport.

Those who attend sports events to watch and support family and friends competing in non-elite levels of competition (e.g., Masters Games, social sports events) are particularly interesting given that sport spectatorship may in such cases be a minor component of the overall experience of the place of competition. It is also intriguing for the very reason that at non-elite levels of competition, such as regional or national Masters Games competitions, there may exist a merging of the roles of competitor and spectator (Ryan & Lockyear, 2002). This describes the propensity for Masters athletes not only to compete but also to support their fellow competitors. The merging of the roles of competitor and spectator, and the camaraderie arising from it, has become a well-recognized element of Masters competition. In contrast, spending time with family may be an important travel motivation for those who participate in small-scale sport events (Carmichael & Murphy, 1996). This motivation is particularly applicable to female participation in sport, including competition and spectatorship, which is more likely to take place with other family members (Thompson, 1985).

The second category presented in Table 6.1, sports fans, is equally diverse in membership. Stewart (2001) describes the diverse manifestations of fan support for sports teams. The most obvious, and those that have received a disproportionate degree of academic and media attention, are 'passionate partisans', who may be described as 'core' (Peel & Thomas, 1991) or 'hardcore' (Stewart, 2001) supporters. The building of personal identity through subculture membership is an important element of the sport experiences of hardcore sports fans. The concept of serious leisure (see Chapter 7, *Recreational sport and serious leisure*) has been applied to football fandoms (Jones, 2000) to situate the behaviours of football fans within the social identity process. Under this analysis the behaviours of football fans include enduring and perhaps inherited support for their team, strong personal identification with group behaviours and the investment of considerable personal effort in fandom membership. Kulczycki and Hyatt (2005) provide a good example of this with their study of nostalgic fans travelling to see ex-Whalers (a disbanded National Hockey League [NHL] team) playing for their new teams. This context of fan behaviour gives rise to a career path involving stages of achievement and recognition (Donnelly & Young, 1988). The hostility of some sports fans arises from 'in-group favouritism' and 'out-group derogation', which are established on group membership based on the team one supports (Jones, 2000).

The 'passionate partisans', whose identities are closely linked to the successes and failures of their team, stand in contrast to other somewhat less fanatical or obsessive supporters. These, according to Stewart (2001), include 'champion followers' (spectators whose support remains in a state of dormancy until the team shows genuine championship potential), 'reclusive partisans' (dedicated supporters who, for whatever reasons, attend games infrequently), 'theatregoers' (who seek the entertainment of sport in the absence of dedication to any particular team) and 'aficionados' (who seek to witness the exploits of the most famous and skilful players without great concern for who wins of loses). The factors that influence spectator attendance are comprehensively reviewed by Borland and MacDonald (2003). They include league position, goals scored and championship or promotion/relegation prospects (Simmons, 1996). Football league attendance is influenced by the score of the last game (Falter & Pérignon, 2000) and transport costs (Borland & MacDonald, 2003), while uncertainty of outcome has been shown to influence attendances at rugby league (Carmichael, Millington & Simmons, 1999) and football (Forrest & Simmons, 2002) games. Wilson and Sim's (1995) research highlights the importance of the championship prospects of the home team (less so the visiting team), the selection of 'star' players, as well as early season and derby games in promoting spectator interest.

How these factors vary between these discrete groups of spectators remains less well understood, although Simmons (1996) demonstrates that the more casual sports fans are more price sensitive than season ticket holders. Borland and MacDonald (2003) also caution that while much is now known about factors influencing spectatorship, the effects of variables such as television broadcasting on match attendance requires more sophisticated research and analysis than that undertaken hitherto. Clearly, therefore, sports fans vary in the extent to which they are motivated to travel in support of a sports team. For some fans, involvement in the sport itself and association with a particular team are the dominant travel motivations. Social identity can be constructed and reinforced through fandom membership, whereby 'sport becomes a pivotal means of signifying loyalty and commitment, producing enduring leisure behaviour' (Jones, 2000). Each of these discrete groups is likely to view sport spectatorship as quite distinct activity sets.

Sport spectators may, then, be further categorized into groups such as 'passive consumers' (Standeven & De Knop, 1999), either connoisseurs or casual spectators who seek out authentic experiences of sport and place (respectively), and 'subculture aspirants' (Hinch & Higham, 2004). In many sports, consumer identification with a sport subculture may be an important motivation for both participants and spectators. Green (2001:5) notes that 'interactions with others are at the core of the socialisation process and provide avenues through which values and beliefs come to be shared and expressed'. Sport tourism may, therefore, be motivated by a celebration of subculture through participation, spectatorship, association or interaction (e.g., through related non-sport activities at the location where the sport or competition takes place) (Green & Chalip, 1998). Business travellers and virtual spectators have been less well researched, yet represent increasingly significant elements of sport spectatorship.

SPORT SPECTATORSHIP AND THE SEARCH FOR AUTHENTIC EXPERIENCES

It is argued here that manifestations of sport spectatorship and support (see Table 6.1) are, to varying degrees, built upon the search for authentic experiences of sport. Event spectators attending Olympic events seek authentic competition in which uncertainty of outcome is uncompromised by bribery, corruption, cheating or drug use (Jennings, 1996). Sports fans seek the authenticity of championship teams competing in balanced and intense leagues. Sports gamblers place bets because they expect authentic competition without undisclosed bias in preparation or performance. The authenticity of sport competition, which can be so compromised by blood doping (e.g., Tour de France cycling), use of anabolic steroids (athletics), bribery of officials (e.g., boxing) or overbearing commercialization (e.g., player strikes and the intrusiveness of sponsors interests), is clearly very relevant to the attractiveness of sports to tourists.

In terms of sport tourism, then, it is important to theorize sport spectatorship as an authentic experience of place. Such a theorization is attempted in detail in Chapter 8 (*Authentic experiences*), and central to this discourse is the role of commodification in the professionalization of spectator sports.

Globalization has given rise to debates surrounding the imposition of global forces in sport and tourism and whether commodification leads inevitably to a homogenization of local culture and regional landscapes (Mowforth & Munt, 1998). This line of argument suggests that the commodification process destroys, or at least significantly alters, the culture of a destination community. In doing so, the authenticity of culturally based tourism products and attractions at the destination is lost (MacCannell, 1976). In the absence of a strong stimulus to travel, the competitiveness of such destinations will be compromised.

In light of this debate it has been argued that sport spectatorship has unique advantages over other types of cultural tourist attractions when considered in the context of commodification (Hinch & Higham, 2006). The key characteristics of sport attractions include uncertainty of outcomes, the role of athletic display, the kinaesthetic nature of sport activities and the visceral nature of many types of sporting engagements. As a consequence, experiences of sport, be they spectator or competitor experiences, can be of high intensity and engagement. These characteristics may explain why sport spectatorship, more than many other types of tourist attractions, is able to withstand many aspects of commodification and, therefore, provide spectators with authentic experiences.

Alternatively, sport spectatorship may require little or no movement in space beyond ones living room, local pub or online betting agency (Weed, 2007). If the activity (sport) can be experienced equally in the company of the appropriate people in a local pub, sports club or public live site, (i.e., the destination/place of competition is irrelevant) then the need to travel and the interests of the destination are drawn into question. However, sport remains a powerful force that invokes travel to places of competition, as in the case of 'event goers' and certain manifestations of sport fanship (Giulianotti, 1996). Sport spectatorship, then, should be theorized as a composite of an activity (a particular sport), people (athletes, fans, supporters, spectators and local residents) and place (the destination/place of competition) (Weed, 2006). Central to this discussion is the role of 'place' in this tripartite.

The interplay of travelling sport spectators and the place of competition is addressed most usefully by Morgan (2007), who adopts a sociological perspective on the management of sport spectator experiences. Morgan asserts that understanding the tourist experience is critical to the status of the destination in the aggregate of the spectator experience. In doing so he highlights two perspectives on the management of spectator experiences:

1. Managerial view: An experience as a type of product or service to provide an added-value offering

2. Consumer behaviour view: An experience as having emotional, symbolic and transformative significance for the individual involved (Morgan, 2007:362)

The former perhaps best describes a commodified product where sport tourists are viewed as a homogeneous group that can be caricatured and catered for in general terms. One size fits all. The latter, by contrast, views the sport tourist experience as a 'subjective emotional journey full of personal, social and cultural meanings' (Morgan, 2007:361) Such an approach, it is argued, is critical if the destination or place of competition is to achieve a standing within the tripartite of 'activity, people and place' that cannot be devalued or dismissed. The commodification of sport experiences through controlling and stage-managed experiences may relegate the live experience of spectator sport to little more than the television viewing experience. Elevating the subjective and emotional elements of the experience as an interplay of a unique sporting occasion, taking place in a local place-situated context that is central to the occasion and in association with the interactions of travelling supporters and local hosts, renders the sport spectator experience unique. In the process, and contrary to concerns about globalization, place competition and the mobility of people and products, the place of competition achieves non-transferable status.

In illustrating a sociological perspective of the visitor experience, Morgan (2007:363) presents an experience space model (Figure 6.1) to explain that 'the experience is created by the interaction between the activities and the

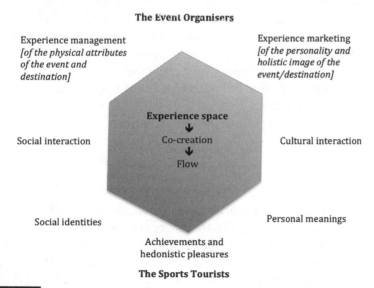

FIGURE 6.1 *The experience space: Interactions between organizers and sports tourists (Source: Morgan, 2007).*

places provided by the destination and the internal motivations and meanings brought by the visitors'. The upper portion of Figure 6.1 illustrates the classic motivational pull factors centred on the physical attributes and image of the destination, which are mediated by destination management and marketing activities. This represents the destination setting within which tourist experiences can be played out. The lower portion of the model depicts the motivations, meanings and identities that tourists bring to the place of competition. In the case of sport tourism, the visitor experience will be heavily influenced by personal meanings and the collective social identities of communities of supporters (Morgan, 2007). The experience space allows for the co-creation of experiences based on social and cultural interactions that represent the interplay of activities and people in a setting that is place-situated.

Morgan (2006, 2007) highlights three internal elements of the spectator experience. The first relates to the personal benefits of *hedonistic enjoyment and achievement*. Novelty, impulse, entertainment and surprise are essential elements of experience that can be achieved in the tourist space. So too, according to Morgan (2007), is total absorption in an activity, which can give rise to the elevated state of 'flow' (Csikszentmihalyi, 1992) (see Figure 6.1). The second is *social interactions*, which lie at the heart of the intense collective experiences of spectator sports. These interactions provide a setting in which individual and social identities are forged and where social and environmental circumstances may give rise to a sense of group identity or 'communitas' (Hinch & Higham, 2006; Weed, 2006, Morgan, 2007; see Chapter 8, *Authentic experiences*). Interactions with local people, both in terms of integration (shared experiences) and differentiation (development of social identity), may be critical elements of the sport tourism experience (Weed & Bull, 2004). The third key element is *meaning and values*. The meanings and values associated with a sport spectator experience are derived from the cultural background of the visitor and their subjective understanding and interpretation of the historical and cultural context of the sport and place where it takes place. 'Sporting allegiances and cultures are therefore deep-set and subtle expressions of personal identity' (Morgan, 2007:368).

Thus, in terms of sport tourism the significance of the place of competition (the destination) vis-à-vis the spectator experience rests with the social and cultural interactions that occur when people travel, tour and gather at places of competition (Weed, 2007). The social experience is place-situated and derived principally from the interaction of hosts and guests. Within this context, hedonistic enjoyment and achievement, social interaction and meaning and values lie at the heart of the sport tourist experience

(Morgan, 2007). This point corroborates the findings of studies of sports fans, which demonstrate the importance of the social experience in terms of travelling for sport spectatorship (Fairley, 2003). It adds emphasis to understanding sport spectatorship in terms of the local experience as a strategy to counter the transportability of sports, sport spectatorship and sport experiences in a global and mobile world (see also Chapter 11, *Modern landscapes and retro parks*).

LIVE AND MEDIATED SPECTATOR INTERESTS

The rise of mediated (televised) sport experiences is a consequence of globalization and professionalization, which has been widely critiqued (Coakley, 2007). Many criticize the supremacy of media interests in professional sport. Indeed sport is replete with examples of gross commercial interests overriding the interests of athletes and live spectator audiences. The running of the 1984 (Los Angeles) Olympic marathon, the first to involve a women's marathon competition at the Olympic Games, is early evidence of such intrusion. The interests of athletes, both in terms of levels of performance and physical well-being, suggested an early morning start to avoid high levels of daily pollution and temperature. However, the men's and women's races started later in the morning to suit television viewing times on the US Atlantic east coast.

Similar consequences have unfolded with the professionalization of Rugby Union in the southern hemisphere. The creation of South Africa, New Zealand Australia Rugby (SANZAR) in 1995 was the result of an agreement of mutual interests between the national unions of South Africa, Australia and New Zealand (professionalization and player retention) and News Corporation (exclusive broadcasting rights) (Smith, 2000). This has affected the scheduling of matches in Australia and New Zealand to suit the convenience of European television audiences, which are a major source of television revenue for News Corp Ltd. This has become a bone of contention as night sport in winter, it is widely agreed, compromises player performance, game strategy and spectator comfort. The 2007 Wimbledon grand slam tennis championship provides an example of the tradeoffs that exist between television and commercial interests and the spectator experience. The championship was thrown into disarray by adverse weather and the playing schedule was compressed to ensure a Sunday men's final (rather than extend the tournament into a new week). This decision, which was influenced by television revenue interests, resulted in two substandard semifinals (Nadal v Djokovic and Federer v Gasquet) that were impacted by player exhaustion and injury. The spectator experiences of those in attendance were compromised by the commercial interests of televised sport. These manifestations of commodification, it can be argued, may compromise the authenticity of sports competitions as well as spectator experiences.

The melting pot of home and away spectators

Historically it could be assumed that the majority of spectators support the home team (due to proximity) while a small body of travelling supporters may invest the time and effort required to attend games and support their team away from home. Globalization and high personal mobility have acted to add complexity to this formula. Firstly, high personal mobility allows for large and increasingly diverse bodies of travelling spectators to arise (Hinch & Higham, 2004). Furthermore, large populations of expatriates living at or near the destinations where their 'home' teams compete may mobilize to support the team representing their place of origin. Australians permanently or temporarily resident in London or elsewhere in the United Kingdom will mobilize in large numbers to support the Australian national cricket team playing at Lords (London). The Tri-nations rugby series experiences high levels of support for the All Blacks in Sydney and the Springboks in Perth (Western Australia) where large expatriate New Zealand and South African populations (respectively) live. It is intriguing to contemplate the authentic experiences these spectators experience when they attend sporting competitions that allow them to support a team representing their place of origin or country of birth as well as to associate with their fellow countrymen in a 'foreign' setting.

While little scholarly work has specifically addressed this manifestation of sport spectatorship, it is probable that these sports experiences allow for the reaffirmation of national and personal identity in a foreign context, albeit one that has become the place of residence for these mobile people. It is likely that for large sporting events expatriates serve as providers of temporary accommodation for friends and family who travel to support their travelling team. Within this context, and within the study of tourism, it is also interesting to contemplate the roles that expatriates play in this respect, whether they function as hosts for their temporary visitors or temporarily act as 'visitors' to their own local community alongside those who are genuinely visiting for the purpose of sport spectatorship. In both cases, the experiences of locally resident expatriates and visitors will be quite different depending on the roles they assume. Like stadium sports, themed pubs and sports bars may serve a similar purpose for expatriate residents. The Walkabout Inn in

Islington and Covent Garden (and now in other parts of London and the United Kingdom) is a popular gathering place for Australians as well as New Zealanders and South Africans in London, serving Antipodean beverages and providing a unique environment for sport spectatorship, one that is also likely to serve interests in reaffirming a sense of personal identity among those in attendance.

In a highly mobile world, the spatial travel ranges and supporter profiles of spectators may have become increasingly complex and confused. The participation of the Brazilian football team (and other teams) in the Germany 2006 FIFA World Cup generated various manifestations of football fanship, the most obvious of which is the domestic Brazilian population, which comes to a standstill to watch their legendary team play on the television. However, this team is associated with other distinct manifestations of team support. One is the collection of individuals who have the wherewithal and are sufficiently passionate in their support to travel from Brazil to the World Cup to support their team. A second may be drawn from the sizable expatriate Brazilian populations resident in European cities such as London, Paris and Rome. These supporters travel considerably less distance but are no less able to reaffirm their Brazilian identity in supporting their team in competition. However, a Brazilian national living in London and travelling extensively on holidays in Europe to destinations in Portugal, Spain or Italy may have multiple layered allegiances during such a competition. When any of the national teams of these countries compete in the World Cup, the allegiances of these spectator groups may prove to be multiple and flexible.

Furthermore, the body of spectators openly demonstrating their support for Brazil during the football World Cup may include football watchers from any country around the world who may be attracted to supporting the team by its historical record of success at the World Cup, its aura or brilliance, its skilful style of play, or the colour, exuberance and intensity of Brazilian football fans. Similarly, as teams are eliminated from competition, 'displaced' fans are likely to adopt their 'next favourite' team as the focus of their support, if only to restore their active spectator interest in the event. When the well-performing Australian team was eliminated from the 2006 FIFA World Cup by Italy, many Australians adopted the Brazilian team as the new focus of their support in the latter stages of the competition. Thus, as a sport competition reaches its climax the bodies of spectators supporting competing teams are likely to become heterogeneous and multinational in collective character as mobile fans engage flexible fandoms to experience high levels of sporting competition (see Case study 6.1).

Case Study 6.1

The changing nature of sports fandom

Ian Jones (Bournemouth University, United Kingdom)

For many sporting events, the crowd – both 'home' fans and those who have often travelled very large distances to watch and support – is an integral aspect of the occasion. This case study explores some of the issues that arise from the nature of fandom and spectatorship within a globalized society and outlines how globalization has led to a change in the nature of the sports crowd, examining the concept of fan identification and the consequences that the changing nature of fan identification may have for fan behaviours. It is based on an extended and ongoing period of ethnographic research exploring the relationships between the fans of Luton Town, a lower-level professional football club in the United Kingdom, and the wider context of European football.

The nature of sports fandom

Sports fandom is generally differentiated from spectatorship in terms of the extent of identification an individual has with a team. Spectators are attracted to the spectacle of the sport itself, whereas the fan will have an emotional involvement with a team or individual. Branscombe and Wann (1992:1017) define sports fan identification as 'the extent to which individuals perceive themselves as fans of the team, are involved with the team, are concerned with the team's performance, and view the team as a representation of themselves'. Essentially, fans identify with the team. This identification has, it seems, until recently, been focused on ascribed factors, for example fans have traditionally identified with a team on the basis of their hometown, or, alternatively, the team followed by their fathers (Jones, 1997). One key informant over ten years ago suggested:

> ... I think you have an allegiance to your local team, and I was brought up locally ... so basically I've been brought up with supporting my home team, you have an allegiance to your local team and it goes beyond just football, it's something to do with the locality of the team, it's your own team as it were.

Yet contemporary interviews with younger football fans have almost invariably highlighted the lack of credibility in terms of supporting lower-level teams such as Luton Town, with the following representing a typical statement:

> I think now if you say you support your local team it's seen as a bit strange – you have to support Man United or Chelsea now as that's what everyone else does – the kids here who follow Luton Town are laughed at basically as it's not seen as proper football.

Thus, the question of whether, as a consequence of such processes, there is a shift from crowds consisting mainly of followers, or what we can define as 'fans', who actually identify with the team on the basis of factors such as the team representing their hometown or place of birth for example, to 'spectators', with much less of an emotional bond to the team? A visit to Luton Airport in 2007 found a group of local residents waiting to check in to a flight to Madrid for a Champions League game. One fan suggested:

> Its quality football, miles better than you'd get at a Luton game, and probably cheaper than going a Premiership match – it's costing us forty pounds for the flight, and only thirty Euros to get in. There's accommodation on top of that, but you don't mind paying that if it's somewhere nice.

When asked about the importance of the game, the fan responded:

> To be honest, as long as it's a good game, I don't really mind what the result is. I just want to see a quality match and you won't get that at the level Luton are.

Whilst there are, clearly, large numbers of fans who still possess allegiance to a team on the basis of a shared common characteristic (such as following your local team), it seems apparent that there is a growth in spectators willing to follow teams on the basis of factors such as success, basking in the reflected (and high profile) glory of those higher-profile teams, with arguably less commitment. As one Premiership fan, 'Aesthetic Relic' noted on a fan message board:

> There are plenty of fans out there who jump ship regularly. The same fans who slag off a player's loyalty saying it's all about the money, yet they do exactly the same thing when the next big investor comes along or a different team starts to win things (Football Forums.net, accessed 24 August 2008).

It could be argued that there is a move in the nature of sport crowds, particularly at the higher echelons of football. It seems possible to subsequently identify two general types of attendee:

1. The highly identified fan, with allegiance to a particular team. Such fans are likely to be relatively faithful and maintain a sense of identification with the team, often overcoming issues such as poor performance, defeat and lack of entertainment to carry on following the team (Jones, 2000) and being motivated by feelings of group affiliation, eustress and self-esteem factors (Wann et al., 2001.)

2. The spectator, who will be more attracted by factors such as entertainment and being able to bask in the reflected glory of supporting a high-profile, successful team. Such spectators are likely to be much more fluid in their support and are likely to demonstrate less commitment (although, as Snelgrove et al. [2008] identify, such spectators may be able to develop and strengthen identities through attendance and thus become committed fans).

Although the categories outlined above are simplistic, they are useful to demonstrate that sports crowds are unlikely to consist of a homogenous group and that differing motivations will exist, and different experiences will result for each type. Ongoing processes of globalization suggest that there may be an ever increasing tendency towards spectatorship, based not on identification with teams or competitors as such, but on the spectacle itself. Alternatively, fans will continue to identify with those taking part, but the basis of such identification will not be the traditionally ascribed ones of locality and family but with greater fluidity of choice and change, perhaps influenced by the high-profile media coverage. As one Luton fan suggested: 'If you live in Luton, it's far easier to watch or read about Real Madrid than it is to get any information about Luton Town'.

Although it is unlikely that sports such as football will ever become spectator-based, rather than fan-based, the growing shift towards high-profile clubs raises the question of the long-term implications for smaller clubs, such as Luton Town, and how they will be able to exist within such a competitive global context.

Selected references

Jones, I. (1997). The origin and maintenance of sports fan identification: A response to Wann, et al. (1996). *Perceptual and Motor Skills*. 85, 257–258.

Jones, I. (2001). A model of serious leisure identification: The case of football fandom. *Leisure Studies*. 19, 283–298.

Snelgrove, R., Taks, M., Chalip, L., and Green, C. (2008). How visitors and locals at a sport event differ in motives and identity. *Journal of Sport & Tourism*, 13 (3), 165–180.

Wann, D., Melnick, M., Russell, G., and Pease, D. (2001). *Sports Fans: The Psychology and Social Impact of Spectators*, New York: Routledge.

Virtual spectatorship

Where spectator demand heavily outweighs ticket supply some interesting variations on spectatorship and experiencing live sport in real time have evolved. Historically, live sports have been contested in stadiums of varied capacities, catering for the live spectatorship interests of an exclusive group of ticket holders. Since the 1950s the experience of live sport has been diversified by radio, television broadcasts, satellite television and the Internet. The overt motivation for sports fans is to watch live sport. The sharing of experiences and social interactions that are associated with intense sport competition are central to the sport experience (Morgan, 2007). Weed (2007), however, highlights that watching sport in the pub can offer many of the same qualities of the sport spectator experience, including experiencing sport in shared company and reliving key moments in the contest after the event (Morgan, 2007).

An interesting variation of both stadium and pub sport experiences is the live televising of sports events in local spaces in immediate or close proximity to the stadium where the event is actually taking place. St. James' Park, the recently redeveloped home of Newcastle United FC, included in its stadium design various corporate facilities as well as public bars where non-ticket holders can experience the game live on television. This is a strategy to serve demand when it exceeds the seating capacity of the stadium, allowing fans to feel the atmosphere of the game at the stadium as it is actually taking place. Some non-ticket-holding fans, the most passionate partisans (Stewart, 2001), will actually travel to the place of competition to experience the atmosphere of the game and join in post-match celebrations. The 2007 European Championship final between Liverpool and AC Milan was contested at the Olympic Stadium in Athens in June 2007. Many non-ticket-holding Liverpool fans travelled to Athens in the hope of getting a ticket to the historic game. Their contingency plan, in the likely event of not watching the game live at the Olympic Stadium, was to watch the game close to the stadium in Athens together with thousands of fellow Liverpool FC supporters and to join in post-match celebrations in the event of a victory. This phenomenon, no doubt a consequence of high contemporary mobility (budget carriers such as EasyJet and RyanAir offer flights to Athens from the United Kingdom for as little as £1.00 excluding taxes), has opened new opportunities for spectators to experience live sports.

THEORIZING LIVE SPORT SPECTATORSHIP IN A GLOBALIZED MULTI-MEDIA SOCIETY

The globalization of multi-media societies has had the effect of rapidly diversifying live sport spectatorship experiences. This trend possibly dates to the inter-war years when political announcements, news flashes and international sports competitions (e.g., world championship boxing) were recorded and delivered to live audiences in public theatres. In the post-war era radio commentaries became the standard means by which the general public could experience live sport. The television era dates to the 1960s and 1970s and the development of both public television broadcasts of domestic and international sports. There soon followed the development of satellite television in 1979 (Halberstam, 1999).

Since these developments, the course of change has been rapid (Figure 6.2). The televising of live sport allows for mass sport spectatorship from the convenience of one's private living room. It has also allowed for the installation of large projection screens in private (e.g., exclusive clubs) and public (e.g., pubs and sports bars) spaces (Weed, 2007). Wider experiences of live sport extend to downloading video clips of significant passages of play (as in the case of the 2002 FIFA World Cup in Korea and Japan) via cellular phones and SMS/TXT score updates as well as video streaming and live blogs mediated via the Internet.

Perhaps the most intriguing variation of live sport spectatorship, one that has not yet fully unfolded, is the phenomenon of big screen live sites. Electronic scoreboards, replay screens and closed circuit television in the major stadiums of the world are recognized as the forerunners of the big screen.

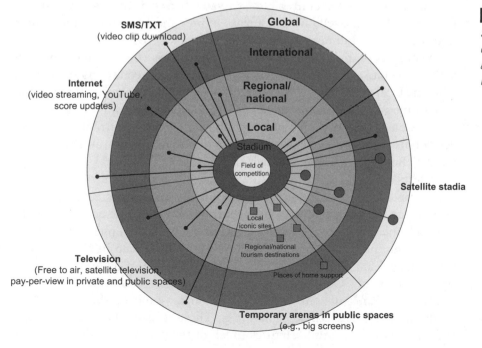

FIGURE 6.2

Spectator experiences of live sport in a globalized multi-media society.

While big screens have become commonplace in major stadiums, their use in public spaces is a relatively recent but rapidly diversifying development. During the 1991 Rugby World Cup in Britain and France, the success of the Manu Samoan rugby team in qualifying for the quarter-finals gave rise to an upsurge in national pride and spectator interest in the south sea islands of Western Samoa. Lack of access to television coverage resulted in the hasty installation of a big screen at Apia Park in the Samoan capital. Apia Park was full of viewers in the middle of the night when Samoa famously defeated hosts Wales in the RWC quarter-finals. This is an early example of the 'satellite stadium' phenomenon (see Figure 6.2), in which big screens are erected in stadiums or arenas that are local to or, in this particular case, far removed from the place of competition.

More recently the big screen spectator experience has evolved further into the temporary construction of viewing facilities in public spaces to essentially extend the stadium spectator experience to non-ticket holders. This has proved an effective means of overcoming the constraints of limited stadium spectator capacities. Again, various manifestations of the big screen phenomenon have emerged in a comparatively short space of time and at a range of spatial levels. Most immediately, the development of big screen viewing venues in local precincts has allowed destinations to maximize the involvement of spectators in large-scale sports events. 'Live sites' have been developed to provide not only a place to watch live sport in close proximity to the actual contest itself but also a place of pre- and post-competition entertainment for the full range of sport spectator types (see Table 6.1).

A corollary of this course of development that has emerged in recent years is the deliberate and strategic decision to situate big screen spectator facilities at iconic local sites. The televising of live sports taking place at recognisable and iconic sites has come to be seen as an effective way of generating destination awareness and place promotion, while contributing to the development of a unique sense of place. Images of marathon runners crossing London Bridge or running through Central Park (New York) and Olympic triathletes sprinting to the finish line at the steps of the Sydney Opera House are examples of this form of place promotion. Situating big screens and public viewing facilities at iconic sites may contribute to the same end. To date the most advanced example of these aspects of the big screen phenomenon was achieved during the hosting of the 2006 FIFA World Cup in Germany (see Case study 6.2). While temporary big screen spectator facilities were constructed in many German host cities during the month-long event, the creation of 'Fan Mile' in Berlin, set amongst some of the great iconic monuments of the German capital (e.g., The Reichstag, Brandenburg Gate and the Victory Column), captures much of the potential of the big screen spectator experience. Indeed, while 74,228 spectators watched Germany play Italy in the World Cup semi-final at the Olympiastadion (Berlin), a further one million fans watched the game live on big screens among Berlin's urban icons, which had been transformed into the setting for the Fan Mile.

Case Study 6.2

Spectator experiences during the Germany 2006 FIFA World Cup

Preparations for the 2006 FIFA World Cup hosted by Germany involved the construction of a number of new stadiums to host World Cup games. It also involved the development of a range of related attractions to encourage the interest, participation and support of the German people as well as to foster international tourism associated with the event. Frankfurt's 'official overture to the World Cup' involved 300,000 people gathering on the banks and bridges of the River Main in Frankfurt on Saturday 3 June to watch the 'Skyarena show', which featured spectacular lighting effects and images being projected onto the city's skyscrapers to a musical accompaniment. Aside from the twelve cities that actually hosted World Cup football games, numerous other cities and regions played host to world cup teams. Trinidad's 'Soca Warriors' were based in Rotenburg-Wümme, for example, and the Swedish national team in Bremen, where official welcomes were held with strong local/regional support. Such were the levels of public support engendered from the start of the tournament that teams such as Ghana were also farewelled by 3,000 supporters in the marketplace of Würzburg after being knocked out of the final sixteen by Brazil.

During the course of the event non-ticket-holding fans were catered for as an important element of the overall spectator audience. In Berlin the Fan Mile dominated the Strasse des 17 Juni between Brandenburg Gate and the Victory Column from 7 June to 9 July 2006. On 7 June 2006 the first event hosted on Berlin's fan mile was a welcome party followed by the kick-off of the World Cup's opening match. Football fans were entertained by musicians from the countries represented by teams at the World Cup, including Nelly Furtado (Portugal), Ronan Keating (Ireland) and the Berlin German Opera Choir and the Berlin Philharmonic Orchestra. Football World Cup

legends such as Pelé (Brazil), Sir Bobby Charlton (England) and Paul Breitner (Germany), among other celebrities, attended the event. Fan Mile also featured the Adidas Arena, a 1:10-scale version of the Olympiastadion, which was located temporarily by Spreebogen Park in front of the Reichstag building to provide up to 8,000 fans with public viewing, shops, a cultural entertainment programme and catering. During the World Cup hundreds of thousands of fans gathered in the heart of Germany's national capital, surrounded by Berlin's historic monuments, to watch matches live on giant screens and savour the football party atmosphere. One million people congregated in Berlin's Fan Mile on 4 July 2006 to watch the FIFA World Cup semi-final between Germany and Italy on twenty-two giant screens.

Similar efforts were invested in other German cities to accommodate high levels of domestic and international spectator interest in the event. Over 15,000 fans followed the match between Germany and Ecuador on giant screens at Leipzig's Augustusplatz on 20 June 2006. In Frankfurt fans from all over the world watched World Cup games in temporary arenas constructed on the banks of the River Main. They watched World Cup games on giant screens situated in the middle of the river on 22-m-long hydraulic poles (televised images were projected to viewing audiences on both sides of the river). As such, ticket-holding fans who were able to attend games live were outnumbered by spectators watching the same games, at the same time, on giant screens located in a number of local and regional public spaces.

The development of big screen spectator precincts at local and recognizable urban sites has spawned some interesting variations of the big screen phenomenon. One such variation is the development of non-local live spectator sites. The development of temporary viewing facilities allows for sports competitions to be transformed from a local/stadium event into wider regional or national sport spectatorship events.

This creates significant opportunities for tourist destinations where large, multi-national and mobile tourists are temporarily based. While many non-urban tourist destinations are unlikely or unable to host live stadium sport, the big screen has emerged as a means by which to capitalize on tourist interests in sports events. This may also be a strategic response to minimize the diversion effects of prominent sports events that may compete with traditional tourist destinations for visitor attention. A further variation of big screen spectatorship at a wider spatial level is the creation of temporary spectator precincts in home countries of nations competing in world championship events. Thus, during the 2006 FIFA World Cup campaign it was common for big screen live sites to be developed both in existing stadiums and public places such as Trafalgar Square (London), Federation Square (Melbourne) and Circular Quay (Sydney).

It is, therefore, important to recognize that the spectatorship experience has expanded far beyond the spatial limitations and elitist confines of the stadium experience (Hede & Alomes, 2007). This expansion of real-time sport experiences has effectively democratized both public access to experiencing sports events and destination capacities to leverage or 'host' (via the creation of temporary viewing facilities and live sites) sports events. Herein lie both challenges and opportunities for tourist destinations that exist and compete within the context of globalized and multi-media societies. The domain of stadium sport as well as new and emerging spectatorship phenomena is interesting to theorize. It would appear that connoisseur sport spectators are those who give priority to live spectatorship in the stadiums and arenas where elite sports contests take place (Standeven & De Knop, 1999). Those who are unable to access limited tickets may choose to travel nonetheless to the place of competition to experience the contest in other ways. This may represent a sizeable group of spectators in the case of historic or important sports events. Thus, the emphasis on spectatorship, which has historically focussed on the highly constrained setting of a stadium, has clearly diffused to alternative forms of live spectatorship in public spaces (Beauchamp, 2008).

While the stadium remains exclusive in terms of ticket-holder access, the spectator experience has rapidly evolved, particularly in less constrained public spaces. This course of evolution is yet to be fully embraced in event management and event bidding processes. In theory, it is conceivable that the development of spectator facilities in dedicated, temporary venues in public spaces will become a legitimate part of the strategic event development process. If so, the historical focus on stadium capacity, the need for infrastructural investment and the prospect of archaic, monolithic and uneconomic stadium legacies following mega sports events may be unlocked. Temporary spectator facilities, the use of public spaces and a focus on remote spectator experiences may be key elements of sustainable stadium development.

It is interesting to theorize that spectatorship in public spaces may become part of the event bidding process, as a means to reduce the burden of stadium/infrastructure investment. It may also be seen as a means to improve equity in the international event bidding process by affording small, poorer and/or peripheral nations and destinations an opportunity to realistically bid to host sports events despite more modest stadium infrastructure. Such a strategy may be supported by innovative means to create unique visitor and spectator experiences through ancillary entertainments aimed at the creation of atmospheres of local festival or carnivalesque (Giulianotti, 1995). The interspersion of the experience of sport with authentic experiences of place through music, atmosphere, food and beverage and personal interaction offers avenues of opportunity in terms of place competition and place promotion. The use of iconic urban monuments and historic sites is now established as a prominent element in this mix (Chalip, 2002). While improving equity in bidding for international sports events, such strategic developments could also form part of the leveraging strategy for major sports events.

The extreme of this theorization is a major sports event played out in a modest or empty stadium, with large and dispersed audiences experiencing the sport competition at specifically selected sites where temporary facilities are constructed. Such sites could include regional tourism or urban destination live sites (Hede & Alomes, 2007) at a range of spatial scales. Variations of this scenario include the use of local blackouts (withdrawn or delayed local television coverage) to promote stadium ticket sales. However, even given this broadcast blackout practice, elite sport has in a number of cases been played in front of rows of empty seats in cases of stadium closure due to fan violence or threats of security disruption. Such scenarios invoke consideration of the potential for remote and big screen spectatorship to allow, for example, developing countries (where stadium facilities are otherwise inadequate) to host major sports events. This does highlight the transportability of sports, which may be seen as both an opportunity and a threat. This may be seen to erode sport tourism as a composite of activity, people and place if place is seen to be expendable or reproducible through the development of live sites. The counter view is that it heightens the need for place to be central to the experience of sport (Morgan, 2007; Weed, 2007).

Selected references

Beauchamp, P. (2008). Event Horizons Expanding. Sunday Herald, September 17, pp. 73.

Fanfest Berlin (2006) http://www.berlin.de/fifaw2006/english/fanfest/index.php. (accessed 17 November 2006)

Hede, A. and Alomes, S. (2007). Big Screens: Exploring Their Future for the Special Event Sector. 4th International Event Research Conference. Melbourne, Australia.

CONCLUSION

The globalization of sports and tourism has had various implications for sport spectatorship as a tourism activity. While multiple and flexible fandoms have emerged, the entrenchment of team loyalties based on social and cultural meanings is also evident. Sport spectatorship in association with tourism experiences in places of competition has become an important means by which to build a sense of national, collective or personal identity in times when globalization has brought unprecedented change to the reference points that once framed peoples' lives. One consequence has been that the identities of individuals or groups of sport spectators have given rise to the search for unique personal or social experiences. This runs counter to the packaging and commodification of sports experiences and promotes the need for sociological insights into the nature of sport tourism experience.

Sport spectatorship offers the potential for unique experiences to be derived from social and cultural interactions, which represent the synergistic interplay of intense sporting activities and the coming together of spectators from 'home' and 'away' in a setting that is place-situated and bounded in space and time. The uniqueness of these social experiences represents a counter to the high mobility and transportability of sport in a globalized world. Thus sports stadiums, be they modern or retro (see Chapter 11, *Modern landscapes and retro parks*), can be reproduced in any part of the world. However, it is the social experience, which is place-situated and socially/culturally constructed, that lies at the heart of the sport tourist spectator experience. Herein lies a key element of sport tourism that, despite (and perhaps because of) globalization and contemporary mobility, cannot be spatially transplanted. The diverse (and diversifying) ways in which live sports may otherwise be experienced present both opportunities and threats to tourism destinations.

CHAPTER 7

Recreational Sport and Serious Leisure

Chapters 5 (*Globalization and the mobility of elite athletes*) and 6 (*Spectatorship and spectator experiences*) explored the travel activities of elite athletes and the spectators who follow them. In contrast, this chapter examines the travel practices of recreational athletes. In doing so, recreational sport is considered to fall under the broad rubric of leisure. It involves freely chosen participation in sport activities primarily for the intrinsic rewards associated with it. While 'having fun' is often the primary reward/motivation for this involvement, there are also more serious motivations/rewards that will be considered. This chapter opens by considering whether travel is a benefit or cost in terms of recreational sport. A leisure constraint framework is used to explore this question with a focus on the negotiation of constraints. Negotiation is then considered in the context of serious leisure and sport subcultures. The chapter closes with a discussion of issues related to identity and commodification.

TRAVEL: A BENEFIT OR CONSTRAINT?

While the travel lifestyle of professional and elite athletes may seem attractive from afar, it presents a serious challenge to these athletes as they seek to perform their sporting endeavours at optimal levels (see Chapter 5, *Globalization and the mobility of elite athletes*). In many ways, travel is a constraint to athletic performance that has to be negotiated and managed in a strategic fashion. Whether travel is a benefit or constraint in the context of recreational sport tourism is not readily apparent nor has it been extensively addressed in the literature. Intuitively, however, the appropriate response would seem to be that 'it depends'.

Leisure constraint theory offers a way of considering whether travel is seen as a benefit or cost for recreational sport tourism. Under this theory, consideration is given to the 'factors that are assumed by researchers and/or perceived or experienced by individuals to limit the formation of leisure preferences and/or to inhibit or prohibit participation and enjoyment in leisure' (Jackson, 2000). An important aspect of this theory in relation to the question of cost or benefit is the idea of negotiation. To a considerable degree, by adopting a leisure constraint framework, the question as to whether travel is a benefit or constraint for recreational sport becomes mute. What becomes important is the nature of the perceived constraint and how prospective participants negotiate this constraint.

Like other forms of leisure, a variety of constraints can be found in sport tourism (Hinch, Jackson, Hudson & Walker, 2006). At its core, though, sport tourism is faced with the constraint of distance. By definition, tourism requires travel between home communities and the tourist destination. The more isolated the destination or the longer the distance to a destination, the greater the constraint (Hinch & Jackson, 2000). While not couched specifically in the terminology of constraints, geographers have captured this concept through the development of distance decay theory, which highlights the inverse relationship between increasing distance and the number of travellers visiting a destination (McKercher & Lew, 2003). Basically, the cost of a journey in terms of time, money and energy tends to increase and therefore presents a higher level of constraint as distance increases.

Figure 7.1 illustrates the key components of leisure constraint theory and highlights the negotiation process that characterizes leisure involvement. At its core is the process of leisure involvement, which begins with motivations that lead to leisure preferences. These preferences are then assessed in the context of interpersonal compatibility and coordination with other stakeholders associated with this leisure activity. Final outcomes are reflected in the level and nature of leisure participation. A parallel hierarchy of

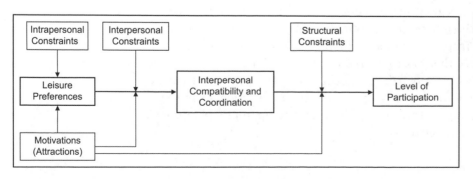

FIGURE 7.1

The hierarchical/ negotiation model (Source: Jackson, Crawford & Godbey, 1993).

constraints operates starting with intrapersonal constraints that relate directly to leisure preferences. For example, if an individual has never been exposed to a sport such as scuba diving, this activity is unlikely to feature as one of his or her leisure preferences. At the next level in this constraint hierarchy are interpersonal constraints, an example of which might be the inability to find others willing to join a kayaking expedition that requires multiple participants. Finally, a variety of structural constraints might be present, such as the cost of the expedition or the time required for its completion. Jackson, Crawford and Godbey (1993) point out that these constraints do not necessarily prevent participation although they may change the nature of that participation. They propose what has come to be known as the 'negotiation thesis' of constraint theory.

This negotiation thesis is highlighted by six specific propositions:

- Participation is dependent not on the absence of constraints (although this may be true for some people) but on negotiation through them. Such negotiation may modify rather than foreclose participation.

- Variations in the reporting of constraints can be viewed not only as variations in the experience of constraints but also as variations in the success in negotiating them.

- Absence of the desire to change current leisure behaviour may be partly explained by prior successful negotiation of structural constraints.

- Anticipation of one or more insurmountable interpersonal or structural constraints may suppress the desire for participation.

- Anticipation consists not simply of the anticipation of the presence or intensity of a constraint but also of anticipation of the ability to negotiate it.

- Both the initiation and outcome of the negotiation process are dependent on the relative strength of, and interactions between, constraints on participating in an activity and motivations for such participation. (Jackson et al., 1993)

While there are a number of factors that influence an individual's ability to negotiate these constraints in the context of recreational sport, one of the most important is the level of commitment to that sport. Stebbins' concept of serious leisure suggests that recreational sport enthusiasts who possess high levels of commitment to their sport are often able to negotiate the classic tourism constraints associated with travel.

SERIOUS LEISURE

The concept of serious leisure as articulated by Stebbins (1982, 1992) has helped to detrivialize the field of leisure studies by allowing it to 'escape the conceptual burdens of enjoyment, freedom and celebrations of choice' (Raisborough, 1999:67). It does this by distinguishing between casual and serious forms of leisure. Examples of the former include popular activities like watching television and activities that tend to be classified as diversions. Examples of the latter, that is, serious leisure pursuits, include playing in a performing amateur orchestra or running in marathons. In brief, Stebbins (1992) defines serious leisure as follows:

> the systemic pursuit of an amateur, hobbyist or volunteer activity that is sufficiently substantial and interesting for the participant to find a career there in the acquisition and expression of special skills and knowledge. (Stebbins, 1992:3)

Gammon and Robinson's (1997) distinction between sport tourism and tourism sport highlights two basic motivational orientations for sport tourism. In their definition of sport tourism, sport is the prime motivation to travel with the touristic element being secondary. In contrast, they distinguish tourism sport in that the holiday or visit, rather than the sport, is the primary motivation. Sport is seen as a secondary or even incidental element of the holiday experience. While both of these types of sport involvement have implications for travel, it is the former that is most salient in the context of leisure constraints and is, therefore, the focus of this chapter.

Distinguishing qualities of serious leisure

There are six unique qualities of serious leisure including perseverance; leisure careers; significant effort based on special knowledge, training or skill; durable benefits; a unique ethos surrounding the activity and a strong personal identification with the pursuit (Stebbins, 1982, 1992). Each of these qualities of recreational sport is relevant in a tourism context.

Development as an athlete requires *perseverance* to learn new physical and tactical skills and to attain the physical prowess required to compete at higher levels within the sport. Success motivates athletes to persevere, with the most important criterion of success being the achievement of personal goals rather than simply winning or losing (Siegenthaler, Gonzalez & Leticia, 1997). Athletes who persevere through their athletic failures or setbacks and the sacrifices that inevitably accompany the time and energy needed to develop competence and expertise in a sporting pursuit are more likely to attain their personal goals than those who do not. They are also more likely to negotiate the constraints that travel may present in extended journeys to national and international calibre activity sites and/or the pursuit of increasingly high levels of competition.

A second distinguishing feature of serious leisure pursuits is a *career-like pattern* of performance and achievement. Such careers are very apparent in sport, with skill levels often being measured in very explicit ways and being rewarded in terms of assignment to competitive hierarchies within a sport. At each level of these competitive hierarchies there are typically direct measures of performance related to wins and losses, goals scored or assisted, race times and an assortment of other statistical measures. There is also an assortment of indirect indicators and attributes, such as the 'competitiveness' of an athlete, that are used as indicators of career stage. Even in athletic activities that eschew such explicit measures of performance, there are important career stages such as the four-stage framework of pre-socialization, selection and recruitment, socialization and acceptance/ostracism in the sporting subcultures of climbing and rugby (Donnelly & Young, 1988). Similar types of careers can be observed in other types of sport subcultures such as surfing, snowboarding and extreme sports. Under a serious leisure framework careers are built around avocations rather than the vocations of work.

The third quality that distinguishes recreational sport as serious leisure is the expenditure of *personal effort* 'based on special knowledge, training, or skill' (Stebbins, 1982:256). While one sometimes hears of 'gifted natural athletes' who do not seem to have to work hard to perform well, such athletes are few and far between. Recreational athletes who are serious are characterized by demonstrated personal effort in their given athletic pursuits. They are committed to the physical and mental training required to pursue and maintain their serious leisure career.

Stebbins (1982, 1992) lists *durable benefits* as the fourth quality of serious leisure pursuits. Such benefits include 'self-actualization, self-enrichment, recreation or renewal of self, feelings of accomplishment, enhancement of self-image, self-expression, social interaction and belonginess (sic), and lasting physical products of the activity' (1982:257). Examples of these benefits can be found in sport (e.g., Green & Chalip, 1998). Wheaton (2007), whose work on sport subcultures has intriguing parallels to the literature on serious leisure, argues that it is 'the "inner" or "felt" body – not the commodified, astheticized, and disciplined body' (p. 298) or in other words, the intrinsic rather than the extrinsic benefits that are most important in terms of the durable benefits.

The fifth quality of serious leisure is the *unique ethos* associated with a particular pursuit. Stebbins (1982) described these as subcultures characterized by special beliefs, values, moral principles, norms and performance standards. There is a particularly rich literature on sport subcultures, such as rugby and climbing (e.g., Donnelly & Young, 1988), snowboarding (e.g., Heino, 2000), skateboarding, (e.g., Beal, 1995) and windsurfing (e.g., Wheaton, 2000). This literature is very consistent in the characterizations of these sports in terms of subculture-specific beliefs, values and behaviours. While Stebbins (1996a) has argued that recreational tourism is different from cultural tourism, his argument is based on a visual and performing or 'liberal arts' interpretation of culture. When culture is viewed as a 'way of life' (Chapter 4, *Culture and identity*), these sporting subcultures and the activities that characterize them can clearly function as cultural attractions.

The sixth and last quality that Stebbins (1982, 1992) used to define serious leisure is that participants tend to *identify strongly* with their chosen pursuits. This is particularly true of sport subculture members who consciously and unconsciously present themselves as subculture members. In her study of windsurfers, Wheaton (2000) concluded that the most important forms of social capital and identity were found in skill and performance of these athletes. Nevertheless, she and others have noted a broad range of consumption markers that have been used to signify sporting subculture membership to outsiders as well as insiders. Examples include the type of equipment used (Yoder, 1997; Heino, 2000), clothing styles (Humphreys, 1997), media consumption and language idioms (Wheaton & Beal, 2003).

Serious leisure typology

Stebbins (1982, 2007) suggested that there are three main types of individuals who tend to exhibit the qualities that characterize serious leisure practices. These include amateurs, hobbyists and volunteers. While Stebbins includes sport examples to illustrate each of these categories, it is useful to expand on the role of sport, particularly as it relates to sport tourism. The first category in this framework is that of modern amateurs found in art, science, entertainment and sport along with a range of other realms. Amateurs are positioned as part of a professional–amateur–public system in which there is interdependency between the parties, with the amateurs tending to serve as a conduit between professionals and the public. Sport is a particularly dynamic realm for amateurism given the professionalization of a broad range of sporting codes over the past century (e.g., rugby union; see Smith, 2000; Higham & Hinch, 2003). As the professional ranks of sport have swelled, the amateur ranks have served as a feeder for professional competitions. Top ranked amateurs participate in elite sports and tend to have many of the same travel opportunities as their professional counterparts albeit on a more limited scale and perhaps a more restricted travel range.

Rather than following a professional tour that may take them all over the world or throughout major regions on a regular basis, top amateurs are likely to play and compete closer to home, as they face greater travel constraints in terms of money and time. One of the results of this more limited range of travel is that they remain identified with their home region.

The second category in Stebbins' (1982, 2007) typology were hobbyists who are defined as 'serious about and committed to their endeavours, even though they frequently feel no necessity or obligation to engage in them' (Stebbins, 1982:259–260). Their participation is, however, regular, systematic and driven by the desire to acquire and maintain unique skill sets. Stebbins' case study on mountain climbers serves to illustrate the nature of this group (see Case study 7.1). In contrast to professionals, hobbyists operate external to professional–amateur–public systems. They tend to lack professional counterparts. Stebbins suggests that one type of hobbyist is the 'active participant' and lists sports like bodybuilding, backpacking, hang gliding, cross-country skiing, surfing and fishing and hunting as examples of this type of hobbyist. Since the publication of his 1982 article, professional competitions have been introduced in many of these sports (e.g., bass fishing competitions; see Yoder, 1997) or they have been professionalized in terms of the development of paid demonstration, instruction and guiding functions (e.g., whitewater kayaking, see Kane & Zink, 2004). To the extent that this has occurred, these sports have shifted towards the amateur category but substantial vestiges of sport hobbyists still exist. Stebbins labels those sport hobbyists who operate under a formal set of rules that structure their contest-like activities as players. The dedication of these hobbyists drives them to seek out geographic locales for participation that advance their serious leisure careers. While the desire to participate in a sport such as windsurfing may be a factor in choosing to live by a suitable site (Wheaton, 2000), where it is not possible to live at the activity site permanently, serious windsurfers will structure their leisure travel accordingly.

Case Study 7.1

Mountain climbing and serious leisure

Robert A. Stebbins (University of Calgary, Canada)

When asked by an interviewer for the *New York Times* (18 March 1923) why he wanted to climb Mount Everest, George Mallory replied, 'Because it is there'. 'There' was not where Mallory lived, however, which was England, but in the case of Everest, it was in Nepal. He was in effect a tourist who journeyed to that county, as he had earlier to other Asian and European countries, to climb a certain mountain. In fact, concerning Everest, Mallory failed to 'summit', as he had twice before (he died during this third attempt), but reaching the peak is not an essential quality of mountaineering, a subtype of hobby generally classifiable as activity participation (Stebbins, 2005).

A distinctive group of people around the world with sufficient money and time for going to destinations away from home travel specifically to climb one or more distant mountains. Not all these people are hobbyists, however, since it is possible to climb some mountains as tourist objectives without the conditioning and knowledge needed in their serious leisure counterparts. Thus, Mount Fuji in Japan, which receives more than 200,000 visitors annually (http://www.mt-fuji.co.jp/info/info.html, retrieved 9 February 2008), has among other trails to the top, a relatively easy one for beginners, for casual leisure participants.

Nonetheless, other mountains that have generated a notable touristic following can only be climbed by those who have a hobbyist attachment to the activity (Stebbins, 2005). That is, at minimum, they must be in the fine physical condition required for success at a given nontechnical climb. Moreover, for technical climbs, they will not only have to be in such condition but will also need the skills, knowledge and equipment of technical climbers. These include knowledge of how to rappel, drive pegs, use rope, employ an ice axe and find climbable routes. Climbing Kilimanjaro, the highest mountain in Africa, is a popular tourist activity, which however takes six to eight days on the mountain to gain the summit, depending on the route taken. Though no technical climbing is involved in the standard route, physical conditioning is imperative. The same holds for Mount Aconcagua in Argentina (13 days on the mountain climbing the standard route) and, whereas this site is less popular than Kilimanjaro, it is also considerably higher – only Everest is taller. These mountains attract climbers in significant numbers, as do some others; among them are Mont Blanc (Europe), Denali/Mount McKinley (Alaska), Aoraki/Mount Cook (New Zealand) and Mount Elbrus (Russia). As with Kilimanjaro, Aconcagua, and Everest, each offers at least one nontechnical route to its summit, routes far more popular than their technical counterparts.

Peak bagging

This is mountaineering language for 'summiting' a particular mountain, usually considered, however, as one of several summits achieved and planned as a personal collection of such accomplishments. The desire to bag peaks motivates touristic mountain climbing. That said some peak baggers are strictly local in orientation, in that they live in a mountainous region and have developed an interest only in summiting the mountains within a day's drive from home. Other baggers, however, though they may have this local interest, also yearn to mount distant peaks in their own country or outside it. And still others may have no local mountains of significant height to climb, a situation Mallory faced as well as Ronald Naar of the Netherlands, who is one of the small international group of 'seven summiteers'.

An elite set of peak baggers, and hence mountain climbing tourists extraordinaire, are those who have climbed the highest mountain on each of the seven continents, collectively known in mountaineering circles as the 'seven summits'. In 1985 American climber Dick Bass became the first mountaineer to climb this group (Bass, Wells, & Ridgeway, 1986), which soon stirred controversy over the identity of the highest peak in Australasia. According to the website statistics, facts and figures of all seven summiteers, 198 people have achieved this distinction as recorded through March 2007 (http://7summits.com/7summits_statistics.php, retrieved 9 February 2008).

Touristic impact

By the mid-1990s, 4,000 people had attempted to climb Everest – of which 660 successfully reached the summit and more than 140 died trying (Shroder, 2008). This record dates to 1921 when the first attempt was made to reach the top. By contrast a tourist website promoting Kilimanjaro claims that this mountain now attracts 15,000 climbers annually (http://alpineascents.com/kilimanjaro-why-climb.asp, retrieved 9 February 2008). The annual number of visits to Fuji mentioned above dwarfs these figures. Yet, all considered, contemporary touristic mountain climbing inspires a sizeable gang of hobbyists to visit the mountainous regions of the world.

These visitors do more for the local economy than simply hiring local guides and porters to assist them in climbing the famous nearby mountain. For example, climbers commonly arrive at their destinations a day to two in advance of the ascent (often to adjust to jet lag) and typically linger a day or two after the descent (often to limber up for the long, sedentary trip home). During this time they usually spend money locally on restaurants and sleeping accommodations. In addition, they use the town's transportation services to the closest airport, bus station or train terminal. Although mountain climbers tend to bring their own clothing and equipment, their guides supply such necessities as tents (where huts are not maintained) and food. The latter is mostly, if not entirely, purchased close at hand.

Conclusion

Bourdeau, Corneloup, and Mao (2004) write that mountain adventure sports in Europe, including mountain climbing, have recently shown dramatic increases in popular interest. One result has been to thrust these activities to the centre of the alpine sport tourism system. It is highly likely that this trend is also evident in other parts of the world where popular climbs are now routinely undertaken.

Selected references

Bass, D., Wells, F. and Ridgeway, R. (1986). *Seven Summits*. New York: Warner Books.

Bourdeau, P., Corneloup, J. and Mao, P. (2002). Adventure sports and tourism in the French mountains: Dynamics of change and challenges for sustainable development. *Current Issues in Tourism*, 5(1), 22–32.

The third type of serious leisure is volunteer activity, which is non-paid activity deemed beneficial to others (Stebbins, 1982, 1996b, 2007). It is characterized by altruism although Stebbins has pointed out that while the initial commitment to volunteer activity may be driven by altruism it is likely that continued involvement will be sustained by self-interest. Another characteristic of volunteer activities is that they are delegated tasks in that they are often assigned by paid staff. Sport has a long tradition of volunteer support that ranges from parents coaching their children's teams through to the administration of high-level amateur sport organizations. As was the case with hobbyists, volunteer roles are changing as sport is increasingly professionalized at the elite levels. In terms of sport tourism, even at a global scale, sporting events tend to rely on volunteers to carry out the 'hands on' aspects of the event. This is especially true in terms of the assorted destination hosting roles that are critical to the experience of the athletes as well as the spectators. Cities which have a strong track record of volunteer support and expertise are much more competitive in the bid processes for these events than those which do not have this volunteer base.

Sport tourism dimensions of serious leisure

One of the most direct ties between sport as serious leisure and tourism is that certain sports are dependent on specific types of environments and, therefore, geographic locations (see Chapter 12, *Place attachment*). This dependence requires travel for the serious pursuit of a recreational sport endeavour. Beyond this place dependence there is the element of place identity. The significance of this element is illustrated in Green and Chalip's (1998) emphasis on identity in their concluding comments on the motivation of female football players to travel to Florida from all across the United States to play in a tournament.

> *Playing* per se *is necessary but probably not sufficient to attract and retain participants. Players seek opportunities to celebrate the identity that they and their fellow players have chosen to share. In the case of the football tournament, women seek more than a chance to play football; they seek an extended occasion and an encapsulated space to be football players.* (Green & Chalip, 1998:285)

While the concept of place identity will be explored in more depth in Chapter 12 (*Place attachment*), at this point it is important to consider identities in the context of serious leisure and sport tourism. Jones and Green (2006) have published the most direct explorations to date on these relationships. They argue that serious leisure and travel to participate in serious leisure are mutually reinforcing activities in the context of sport tourism. This mutual reinforcement is fostered in five ways, which include the following:

1. Offering a context through which to construct and/or confirm one's leisure identity;

2. Providing a time and place (and perhaps liminoid space) to interact with others sharing the ethos of one's chosen activities;

3. Providing a stage on which to parade and celebrate a valued social identity;

4. Creating another step in one's leisure career; and

5. Affording a means by which to signal one's career stage to others (Jones & Green, 2006:43).

First, sport tourism provides a context for individuals to construct their social identities. There tends to be a greater opportunity to construct a preferred identity in the realm of leisure than in the realm of work, given the fundamental choices afforded by leisure. In adopting a serious leisure lifestyle through sport, an individual is able to influence the construction of his or her social identity. Travel associated with a serious sport pursuit has long been used as a 'bonding' opportunity for teams involved in competitive sport and can serve a similar socializing function for other types of serious recreational athletes. Jones and Green's (2006) analogy of a language training course with its benefits of immersion is paralleled by the socialization benefits of travel for serious leisure. Such activity-based travel serves as an intensive course in the sporting subculture away from the normal distractions of an individual's day-to-day life.

Second, the travel associated with serious sporting pursuits provides a space for subcultural interaction. In doing so, these spaces become infused with meaning, thereby becoming places of identity for travellers. Rather than shifting between work and leisure identities as one does at home, sport-related travel allows an individual to focus on his or her sport identity.

Third, sport tourism destinations become stages for the display of sporting identities. Sport tourists are simultaneously escaping from their home-based identities and seeking out their serious leisure identities. In doing so, they have the opportunity to parade and celebrate sporting identity. Green and Chalip (1998) also suggest that the destination acts as a form of 'encapsulated space'. Sport tourism destinations function as subculture 'hot houses' that provides fertile grounds for identity construction and sources of subcultural capital. Wheaton (2007:299) goes so far as to suggest that these leisure spaces are 'not just an "escape" from everyday life, but a place for critiquing it'. As such, these spaces play a critical role in the construction of social identities.

Fourth, a visit to a sport tourism destination may signify a critical event in an individual's leisure career. Progression through a competitive hierarchy that characterizes a sport will often be marked by a sequence of local, regional, national through to international competitions. While the nature of this competitive hierarchy means that relatively few participants have the opportunity to play at an international level, it is not necessary that a serious leisure career reach this level of attainment. For some, participation at a regional event will represent the height of their achievement. For sport hobbyists who fall into Stebbins' (1982) description of a collector, career milestones may be signified by visits to designated areas (e.g., climbing mountains on each continent). Similarly, visits to sites of special significance for a particular sport, for instance, a golfer playing on the old course at St. Andrews, Scotland, may be seen as a pilgrimage of sorts that demonstrates the commitment of an individual to his/her sporting career.

Finally, not only does sport-based travel potentially mark progression on a leisure career ladder, it also serves as a signifier of career attainment. The travel portfolio of a member of a sporting subculture has social capital. For example, windsurfers gain social capital from the consumption of travel-related articles in magazines dedicated to their sport (Wheaton & Beal, 2003). In their study of international participants on a kayaking package tour in New Zealand, Kane and Zink (2004:342) concluded:

The prestigious 'capital' value of this tour destination, and of participants' previous tours indicate that, for the participants, package adventure tours were markers in their serious leisure career.

Visits to sites of importance within a subculture serve to signal one's status as an insider and to varying degrees they serve to highlight one's status within this subculture. Like the hardware that often symbolizes championship performances in traditional sport competition, 'travel trophies' that serve as displays of visits to important destinations in a particular sporting world are often highly valued. Such souvenirs may take the form of photos displayed on personal blogs, t-shirts or team jerseys highlighting the event or destination, custom made equipment or numerous other tangible tokens from the destination.

IMPLICATIONS FOR SPORT TOURISM

While the theory of serious leisure has gained considerable traction with researchers studying in the realm of leisure, it has not been widely used in the study of sport. Sport sociologists have, however, studied sport subcultures in a way that is comparable to serious leisure. In both realms, issues of identity and commodification have been raised in the relation to sport tourism.

Issues of identity

At the core of both areas of study is the belief that the leisure activity, be it sport or some other form of leisure, plays a central role in the development of identity. Under the serious leisure approach, identity formation is imbedded in the six defining qualities that Stebbins (1982) outlines. From a sport subculture perspective, the idea of a career-like structure and a distinct ethos related to the activity is emphasized. Sport sociologists like Donnelly and Young (1988) used similar terminology to describe how recreational athletes involved in climbing and rugby used the respective sport subcultures for the construction and confirmation of their identities while focusing primarily on sport tourism. Green and Chalip (1998) drew heavily on the sport subculture literature in their study of a women's football tournament in Florida. In contrast to existing studies in sport sociology, however, they consciously considered the role of place in the identity making process associated with the subculture of women's football in the United States. At the heart of this identity building process was the provision of a stage or encapsulated space within which to celebrate one's identity as a female football player. They concluded that in this instance, the attraction of the event was the celebration of a subculture rather than the place, the hosts or even the sporting activity itself.

> *Although the compact geography of Key West certainly facilitates*
> *social encounters, nothing that goes on at the tournament depends on*
> *the Key's geography or location… Site and culture may be facilitative,*
> *but they are peripheral. The fundamental attraction is neither the*
> *place nor its people; the fundamental attraction is the other players*
> *who attend. The event itself is more important than the destination.*
> (Green & Chalip, 1998:286)

Similar studies are needed of other types of participatory sporting events to see if this result holds true across a broad range of sport tourism activities, thereby confirming the transportability of such events.

Serious leisure scholars and those who study sport subcultures tend to agree that while identity may be strongly influenced by one's leisure or sport avocation, this is moderated by the other social roles that an individual may hold. For example, in their study of serious leisure related to dog sports, Gillespie, Leffler and Lerner (2002) note that considerable identity negotiation may be necessary around the boundaries of 'real life' and these 'greedy avocations'.

> *Serious leisure generates its own social identities, including patterns*
> *of time allocation, expenditures, family relationships, and norms. Its*
> *demands and those of the 'real world' sometimes conflict. In these*
> *conflicts, priorities, rules and relationships are actively negotiated by*
> *participants, sometimes leaning toward the demands of the dominant*
> *culture, sometimes not.* (Gillespie et al., 2002:300)

The implication of this from a sport tourism perspective is that sport travellers are not simply reinforcing a countercultural identity through their activities. In fact, they are simultaneously resisting and reproducing dominant culture.

Much of the identity making power of serious leisure and sport subcultures is based on insider and outsider groups or the dichotomy between us and 'others' as raised in Chapter 4 (*Culture and identity*). However, there appear to be a few cracks in this basic dichotomy. Michele Donnelly (2006) criticizes sport subculture literature for its tendency to define insider authenticity based on a presumed core of insiders. She sees this as contradictory in as much as subcultures themselves are born on the margins of dominant society. Margins of a subculture are, therefore, deserving of more in-depth study and may very well be dynamic regions of identity formation, which reveal the error in the oppositional nature of insider/outsider categorization that has dominated the literature to this point. In a sport tourism context, the complexity of these insider/outsider identities is highlighted by the layers of subculture and geographic insider/outsiderness that interact when subculture members participate in their sporting activities while they are away from home.

Wheaton (2007) adds to this critique of the sport subculture literature by suggesting that the traditional ways of defining a subculture in terms of difference and resistance are being eroded in a post-modern society.

> *Neo-tribes suggest a postmodern 'pick and mix' world of consumer choice in which we are free to choose identities, ignoring the structural constraints that underpin identity choices and create lifestyles.* (Wheaton, 2007:290)

She describes the emergence of post-subculturalists who shift between sporting subcultures, thereby problematizing the basis on which sport scholars have been defining subculture and de-centring identity. Tourism, with its ability to facilitate the escape from the social roles that one is expected to fulfil at home, along with its convenient packaging of sport, provides an accessible realm for such de-centring of identity. It provides individuals with an opportunity to experiment with their sporting identities in ways that are not possible at home.

Crosset and Beal (1997) suggest that the use of the term subculture in sport is most applicable in situations where a sport such as body building is marginalized within the dominant culture. The term becomes less applicable as these sporting activities are accepted as legitimate activities by dominant culture even though they are rather specialized. Subcultures are all in various stages of losing their countercultural status. As an alternative to the subcultures, Crosset and Beal suggest that cultural studies scholars should consider the merits of studying 'social worlds and sub-worlds', which is consistent with the serious leisure terminology used by Stebbins (1982, 2007). These social worlds are defined as large and highly permeable, amorphous and spatially transcendent forms of social organizations made up of people sharing common interests and common channels of communication. As such, they offer advantages for inquiry into this dimension of sport tourism activity relative to the traditional focus on subculture.

Issues of commodification

Commodification has been a major theme in the sport subculture literature. While subcultures were often reported to have originated as a form of resistance to mainstream sports characterized by high levels of consumption, these subcultures are often distinguished by their own form of consumerism.

For example, Wheaton (2000:261) argues that the 'consumption of objects—specifically the equipment or kit—is central to windsurfing and other new individualized 'lifestyle' sports'. Despite this characteristic of consumption, she argues that members cannot 'buy' their way into a subculture. They must back up their consumer goods with a sport performance level that matches or surpasses the level of their equipment. Interestingly, her work suggests that different windsurfing sites have different standards of conspicuous consumption. This view suggests that sport subcultures have a geographic layer that is intertwined with their other cultural dimensions.

Wheaton and Beal (2003) highlight another aspect of this culture of consumption in extreme sport. They found that windsurfers and skateboarders consumed subcultural media magazines in order to obtain insider information and therefore status. In particular, they were interested in travel advertisements. Featured locations were deemed to be authentic in terms of an idealized windsurfing lifestyle. Clothing advertisements depicted similar idyllic locations in an effort to sell their product lines. In his article titled 'Shredheads go mainstream? Snowboarding and alternative youth' Humphrey (1997) traced the evolution of snowboarding from its counterculture roots to its current position as a mainstream sport characterized by the consumption of travel, equipment and clothing. Even while members were focused on the development of a countercultural image, commercial ski resorts began to actively cater to the demands of this new 'market' (Hudson, 2003). Michele Donnelly (2006) points out that despite his countercultural rhetoric, Jake Burton who is recognized as the inventor of modern snowboarding, is in fact a major beneficiary of the commodification of the sport as the owner of one of the most popular and profitable manufacturers of snowboards and snowboarding gear.

Tourism is a manifestation of commodification. The sport tourism industry packages sporting activities, place and the social interactions in return for a fee. The intent of the industry is to earn a profit by providing satisfying sport experiences to individuals away from their home environment. While some (e.g., Heywood, 1994) imply that such commodification undermines the integrity of the activity, others (e.g., Green, 2001) simply recognize the existence of this process without suggesting that it undermines authenticity. In the latter instance, Green has argued that sport subcultures and identities can be effectively leveraged to promote sporting events like the Gold Coast Marathon and the Australian Motorcycle Grand Prix. Event hosts who leverage events in this way not only enjoy higher net benefits in the destination but can potentially provide improved leisure experiences to the visiting sport tourists.

While the concept of serious leisure suggests that individuals may expend significant amounts of money in the pursuit of their leisure patterns, there has been little exploration on the implications of this process. Yoder's (1997) ethnographic study of the relatively new but increasing popular sport of competitive bass fishing is an exception. Yoder (1997:415) suggests:

Tournament bass fishing deviates significantly from the conventional model of serious leisure that consists of professional, amateurs and publics. It is a highly structured sport heavily dominated by national fishing organizations, event promoters, and the manufacturers and distributors of sporting goods and services.

He goes on to outline the emerging and significant role of commodity agents, such as equipment manufacturers and event sponsors, in terms of influencing the consumption of serious amateurs and the public associated with the sport. He also highlights the diversification of the professional ranks of the sport with the emergence of demonstration bass fishers along with those who earn their living from their competitive winnings. While he does not emphasize the spatial dynamic within the sport, it is clear that a geographic hierarchy exists from local- through to state-, regional- and national-level competitions in the United States. Yoder concludes:

The relationship between commodity agents and amateurs/publics fosters the development and maintenance of the sport's unique ethos. In return, the relationship is supported by the social world that develops around the ethos. Commodity agents depend on amateurs/ publics to consume their products. Amateurs/publics depend on the producers to supply them with goods and services they believe are necessary for participation. (Yoder, 1997:423)

One of the significant concerns Yoder raises is that there have been few rules established in the sport to ensure that competition outcomes remain difficult to predict and that they rely more on the fisher than the equipment. Essentially, he suggests that there is a conflict between the interests of equipment manufacturers with their motivation to sell the latest technical innovations relative to the competitive essence of the sport. A similar concern exists more broadly in terms of the travel industry that supports sport tourism. The question must be asked as to whether the tourism trade will operate in a sustainable manner or will they promote overuse of a sporting resource, because it is in their short-term financial interest to do so?

Another challenge of the commodification of sport though tourism is the apparent contradiction between adventure and safety that exists in the context of adventure tourism. Kane and Zink's (2004) study of international kayakers participating on a package kayaking tour of New Zealand provides useful insight into this issue. They described the tour as follows:

> ... *a consumable package of perceived safe experience from which participants could produce stories of adventure, implying unsafe experience. Specifically in their 'way of thinking' a package adventure tour was a mechanism to increase experience and critically create stories of 'symbolic capital', with the potential to improve their status in their serious leisure of kayaking.* (Kane & Zink, 2004:342)

At some level, all of the participants or clients on the tour were purchasing a degree of safety in their adventure. However, this commodification of risk and safety was rationalized in the narratives of the experience that were being developed throughout the trip and that would be retold on their return home. Relatively safe events would become near disasters and professional guides would become just 'a bunch of kayakers'. The question then becomes how the operator balances these conflicting demands for risk and safety. How do you 'package' extreme sport travel experiences in a way that is commercially viable?

CONCLUSION

Recreational athletes are an important consideration in the study of sport tourism. While they seldom have the high profile of elite athletes or the spectators who attend elite events, they represent a substantial portion of sport tourists. Leisure constraint theory provides a useful framework for understanding the travel behaviours of these individuals. One of the most insightful elements of this theory is the idea of negotiation – that even if the costs of travel are seen as a constraint, individuals can negotiate through or around these barriers. This is especially true for individuals who take their recreational sport seriously. Stebbins' (1982, 1992, 2007) concept of serious leisure shows that qualities like perseverance and a strong identification with the sporting activity can help individuals to surmount obstacles, such as travel, that might otherwise prevent them from participating. More work is needed to consider the relevance of this body of research relative to the subculture research found in sport. Green and Jones (2006) have moved in this direction. Their theoretical discussion of sport-based serious leisure and the associated travel to participate in sport tourism provides fresh insight into sport tourism due in part to their success at drawing on the sport subculture as well as the serious leisure literature.

Serious leisure provides a very powerful framework for inquiry related to sport tourism of a recreational nature. One of the most promising lines of inquiry addresses issues of identity as raised in Chapter 4 (*Culture and identity*). The theory of serious leisure has intriguing parallels with investigations into subculture that have been popular in the realm of sport. An additional advantage that it offers is its potential to combine considerations of personal identity with considerations of place. It also offers the potential for insight into the changing patterns of mobility of recreational athletes. A second line of inquiry that is highlighted in the chapter relates to issues of commodification. While these issues are relatively transparent in professional sport, they are much less so in terms of recreational sport travel. Further consideration is required to develop insight into the nature and implications of commodification in this realm.

Finally, it should be recognized that serious leisure is but one major category of recreational sport. Stebbins (2007) presents a serious leisure perspective which recognizes the categories of 'casual leisure' and 'project-based leisure' in addition to 'serious leisure'. These additional categories merit further attention by researchers as much recreational sport undertaken while travelling cannot be classified as serious leisure. Insight into these types of recreational activities will provide a more complete understanding of sport tourism phenomena.

PART 4

People

Authentic Experiences*

CONTENTS

One of the fundamental criticisms of tourism is that it leads to pseudo-events that fail to reflect the true culture of a place (Boorstin, 1964). This criticism suggests that in the process of catering to visitors, tourism operators create packages and foster experiences that corrupt the cultural essence of the attraction. In effect, the destination becomes a stage featuring performances by hosts who are removed from their real lives, their real homes and their real culture.

As a result, tourist experiences are diminished. Typically, the tourism industry has been blamed for this erosion of authenticity, and increasingly the industry itself has identified inauthenticity as an issue. Gilmore and Pine (2007) capture this sentiment with their message that authenticity is what consumers want and, by extension, what producers should be providing. In this chapter, we argue that sport offers unique qualities relative to other types of cultural tourist attractions in terms of facilitating authentic tourist experiences. We do this by positioning sport as a cultural tourist attraction and highlighting the challenges of commodification. The balance of the chapter uses Wang's (1999, 2000) framework of authenticity to demonstrate the relevance of sport attractions as agents for authentic tourist experience.

SPORT AS A CULTURAL TOURIST ATTRACTION

Sport fits nicely under Leiper's (1990:371) framework of a tourist attraction, which he defines as '… a system comprising of three elements: a tourist or

---

* This chapter is extensively derived from Hinch, T.D. & Higham, J.E.S. (2005). Sport, tourism and authenticity. *European Sports Management Quarterly*, 5(3): 245–258. Special issue: Sports tourism theory and method. Guest editor: Mike Weed.

human element, a nucleus or central element, and a marker or informative element. A tourist attraction comes into existence when the three elements are connected'. In the context of sport, the human element includes competitive and elite athletes, spectators and an assortment of supporting personnel. Markers take the form of advertisements and various media representations of sporting places. The nucleus is where sport is produced and consumed. It is where the games, activities and competitions that characterize sport are played and otherwise engaged in.

It is our contention that all sports, both urban and nature-based, are cultural manifestations and therefore are potential cultural attractions. For example, Bale (1994) argues that sports are not natural forms of movement but rather form part of a cultural landscape. Even sports that take place in supposedly natural environments actually take place in environments that are subject to cultural modification. Golf courses, for instance, are designed, maintained and otherwise used by humans clearly making them a part of a cultural landscape (Priestley, 1995).

A sport attraction is also a cultural attraction to the extent that sport identities (see Chapter 4, *Culture and identity*) are a reflection of the culture in a place. These identities represent the way communities are perceived and are projected based on prevailing social and ideological values and practices (McConnell & Edwards, 2000). In his book *Travels with Charley*, novelist John Steinbeck (1963) suggests that visitors can obtain a sense of local culture by going to a local pub on a Saturday night or to a church service the next day. In both cases, the visitor is able to share in local celebrations that reflect an important dimension of the culture of a place. The pub and the church service function as recognized 'windows' or perhaps even 'portals' into the backstage of a destination. A similar argument can be made for sport events and activities, as sport is one of the ways in which humans develop their personal and collective identities. Nauright (1996) goes as far as to claim that in '… many cases, sporting events and people's reactions to them are the clearest public manifestations of culture and collective identities in a given society' (p. 69). Notwithstanding this perspective, processes of globalization have challenged the traditional view that sport 'embodies local culture' (E. Cohen, personal communication, 12 June 2007). This is especially true in the context of sports like football with its global appeal, global competition, worldwide media distribution and the global mobility of its elite players. Yet, even in the case of football, there are local variations in style and passions that are consistent with Maguire's (1999) argument that there are increasing varieties even in the face of diminishing contrasts as the local negotiates its place in the global (see Chapter 2, *Sport and tourism in a global world*).

For example, a visitor will experience a significant aspect of Canadian culture by attending an ice hockey game while in Canada (Gruneau & Whitson, 1993). More generally, visitors who attend local sporting events, participate in local sport activities or visit local sites to venerate sports/people are afforded a unique opportunity to access the backstage of a destination. Furthermore, their visit is not likely to be as intrusive as visits to many other cultural sites because these elements of sport experience, despite their cultural significance, tend to be viewed as being within the public rather than private domain.

COMMODIFICATION

Tourism is a business. Tourism operators, governments, local hosts and tourists tend to rationalize their decisions in economic terms and behave as actors in a common market (Pearce, 1989). The fundamental rationale for tourism development is an economic one; destinations and providers of tourism goods and services seek net economic gains. Tourism activities are, therefore, a form of commercial exchange.

Destination resources such as attractive climates, beautiful landscapes and unique local cultures are packaged in a multitude of ways that are designed to provide leisure experiences for visitors. These experiences are exchanged for the visitors' economic resources, which are usually collected through an assortment of fees charged for tour packages, attractions, accommodation, food and beverages, transportation, souvenirs and other visitor-related products and services as well as through avenues of government taxation. Cohen (1988:380) described this exchange as a form of commodification or

> ... *a process by which things (and activities) come to be evaluated primarily in terms of their exchange value, in a context of trade, thereby becoming goods (and services); developed exchange systems in which the exchange value of things (and activities) is stated in terms of prices form a market.*

Commodification has drawn considerable attention from critics of tourism who suggest that selling landscapes and culture in this type of exchange is somewhat akin to prostitution in that by engaging in these transactions, the destination is sacrificing part of its soul (Greenwood, 1989). The commodification of local culture is seen as especially challenging given the intrusive nature this can have in terms of the backstage of a destination. Sport is rapidly moving toward a similar degree of commodification as reflected, for example, in the trends towards professional competition, commercial intrusion, increased media involvement and the emergence of transnational sport equipment manufacturers. McKay and Kirk (1992:10) argue that '[w]hereas cultural activities such as ... sport once were based primarily on intrinsic worth, they are now increasingly constituted by market values' (*see* Case study 8.1).

Case study 8.1

Promotional culture, indigenous identity, and the All Blacks Haka: Questions of commodification and authenticity

Jay Scherer (University of Alberta, Canada)

This case study examines issues of commodification and authenticity as they relate to the production and consumption of sport experiences that are increasingly mediated and incorporated into a global promotional culture. On 16 June 2007, Italian truck manufacturer Iveco, a multinational corporation with little or no connection to the sport of rugby union (or to New Zealand for that matter) became the official global sponsor of the All Blacks. In doing so, Iveco joined a host of other corporations including adidas, Coca Cola, Ford, Wheet-Bix, Steinlager and Mastercard in articulating their brand with the All Blacks, and by extension, New Zealand identity. These issues speak precisely of the impact of globalization on rugby as the New Zealand Rugby Union (NZRU) and its corporate 'partners' aggressively pursue new revenue streams and global audiences (Hope, 2002; Scherer, Falcous, & Jackson, 2008). A corollary of the exponential increase in the marketing of the All Blacks, however, has been the intensive commodification of Māori culture and specifically the Ka Mate haka, which is performed by the All Blacks prior to each test match. For example, to anoint their global sponsorship, Iveco recently released three versions of a televised advertisement, which aired in Italy, Spain, Great Britain, and New Zealand and featured several All Blacks of Polynesian, Māori and Fijian descent performing the Ka Mate haka to equate the power of the All Blacks with the 4WD Iveco Stralis. Revealing the ongoing erosion of the territorial frontiers of the global advertising industry, the Iveco All Blacks campaign, which so heavily commodified the Ka

Mate haka and Māori culture, was developed and produced by the Domino advertising agency, in Italy.

Iveco's sponsorship of the All Blacks has seemingly extended well beyond a simple partnership between the NZRU and a multinational corporation. More specifically, in 2007 various aspects of Māori culture, including the Ka Mate haka, were central to the Notte Bianca (an annual all-night cultural festival) which was hosted in Rome to promote not only Iveco but also New Zealand, which exists as a 'brand state' (Van Hamm, 2001) in the competitive and lucrative global tourist market. An Iveco press release noted:

> Iveco and New Zealand's Embassy in Rome will lead the public all the way to New Zealand, accompanied by the Haka dance that will introduce the Māori cultural identity ... In the collective ritual of the Haka dance, Iveco will join the Māori people in confirming the values (Commitment, Reliability, Performance and Team Spirit) that it shares with the New Zealand rugby team, the All Blacks ... During the Haka dance, the streets of Rome will become a marae, the traditional open-air space in which social ceremonies are held. The shouts and foot-stamping will reaffirm the endurance of the Māori cultural heritage; watching this spectacle ... onlookers will witness an identity and values whose power remains undiminished even in today's world. (Iveco, 2007)

It can be suggested, then, that Māori culture and the New Zealand state have been incorporated into commercial enterprise, market dynamics and a global promotional culture in which almost every element of social and cultural life has become a sales pitch and where consumer identities have become the currency of everyday life. What is plainly visible here is not only the ongoing delocalization of Māori identity and culture but also the possibilities of vicariously experiencing the world's geography:

> The interweaving of simulacra in daily life brings together different worlds (of commodities) in the same space and time. But it does so in such a way as to conceal almost perfectly any trace of origin, of the labour processes that produced them, or of the social relations implicated in their production. (Harvey, 1990:300).

Following Harvey (1990), these broad cultural-economic conditions are clearly of interest for sport tourism scholars and students interested in the critical study of globalization and the increasing premium that is being placed on the production of 'authentic' Indigenous traditions and heritage experiences for the consumption of global audiences, sports fans and tourists. More importantly, however, these issues are of paramount importance for Māori who are witnessing an exponential growth and interest in the use of Māori imagery, symbols and designs to promote commercial products and specific places as tourist destinations (Solomon, 2007). These developments have, incidentally, galvanized many Māori who are concerned with the misrepresentation of their culture and are at the core of Māori struggles over the legal protection and identification of intellectual property rights, a reminder of the different types of claims being placed on identity and 'authenticity' in the global economy.

Two sport-related examples point to the relevance of these issues. In 1999, adidas released a widely acclaimed television commercial entitled 'Black'. The commercial was based largely around the spectacle of the Ka Mate haka and Māori culture: it was developed as a 'primal, scary ad' (Primal Team, 1999:22) to reach adidas's company-wide global target market of 14–25-year olds in over 70 countries around the world. Despite going to extensive lengths to produce 'authentic' representations of indigenous culture, including consulting with some Māori and transforming the commercial set into a marae [communal meeting place], the advertising executives decided to

technologically enhance the commercial by adding a simulated moko (facial tattoo) to the main warrior who features so prominently in the ad. The commercial's stereotypical imagery, including the fabricated moko were, however, greeted with derision from some Māori who argued that indigenous culture cannot simply be haphazardly simulated and inserted into commercials that are controlled by non-Māori. Referring specifically to the use of the moko, lawyer Maui Solomon explained:

> The tau moko is not just the individual lines on the face it tells a whole story of that person's heritage, of the marae of the tribe … it's part of that collective right … the person carries all of that mana, all of that heritage, all of that tradition. So, it is wrong for me to go and try and copyright an ancestor figure that's been carved on a tree because I've got a company and I want to use it on a logo because that belongs to my collective, it belongs to my iwi. (Solomon, cited in Jackson & Hokowhitu, 2002:136)

Finally, in 2005 thousands of rugby fans travelled to New Zealand to support the British and Irish Lions rugby team. A key component of their sporting and cultural experiences consisted of not only watching or attending the various rugby matches but also consuming the advertising and marketing for the Lions tour, which was laden with indigenous imagery. One of the most significant campaigns was adidas's 'Stand in Black' promotion that consisted of the placement of a number of 'Haka Man' statues around New Zealand. One of adidas's statues on Watchman Island was, however, unceremoniously toppled by a local Māori group who considered the statue to be culturally insensitive. Beyond this, it is important to note that even a number of high-profile All Blacks, including Byron Kelleher for example, have recently suggested that the performance of the Ka Mate haka prior to each match is little more than a promotional stunt and no longer reflects the values of the All Blacks. Regardless, these actions and claims clearly raise a number of complicated questions pertaining to the production of 'authentic' advertising and sport tourism experiences, especially in light of the growing concerns of indigenous peoples in terms of how they are represented in contemporary marketing campaigns.

Selected references

Jackson, S. and Hokowhitu, B. (2002). Sport, tribes and technology. *Journal of Sport and Social Issues*, 26, 2: 125–139.

Scherer, J., Falcous, M. and Jackson, S. (2008). The media sports cultural complex: Local-global disjuncture in New Zealand/Aotearoa. *Journal of Sport & Social Issues*, 32, 1: 48–71.

Solomon, M. (2007). A long wait for justice. In *Resistance: An Indigenous Response to Neoliberalism*, (M. Bargh, ed.) pp. 75–84, Wellington: Huia Publishers.

Sport tourism represents but one of the many ways in which sport is being commodified. The question remains, however, whether this commodification is destroying the cultural meaning of sport in tourism destinations. Stewart (1987:172) suggests that this is the case by arguing that

> *Social hegemony of the commodity form is apparent as the practice of sport is shaped and dominated by the values and instrumentalities of the market … the idealized model of sport, along with its traditional ritualized meanings, metaphysical aura, and skill democracy, is destroyed as sport becomes just another item to be trafficked as a commodity.*

But has this idealized model of sport ever really existed? If sport is recognized as being dynamic in nature, then change is a normal part of its evolution. The types of change that Stewart has highlighted are consistent with the changes that characterize globalization more generally (see Chapter 2, *Sport and tourism in a global world*). While these changes certainly present issues in terms of the way sport has traditionally been viewed, they do not necessarily destroy its cultural essence.

So while recognizing the potential negative impacts of the commodification of culture for tourism, the process itself is not automatically destructive. For example, Cohen (1988:383) argued:

> *Commodification does not necessarily destroy the meaning of cultural products, neither for the locals nor for the tourists, although it may do so under certain conditions. Tourist-oriented products frequently acquire new meanings for the locals, as they become a diacritical mark of their ethnic or cultural identity, a vehicle of self-representation before an external public.*

These observations resonate particularly well in the context of sport-based attractions. Notwithstanding the globalization of many sports, attractions based on local sporting events, activities and nostalgia tend to reflect local culture whether it is manifest in unique playing styles, emotions or fundamental values. For example, tourists attending an amateur thakrow competition in a Thai village achieve first-hand insights into local styles of play, just as those experiencing genuine Thai boxing competitions are ruthlessly exposed to unique local values and emotions. The same may be said of most sports, from village cricket in rural England to Melbourne's Australian Football League (AFL) competition.

In contrast to many types of cultural attractions, those based on sport tend to be more robust and resilient to the potential compromises of commodification. For instance, one of the characteristics of sport is that the display of physical prowess is an integral part of many sporting activities (Loy, McPherson & Kenyon, 1978). Display suggests that in addition to the athletes producing live sport, there is an audience that views or consumes it. Spectatorship, therefore, is a natural part of sport events, especially at more competitive levels. This is not to suggest that spectatorship is universal. There is, in fact, a broad range of spectator interest in events. Events that are recreational in nature or which are being contested by players in their early stages of skill development are likely to attract fewer spectators than elite competitions (Hinch & Higham, 2004). Yet even these types of events can attract a loyal following of family and friends. Carmichael and Murphy (1996) provide clear evidence of high levels of spectator travel for youth, recreational (non-competitive) and non-elite sports in Canada.

Furthermore, the suggestion that the locals tend to view tourist-oriented products as diacritical marks of their cultural identity fits very well with the view that sport is a major determinant of collective and place identity (Nauright, 1996; Bale, 1989). In hosting visiting spectators and sports enthusiasts, the collective identity of the locals may be used by tourism marketers to influence destination image (Whitson & Macintosh, 1996). Finally, despite the challenges of commodification in terms of the changes that it inevitably brings to the meaning of these tourism products, it is unlikely to destroy the authenticity of sport given the uncertain outcomes associated with sporting competitions. While the commodification of sport has been accompanied by entertainment and spectacle, as long as the outcomes of these competitions remain uncertain, authentic sport experiences are likely to be the result.

In this sense, sport-based attractions avoid the challenges of staged authenticity that characterize other cultural tourist attractions such as indigenous dance performances. Exceptions to this type of authenticity include both overt and covert staging. Examples of what are generally considered to be overt staging include demonstrations or performances such as Thai Boxing matches performed for tourists in Pattaya, Thailand and the popular World Wrestling Entertainment (WWE) matches in North America which are scripted in advance. Examples of covert staging include resort golf courses intentionally designed to facilitate low scores and bulls that have been bred to favour dramatic kills by matadors. While these types of examples are the exception rather than the rule, the illegal use of steroids represents a form of covert staging that appears to be much more pervasive. It provides unfair advantages to dishonest athletes thereby undercutting the advantages of uncertain outcomes and the essence of fair competition in sport (E. Cohen, personal communication, 12 June 2007). More generally, however, sport attractions offer the promise of authenticity, which is increasingly rare in other types of cultural attractions.

AUTHENTICITY

The role of authenticity in tourism has been a subject of interest to academics for over four decades. Boorstin's (1964) criticism that tourism fosters pseudo-events highlighted the issue of the real versus the fake in tourism. This was followed by a body of work by MacCannell (e.g., 1973, 1976) in which he argued that the search for authenticity is one of the main motivations for travel. His contributions included the concept of staged authenticity based on Goffman's (1959) idea of the front versus back regions of social places. An example of this form of authenticity is an organized tour of a sports stadium or arena that provides access to the players' changing rooms (e.g., tours of Wembley Stadium, Wimbledon Lawn Tennis Club). While giving the impression that these tours provide a glimpse into the backstage of a destination, the management of these tours really means that the locker rooms are extensions of the front stage at least at the time of the tour.

Taylor (2001:10) captures the essence of this view of authenticity in his suggestion that tourists '... are driven by the need for experiences more profound than those associated with the "shallowness of their [modern] lives"'. They are searching for real things, real people and real places. Unfortunately, the paradox inherent in tourism is that genuine authenticity is virtually impossible to find as the very presence of a tourist destroys the purity of the toured object, whether it is a thing, a person or a place (Cohen, 2002). All tourist attractions are, therefore, contrived to some extent, although this disturbance would seem to be mitigated in the case of objects for which public display is a core component.

An interesting variation of the basic concept of authenticity is emergent authenticity. Cohen (1988:379) describes this as 'a cultural product ... which is at one point generally judged as contrived or inauthentic may, in the course of time, become generally recognized as authentic'. Disneyland is a good example, as it was initially viewed as being inauthentic but then 'emerged' as an authentic representation of American culture (Johnson, 1981).

Increasingly, the view that most tourists seek objective authenticity is being challenged. It is argued that rather than seeking authentic objects, tourists tend to be seeking enjoyable and perhaps meaningful experiences (Cohen, 1995; Urry, 1990). Often the search for objective authenticity seems to fall outside of the motivations for mass tourism (Wang, 1999). Popular tourist activities such as visiting amusement parks are more about entertainment and pleasure seeking. The extent that authenticity is important to tourists depends in a large part on their personal perspective (Boniface & Fowler, 1993). As a result of these developments, the focus in the literature is changing from the authenticity of the toured object to the authenticity of the experience of the tourist.

At the same time that it was being recognized that there were a broad range of travel motivations beyond the 'search for authenticity', post-modern scholars were also questioning the very concept of authenticity itself. Harvey's (1990) discussion of simulacra – as a copy of the original that never existed – highlights this perspective, as does Baudrillard's (1983) concept of hyperreality in which the real and the fake are indistinguishable. The arguments of these authors suggest that it is unrealistic to expect that truth or knowledge can be objectively assessed in terms of time and place. For example, Featherstone (1991:99) argues that the post-modern city is characterized by '"no-place space" in which the traditional senses of culture are decontextualized, simulated, reduplicated and continually renewed and recycled'. Notwithstanding these thought provoking intellectual perspectives, the ever growing popularity of various travel guides, such as the *Lonely Planet* series, suggest that there remains a genuine quest for real experiences.

Wang's perspective of authenticity

Wang's (1999, 2000) review of authenticity in a tourism context recognizes the criticisms of post-modern scholars while at the same time offering a constructive perspective of authenticity as tourists experience it. He provides a pragmatic framework, which is used to consider the merit of sport as a tourist attraction for the balance of this chapter. His framework has been adopted for two key reasons. The first is that Wang recognizes the criticisms of post-modern scholars. Rather than abandoning the concept of authenticity, Wang has developed a typology that includes 'existential authenticity'. This form of authenticity is concerned with the state of being of the tourist rather than the object of the tourist visit. From this perspective, tourists judge authenticity on the basis of their experience. The second reason for adopting Wang's framework is that it provides an intriguingly good fit for the examination of sport. It serves as a useful heuristic to gain insight into sport tourism experiences that, to this point, have not been highlighted in the literature.

Wang (1999) suggests that there are at least three different ways of thinking about authenticity in a tourism context. The first type of authenticity is labelled 'objective authenticity' in reference to the authenticity of the original. This is the type of authenticity on which Boorstin's (1964) critique of tourism was based. It is best illustrated by the example of a museum curator who verifies whether a particular artefact is genuine or not. Similarly, a painting may be objectively judged to be real or fake. While this type of authenticity has application in the realm of sport museums (e.g., whether a uniform on display at the *World of Rugby* museum in Cardiff was actually worn by a specific individual in a particular championship game), it is of limited value in the context of contemporary sport. If sporting codes are recognized as dynamic things, claims that the objective authenticity of a sport has been corrupted due to a break from tradition cannot be given credence. In practice, there are few situations in which the toured object (i.e., sport) can be objectively judged in terms of authenticity.

The second type of authenticity in Wang's (1999) framework is labelled constructive authenticity. This refers to

> ... *the authenticity projected onto toured objects by tourists or tourism producers in terms of their imagery, expectations, preferences, beliefs, powers, etc. There are various versions of authenticities regarding the same objects. Correspondingly, authentic experiences in tourism and the authenticity of toured objects are constitutive of one another. In this sense, the authenticity of tourism objects is in fact symbolic authenticity.* (Wang, 1999:352)

Constructive authenticity recognizes that tourists adopt different meanings of reality based on their particular contextual situation. 'Authenticity is thus a projection of tourists' own beliefs, expectations, preferences, stereotyped images, and consciousness onto toured objects, particularly onto toured Others' (Wang, 1999: 355). Rather than searching for authenticity in the 'originals', under this interpretation, tourists search for 'symbolic' authenticity. Toured objects are viewed as authentic because they are seen as signs or symbols of the real. This distinction accounts for the influence of tourism promotions and the preference of most tourists for a nostalgic or sanitized version of reality. Constructive authenticity, while still focused on the toured object, provides a broader interpretation of authenticity and allows its application across a wide range of tourism activities. From a sport attraction perspective, it helps to explain the influence of mass media and tourism marketing. Attendees at sporting events seek the symbolic authenticity that has been projected by the media prior to the event. The media tends to confirm these symbols during their subsequent coverage of the event. For example, visitors to the Olympic Games may achieve a sense of authenticity when they see the Olympic flame with all of its associated symbolism as represented in the media. Similarly, active sport tourists assess authenticity, at least in part, based on the expectations fostered through the promotional messages of equipment manufacturers and destination marketers. Sport tourists judge the authenticity of sports halls of fame based on imperfect memories from their youth in combination with nostalgic narratives found in the popular media and the interpretive statements of the museum curators. Alternatively, sport tourists may construct authenticity on the basis of their own sporting experience or their experience in other realms of life. For example, the fact that someone has been injured in a competition may, for some, serve to confirm the authenticity of the event (E. Cohen, personal communication, 12 June 2007).

Wang's (1999) last type of authenticity is presented in direct response to the dismissal of the concept by post-modernist writers. Rather than judging authenticity on the basis of the toured object (e.g., sport attractions), authenticity is assessed on the basis of the reality of the tourist experience. It is this engagement in experience that makes sport such a robust type of attraction. Wang calls this existential authenticity, which he describes as:

> ... a potential existential state of Being that is to be activated by tourist activities. Correspondingly, authentic experiences in tourism are to achieve this activated existential state of Being within the liminal process of tourism. Existential authenticity can have nothing to do with the authenticity of toured objects. (Wang, 1999:352)

While there is no unified post-modern critique of authenticity, Eco's (1986) discussion on 'hyperreality' is typical of this position. By deconstructing the boundaries between the copy and the original, Eco undermines the central arguments of Boorstin and MacCannell in relation to objective authenticity. Eco argues that Disneyland was born out of fantasy so that there is, in effect, no 'original' upon which to make an assessment of authenticity. Others have observed that in a post-modern world, tourists seem to be more interested in seeking authentic experiences than authentic objects or Others (Butler, 1996; Cohen 1995). Wang (1999) proposes existential authenticity as a concept that can provide insight into the motives of tourists in a post-modern world. He describes existential authenticity as a 'special state of Being in which one is true to oneself, and acts as a counter dose to the loss of "true self" in public roles and public sphere in modern Western society' (Wang, 1999:358). Tourists search for this 'true self' in travel settings where they are less constrained by the 'roles' that they must play in other dimensions of their post-modern lives. A similar argument can be made in terms of sport settings.

Tourism allows individuals to transcend their daily lives. The examples of tourism activities that Wang (1999) used to pursue this type of authenticity include mountaineering and adventure travel, the former being a particular type of sport and the latter manifest in many sports. One of the things that makes sport a likely activity for tourists to have authentic experiences is its high propensity for engagement. Examples of this engagement range from 'flow experiences' often associated with sport (Csikszentmihalyi, 1975) to the engagement that comes with being a member of a sport fandom (Jones, 2000). Sport attractions are also distinctive given their emphasis on performance, competition and uncertain outcomes. From an experience perspective, these characteristics mean that each sporting event and activity has the potential to be unique and engaging in its own right.

Wang (1999) describes two additional dimensions of existential authenticity that have relevance for sport tourism. The first is intra-personal and the second inter-personal in nature. Intra-personal authenticity is expressed in part through bodily feelings. The body is used both in the 'display' of personal identity in terms of health, vigour, movement and other physical characteristics and in all sensory perception. Lefebvre (1991) uses the example of individuals on a beach to illustrate that this space serves to alter routine experience through recreation and playfulness thereby fostering existential authenticity. Other sport spaces provide comparable opportunities for tourists to have authentic existential experiences in terms of bodily feelings. This is true both in terms of the relevance of display in sport and in terms of its kinaesthetic nature. Tourists who are normally confined to sedentary jobs, where their bodies are often ignored, have a much greater opportunity to experience intense feelings of bodily awareness when they are involved in active sport while on their vacations.

Another variation of intra-personal authenticity is 'self-making'. This form of authenticity concerns tourist experiences that build self-identity and are often associated with adventure travel (see Chapter 4, *Culture and identity* and Chapter 7, *Recreational sport and serious leisure*). In this case, adventure is used to compensate for the boredom often found in other realms in one's life. Once again, sport offers an attractive opportunity as a tourist activity due to the risks associated with unknown outcomes and the competition that is inherent within sport. While mountaineering is a classic example (Wang, 1999; Case study 7.1), a broad range of extreme sports could be included. It is also important to note that different individuals will perceive risk and adventure in different ways. Thus, the risk for a novice skier on the 'bunny slope' may serve the same function in terms of facilitating an authentic existential experience as a technically challenging climb for an experienced mountaineer.

Wang (1999) described inter-personal authenticity in terms of family ties and touristic communitas. In the case of the former, he argued that the classic family vacation provides the opportunity to strengthen the social bonds between parents and their children and between siblings. Vacations take the family away from the routine of work and school, thereby affording the opportunity to play with each other away from the home environment. Sport-based tourist attractions represent a unique opportunity to explore these bonds whether it is through the informal sharing of sport passions or the more formal generational transfer of sport skills.

In the case of touristic communitas, the advantages of sport are even more evident. Wang (1999) draws a parallel between touristic communitas and pilgrimage. He argues that just as pilgrims confront one another as social equals based on their common humanity, there are other types of tourism activities that promote a similar type of experience. He uses Lett's (1983) ethnographic study of charter yacht tourism in the Caribbean to illustrate his claim. In this sport example, it is argued that the social hierarchies found in the regular day-to-day lives of these individuals do not dictate the inter-relationships between members of this subculture. There are numerous other examples of these types of sport subcultures that are closely tied to sport attractions, particularly those associated with 'participation and pleasure' sports (Coakley, 2004), as opposed to 'power and performance' sports. The subcultures associated with the sports of snowboarding (Heino, 2000) and windsurfing (Wheaton, 2000) serve to illustrate this view. It should be recognized, however, that while these sport subcultures may not have the same hierarchical social structures as found in other dimensions of their members' lives, there is often a unique hierarchy that exists within the subculture itself (Donnelly & Young, 1988). The key point, however, is that these sport subculture hierarchies are in fact distinct, thereby allowing an individual who may be frustrated in terms of his/her status at work to develop a sense of identity through membership in a sport subculture community.

CONCLUSION

The objective of this chapter was to demonstrate that sport-based tourist attractions have unique qualities that facilitate authentic tourism experiences. Positioning sport as a tourist attraction is a form of commodification, but the natural role of display in sport and the ability of sport attractions to align collective identity and destination image help to protect sport's cultural 'soul'. Similarly, an assessment of sport in terms of Wang's (1999) three types of authenticity suggests that sport attractions have distinct advantages in terms of constructive or symbolic authenticity as well as existential or experience-based authenticity. Uncertainty of outcomes, the role of athletic display, the kinaesthetic nature of sport activities and the tendency for strong engagements in sport represent some of the key characteristics of sport that protect cultural authenticity. To the extent that sport attractions can facilitate authentic cultural experiences, the likelihood that tourism and, more importantly, local culture can be sustained in a destination is greatly enhanced.

Temporary Sport Migrants

Tourism is just one type of mobility. It occurs for a relatively short duration and is characterized by a return to the point of departure, that is, one's regular place of residence (Chapter 3, *Sport and contemporary mobility*). Tourism researchers have tended to focus on short-term visitors. Tourists who are in a destination for extended periods of time have received much less attention. This approach has constrained insight into the broader spectrum of tourism activity. A case in point is the lack of understanding of temporary sport tourism migrants.

In adopting a mobility perspective, the barriers associated with traditional tourism research approaches are reduced. The challenge becomes one of distinguishing between permanent migration and temporary migration. The merit of doing this in a sport tourism context is particularly strong given the high profile, but often temporary, migrations of professional athletes involved in the production of sport. Just as fascinating is the growing trend of youth travelling for extended periods feeding their appetite for sport and adventure. Bell and Ward (2000:94) have argued that many long-distance moves are motivated by social, physical or service amenity consumption, rather than being driven by production. This seems particularly true in the context of sport-based travel, although a variety of hybrids that combine production- and consumption-oriented migration have emerged. Table 9.1 contrasts key characteristics of permanent and temporary sport migrations.

Permanent migration is characterized by a conscious change of primary residence with no intention to return permanently to one's original home. The move is seen as being permanent, usually involving a single transition from locations A to B with minor variations in travel flows across seasons. In contrast, temporary migrations are characterized by less emphasis on primary residence, an intension to return home, varying durations of stay, repetitive

Table 9.1	Travelling Sport Workers Versus Working Sport Tourists	
	Type of Mobility	
	Permanent Migration	**Temporary Migration**
Definition	**Permanent Change of Usual Residence**	**Non-Permanent Move of Varying Duration**
Key concepts		
• *Primary residence*	Integral concept	Less centrality
• *Return*	No intention to return	May involve a return 'home'
Key dimensions		
• *Duration*	Lasting relocation	Varying duration of stay
• *Frequency/sequence*	Single transition from A to B	May be a repetitive and/or sequential event; A to B to C to A
• *Seasonality*	Minor seasonal variation	Coincides with sport seasons

Source: Adapted from Bell & Ward, 2000

and/or sequential moves and surges and ebbs of mobility that coincide with sport seasons. While these temporary migrations may sometimes turn into permanent moves, research has suggested that whether it is northern 'snow birds' wintering in the southern United States (McHugh, 1990) or temporary labour migrants working at ski resorts in Sweden (Lundmark, 2008), they are unlikely to become permanent migrants to the destination. Such findings imply that temporary migrants are a distinct group that merits further attention.

In this chapter, we examine traditional perspectives of sport tourism related to temporary migrations and the new realities presented by the globalization of sport. Temporary sport migrations of production and consumption are considered followed by a discussion of sport migrants of the middle ground – a growing group of migrants that represents a hybrid of consumption and production motivations.

CHANGING PERSPECTIVES OF THE BOUNDARY BETWEEN TOURIST AND MIGRANT

Cohen's typology of tourists

Cohen's (1974) seminal paper *'Who is a tourist? A conceptual clarification'* provided a framework of tourism types that still shapes our understanding of tourists. It has, in effect, set many of the parameters for the populations that have been studied by tourism researchers over the past 35 years. In this conceptualization, Cohen (1974:531–532) isolated six dimensions of a tourist. First, the tourist was seen as a temporary traveller with a permanent residence to which he/she would return. Second, tourists are voluntary travellers who exercise choice in terms of where and when they travel. Third, tourists were identified by being on a round trip. Not only did they have a permanent residence at their point of origin but they also return to it at the conclusion of their trip. Fourth, a tourist is on a relatively long journey and not a short excursion or day trip. Fifth, a tourist trip is non-recurrent. Under this parameter, members of a family who travel to their second home on a regular basis are not tourists. Sixth, tourist trips are non-instrumental. The trip is not a means to another goal such as business development. In his detailed explanation of these dimensions, Cohen recognized the fuzziness of some of these categories but used them to clarify the distinction between tourists and the many other types of travellers that exist. This conceptual framework has served as a reference point for tourism scholars who have followed although it has been modified along the way.

In an early criticism of Cohen's framework, Jaakson (1986) argued against the dismissal of second home owners as tourists on the grounds that they take recurring trips to the same place. Jaakson's argument was that these second home owners constituted an important component of domestic tourism. To ignore second home owners would limit our understanding of travel, infrastructure and behaviour. In addition to this type of questioning of the premises that underlie Cohen's typology, the environment in which tourism operates has changed dramatically over the past 35 years. At the heart of these changes are globalization processes that have altered the global context in which this framework was developed. As argued in Chapter 3 (*Sport and contemporary mobility*), the concept of mobility offers a new and more inclusive perspective of tourism and travel.

The problem with dichotomies

One of the more powerful illustrations that has been used to argue the close relationship between sport and tourism are the labels found on the score boards in many arenas and stadiums throughout the world – home and visitors (Hinch & Higham, 2004). These labels parallel the long accepted tourism dichotomies of host and guest (Smith, 1978, 1989) and of home and away. It is becoming increasingly clear, however, that global processes have blurred the lines between what were once thought of as exclusive domains. For example, how do you determine permanent versus temporary migration in a typical ski resort community? While a first time visitor on a one-week vacation package may be easy to classify as a guest and a long time resident homeowner may be seen as a host, this excludes the multitude of individuals who fit somewhere in between. What is the status of second home owners who spend four months a year in the community or time-share condo owners who spend two weeks a year in the community? Do these home owners 'trump' long-term renters or hospitality workers from overseas who are on temporary work visas? As Perdue (2004) pointed out in his analysis of Colorado ski resort communities, there is a wide variety of stakeholders that go beyond the simple dichotomy of hosts and guests. Each stakeholder group has their own needs and interests which may or may not coincide with those of the other groups.

Another dichotomy that has been complicated by globalization is the opposition that is inferred between the destination and the origin. Changing perspectives in this relationship are due, in part, to the blurring of the boundary between hosts and guests along with their perspectives of home. Bianchi (2000:109) argues that tourism destinations have

> … become sites of encounter situated at the interface of travelling-dwelling, out of which there emerges a number of hybrid practices and cultural forms with varying degrees of rootedness.

Increased mobility has meant that it has become much more difficult to identify the 'other' in a tourism destination while at the same time, the emergence of tourism and sport diasporas has complicated the concept of home. Being 'local' in a globalized world is also often seen as an indication of social deprivation and degradation (Bianchi, 2000). The 'local' is, therefore, in a constant struggle to distinguish itself from competing destinations but at the same time, to demonstrate that it is part of the global network. In seeking this balance, the local has built a multitude of global networks including those related to sport and tourism. The result has been an erosion of many of the traditional boundaries that distinguished one community from another.

The traditionally held dichotomy between work and leisure/tourism has also been challenged by the process of globalization. Until recently, tourism has been studied in opposition to work (e.g., Graburn, 1989). It is generally seen as falling under the realm of leisure or time free from work and other obligations. While it is recognized that business activities have a very significant travel dimension, the concept of tourism is often associated more generally with leisure and separated from work. This dichotomy is increasingly being challenged by authors such as Uriely (2001:6) who has presented a list of variations between travelling workers and working travellers. These variations include

1. Travelling professional workers, who are mainly oriented towards work-related purposes and engage in tourist-oriented activities only as a by-product of their excursion;

2. Migrant tourism workers, who travel in order 'to make a living' and 'have fun' at the same time;

3. Non-institutionalized working tourists, who engage in work while travelling in order to finance a prolonged trip; and

4. Working-holiday tourists, who perceive their work engagement as a recreational activity that is part of their tourist experience.

Table 9.2 illustrates these variations as they relate to sport tourism.

Working sport tourists tend to be motivated by their sport and touristic interests. Work is seen as a recreational activity that is part of the tourist experience. An example of an individual in this category would be a minor league professional rugby player from Australia who plays a season in the United Kingdom not to advance his rugby career so much as to enjoy the cultural experience of living in the United Kingdom. In contrast, an example of an individual fitting into the non-institutional working tourists would be a South African working as a fruit picker to help finance her surfing tour of Australia. Migrant sport tourism workers would include seasonal hospitality workers in mountain resorts, many of whom pursue their outdoor sport passions during their free time in these resort areas. Finally, an example of a travelling professional sport worker is a professional tennis player who travels the globe to compete at major competitions (see Chapter 5, *Globalization and the mobility of elite athletes*).

The dichotomy between work and leisure/tourism is most directly challenged in the working-holiday sport tourist category. Bianchi's (2000:107) argument that tourists often 'engage in periods of work within tourism destinations as an integral part of the touristic experience' suggests that more attention needs to be given to this group. As traditional dichotomies are eroded through globalization processes, sport tourism destinations have become '… a series of fluid social formations through which geographically mobile capital, tourists, migrants and workers move and articulate with local and regional social formations' (Bianchi, 2000:118). The social structure of these destinations is much more complex than the simple home–away, host–guest, and work–leisure dichotomies would suggest.

TEMPORARY MIGRATIONS OF CONSUMPTION AND PRODUCTION

Migration has typically been studied from the perspective of labour movements associated with production. Permanent migrations tend to be

Table 9.2 Types of 'Travelling Sport Workers' and 'Working Sport Tourists'

	Types of Sport Travellers				
	Working Sport Tourists		**Travelling Sport Workers**		
Dimensions of Comparison	**Working-Holiday Sport Tourists**	**Non-Institutionalized Working Sport Tourists**	**Migrant Sport Tourism Workers**	**Travelling Sport Workers**	**Travelling Professional Sport Workers**
Work and touristic motivations	Work is grasped as a recreational activity that is part of the tourist experience	Work in order to finance a prolonged trip	Travel in order to 'make a living' and 'have fun' at the same time		Travel in order to pursue a sport career
					Engage in tourist-related activities as a by-product of the excursion
Work characteristics	Unskilled but usually recreational manual labour	Unskilled and usually unpleasant manual labour	Skilled or semi-skilled work in the tourism economy		Professional, official role, or business-related work
	Extraordinary work	Occasional work	Repetitive seasonal employment		Repetitive, career-related work
	Unpaid work	Low-paid and non-prestigious work	Unsecured and low-paid employment		Prestigious and well-paid work
Demographic profile	Middle-class young adults	Middle-class young adults	Lower-middle class or working-class single and unattached adults Periodically unemployed in their home societies		Middle-, or upper-middle-class adults

Source: Adapted from Uriely 2001

motivated by the search for a better livelihood. The study of temporary migrations from a production perspective typically focuses on seasonal workers such as fruit pickers who supplement a local labour pool that is either too small or not interested in meeting the labour requirements of the industry. However, Bell and Ward (2000:94) point out that 'an increasing proportion of longer distance moves are motivated by the search for social, physical or service amenity and hence consumption – rather than production led'. This applies aptly in the context of sport and tourism.

Temporary migrations for consumption of sport

There are two long-standing temporary migrations featured in the tourism literature that have considerable relevance to sport. The first concerns temporary migration to second homes while the second concerns seasonal migrations by retirees as exemplified by 'snowbird' migrations in North America. There is, of course, substantial overlap between these categories.

Despite Cohen's (1974) reluctance to treat second home owners as tourists, their sheer volume and the fact that they must leave their primary home to visit their second home suggests that this migration is worthy of study (see Chapter 10, *Transnationalism, migration and diaspora*). While there are a growing number of second homes located in urban areas, the vast majority are located in peripheral areas that balance the desire for ease of access with proximity to natural amenities (Müller, 2007). Second homes are places of recreation which often takes the form of outdoor-related sport pursuits that are constrained at the primary residence. In arguing for the importance of second homes in New Zealand, Kearns and Collins (2006:230) suggest that they offer

> … *opportunities to escape the rigours of urban life, and experience elements of the natural environment: sun, wind, water and the rhythms of the tide … [and that they are]… centred around escaping the city in order to participate in outdoor recreation in uncrowded landscapes, especially in summer.*

A closely related consumptive form of temporary migration is that of snowbird or seasonal retiree communities. This group consists of individuals who have significant financial resources but are not constrained by work obligations due to their retirement status. The snowbird moniker is derived from the North American situation where the migration of retirees mimics the natural north/south winter migration of various bird species. These temporary migrants take up residence in second home condominium developments or trailer parks with like-minded individuals. In addition to the allure of warmer climes the '… three most distinguishing elements of this snowbird lifestyle are the very high levels of importance given to: (1) the pursuit of recreation activities, (2) social interaction among snowbirds, and (3) geographic mobility' (Mings, 1997:170). As in the case of the sporting activities engaged in by second home users in general, those pursued in seasonal retiree communities are recreational in nature, including walking, cycling, swimming, fishing, golfing and bowling (Mings, 1997; Martin, Hoppe, Larson & Leon, 1987).

Temporary sport production migrations

Production-driven sport migrations are one of the defining characteristics of the globalization of sport. This is particularly true in the realm of professional sport where athletic careers are often defined by a series of temporary migrations (see Chapter 5, *Globalization and the mobility of elite athletes*). It is also evident in the context of professional hospitality workers who help to produce sport tourism experiences in the resort industry.

As professional sport has grown, the demand for elite athletes has outstripped local supply. Professional sport enterprises have progressively expanded their search for athletic talent from local to regional and from national to global. This has been done in conjunction with the emergence of global sport media and a dynamic environment of increased personal communication, transportation and finance. Evidence of intercontinental migrations of professional athletes can be found in all major professional sports including football, basketball, baseball and hockey. In sports such as cricket and rugby, there is a seasonal exchange of athletes between the northern and southern hemispheres while other sports such as golf, tennis, skiing and motor sports have commodified their activities in the form of professional tours that make their way around the developed world throughout much of the calendar year (Maguire & Bale, 1994). The days of exceptional athletes developing their skill sets and then practicing their sporting profession near their birthplace have long since passed.

Maguire (1999:105) presents a typology of sport labour migration consisting of pioneers, settlers, nomads, returnees and mercenaries. Pioneers often emigrate for non-sport reasons such as religion and seek 'to convert the natives to their body habitus and sport culture'. Settlers are sport migrants who settle permanently into their new homes. Nomadic cosmopolitans move from destination to destination plying their sporting trade with a 'desire to explore the experience of difference and diversity' (Maguire, 1999:105) associated with these places. Returnees are those who are constantly attracted back to their 'home soil' as exemplified by athletes involved in sport circuits associated with golf, tennis, skiing and motor sports. However, the most prominent category in this typology is the mercenary group. This is the high-profile group of athletes who 'are motivated more by short-term gains and are employed as "hired guns"' (Maguire, 1999:105).

These sport tourism migrants are part of the complex political economy that has accompanied globalization. Professional sport migrations are impacted by and in turn impact the political, cultural, economic and geographic dynamics of today's global realities. For example, these temporary sport migrations are closely tied to free trade agreements and associated national and international labour laws. The relatively restrictive European football transfer system was successfully challenged by Jean-Marc Bosman in the European Court, thereby securing the much freer movement of players within the European Union (EU) (Maguire & Stead, 1998). Similar advances in free agency rights have been established in other leagues such as the National Hockey League in North America. Perhaps due to their relatively short sporting careers, athletes have tended to respond to a more flexible environment by selling their talents to the highest bidder. Likewise, professional sport franchises continue to trade and sell the services of these athletes in pursuit of the 'best interests of the team'.

As a result, professional athletes have become very mobile. This mobility has brought a variety of challenges with it, including the capacity of athletes to adjust to different cultural arenas and the erosion of their sense of attachment to the places in which they play. From the perspective of their hosts, the increasing presence of international players has challenged traditional constructions of national and team identity. It has also caused issues in terms of the divorce between sport development systems in the country of athletic origin and the places of production in terms of the professional leagues that these athletes now compete in. Exporting regions lose the economic benefits of the commodification of their native athletes while importing regions face restricted opportunities for home-grown talent.

Hospitality workers at resorts are another type of migrant group that is involved in the production of sport experiences. In their study of a sport-related Hawaiian resort, Adler and Adler (1999a) identified two types of hospitality workers that have particular relevance in terms of the production of sport experiences: new migrants and managers. The new migrants group occupied the lowest rung of the occupational hierarchy at the resorts. They had arrived from countries characterized by low standards of living and were focused on improving the prospects of their families. While they did not necessarily have a direct interest in sport, their willingness to take on menial positions was critical to the functioning of these resorts. The various managers of these resorts were also characterized as temporary migrants. Although they enjoyed a much more elevated status at the resort, they seldom worked in one location for more than a few years if they harboured any ambitions of moving up their corporate and/or career ladders. Their administrative skills are critical to the delivery of sport and hospitality services at the resort.

From an industry perspective, each of these groups has a variety of advantages and disadvantages. For example, in a report on the merits of foreign workers from Argentina and Brazil at a US ski resort, the benefits for the resort were described in terms of the workers' culinary skills, good will, stimulation of other workers and overall impressive work ethic (Bearns, 2003). The disadvantages of this workforce were outlined in terms of their lack of preparation for the winter climate, language barriers and the lack of support available to these temporary immigrants outside of the work place. In terms of the migrant managers, their international origins and experiences helped them to understand and connect with their international sport tourism clientele (Bianchi, 2000) while the disadvantage was that a dependence on such migrants deprived the locals of the likelihood of working their way into these positions of management. Perdue (2004) has also pointed out that in the case of the ski resorts in Colorado, the interests of these types of migrant employee groups do not necessarily coincide with the interests of other resident groups or guests in the community. One explanation for this disjuncture is that despite the critical contribution that each of these groups makes to the destination, they have different levels of commitment, attachment to place and perhaps more tellingly, power.

MIGRANTS OF THE MIDDLE GROUND – HYBRIDS OF CONSUMPTION AND PRODUCTION

The Endless Summer, a popular film released in 1964, followed a small group of surfers as they traversed the globe on a quest for the perfect wave (Ormrod, 2005). Their search epitomized early temporary migrations for sport consumption. In reality, however, very few people have the financial resources to pursue such adventures. While the search for the 'perfect wave' may remain a powerful motivation for sport migration, it is almost always accompanied by significant costs that mean that travellers need to seek work.

It is this hybrid of sport migrations characterized by leisure and work or by consumption and production which we now address.

Seekers of sport and adventure

Adler and Adler's (1999a) sociological study of the large Lukane Sands resort property in the Hawaiian Islands provides considerable insight into this type of temporary migration. In their analysis of the social worlds of the employees at the property, they labelled one of the major groups 'seekers', whose 'interests lay in maximizing their immediate life satisfaction' (Adler & Adler, 1999a:35). Seekers are escaping from the daily routine. Adler and Adler argue that seekers '... pursued alternative lifestyles and careers, shaped by their intense focus on recreation [sport]. They explored all corners of the world looking for paradise' (Adler & Adler, 1999a:35). Seekers were predominantly male and held a variety of sport and recreation as well as unskilled positions at the resort. Many of them travelled a circuit that took them to some of the worlds' most attractive sporting sites, which not surprisingly, coincided with the location of other tourism resorts where they could find similar types of employment.

Seekers are motivated by their leisure passions, with those related to sport taking centre stage. Adler and Adler (1999a:40) suggest that this group

> ... travelled for adventure, to experience danger, to endure harsh conditions, and to overcome heroic obstacles. They were also driven by the sheer physicality of the experience, the need to challenge and use their bodies. Many spoke about 'testing,' 'strengthening,' or 'tuning' their physical selves, focusing their identities in their bodies.

Their resort employment was primarily a way of facilitating their sport and travel interests. Despite this emphasis on the consumption of sporting experiences rather than work career-oriented production, their work was important to them. Bianchi (2000:124) suggests:

> [a]lthough the specific content or nature of work is not of paramount importance for migrant tourist-workers, it is not purely a means of securing their material subsistence, but undertaken as part of a broader recreational experience in which they can indulge in certain social, artistic and sensual pleasure amongst similar groups of like-minded individuals.

Seekers not only enjoy the benefit of income that allows them to pursue their sporting lifestyle, they also enjoy benefits in the form of seasonal employment, non-standard work hours, access to like-minded sporting communities and the respect and often the envy of vacationing sports enthusiasts (Boon, 2006). Their employers enjoy a labour pool that 1) extends beyond the often limited local supply; 2) features workers who often see the seasonal nature of the job as a positive rather than a negative feature; 3) consists of workers who enjoy flexible and/or non-standard hours that enable them to pursue their own leisure interests during the regular work day and 4) provides the intangible benefit of workers who relate well to guests in terms of their sport interests, international perspective and knowledge of local sport sites. Boon's (2006) analysis of the work environment of temporary sport migrants in Queenstown, New Zealand, articulates these benefits in the context of resources available to both the workers and their employees (Figure 9.1).

Adler and Adler (1999b:384) identify six subgroups of seekers based on their level of commitment to this lifestyle. Timeouters were those individuals taking a short break from the pursuit of more traditional career and life goals. Typically, this break came after completing a post-secondary degree or

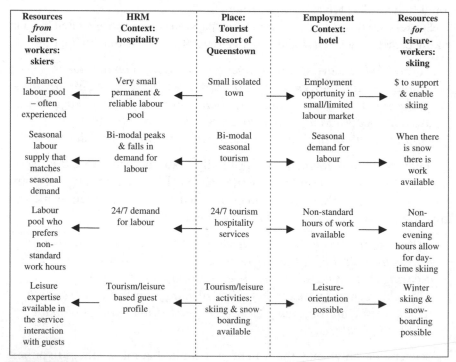

Resources *from* leisure-workers: skiers	HRM Context: hospitality	Place: Tourist Resort of Queenstown	Employment Context: hotel	Resources *for* leisure-workers: skiing
Enhanced labour pool – often experienced	Very small permanent & reliable labour pool	Small isolated town	Employment opportunity in small/limited labour market	$ to support & enable skiing
Seasonal labour supply that matches seasonal demand	Bi-modal peaks & falls in demand for labour	Bi-modal seasonal tourism	Seasonal demand for labour	When there is snow there is work available
Labour pool who prefers non-standard work hours	24/7 demand for labour	24/7 tourism hospitality services	Non-standard hours of work available	Non-standard evening hours allow for day-time skiing
Leisure expertise available in the service interaction with guests	Tourism/leisure based guest profile	Tourism/leisure activities: skiing & snow boarding available	Leisure-orientation possible	Winter skiing & snow-boarding possible

FIGURE 9.1 *Resources from and for skiing leisure workers in Queenstown (Source: Boon, 2006).*

diploma. A second type of seeker was a transient group. While their stay at any one resort property was limited, they tended to move on to another property in order to accumulate different sporting experiences. Mid-length seekers committed to a resort area for anywhere from one to ten years. At some point during their migration, they become dissatisfied with their life-style and return 'home' to take up more traditional life roles. Come-and-goers stay for five to ten years and while they demonstrate considerable commitment to their new sporting home, they are drawn back to their original home by major life changes or family crises back home. Permanent seekers 'make transience a way of life, but they established a regular home base, to which they returned annually' (Adler & Adler, 1999a:385). Finally, career seekers made a conscious decision to maintain an alternative lifestyle based on their leisure passions. Many of them obtained jobs that capitalized on their sporting passions whether it was working as sport instructors at the resort property or becoming entrepreneurs with their own sport-based businesses.

The challenges of being a seeker

Seekers pursue experiential rather than material goals. In his description of migrant tourist workers, Bianchi (2000:127) sees this lifestyle as 'a form of resistance to the intensification of the commodification of time in post-industrial capitalism, in which not only our working lives but also our leisure has become increasingly dictated by the market'. Despite the important role that they play in the tourism industry, 'they also resist attempts to regulate their movements and define the appropriateness of their behaviour, in the same way that earlier tramps challenged the localizing strategies of trade unions and the state' (Bianchi, 2000:127). A key characteristic of forsaking, at least temporarily, the normal trappings of traditional careers and lifestyle is the non-traditional approach to time. In contrast to this view of seekers as resisters of the commodification of time, Adler and Adler (2001) suggest that the employees in sport-based resorts lose control of their time. They argue that in creating at 24/7 year round leisure experience for resort guests, the work schedule of employees is desynchronized from their schedule at home. They describe this phenomenon as the tendency toward 'incessant' time in which commercial activity expands around the clock. In facilitating the vacation experience of resort guests the daily, weekly and seasonal schedules of resort workers are disrupted. This apparent contradiction between resisting the commodification of time and being an instrument for this commodification is avoided at the personal level for 'seekers' to the extent that the schedules they keep truly accommodate their sport passions.

Another challenge faced by temporary sport migrants exists in the realms of community and citizenship. Bianchi (2000:114) suggests that temporary migrant communities '… reflect social relationships which are based upon a series of episodic relations amongst individuals with shared interests and lifestyles, rather than attachment to a specific place associated with a stable and enduring identity'. Almost by definition, they are not able to develop roots in a destination. They abandon traditional family roles in favour of fluidity and flexibility. Friendships are transitory, tending to be formed quickly, be shallower and of shorter duration than typical friendships. Friendship networks 'formed around their serious leisure interests such as mountain biking, scuba diving, and windsurfing' (Adler & Adler, 1999b:49), and they connected to worldwide networks of like-minded individuals.

Seekers based their identity on their sporting pursuits.

They pursued this route to deepen their intrinsic selves through a heightening of experience, skill development, and self-actualization. In so doing they invested in their social and physical selves, enriching their cultural capital in the most portable space possible: their embodied, corporeal beings. (Adler & Adler, 1999b:51)

Rather than defining themselves in terms of their material possessions or financial wealth, seekers identified themselves in terms of what they had done and what they could do relative to their sport and travel passions. Bianchi (2000) sees migrant tourist employees as post-industrial drifters, with the difference being that they are drifters by choice. Their identity is less tied to their work than to their sporting interests. While these types of views are consistent with post-modern perspectives, vestiges of modernity remain. For example, Clarke's (2005) study of British working holiday-makers in Australia reported the phenomenon of 'dwelling-in-travelling' in which transients established resident-like ties to the local community even though their stay was temporary in nature. Practices such as these demonstrate that seekers reflect notions of post-modernity in their fragmented lifestyle and mass-media-driven culture. But despite these vestiges of post-modernity, Adler and Adler (1999b:53–54) suggest that seekers have not lost their sense of self. In fact, they suggest that 'the selves of transient resort workers in the post-modern era have adapted and thrived, emerging with renewed self-orientation and stronger driving center' and that '… the core self has adapted to contemporary conditions and thrived'. Case study 9.1 provides insight into the complex relationship between leisure, work and travel that is reflected in the lifestyles of these individuals.

Case Study 9.1

Transient workers in Queenstown and Whistler

Tara Duncan (University of Otago, New Zealand)

Terms such as migrant workers (Bianchi, 2000), working tourists (Uriely and Reichel, 2000; Uriely, 2001) and even the ubiquitous backpacker can all be used to try and 'pigeonhole' the transient workers who spend an extended amount of time in specific destinations in order to engage in sporting activities or a sporting lifestyle. In this case study, the focus will centre on groups of young people found in two main destinations, Queenstown in New Zealand (Boon, 2006) and Whistler in western Canada (Duncan, 2007).

It is worth noting that in much academic literature, work is seen as opposite to leisure (Adler & Adler, 1999a; Guerrier & Adib, 2003; Urry, 2002). As Boon (2006:596) suggests, leisure is more than just a personal or social experience; it is also a major industry grouping responsible for significant levels of economic activity – both through spending and employment (see Kraus, 1994). In the case of these two destinations, tourism is one such leisure industry and it is through these complex aspects of leisure, work and travel that these destinations are attractive to those looking to spend a protracted amount of time engaging in work so that they may also engage in particular types of lifestyles.

This distinction between work and leisure becomes ever more blurred (see Bianchi, 2000) when considering groups of (often Western) young people whose mobility, resources and motivations lead them to travel the world at various points in their lives. Research such as Adler and Adler's (1999a) in Hawaii illustrates how some groups of workers, one of which they label Seekers, were seen to pursue 'a leisure ethos that sublimated work to its service. Their lives, goals, and identities were shaped by their leisure, their clear central life interest, giving them a leisure-driven work culture' (Adler & Adler, 1999a:394). Wyn and Willis (2001) in their research on young Australians in Whistler also suggest that young people now have a more flexible attitude to their careers and so define themselves in terms of mixed patterns of job and life commitments, where work and leisure complement each other profitably and where leisure is not the part of life on which they mean to miss out.

If this is defined in terms of their working lives, then living and working in destinations such as Queenstown and Whistler can suggest that these young people look to reconcile the work they do with an identity (and so lifestyle) that they can accept, either by interpreting their paid work positively or by discounting the importance of paid work as the basis of lifestyle and identity (see Leidner, 1991:154).

As Byron, an HR manager, said of the young people who come to work in Whistler,

> *youth today ... are looking for a total life experience so when they come to a ski resort they're not really taking a year off to learn how to ski, they want something that will still fill their resume or prove positive in terms of life experience*

In Queenstown, an HR manager at one of the hotels said,

> *I know that all these people are going to come through my [training] courses and they will probably only be with us three months, six months, maximum a year ... but it's just something that you have to do. You have to continually train your staff so that they can meet your expectations and also develop themselves as well. ... (Boon, 2003:133)*

From the employers' perspective, it is the recognition that for many of the young people coming to work in these destinations, lifestyle is an important aspect but, as Drake International (n.d.:11) point out, key features such as work/life balance and professional growth and development are equally important to this group of young people (who often fit into the 'Generation Y' category). This comes through in Whistler where respondents talk about how the lifestyle they have experienced in the destination will affect their lives after they have left.

I've more come here for the lifestyle, the ski village lifestyle... not having too many responsibilities, looking after myself. Yeah, I think this is another thing I am going to take away from travelling in general, like my views on this have completely changed, it's like about a work life balance ... (Grace, aged 23).

Yet, in both Whistler and Queenstown, there are those who come specifically for the sporting opportunities. Ben explains that the reason he came to Queenstown was

Skiing basically. I came back from overseas ... spent a lot of time skiing in France then came home and thought what am I doing home... So I came down seven years ago for skiing and work and to have a look around ... It's good it's good. The lifestyle. If you are in to mountain biking and skiing and all that sort of thing it's great (Boon, 2006:599).

In Whistler, comments such as 'I came for the mountain lifestyle' or 'I love getting to do something I love [snow-boarding]' were common. Others, such as Veronica, saw the skiing as a reason to come, 'I went to Whistler specifically because ... I wanted to do a ski season'. For some then, the sporting element is their motivation; by gaining employment in a ski resort, these young people can combine their passion (skiing or snowboarding in these instances) with the paid work that supports this passion (see Richards 1996, Boon 2006).

For many of the young people involved, it is the combination of money, time and availability of particular activities that draws them to these destinations. Here again, the complex nature of what 'leisure' is comes to the fore. In this respect, the destination becomes a crucial aspect for the temporary worker. Destinations such as Queenstown and Whistler attract millions of tourists every year. As such, they have an infrastructure that can provide young people looking to live a sporting lifestyle with the flexibility to achieve this very lifestyle. The tourism and hospitality industries offer the flexibility of work and time whilst offering the incentives of money. The destinations, by having these industries also offer the personal and social aspects of leisure through the ability to ski/snowboard when not working and the ability to socialize with work colleagues, other transient workers and tourists. Thus, leisure becomes the 'activities [that] are inscribed and structured habits of thought and behaviour which contribute to our ways of seeing ourselves and others, to a making sense of our social relationships, and to the piecing together of some notion of what we call 'society' (Hill, 2002:2).

In conclusion, and as Boon (2006:604) suggests, 'it is now possible to acknowledge the idiosyncrasy and heterogeneity of contemporary working lives'. The centrality of leisure in many young people's life choices (see Wyn & Willis, 2001) suggests that the relationship between leisure, work and travel is more complex than previously assumed. As the boundaries between work and leisure continue to become blurred (see Bianchi, 2000; Urry, 2002) and as more and more young people engage in these sporting lifestyles on a longer-term basis, the question becomes, when does this leisure-work lifestyle become a career (see Boon, 2006)? Many of the transient workers in these destinations can be seen to be in the middle of transnationalism (see Conradson & Latham, 2005; Clarke, 2005) and as such, have distinct experiences where their time travelling, working and living is often dominated by their leisure (and so often, sporting) interests. In researching these areas, the focus should evolve from understanding these young people only in terms of their mobility to something that considers how their sense of everyday life, in the contexts of living, working and playing, is constituted by and in these destinations whilst also impacting upon those communities where they perform these 'everyday' lives.

Selected references

Duncan, T. (2007). *Working Tourists: Identity Formation in a Leisure Space*. London: University College London.

Boon, B. (2006). When leisure and work are allies: The case of skiers and tourist resort hotels. *Career Development International* 11(7): 594–608.

Hill, J. (2002). *Sport, Leisure and Culture in Twentieth-Century Britain*. Basingstoke: Palgrave.

CONCLUSION

Heightened contemporary mobility has challenged the way we understand tourism. One of the ways in which it has challenged our understanding is by blurring the temporal boundaries that have traditionally been used to define tourists. More specifically, new perspectives on mobility highlight the need to develop an understanding of temporary sport migrations and people who undertake these migrations.

Leisure consumption is a major driver of many temporary sport tourism migrations. Individuals who are relatively free of temporal constraints (e.g., retirees) and financial constraints are often privileged to own or rent second homes in desirable regions of the world. Typically, these second homes provide their owners with access to recreational and sport amenities that they do not have at their primary residence. As such, the temporary migrations that these individuals undertake are characterized by their involvement in a broad range of sporting activities.

At the other extreme, a significant proportion of temporary migration is driven by production as people pursue their livelihoods related to sport. Professional athletes represent one of the most mobile and certainly high-profile groups in this category. They respond to very dynamic markets for their services, which increasingly see them migrating to international destinations during one or more sporting seasons. While having a much lower profile, there is also significant production-related temporary migration in the form of managers and hospitality workers who form the staff complement of sport-based resorts.

Like many other proposed dichotomies, the suggestion that temporary sport migrations are characterized by a dichotomy of those related to consumption and those related to production is false. The reality is that there are many sport tourists who may be driven by their search for the perfect 'wave' who combine their sporting passions with paid employment during their temporary residence. A particularly interesting characteristic of this group is their pursuit of the 'physicality of the experience' and their focus on their physical identity (Adler & Adler, 1999b:35). In many ways these seekers are products of the globalization processes as they seek to make sense of a very dynamic world. While their decision to abandon traditional roles at home in favour of fluidity and flexibility is consistent with post-modern perspectives of identity, the fact that such migrations are temporary suggests that these individuals are still anchored in the modern with a strong sense of self.

CHAPTER 10

Transnationalism, Migration and Diaspora

The discussions presented in this chapter are anchored in the globalization of sport and tourism and the consequences for migration and long-term or repeat travel. Coles, Duval and Hall (2004:463–464) have criticized the lack of discipline-based efforts to 'understand the range of mobilities prevalent in more or less globalised environments'. They argue that very little scholarly effort has been directed towards connecting micro- and global levels of human movement. As a consequence, there exist 'fairly substantial gaps in our knowledge of tourism as a representation of contemporary social systems' (Coles et al., 2004:464). While tourism phenomena have evolved with advancing transport technologies to incorporate same-day travel across expanding spatial scales (Coles et al., 2004), it is also necessary to conceptually integrate understandings of tourism within a range of mobilities undertaken by individuals across the spectrum of longer-term temporal scales.

The manifestations of mobility addressed here relate to the medium- and long-term temporal scale and thus include phenomena such as seasonal patterns of mobility, repeated and regular migrations that persist over the long term (e.g., the use of second homes), sport and transnationalism, migration and diaspora (Figure 10.1). Long-term return visitation is differentiated from seasonal migration (see Chapter 9, *Temporary sport migrants*) in this chapter. While many people of different ages engage at some stages of their lives in transient lifestyles, perhaps as members of mobile seasonal workforces, long-term return visitation as it is addressed in this chapter considers those who engage in regular and routine travel from one place that they consider to be 'home' to one or more other places in which they may feel equally at home. Migration, return migration, transnationalism and diaspora represent different manifestations of the interface of activity, people and

CONTENTS

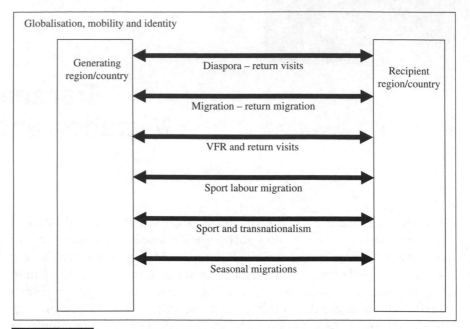

FIGURE 10.1 *Sport mobility in the medium- and long-term temporal dimension: Transnationalism, migration and diaspora.*

place, with important implications for globalization, mobility and identity. This chapter explores these mobility phenomena in terms of links between places, migration and return travel, tourism development and other connections between places (e.g., social, cultural, political). Each represents quite distinct manifestations of sport, mobility and identity, with implications for the evolution of sports over time and the development of tourism.

GLOBALIZATION AND THE MOBILITY OF SPORTS

Sport as culture is closely linked to tradition and identity. In the latter part of the eighteenth century, when many Scots emigrated from the Highlands following the Rebellion of 1745 (Webster, 1973), various aspects of Highland culture and tradition were relocated with them. The Highland Games are iconic athletic events in Scottish communities that have been transplanted with the Scottish diaspora into new world communities in the United States, Canada, New Zealand and elsewhere. One of the key drivers of the continuity of these events is a desire to perpetuate Highland traditions, dress, culture and music in the interests of personal and collective identity (Jarvie, 1989,

1991, 2006). Many have evolved into iconic tourist attractions in their own right (Donaldson, 1986). In a global world, sport has been elevated as a mechanism for retaining tradition and building identity (see Chapter 4, *Culture and identity)*.

Migrants have historically taken with them sports as cultural artefacts and reminders of home. Examples of sports taken abroad with military personnel are commonplace. British troops contested games of football with their German adversaries when short ceasefires allowed battle-weary soldiers to emerge from the western front trenches of World War I. New Zealanders who travelled to the theatres of two World Wars in Europe (1914–1918 and 1939–1945) took with them the game of rugby, competing against teams from other allied forces in France, Egypt, Turkey and Lebanon. Klein (1994:186) notes that 'it was through US military and economic presence (including in the early twentieth century a string of marine invasions in Central America and the Caribbean) that the game (of baseball) spread'. Similarly baseball was introduced into Mexico by the employees of early US multinational companies in the 1880s, Venezuelans learned the game from US involvement in the petroleum industry and US naval personnel forced the game upon the Japanese from 1945 (Klein, 1994). Students who studied in the US returned to Cuba with the game of baseball in the 1860s. Cubans learned and mastered the sport and then exported it to other Caribbean islands including the Dominican Republic in the 1880s. Cubans fleeing domestic turmoil in the 1890s took the game to Yucatan, while Panamanians received the game from the international workforce that undertook the building of the Panama Canal (Klein, 1994).

Maguire (2002) used the term sport migrant 'pioneers' to describe those with the necessary passion who seek to transplant their sport into new parts of the world. He argues that Canadian migrants in Britain performed this role in the 1990s with the sport of ice hockey. The mobility of sports may also be facilitated by tourism. Tourism may exert considerable influence over the development of sports in many parts of the world. Golf has been systematically imported into many hot climate destinations as a tourism development strategy in recent years (Priestley, 1995; Bartoluci & Čavlek, 2000). In the process the development of golf courses and resorts has created what Bale (1989) refers to as sportscapes; standardized cultural landscapes of sport.

A reciprocal relationship exists between the dynamics of tourism and evolution of many sports (Hinch & Higham, 2004). Tourism provides the opportunity for leisure activities to be popularized (de Villiers, 2001), golf, tennis and a range of beach and water sports being obvious examples. While tourism may introduce sports into new areas, it may also serve as a force for innovation in sport. Innovation in competitive sport is constrained by formal rules and regulations governing league competitions. Recreational sports are less restricted. Both competitive and recreational settings are influenced by external trends associated with the economy, politics, society, technology and the natural environment. However, the reason that recreational sport is more conducive to innovation is that experimentation is less restrained in leisure and tourism settings. Keller (2001) also argues that the change in location and uninterrupted free time that tourists enjoy while on holiday provides a setting that is conducive to experimentation and trying something different. Tourism may, therefore, also be an agent for the development of new or hybrid sports as well as the spatial diffusion of sports (Hinch & Higham, 2004).

MEDIUM- AND LONG-TERM RETURN TRAVEL PATTERNS

Seasonal migration is an increasingly widespread phenomenon (Hall & Williams, 2000). Such migratory patterns may be associated with the pursuit of out-of-season sports, outdoor pursuits and healthy lifestyles, often in association with advancing age and retirement. Historically, the most prominent manifestation of seasonal migration is the tendency of those who live in Northern European countries and the colder states and provinces of the United States and Canada to migrate seasonally to condominiums on the Costa del Sol and to the sunbelt states of the southern United States, most typically Florida. The rental of condominiums and purchase of timeshare accommodation are manifestations of long-term repeat mobilities that are in some instances built upon continuing participation in outdoor summer sports. Similarly, many retired New Zealanders migrate seasonally to rented apartments or second homes on Australia's Queensland coast or undertake regular winter holidays in the islands of the South Pacific. These patterns of mobility represent an escape from winter climates and the opportunity to continue to play sports and engage in leisure and recreational activities of preference.

In an increasingly mobile world, young sports participants have demonstrated a propensity for foregoing or withholding the obligations of career path development and family commitment to pursue their sporting passions in different prominent locations around the world (see Chapter 9, *Temporary sport migrants*). These patterns of mobility are undertaken by elite and recreational sports people and in both cases involve year round participation (e.g., seasonal travel between the hemispheres), either as professional athletes or as members of a mobile seasonal workforce. A further and distinct manifestation of recurrent seasonal migrations involves the mobility of athletes seeking to establish or perpetuate competitive careers. This revolves around the search for 'off season' competition with the aims of keeping fit, rehabilitation from injury or to develop career experience as either players or managers.

Cohen (1974) suggests that the use of second homes should be excluded from the study of tourism because the 'tourism' component of such use is marginal at best. This is a point of subsequent debate (Jaakson, 1986) as it is apparent that the use of second homes is an important aspect of the realm of domestic and, increasingly, international tourism (Müller, 2004). Indeed Jaakson (1986:388) describes the second home owner as a '"permanent tourist", someone who is in a perpetual state of travel anticipation'. Hall (2004) makes a strong case for the inclusion of second home use, as well as other forms of contemporary mobility, within the social science of tourism.

Second home use is characterized by recurrent travel flows but may also be manifest in terms of the use of second homes by a range of other users (visiting friends, other family members) as well as rental tenants. Therefore, second homes in Central Otago (New Zealand), while commonly used by owners for summer/Christmas holidays, have become widely used in winter and spring as rental properties that are made available to seasonal ski field employees and/or recreational and competitive skiers and snowboarders. While Greer and Wall (1979) found that the use of second homes by those resident in Toronto were typically to residences within a 75–100 mile radius of the city, it has become much more common for second home use to incur cross-border travel, including from the United States to Canada and across European borders (Müller, 2004). Increased mobility has transformed the second home phenomenon from a largely domestic activity to one that is international in scope (Tress, 2007).

The terms used to describe second homes vary considerably between different parts of the world. Interestingly, with each there are likely to be associations with outdoor activities, recreational pursuits, healthy lifestyles and sports. These include condominiums, cottages, holiday homes, vacation apartments and timeshares, summer and winter cottages, weekend residences (often beach homes), country houses and ski chalets (Jaakson, 1986). Each is commonly associated with particular landscapes and climatic regions. Thus, in Canada, 'by far the majority of second homes have a lake or other waterfront setting. The term 'cottage' has an immediate meaning for most Canadians, and brings with it widely held associations' (Jaakson, 1986:371). The Canadian summer cottage has for generations been a venue for boating, fishing, swimming, waterskiing, snowmobiling, skiing and snowshoeing. The Norwegian winter equivalent is a place of skiing and snowboarding and other snow/ice sports and activities. The link between second home use and a wide range of outdoor sport that vary across the seasons (e.g., skiing, snowboarding, kayaking, mountain biking and rafting) is commonly associated with second home use in parts of New Zealand.

Jaakson (1986) notes some interesting aspects of second home ownership and use of relevance to this discussion. He observes the 'inversion' that takes place between principal and second homes insofar as the former is 'work-oriented' and the latter is 'leisure-oriented'. This in itself implies not only the importance of recreation and physical activity at the second home but also alludes to the labour market requirements of such destinations (*see* Case study 10.1). The blurring of the dividing line between work and leisure, then, should not be obscured. However, the availability of sport/recreation amenities (Müller, 2006) and lack of time constraints are important aspects of second home use and inversion (Jaakson, 1986). The contribution of second home use to identity is also highlighted in the Canadian context. This is attributed to long-term continuity of second home ownership and return travel (many second homes are owned on an intergenerational basis) as well as the passing of techniques and skills between generations of sport participants (Jaakson, 1986).

Case Study 10.1

Second homes and sports-related mobility to the Tärnaby/Hemavan ski resort in Northern Sweden

Dieter K. Müller (Umeå University, Sweden)

Second homes are at the intersection of migration and tourism, implying various causal relationships between them (Hall & Williams, 2000; Hall & Müller, 2004). For example, second home tourism entails the movement of labour into destination areas, and second homes in amenity-rich areas can be converted into future permanent homes for retirement.

This is not least applicable to skiing destinations in attractive mountain locations. Indeed, Lundmark and Marjavaara (2005) demonstrated that ski resorts were the primary location factor for purpose-built second homes in the Swedish mountain range. Moreover, second homes in these ski resorts are usually owned by a well-off share of the population (Müller, 2005). This case study presents the situation in the ski resort of Tärnaby/Hemavan in Northern Sweden. The

destination is located close to the Norwegian border just south of the Arctic Circle, and owing to its remote location, it is a secondary winter destination only. Indeed, the area caters for less than 3% of all alpine skiing in Sweden. Nevertheless, the opening of an airport with direct connections to Sweden's capital Stockholm, as well as an increasing interest from Norwegian investors in the region, has entailed a boom not least regarding the construction of new second homes. The results presented here are drawn from a database study of the area covering the period 1991–2000 (Müller, 2006).

The Tärna/Hemavan destination has only about 1600 registered inhabitants, while the privately owned second homes amount to almost 2100. This implies a dramatic population increase, particularly during the winter season, lasting from late September until May. A majority of this temporary population is usually permanently residing along the coastline of Northern Sweden about 400 km away from the destination. The second homes are used about 30 days per year by their owners, and their consumption is estimated to be equivalent to that of almost 90 permanent households in the region (Jansson & Müller, 2003). However, second home owners are often accompanied by friends and relatives. Hence, the average number of users of a second home is almost 6 persons at a time.

Moreover, more than 60% of the second homes are sometimes let or lent to other households/friends, implying a far higher occupancy rate. Hence, second homes are the dominant form of accommodation in the area. In summary this means that during peak season, usually around the Easter holidays, the number of people in the area is greater than 15,000 when considering both hotel guests and seasonal labour, which in the current case number less than 100 (Lundmark, 2006). This makes the resort an important seasonal node in the area.

Tärnaby/Hemavan has a stable population development not only owing to in-migration but also to a relatively young population (Müller, 2006). In contrast, many other areas in the northern Swedish periphery are suffering from out-migration. Altogether, 480 individuals migrated into the resort between 1991 and 2000. About 25% were aged below 19 years, indicating the rather selective attractiveness of the mountain resort. A majority of in-migrants moved from the coastal parts of the county; meanwhile, 139 were enticed to leave a residence in southern Sweden for a life in the northern periphery.

The study revealed the role of second homes in attracting population to Tärnaby/Hemavan (Jansson & Müller, 2004). Altogether 29 households representing about 20% of all in-migrants already owned a second home in the area prior to the relocation of the primary residence into the area. Although unclear from the survey, it can be assumed that a majority converted their second home into a primary home.

The importance of skiing and other forms of tourism was also demonstrated by the occupations of the in-migrants. Hence, 179 out of 480 individuals were employed within tourism, often directly after moving to the resort. This group constituted a third of the total labour force involved in tourism, making the in-migrant group an important pillar of the local tourism industry. Particularly the hotel and restaurant sector employed in-migrants, but also tourism operators and services geared towards alpine skiing and snowmobiling

had newcomers among their staff. Retailing was also another important labour market sector for in-migrants. Interestingly, it was not the group of second home owners who took up employment in tourism. They had obviously other opportunities to make a living in the area and were thus not forced into this rather low-income sector.

Many of the in-migrants had no experience of tourism-related work prior to arrival in Tärnaby/Hemavan, and indeed not all remained in the sector for any longer period of time. Almost 50% had left the sector at the end of the studied period.

Hence, tourism development forms an important precondition for in-migration to the area in that it provides service jobs with relatively low entrance barriers. Young age, low incomes, limited education and frequent employment changes among the newcomers point at migration motives that are not necessarily production-led. Instead, it can be concluded that in-migration to Tärnaby/Hemavan is mainly consumption-led, acknowledging the amenities of the mountain resort including skiing and plentiful outdoor activities that attract young households into the area. Moreover, second homes form an important anchor for future in-migration, although they are no necessary precondition.

Selected references

Jansson, B. and Müller, D.K. (2003). *Fritidsboende i Kvarken*. Umeå: Kvarkenrådet.

Lundmark, L. (2006). Mobility, migration and seasonal tourism employment. *Scandinavian Journal of Hospitality and Tourism* 6(3), 1–17.

Lundmark, L. and Marjavaara, R. (2005). Second home localizations in the Swedish mountain range. *Tourism* 53 (1), 3–16.

Müller, D.K. (2005). Second home tourism in the Swedish mountain range. In *Nature-Based Tourism in Peripheral Areas: Development or Disaster?* (C.M. Hall and S. Boyd, eds.), (pp. 133–148). Clevedon: Channel View.

Müller, D.K. (2006). Amenity migration and tourism development in the Tärna mountains, Sweden. In *Amenity Migrants: Seeking and Sustaining Mountains and Their Cultures* (L.A.G. Moss, ed.), pp. 245–248. Wallingford: CAB International.

Recurrent return visits are also a common feature of some seasonal sports and recurring sports events. Long-term repeat and return travel patterns are associated with participation and spectator sports that achieve high participant loyalty whether they are competitive or non-competitive. Multi-sport and endurance events that take place in unique and attractive physical environments, for example, typically have loyal participants who return annually to contest events, either to win (or compete strongly) or to participate as a means of building personal or collective identity. The arduous Speight's Coast-to-Coast (New Zealand) multi-sport event celebrated its twenty-fifth anniversary in 2007 and it was noteworthy that many who contested the first event in 1983, despite the highly demanding nature of the event, returned once again as participants. Some had competed in the event every year since its inception, and many travelled internationally to this event as competitors.

Such events may assume the importance of an annual pilgrimage for some athletes and participants, both competitive and non-elite, who generally bring with them large numbers of support crew as well as family and friends as spectators. In contrast, spending time with family may be an important travel motivation for those who participate in small-scale sport events (Carmichael & Murphy, 1996), particularly female participants (Thompson, 1985). In an increasingly mobile world, it also transpires that popular sports events may shape many elements of future decision-making. Carmichael and Murphy (1996) provide one of the few empirical studies into future behavioural intentions towards a place following participation in small-scale sports events; financial investment, the development of business interests, repeat leisure travel, permanent migration (i.e., lifestyle choice) and retirement planning.

The factors that feature in the recall phase of the sport experience as they relate to future repeat visitation and patterns of mobility remain poorly understood. These factors are certain to differ between sport tourist types. High-performance athletes are likely to be influenced by the standard of training facilities, personal performance and the outcome of the sport contest (Maier & Weber, 1993). The experiences of event spectators may be judged by casual spectators based upon the uniqueness of the sport experience, while more serious sports fans may evaluate the sport experience based on opportunities to enhance social identity and self-concept (Gibson, 1998; Morgan, 2007). By contrast, those pursuing general holidays with some incidental sport content may assess the uniqueness of the touristic experience of the destination in the recollection phase (Glyptis, 1982). In each instance, perceptions of the destination and the propensity for repeat travel are likely to be influenced by different factors.

SPORT AND TRANSNATIONALISM

At another spatial level, sports migrations may be specifically considered in terms of inbound and outward travel across national borders. The social and cultural connections that exist between transnational communities provide considerable insight into contemporary migrations. As Coles et al. (2004:468) note, 'The past decade has seen a new shift towards the adoption of a transnational approach to explaining globalised, interconnected migrant identities'.

Transnationalism may be understood in terms of the development and maintenance of networks across national borders. Coles et al. (2004:469) explain that 'in various research centred on migrants, emigrants and the processes of social adaptation and adjustment, transnationalism is used as a sweeping conceptual framework that attempts to make clear the inter-connected social experiences that define … migration'. A transnational approach fosters understanding of the movement of mobile people across national borders and highlights the implications arising from such patterns of mobility, including the development and maintenance of interconnected social networks. Duval and Hall (2004) argue that transnational communi-ties account for a significant proportion of temporary mobility, as such activity is based on previous, multiple and perhaps inter-generational migrations, social relationships and transnational identities.

This approach provides an interesting perspective on sports mobility. Thus, countries like Cuba have been traditionally viewed as a source of professional baseball players and boxers, among other sports. Yet Arbena (1994) points out that during the period from 1930 to 1960 many North American professionals played baseball in Cuba and the Dominican Republic in order to both supplement their incomes and remain physically fit during the off season. Arbena (1994:101) notes that 'since the 1970s higher salaries in the majors have reduced North American participation in Latin American winter ball, though a number of younger players still use the opportunity to work on their game and potential managers seek to develop and demonstrate their leadership capabilities'.

Thus while sports migrations are, most prominently, constituted by elite athletes migrating from donor countries to the most financially powerful leagues of Europe and North America, such transnational mobilities also involve reverse flows. Others may pursue their careers in foreign countries due to changing political circumstances, in either the originating or receiving country. 'A historical example is to be found in the visits to Mexico of Spanish bull-fighters (*torero*s) beginning in the late nineteenth century after the reestablishment of the *fiesta brava* following several decades of liberal suppression of this "violent" Hispanic festival' (Arbena, 1994:99–100). Others may give priority to lifestyle or changes in lifestyle, perhaps with a view to prolonging a professional sports career. Obtaining a taste of regional European lifestyles is an important factor in the decision-making of southern hemisphere rugby players.

With transnationalism come the associated phenomena of visiting friends and relatives (VFR) and return visits. Duval (2004) defines VFR trips as essentially travel initiated by an obligation or desire to be with family or friends. Historically, VFR has been treated as a marginalized form of tourism because it was perceived to be of low value and unresponsive to the marketing efforts of destination organizations (Seaton & Palmer, 1997). However, Duval (2004) situates VFR and return visits within a framework of transnationalism and in doing so views VFR and return travel through the broader lenses of the interconnected social and cultural experiences that commonly define the lives of migrants.

Sports migrants are likely to receive family and friends as VFR travellers. Perhaps of equal interest to scholars is the phenomenon of return visits (Duval, 2004). In the sport labour migration context return visits may relate to sports migrants returning (when opportunities arise) to the place of origin to undertake obligatory or desired family commitments. It may also entail a return to places of competition from the place of origin, perhaps in order to maintain or strengthen social ties or to take up career opportunities, following the completion of competitive sports careers.

Duval (2004:260) points out that 'conceptualizing the return visit requires a deeper understanding of how individuals place themselves within the context of two localities, one of which is their place of birth ... and the other is their current city or country of residence'. Thus, rather than focusing on the motivations and experiences of those who visit friends and relatives, Duval (2004) argues the case for understanding VFR and return visits in terms of the transnational identities that exist as a result of global migrant activity regardless of the political boundaries between nation states. So, for example, Hall and Duval (2004:78) note that migration is an inherent feature of Polynesian people and that '... while islander populations are highly mobile in terms of employment and education, substantial links of kinship and relationships to village and land remain'. Given that sport labour migration is a very prominent manifestation of the mobility of Polynesians, particularly young males, it is interesting to contemplate the VFR and various forms of return visits that may characterize this unique form of mobility.

SPORT AND LABOUR MIGRATIONS

The recruitment and retention of sports people is a common form of labour migration in many parts of the world. The migrations of elite athletes take place at three spatial levels: national, international and transcontinental (Maguire, 1999). American football, baseball, ice hockey and football are sports for which the professional player catchments are global (Bale & Maguire, 1994). Football drives intercontinental sport labour migration flows from Africa to Europe as well as intracontinental flows from central to southern Africa (Cornelissen & Solberg, 2007). Sports labour migrations also take place across a range of temporal dimensions. Those pursuing professional careers in sports such as baseball and basketball are likely to engage in long-term migrations during careers that may span several teams. Semi-professional basketball players commonly migrate between short-term contracts under which they may compete in leagues in such countries as the United States, Australia, Turkey and Brazil. The leisure travel preferences of athletes living and competing in foreign countries are poorly understood.

Another common temporal dimension of sports labour migrations relates to diurnal or seasonal timeframes. It is noteworthy that many sports, particularly those that take place in built (stadiums and arenas) rather than natural settings have been largely freed from seasonal constraints (Higham & Hinch, 2002). However, many outdoor and nature-based sports remain subject to seasonal cycles. Thus, sports such as snowboarding and skiing are associated with shorter-term, seasonal sports labour migrations. Such migrations include not only those who seek competition on the snowfields of the northern and southern hemispheres but also those who engage in snow sports recreationally, who may seek employment at ski resorts on a seasonal basis to finance the pursuit of their sporting passions (see Chapter 9, *Temporary sport migrants*). The America's Cup and other professional sailing regattas are useful examples of seasonal sport competitions that are associated with high levels of seasonal mobility and a blurring of the distinction between work and leisure, production and consumption.

The short-term temporal dimension of sports labour migration, while also operating within competition seasons, extends over periods of several days. Many sports require competitors to adopt mobile lives as they migrate between sites of competition to contest tour events and/or qualifications tournaments. Entry into the golf majors (British Open, US Open, US Masters and Professional Golfers' Association [PGA] Championship) requires professionals to compete on PGA tour programmes in Europe, Asia and/or North America. Within the golf season, competitors migrate from one place of competition to another, often staying only 5–6 days in any one destination. Tennis players seeking a world ranking or trying to advance their ranking must adopt a nomadic existence as they follow the PTA tour circuit (Maguire, 1999). New Zealanders who compete in rowing spend the period from April to September based in Europe for the summer rowing season, living and training in the United Kingdom or Germany and travelling widely across Europe for regular competition. The migratory lifestyles of individual sports people (e.g., squash players, triathletes, surfers, skiers) and team personnel (e.g., beach volleyball, football, basketball and baseball teams) reflect this high mobility as they travel either in search of competition or to meet the playing schedules of league competitions.

Maguire (1999) refers to the 'figurational dynamics' that exists at the various destinations to which athletes migrate or travel to compete (Figure 10.2). Such dynamics differ markedly between places and clearly influence the experiences of mobile sports people. 'Sports migrants … have to do their body work in various locations and, as a group, experience varying degrees of exploitation, dislocation and cultural adjustment' (Maguire, 1999:99). Labour rights are a central element of sports migrant experiences and, according to Maguire (1999), vary considerably between places. The employment rights of Australian rugby league players are, due to salary cap constraints, quite different from the freedom for individual athletes such as

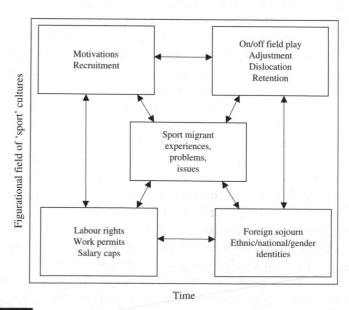

FIGURE 10.2 *Sport migrant experiences, problems and issues (Source: Maguire, 1999:99).*

tennis and golf players. Player draft programmes, in which emerging, typically college athletes are assigned to a particular team, may compromise the freedoms and mobility of sports people.

The experiences of sports migrants vary considerably in terms of the levels of payment, employment conditions and the retention of important freedoms. Living experiences and different player and team cultures may require migrant players to adapt to alien and unfamiliar living, training and competition contexts. 'Sport labour migration, then, is not a uniform experience. It has its own highly differentiated political economy that reflects its position as part of the global sport system' (Maguire, 1999:101). There are many examples of Polynesia sports stars competing in professional, typically power and performance sports ranging from boxing and American football to rugby union and rugby league, who have struggled to adapt to alien living circumstances while seeking to compete abroad. The case of Jonah Lomu (Rugby union) is not uncommon. Despite numerous contract offers to play professional American football, rugby union and rugby league (in the USA, Europe and Australia, respectively) Lomu has played out his career in his native New Zealand (aside from one northern hemisphere season playing rugby union in Cardiff Wales as part of an attempted comeback). The important functions of family and home are a common element of Polynesian cultures, which may challenge the mobilities of some talented athletes.

Some of the underlying factors relating to migration are nicely articulated by Osella and Gardner (2004). These authors identify three inescapable elements of migration including *transformation, ambiguity and power*. First, migration requires transformation by individuals, groups or states in response to the forging of new identities as well as the challenging and changing of existing orders. Second, migrants are required to transform themselves in ways that may result in compromise of competing ideals and values. Migration involves inevitable exposure to new experiences and ideologies that may invoke ambiguous or uncertain responses. Finally, migrants are subject to changing relations of power between places of origin and new places of residence. These may be expressed in exchanges between different states, migrant and non-migrant groups, families and individuals. These aspects of migration begin to explain some of the considerable challenges that have to be negotiated by sports labour migrants. In addition, Maguire (1999) identifies that global sport migrations are predominantly, although not exclusively, male. This raises the important point that many of the experiences, issues and problems associated with sports labour migration may differ markedly on the basis of gender.

The high mobility of contemporary sport labour markets also has significant implications for 'donor' countries (Magurie, 1999). Sport labour migration brings with it the inevitable loss of sporting talent from countries and regions of origin. The loss of Cuban baseball stars to the United States and South American football stars to Europe represents a haemorrhaging of player talent. This loss is typically from less developed to developed countries where economically powerful leagues are able to procure talent on financial grounds. However, this is not exclusively the case. A pattern of player mobility associated with professional ice hockey has been from Scandinavia to the National Hockey League (NHL) (North America). Scandinavia has also been a nursery for professional football players who migrate to southern and western European leagues. The professional rugby union player ranks of New Zealand, Australia and South Africa have also been depleted to serve the interests of foreign clubs predominantly in England, France and Japan. While salary differentials may be an important factor driving these sport labour migrations, other factors include lifestyle, longer-term career opportunities, the stimulation of new competition challenges and the desire to play against the best players in the world (Stead & Maguire, 2000).

Thus the high mobility of sport labour markets has implications for both origin and destination regions. It is the country or region of origin that invests in the production of athletic talent. The extent to which those countries or regions, national unions or clubs are compensated for the loss of athletic talent in a more global sport market no doubt varies in different sporting and national contexts. Maguire (1999:101) notes that 'not only is the indigenous audience denied access to the talent nurtured and developed in their country, but, in some instances, such as with African national football teams, sports lose some of their quality performers when the demands of European clubs clash with international matches'. The expanding flow of elite rugby talent from the South Hemisphere to the local rugby clubs such as Marseille, Toulon, Saracens, Munster and Newcastle has seriously eroded the player-base from which the national teams of New Zealand, South Africa, Australia and Argentina are selected. However, it is also noteworthy that the playing ranks of Tonga, Samoa, Fiji, Tokelau, Namibia and Zimbabwe have been exploited by these same countries. Clearly, as Maguire (1999) points out, mobile sport labour markets have implications for national representation and identity, with dependence relations existing on a range of spatial levels.

Sport labour migrants

As a rule, very little is known about sport migrant workers. On the most obvious level, the fortunes of sport labour migrants are commonly measured in terms of success on the fields of competition. As such, the fortunes of the very few most gifted and successful athletes are much more visible than the many who fail to establish long and successful professional careers. Less is known about sport labour migrants in terms of their backgrounds and their career experiences as well as how their careers impact upon themselves, their families, their homelands and their adopted societies. At the receiving country, player quotas, cultural distance, language barriers and nationalistic sentiments are factors that may influence the experiences of sport labour immigrants (Arbena, 1994). Players may be subject to prejudice based on compromised playing styles that form an important aspect of national identity. Klein (1994:188) notes the Dominican Republic resentment of US neo-colonialism through the sport of baseball. The Latin American preference for 'artistry over brute force was responsible for Roger Maris (the same who would in 1961 break Babe Ruth's single season home run record) being dropped from the Dominican team in the late 1950s when he was considered a legitimate power hitter in the United States'.

The case of Tongan migrants in Australia, and the role of sport in the lives of those migrants, is an interesting case study. Lee (2003) reports on the challenges that are negotiated by Tongan migrants as they seek to counter the dilution of their Tongan culture while assimilating into a new society. The reassertion of Tongan identity involves the demonstration of values such as respect and humility (Lee, 2003) but extends wherever possible to dress, music, dance and food. Tongans living in Melbourne will choose to reside in close proximity to fellow Tongans and will congregate at the same church as their fellow villagers or extended family. Regular return visits to Tonga are an essential element of this process. While negotiating complex elements of identity, Tongans living in Australia are also subject to negative stereotypes, such as the 'illegal immigrant' stereotype that has persisted in Australian and New Zealand media (Lee, 2003).

It is important to understand the unique socio-cultural needs of different sport labour migrants. Knowledge transfer, rituals and ceremonies, social interactions and family commitments including visits and financial remittances that migrants may need to fulfil are likely to contrast markedly between different groups. During professional sports careers these interests might focus on the obligations and preferences of athletes in terms of maintaining social relationships with kinsfolk who remain in the country or region of origin. Equally important questions exist in terms of the challenges of reverse culture shock and social reintegration for those who have, by virtue of a transnational professional sports career, developed multiple identities and complex social networks. Lee (2003) and Duval (2004) both report significant problems encountered by Tongan and Commonwealth Eastern Caribbean (respectively) migrants temporarily returning home. Interestingly, Duval (2004) notes that the alienation felt by these returning migrants was not dissimilar to the negative sentiments often perceived by tourists who visit unfamiliar places.

Non-elite sport and labour migration

Aside from the migrations of elite athletes, very little is known about the role of sports in the motivational set of non-elite labour migrants. Herein lies an aspect of sport and mobility that justifies an empirically directed discourse. Mason (2002) describes the phenomenon of overseas experience (OE), which emerged as a form of migration in the latter half of the twentieth century and is pursued by a large proportion of young (and increasingly not so young) Antipodeans. Commonly the OE is undertaken following the completion of high school or tertiary degrees and usually to bases in the United Kingdom, historically London, but more recently other places such as Edinburgh and Cardiff. It is noteworthy that with changing costs, conditions and requirements of United Kingdom visa and work permit applications many New Zealanders undertaking an OE have in more recent years chosen to base themselves in European countries or in North America or Australia.

Mason (2002) describes the OE as a long-standing form of population mobility that demonstrates aspects of both tourism and migration. In many respects the OE has much in common with the 'gap year' undertaken by many young British students. Jamieson (1996) explains that one of the key elements of these migrations is the acceptance of financial hardships and casual labour in return for both a sense of freedom from social and work constraints as well as the ability to dispense with work commitments temporarily in order to assume mobile lives, to engage in cheap travel and to experience the cultures of exotic places. Escape from the home environment, work and career path commitments and social constraints are an important aspect of the OE (Ryan, 1997). So too, no doubt, is the demonstration of personal, financial and decision-making independence.

Interestingly, Mason (2002) notes that those who engage in the OE are typically aged between 18 and 30 years and are in the most healthy and active years of their lives. This raises interesting questions as to the role of sports in motivating the locations where those engaging in an OE choose to live and work, the destinations that they travel to, and the activities that they engage in during time spent abroad. The significance of national sports tours and, therefore, opportunities to experience and support one's compatriots in international sports competition is unknown. What is known is that when the New Zealand All Blacks tour and play in Europe, they are supported by hordes of expatriate New Zealanders, many young temporary migrants engaged in their OE. It is also probable that young migrants choose destinations where they can continue to engage in their own sporting pursuits of preference. The strong club rugby competitions of Britain, Ireland and France are no doubt attractive to many young New Zealanders living temporarily away from home. Those who are sufficiently skilled and dedicated may see club representation as a means of supplementing their income, perhaps also as a stepping stone to a professional or semi-professional contract or non-sporting career opportunities. The preference of many young Australasian migrants to be based in the Rocky Mountain states and provinces of the United States and Canada, particularly Colorado and British Columbia, is no doubt due in large part to the sports participation and seasonal labour opportunities associated with winter sports resorts (see Chapter 9, *Temporary sport migrants*).

SPORT AND DIASPORA

A quite distinctive manifestation of sport tourism is the mobility of sports associated with diasporas (Hinch & Higham, 2004). The transplanting of sports in association with diasporic communities and the implications for sports and tourism management offer interesting avenues of discussion. The migration of European nationals into the colonies of the imperial empires is associated with the relocation of national sports. Sports such as horseracing (Hong Kong and Singapore), cricket (India, Pakistan, Australia, New Zealand, South Africa and the Commonwealth Caribbean) and football (South American countries) have been transplanted by migrant communities.

Coles et al. (2004:471) describe diaspora as 'diffuse transnational communities bound by a common perception of their origins'. Those claiming Scottish ancestry are common in parts of North America, South Africa, Australia and New Zealand. London, New York and Melbourne all have distinctive diasporic communities, be they Irish, Italian, Croatian or Lebanese. Diaspora describes 'groups of people scattered across the world but drawn together as a community by their actual, perceived, or imagined common bonds of ethnicity, culture, religion, national identity and sometimes race' (Coles et al., 2004:471). However, it is important to note that migration histories, attachments to their home countries and experiences in their adopted countries differ markedly between members of a given diaspora (Coles & Timothy, 2004). Despite common diasporic origins, members of the Irish communities of London, Boston, Melbourne and Tokyo will, despite common elements, be quite heterogeneous entities.

The links between diasporic communities and sport are intriguing. Sikhs brought with them to the cities of the midlands and north of England not only distinctive Punjabi cuisine, among other things, but also the established cricketing art of spin bowling. Similarly, Mexican migrants in the United States prevail in the sport of boxing and Dominicans in New York bring unique skills to bear in baseball. Melbourne and Sydney have also become the bases of Australian football due in large part to the large European expatriate communities in those cities. The Croatian, Italian, Greek and Turkish expatriate communities in Australia have developed close links with a range of local football clubs in Melbourne and Sydney. The descendants of European immigrants have populated the Australian national team which performed with distinction at the 2006 Fédération Internationale de Football Association (FIFA) World Cup in Germany. Ironically, many of these Australian national team players now live and play professionally for European clubs.

Thus, diasporic communities have transplanted, retained, adopted and adapted different sports to suit their own geographical contexts. Furthermore, as with most diasporic communities, the search for identity, independence and, in some cases, ultimately, nationhood is commonly the case and sport is a prominent mechanism for achieving these goals. The cricket pitch is a stage upon which Australians have historically strived to demonstrate dominance over and, therefore, autonomy from the colonial apron strings of England. Similarly, the sport of rugby became a symbol of apartheid as well as religious and racial superiority in South Africa up until 1992, which has understandably proved a difficult history to disassociate from (Nauright, 2001), while the same sport soon became a symbol of integration and collective endeavour in New Zealand's early colonial years (Booth, 2000).

CONCLUSION

Identity is influenced by many cultural attributes but sport certainly appears to be one of the most dominant. Nauright (1996:69) suggests that not only is sport a factor in the process of constructing place identity but that it is one of the clearest indicators of collective identity. The role of sport in the construction of collective identity is not, however, restricted to high-profile sporting competitions. Sports and leisure pursuits that occur on a daily basis in local communities are also important (Nauright, 1997; Harohousou, 1999). The relationship between sport and identity as it applies to mobile people is yet to be fully and critically considered, although some existing studies do whet the appetite for such explorations. Lanfranchi (1994), for example, provides an intriguing review of the French national sports of football and rugby as they relate to mobility and identity. 'French roots are idealized in rugby union. A national self-defined style exists in rugby (*the rugby-champagne*)... Football is too urban, too permeable to minorities; sons of immigrants, sons of the colonies, mercenaries from all parts of the world are unable to reflect the soul of the population' (Lanfranchi, 1994:66).

Many unanswered questions surround the phenomenon of sport labour migration. As with all forms of tourism and mobility, it is critical to understand the 'push' and 'pull' factors associated with the motivations to leave one place and travel to another, regardless of the duration of absence from the generating region or country. It is most evident that economic and political factors in both generating and receiving countries are key factors (Williams, 1994). So too, according to Arbena (1994), are cultural and historical factors. The study of tourism tells us that the experiences of those who leave home, and their overall assessment of those experiences as good or bad, valuable or otherwise, are determined by various factors in both origin and recipient countries. Arbena (1994:108), with reference to baseball in Latin America and drawing on the work of Klein (1991), suggests that mobilities associated with sport can be '... at one and the same time a source of exploitation and development, of cultural colonialism and nationalism, of domination and creativity, of humiliation and pride, of hegemony and resistance'. This statement, more than most, captures the forces and counter forces at play in sport, tourism and contemporary mobility in a global and highly mobile world.

PART 5

Place

CHAPTER 11

Modern Landscapes and Retro Parks

On 5 July 2007 the transport infrastructure of central London came to a standstill as roads were closed and commuter traffic flows redirected for the start of the 2007 Tour de France. A sports event synonymous with the rural landscapes of France, the Pyrennes and the Champs Elysées, now starts in the shadows of Nelson's column, Victory Gate, Whitehall and the Houses of Parliament in Westminster. Sports such as the Tour de France can contribute to the construction of place identity (Hinch & Higham, 2004). It is ironic that after centuries of military conflict between the French and the English, from the Norman conquest (1066) to Agincourt (1415) and the campaigns of the Duke of Marlborough (1704–1709) and Lord Nelson (1798–1805), the Tour de France should start in Trafalgar Square, a site that commemorates England's greatest naval victory over the French in 1805. Such are the landscapes of sport in a global world.

It has been argued that sport is a form of culture and, therefore, the landscapes of sport are cultural landscapes (Bale, 1989). As such, the landscapes of sport are open to cultural interpretation. Ramshaw (2006) uses the English village green and the frozen Canadian farmyard pond as examples of the reinterpretation of natural environments as part of the human sporting landscape (as cricket and ice hockey venues, respectively). Correspondingly, Bale (1993) discusses the cultural interpretations that may be imposed upon built sports places, namely the modern stadium. Bale (1993) uses metaphors as a way of attributing meanings, and therefore beliefs and attitudes, to a stadium. They include the stadium as a park or garden (the sacred turf that without careful maintenance will be returned to nature), machinery (the site of sport production), cathedral (where religious ceremonies are performed) or, from Foucauldian or neo-Marxist perspectives, the stadium as prison (where discipline and control are imposed upon large gatherings).

CONTENTS

Sports places are, therefore, heavily influenced by cultural interpretations of the landscape. This may include the modification of the environment to create sport facilities and the amenities and infrastructure required by those who engage in sports as well as the use of subjective interpretations of the sport landscape to give meanings to place (Hinch & Higham, 2004). Indeed, 'like most other professional sports both cricket and ice hockey have moved to environments that are more suited to spectator sport, and locations where the eccentricities of the sport's natural environment can be mediated' (Ramshaw, 2006:1). It is useful to consider the landscapes of sport based on the consideration of those that take place in natural settings and those that take place in constructed or built venues. This chapter discusses cultural influences on the natural and built landscapes of sports places.

NATURAL LANDSCAPES OF SPORT

The term landscape is often used to imply naturalness (Bale, 1994). The natural landscapes of sport represent a negotiation of nature conservation and cultural influence. Sports are not natural forms of movement. Thus, 'the landscape upon which such body culture takes place is part of the cultural landscape' (Bale, 1994:9). Sports that rely on natural elements (e.g., snowboarding, golf and mountain biking) take place in environments that are subject to varying degrees of anthropogenic change (Hudson, 1999; Hinch & Higham, 2004). For example, Priestley (1995) warns against being fooled by the 'green' appearance of golf courses. It has been noted previously that the rapid development of golf courses around the world over the last twenty years represents a powerful force in standardization (contributing to the loss of biodiversity), environmental modification, and wider ecological impacts associated with high water demands and the use of herbicides and pesticides (Priestley, 1995). The landscapes of sport represent a blurring of the natural and cultural influences of sport and the trend towards standardization (Bale, 1989).

Bale (1989:142) notes that 'inevitably, the growth and continuing locational adjustments made by modern sports have created significant changes in the landscape'. Many locational and landscape changes are temporary and reversible. Triathlons, marathons, cycle races, car rallies and festival or exhibition sports are often conducted on circuits that are regularly modified and courses or courts that may be constructed with varying degrees of permanence. The impacts of these sports, which may include a sizeable body of spectators, are rapidly dispersed at the conclusion of the contest (Hinch & Higham, 2004). Even the lifecycle of a modern stadium may be surprisingly temporary given the changing demands of sports and the high mobility of professional sport franchises (Stevens, 2005). Other sports, particularly those that require permanent and dedicated facilities, or those that are constructed in fragile natural environments, may have longer-term or irreversible impacts on the landscape. The development of ski resorts and winter sport facilities in fragile alpine ecologies is one example. Indeed concern for the development of alpine resorts has seen stagnation of ski markets in Europe and North America (Flagestad & Hope, 2001).

SPORTS AND GLOBAL ENVIRONMENTAL CHANGE

The heavy cultural footprint of sports that take place in natural areas presents a complex conundrum. One aspect of this complexity is access to finite landscapes. 'Sports like hang gliding create pressure on rural hill and scarp country, surfing on beach areas, skiing has placed pressure on mountain regions and water sports compete with one another for precious room on the limited amount of suitable inland water space' (Bale, 1989:163). Nature-based sports often take place in environments that are fragile and sensitive to disturbance (Hall & Page, 1999). Such ecologies are increasingly prominent within the discourses on biodiversity conservation. These concerns are particularly pressing in a sport context because of the dynamic nature of sport and the speed with which new sports are developed and diffused. The transition from innovation in sport to mass participation and from alternative to mainstream sport can be very rapid (Standeven & De Knop, 1999). With specific reference to sport, Hinch and Higham (2004:187) note that 'as sports institutions, media, equipment clothing manufactures and the tourism industry interact, extreme sports tend to shift from subculture to mainstream'.

The globalization of environmental issues has also shaped the modern landscapes of sports events. Irreversible environmental impacts in the mountain ecologies of Albertville's 1992 winter Olympics (May, 1995) reflect the unsustainable practices of the past. In response to growing concerns for global environmental change, the organizing committee of the 1994 Lillehammer Winter Olympic Games pioneered new approaches to environmental management (Kaspar, 1998), focusing on such concerns as waste management and post-event development redundancy (Lesjø, 2000). The Olympic Environmental Charter was then amended to require environmental protection policies in future games. 'The widespread environmental damage at the 1992 Albertville and the Savoie Region Games, and the subsequent 'green' (white) Games of Lillehammer, Norway (1994) were the historical benchmarks for the development of this policy' (Cantelon & Letters, 2000:294). The Sydney 2000 Olympic Games represent a shift towards ecological restoration and biodiversity conservation as an integral part of the Olympic Games development programme (OCAa, 1997; OCAb, 1997). This represents a paradigmatic shift from impact mitigation to proactive environmental stewardship and habitat creation (Chernushenko, 1996; Cowell, 1997), albeit with a local focus. The landscapes of sports are now increasingly situated within the context of global environmental change.

Biosecurity and global biodiversity loss

One example of this global environmental framework is the issue of biodiversity loss. With reference to biosecurity concerns, Hall (2005:330) notes that 'increased movements of people across political and physical borders may have a number of unintended and unwanted consequences'. Biosecurity issues relating to sport and tourism include the translocation of pests and disease pathogens through transport systems, travellers (participants and spectators) and perhaps sports equipment. The relocation of unwanted pests and diseases can have serious consequences for ecological systems, humans and animal populations as well as entire economic sectors such as farming (e.g., animal disease) and export sectors (e.g., fruit and produce subject to insect blight).

At the competitive or elite levels of sport, measures including competition regulations, are often in place to address biosecurity concerns. Perhaps more pressing is the management of biosecurity issues in association with recreational and participation sports. Invasive algae and water weeds can be readily relocated between water systems and water catchments through the use of water sports equipment such as kayaks, paddles, fishing equipment, clothing and boats of all description. The highly invasive and suffocating water algae Didymo (*Didymosphenia geminata*) can be transmitted between water systems in different parts of the world through a single droplet of water or on contaminated and untreated dry clothing (Biosecurity New Zealand, 2007). Similarly, the spread of disease pathogens such as giardia is commonly associated with inappropriate human waste management in nature-based sport, tourism and recreational contexts. The movement and temporary accommodation of people as spectators may also pose disease threats, especially where toilet, food and other public health facilities are inadequate.

Many sports involve the use of animals either as competitors (e.g., greyhound racing, pigeon racing), partners to human competitors (e.g., horse racing, equestrian, dog trials, sledge racing) or as the captive or wild targets of competition (e.g., big game fishing, hunting and rodeo). Some of these sports require the relocation of animals either regionally, nationally or internationally to places of competition. The Olympic equestrian competition, for example, requires the relocation of horses to places of competition in strict adherence to domestic quarantine regulations to reduce the risk of the spread of diseases such as foot and mouth disease, rabies and bovine tuberculosis. Biosecurity issues such as these require close management based on a widespread appreciation of biosecurity, quarantine and other prevention and control measures.

While biosecurity concerns may have significant consequences for human health, animal mortality and the robustness of ecological systems, there are many other biodiversity issues associated with sport and the mobility of participants and spectators. High participation and spectator sports require facilities that may demand the large-scale modification of natural or built environments. Increasingly, the construction of sport and spectator facilities requires that careful consideration is given to location, environmental design and energy efficiency, incorporating long-term sustainable planning (e.g., multi- or alternative use facility design). Similarly, some nature-based sports have come under close scrutiny in terms of concerns for environmental modification and impact. Marine sports (e.g., scuba diving) and alpine sports (e.g., snowboarding and ski disciplines) take place in fragile ecologies and often require and/or result in extensive land- or seascape modification. The anchorage of vessels at dive sites has been a widely recognized issue associated with scuba and free diving, particularly at fragile coral reef sites (Cater & Cater, 2007), as well as potential impacts on incidental or non-target species of marine life (Buckley, 2001). The use of fragile ecologies, in some cases involving considerable bodies of spectators, is also a common aspect of many sports. The search for remote, aesthetic and physically demanding environments for the purposes of multi-sport and endurance events has brought pressures upon areas designated primarily for conservation and biodiversity protection.

The production of artificial sports facilities that deflect demand from natural environments is perhaps one response to environmental impact and biodiversity concerns. Artificial surf waves, climbing walls and constructed ski slopes may deflect the pressures of use from natural areas, although alternatively they may function as high-access introduction points for entry in a particular sport, which ultimately leads to the search for natural settings against which participants can test and enhance their developing skills. Many extreme sports, which offer little potential for artificial design, perhaps represent a counter trend towards sports that are entirely dependent on nature. Participation in these sports may represent a search for authentic experiences that cannot be replicated in artificial settings (see Chapter 8, *Authentic experiences*).

Responses to environmental and biodiversity concerns, therefore, tend to focus on the development of regulations and imposition of management interventions. Biosecurity strategies may include pre-border initiatives, such as identifying high-risk countries of origin, unwanted organisms and pathways of introduction, and educating athletes and spectators on biosecurity issues and responses. Disseminating quarantine requirements and auditing levels of compliance with biosecurity standards have become increasingly important (Hall, 2005). So too have arrival information services, border controls, eradication and containment strategies and strict policing. Post-border management interventions may include placing limits on numbers of participations, restrictions on the duration, timing and frequency of sport competitions, as well as restrictions on permissible equipment. Where biodiversity issues exist in consumptive sport, catch limits, size limits, legal and non-legal target species, open and closed seasons, exclusion zones, policing, limitations on equipment and law enforcement activities have become increasingly commonplace.

Sport, tourism and climate change

The Intergovernmental Panel on Climate Change (IPCC) and the Stern report (2006) projections on climate change signal an austere warning for changes in earth surface air temperature, ocean temperature, sea level, ecological systems and climatic variability. However, it is generally accepted that the consequences of climate change will be wide in regional variation in terms of changes in air temperature, wind, rainfall, temperate, humidity and cloud patterns (de Freitas, 2005). Evidence to date supports the likelihood of high climate change variability, including changes in the frequency, intensity and duration of extreme weather events, such as cyclones, floods, droughts and heat waves. The temporal manifestations of climate change will also vary giving rise to new seasonal variations in the attractiveness of places (Hall & Higham, 2005). Physical, aesthetic and environmental consequences of climate change will influence the attractiveness of destinations as places to visit, possibly to the point of reformulating established and dominant patterns of mobility (Hall, 2005).

It is difficult to envisage any sports that are not subject to some degree to the uncertainties of climate change. For example, ski slopes lacking the requisite snow cover have become an increasingly common occurrence, particularly at lower-elevation ski resorts (Viner & Agnew, 1999). The risks of land instability in alpine areas have become more acute due to the melting of permafrost (Hall, 2005). In both cases, new images of destinations and activities may be developed or reinforced. Snowmaking equipment now forms a central element in the landscapes of many winter sports. However, the financial costs of adequate snowmaking facilities, as well as the energy and water resource costs of snow production, pose additional issues in a time of heightened climate change concern.

The direct consequences of climate change may extend to comfort levels, health concerns or risks for sport participants as well as changes in the comfort levels of both athletes and spectators. Elements of facility design (e.g., retractable stadium roofs, climate-controlled venues) and sport science responses (e.g., relating to athlete hydration and body temperate) are already evident. Direct consequences may extend to the abandonment of activities either at certain locations or altogether or the relocation of activities from one location to another. This may pose a direct threat to locations of tradition as activities become increasingly marginalized. It may also present opportunities for existing resorts to respond to climate change or for new locations to capitalize on emerging opportunities relating to new or existing activities and experiences. The shift in focus from winter sport resorts to all-season, multiple use (including multiple sports) resorts is a case in point (Hudson, 2003).

The indirect consequences of climate change on sport and mobility are also foreseeable to an extent. Hall and Higham (2005:15) note that 'at a broad scale of analysis climate change will likely mean not that people will stop travelling but that they will change their travel preferences in both space and time'. Thus, climate change will result in reformulated social, economic and regulatory conditions that influence patterns of mobility, including those relating to sports. This may include the abandonment or reduction of visits to certain destinations for specific purposes. Sports that take place in natural settings, generally set in peripheral locations that are removed from major markets, are perhaps most susceptible to the likelihood of regulatory regimes to counter carbon emissions from long-distance travel and related factors that are now known to contribute to atmospheric change (Hall & Higham, 2005). The replacement of multiple short-duration visits to sports resorts with less frequent, longer-duration visits to reduce the carbon footprint of repeat travel may be another response to climate concern. The advantages of proximity to airports and cheap air travel routes may be countered as travellers seek to engage in modes of transport that are less heavy in carbon emissions.

Responsiveness to climate change is increasingly apparent in the landscape elements of sport (*see* Case study 11.1). Stadiums are more likely than in the past to be built in association with public rather than private transport accessibility in an attempt to reduce the carbon footprint of transport. Manchester

City Football Club (MCFC) has recently submitted to the Manchester City Council (MCC) a proposal to make The City of Manchester Stadium the first sports stadium in the world to be powered solely by renewable energy. This proposal is closely linked to the Manchester Sportcity programme. The Sportcity renewable energy initiatives include an 85m-high wind turbine and solar panels, sufficient to provide the energy requirements of the stadium and power 4,000 homes in the vicinity when the stadium is not in use. While this initiative has been positioned foremost as an example of leadership in climate change initiatives, it is also noteworthy that it continues a long history of energy production in East Manchester, one of the first industrialized cities.

Case Study 11.1

The 2006 FIFA World Cup and climate change

Mass public events consume considerable energy resources, mostly through transport, stadium floodlighting and illumination. Climate change planning for the 2006 Fédération Internationale de Football Association (FIFA) World Cup hosted by Germany was documented in the 'Green Goal' (2004) report, which predicted greenhouse gas emissions equivalent to 114,000 tonnes of carbon dioxide in the absence of climate change initiatives. FIFA (2004) documented an energy target of a 20% reduction in energy consumption at World Cup stadiums. This target was not met although an overall energy consumption reduction of 13% was achieved. Measures that contributed to this result included the installation of solar power amounting to 2.5 million kilowatt hours of electricity at World Cup sites including Kaiserslautern and Dortmund. It has been estimated that the positive energy legacy of this investment will equal the total energy budget of the 2006 FIFA World Cup within five years. Thirteen million kilowatt hours of certified green electricity from hydropower were purchased from Switzerland between January and June 2006 and assigned to the World Cup.

Stadium design for the Football World Cup considered the carbon footprint of journeys to and from venues. The organizing committee established a target of 50% of all spectators arriving at venues by public transport, a target that was surpassed (57% of all journeys to World Cup stadiums were on public transport while a further 6% arrived on foot and 11% by coach). The scepticism surrounding carbon offsetting notwithstanding (Monbiot, 2007), the event organizers purchased €500,000 of carbon offsets in India and South Africa, which were estimated to save 100,000 tonnes of carbon dioxide entering the global atmosphere (FIFA, 2004)

Other initiatives relating to resource conservation were implemented in advance of the 2006 FIFA World Cup. Rainwater harvesting systems were installed at stadiums in Berlin, Nuremberg and Stuttgart, and water-saving toilets and the deployment of dry urinals at some stadiums were also used to reduce water consumption. Fundamentally, Green Goal (2004) represents a pioneering initiative relating to the use of scarce resources in the hosting of a sports mega-event. Stadium design, energy efficiency initiatives and the use of carbon neutral power sources during the 2006 FIFA World Cup in Germany demonstrate a new commitment to the landscapes of sport in light of climate change and concerns for the conservation of scarce resources.

Source

FIFA (2004). Green Goal: The environmental concept for the 2006 FIFA World Cup.
http://www.oeko.de/oekodoc/292/2006-011-en.pdf (retrieved 21 October 2008).

BUILT LANDSCAPES FOR SPORT

An interesting discourse in the sports literature relates to whether globalization is leading toward a homogenization of sport culture or whether resistance, be it local, regional or national, will retain or enhance differences between places (see Chapter 2, *Sport and tourism in a global world*). The emergence of homogenous sportscapes, including the precise and standardized spatial elements of sports fields (Bale, 1993) as well as increasing uniformity in stadium design are evidence of global standardization. Hinch and Higham (2004) argue that within a tourism context, the trend towards a homogeneous global sports culture would, to some degree, act as a disincentive to travel for sport. 'Homogenisation heralds the advent of an era dominated by creeping global standardization. Heterogenisation, however, rejects the influence of global technologies and products in favour of stressing the inherent uniqueness of localities' (Silk & Jackson, 2000:102).

The modern stadium is an intriguing subject of debate regarding globalization and the homogenization of the sportscape. The term sportscape has been used in the geography of sport to describe the highly modified and technologized sports environment (Bale, 1994). While there are manifold ways in which sports can infuse space with meaning, Bale (1989) notes the emergence of sportscapes as a counter trend, to the point that sportscapes give rise to a sense of 'placelessness' (Relph, 1976). Bale (1989) observes that 'in the twentieth century sportscapes rather than landscapes have tended to characterize the sports environment' whilst also noting that '... the degree to which the natural environment needs to change varies between sports' (Bale, 1989:145).

Sport is relatively unique insofar as it is subject to relentless pressure to make one place of competition exactly the same as another (Bale, 1989). The various forces driving the creation of sportscapes are diverse. Much justification for the creation of sportscapes is derived from athletic demands. The standardization of playing fields and sites of competition is driven by the need to foster even competition between places and performance record keeping (i.e., creating 'level playing fields'). This trend now extends to the neutralization of local weather conditions (e.g., through the development of retractable stadium or arena enclosures), formerly regarded as a defining element of home ground advantage. The desire to foster improved athletic performance is also a factor of relevance to this discussion. Technological demands relating to the standardization of the television broadcasting of live sport (e.g., venue flood lighting), and media reporting, are also global forces driving the creation of sportscapes.

Globalization and mobility have combined to create new and heightened spectator and participant demands for comfort and safety in the sport experience. Indeed Bale (1993) uses the 'stadium as theatre' metaphor to highlight various important elements of the spatial dynamics of the stadium. One key element, of course, is the use of 'actors' and 'audience', which is common to theatre and stadium. Another is the hosting of spectacles. Again, both stadiums and theatres are places where spectacles are planned and staged (Bale, 1993) and where audiences are segmented based on rank or class. An interesting aspect of the 'stadium as theatre' metaphor is the 'move in spectating behaviour towards ritual' (Bale, 1993:320) in which the behaviours of the audience are transformed from the individual to the collective. The counter trend to create segregated, seated and passive spectator experiences, as epitomized through the British Government's response to the Taylor Report (1990), is another example of standardization in the built sports environment.

Trends that run counter to globalization and homogenization are also evident (Maguire, 1999). Maguire (1999:213) suggests that globalization should be understood as a balance between 'diminishing contrasts and increasing varieties'. The view that in sport the forces for homogeneity and heterogeneity coexist is widespread (Merkel, Lines & McDonald, 1998; Washington & Karen, 2001; Harvey & Houle, 1994) (see Chapter 2, *Sport and tourism in a global world*). Regionally or nationally distinct sports (Rowe *et al.*, 1994), the negotiation of introduced sports (Jackson & Andrews, 1999), resistance to new sports (Sugden & Tomlinson, 1996) and the biases of regional and national media representation in sport (Bernstein, 2000) all point towards the power of local/regional and national negotiation and resistance in the globalization of sport. The same, it might be argued, applies to the modern landscapes of sport, where the forces of homogeneity and heterogeneity are continually being negotiated at the local level.

RETRO PARKS

Nostalgia plays a critical part in identity creation and authentic experiences. It is an important determinant of personal and social identify (Davis, 1979) as it is a factor that influences 'how one defines and views oneself in the past, present and/or future' (Fairley & Gammon, 2005:183). Fairley and Gammon's (2005) writing on sport and nostalgia addresses this subject in two parts; nostalgia for sport place or artefact and nostalgia for sport experiences. Elements of the sport landscape ensemble as they relate to sport place and artefact have expanded in recent years to include halls of fame, sports museums and stadium tours, all of which represent the creation of heritage or nostalgic experiences. Of particular relevance to the discussions presented in this chapter, however, are changes to the collective ensemble of the sports place. The creation of spaces of consumption, tourist and entertainment enclaves in inner city settings, has seen a move towards urban sports places. Indeed, in some cases the development of sports venues in inner city locations has taken place in spite of compromises to the spatial elements of the sports stadium (*see* Case study 11.2).

Case Study 11.2

Retro ballparks and the changing urban landscape
Dan Mason (University of Alberta, Canada)

Cities throughout the world, including those in North America, have moved away from traditional industrial economies towards more flexible, service- and consumption-based economies (Fainstein & Campbell, 2002). As a result, industries such as tourism have emerged as particularly critical ways in which cities have reinvented themselves in light of economic decline (Kotler, Haider & Rein, 1993). Within this context, cities have also attempted to reinvigorate their downtown cores through the development of tourism bubbles that create consumption destinations for visitors and locals alike (Hannigan, 1998). In doing so, cities are repositioning their downtowns as exciting places to visit, work and invest and are attempting to project a new image that counteracts notions of downtowns as decrepit, dangerous areas of a city. Thus, the goal is to create recreational and entertainment amenities that will make downtowns vibrant hubs of activity.

Many cities throughout North America have used the construction of a major-league sports facility as an anchor of such development, where games played throughout the season ensure that visitors will be present and that activity will be going on in the local area. Typically called stadium or arena districts, these areas feature other amenities such as movie and performing arts theatres, retail, dining and hotels. Using this strategy, cities like Baltimore, MD, and Indianapolis, IN, have developed long-term urban development plans that feature multiple major sports infrastructure development projects (Euchner, 1992; Rosentraub, 1997).

This strategy emerged during the early 1990s and continues today. While many early sports facilities had been sited in or near downtown cores, by the 1950s larger, multipurpose facilities were being built in suburban locations, designed for ease of access to major roadways (Ritzer & Stillman, 2001). A milestone in the trend to relocate sports facilities back to downtown occurred with the construction of Oriole Park at Camden Yards in 1992 (OPCY). The facility, designed to host the Baltimore Orioles of Major League Baseball, was significantly different from its predecessors. It was not designed for uses other than baseball and attempted to integrate more seamlessly into the surrounding urban landscape. It was built using brick that matched other surrounding buildings, including the massive B & O Warehouse that, rather than being demolished, became a backdrop for the stadium and home to offices and meeting areas for the team and fans (Richmond, 1995).

OPCY was also different from the stadiums built during the 1970s and 1980s, in that its designers deliberately tried to capture design elements of bygone baseball fields, which often featured asymmetrical fields and facility dimensions as they were forced to fit into the surrounding urban environment. The ballpark featured many nostalgic elements, including exposed beams and the aforementioned use of brick. The facility was an immediate success and became another component of the city of Baltimore's broader Inner Harbor development.

Despite paying homage to bygone facilities, OPCY was clearly designed to maximize revenues for the team, with an emphasis on premium seating and maximizing other ancillary revenues (Ritzer & Stillman, 2001). Seeing the success of OPCY, it did not take long before other major league baseball (MLB) teams and cities began clamouring to build their own baseball parks as part of larger, integrated urban development projects. Notably, Cleveland opened Jacobs Field in 1994, which would ultimately be accompanied downtown by a new basketball arena, football stadium, and the Rock and Roll Hall of Fame and Museum. Through the present, no less than fourteen new facilities have been built for MLB teams in the United States. These developments have attempted to create a nostalgic sport experience through unique stadium features (Rosensweig, 2005).

These new retro ballparks can be considered 'hybrid' facilities that feature state-of-the-art design, modern amenities, while still emphasizing historic elements. Some have considered this a process of 'reenchantment', where appeals to the memories of baseball fans have been exploited to maximize revenues (Ritzer & Stillman, 2001). Seen in this way, cities and teams have been able to tap into nostalgic elements associated with their local teams and community in order to create the sports facility as a destination for tourists and locals alike.

Fairley and Gammon (2005) identified that there are two ways in which nostalgia has been leveraged for sport tourism; one relates to nostalgia for sport place (or artefact), while the other relates to the social experience itself. While the former is clearly being employed with the design of retro ballparks, the manner through which the latter is being leveraged is less clear (Mason, Duquette & Scherer, 2005). As cities build their own nostalgia-linked retro ballparks, it will become increasingly difficult for cities to differentiate themselves from others as each city will provide a similarly 'unique' fan experience at their respective retro ballparks. Previous work on sports fans (Fairley, 2003) has suggested that many fans are interested in attending sporting events due to the social experience of attending the games with their peers. As a result, cities interested in gaining competitive advantage using sports facility-based tourism might be encouraged to better understand and exploit any unique links the city has to a specific sport, and focus on creating a fan experience that might be more difficult for other cities to reproduce elsewhere. In other words, the nostalgic association with the sports experience must be better grounded in the local experience and not simply provide a generic nostalgic experience that can be achieved elsewhere. If it does not, then other cities can reproduce a similar tourism experience and any competitive advantages for the city will be lost.

Selected references

Euchner, C.C. (1993). *Playing the Field: Why Sports Teams Move and Cities Fight to Keep Them*. Baltimore: The Johns Hopkins University Press.

Fairley, S. (2003). In search of relived social experience: Group-based nostalgia sport tourism. *Journal of Sport Management*, 17, 284–304.

Fairley, S. and Gammon, S. (2005). Something lived, something learned: Nostalgia's expanding role in sport tourism. *Sport in Society*, 8, 182–197.

Mason, D.S., Duquette, G.H. and Scherer, J. (2005). Heritage, sport tourism and Canadian junior hockey: Nostalgia for social experience or sport place? *Journal of Sport Tourism*, 10, 253–271.

Ramshaw (2006) identifies that 'a trend of revisiting antiquated sports landscapes has begun in earnest' in which 'stadia and sporting events are being placed in a nostalgic or heritage-based light', creating new sports landscapes in the process. In times of upheaval it is common to revisit or reinterpret the past as a strategy for coping with uncertainty in times of rapid change (Hewison, 1987). Ramshaw (2006) hypothesizes that this perhaps explains the growing prominence of heritage in sport given the upheavals of professionalization, sport labour and team franchise mobility, industrial action and steroid use in contemporary sport. He refers to this as the 'heritage industry of sport' (Ramshaw, 2006:1). Manifestations of the heritage industry of sport include the rise of television networks such as ESPN Classic, which are dedicated to replaying historic sports events and championship contests, as well as the growth of heritage sports apparel and the use of historic team uniforms by professional teams to mark anniversaries or milestones of team or club significance (Ramshaw, 2006).

The creation of 'retro parks' such as Oriole Park baseball stadium at Camden Yards (Baltimore, USA) in 1992 is, quite literally, concrete evidence of the heritage industry that has been embraced by some professional sports since the early 1990s. OPCY stadium stimulated the redevelopment of Baltimore's inner harbour and the creation of a 'tourism bubble' of service provision, entertainment and consumption. The move away from multipurpose stadiums to the construction of a unique, single-purpose retro park represented an attempt to build the Orioles' fan base, attract new fans and corporate clients and create visitor interest among non-resident sports fans and tourists. This template has become widely adopted in subsequent years (Table 11.1) to the point that some see OPCY as the original or authentic retro park (Ramshaw, 2006). Menefee (2005) examined attendance, winning percentage, revenue and team value comparing baseball teams using

Table 11.1	North American MLB Franchises that Redeveloped Retro Stadiums Between 1992 and 2004		
Franchise Stadium Name		**Year**	**Capacity**
Baltimore Orioles Oriole Park at Camden Yards		1992	48,876
Cleveland Indians Jacobs Field		1994	43,405
Texas Rangers Ameriquest Field		1994	49,115
Colorado Rockies Coors Field		1995	50,445
Atlanta Braves Turner Field		1997	50,096
Seattle Mariners Safeco Field		1999	47,116
Detroit Tigers Comerica Park		2000	40,120
Houston Astros Minute Maid Park		2000	40,950
San Francisco Giants SBC Park		2000	41,503
Milwaukee Brewers Miller Park		2001	42,400
Pittsburgh Pirates PNC Park		2001	38,496
Cincinnati Reds Great American Ballpark		2003	42,271
Philadelphia Phillies Citizens Bank Park		2004	43,826
San Diego Padres Petco Park		2004	42,445

(Source: Menefee, 2005:33)

multipurpose stadiums and those that had relocated to retro parks in the 1992–2004 period. Three of these variables, the exception being winning percentage, were increased at a higher rate for teams that had built retro stadiums. Menefee (2005) reports that in the first season in new retro stadium facilities average attendance across all fourteen franchises increased by an average of 9725 fans per game. While average total attendance did then decline over time, the sustained increase in average attendance (SIAA) for MLB franchises playing in retro stadiums remained consistently higher than the average increases for franchises not playing in retro stadiums (Menefee, 2005).

At a more general level Ramshaw (2006) identifies three reasons that explain the interest in creating retro parks in North America. First, while many North American cities have undergone economic, social and environmental transformation in the last two decades, including the loss of many primary industries, the creation of retro parks offers the opportunity to engage in urban regeneration while creating heritage landscapes and centres for consumption. Furthermore, heritage or retro sports landscapes offer simplicity and comfort and as such 'reject the codified nature of modern professional sport, and look to a time (real or imagined) when the ways and places where sport was played were uncomplicated and serene' (Ramshaw, 2006:2). Ramshaw (2006) notes that the popularity of retro parks may be interpreted as a rejection of the upheavals and uncertainties of modern sport and the compromise of traditional values of sport competition. The sport experience is perhaps well served by links to the heritage and identities of traditional sports. Thirdly, sports teams provide a tangible link to the identity of the places they represent, and as such the images, memories, nostalgia and perhaps even fiction associated with sports spaces (e.g., stadiums) create connections with the past that have a strong appeal for some sport spectators.

These points help to explain the existence of a trend that runs counter to the development of homogenized sportscapes (Bales, 2003). It is this counter trend that, according to the evidence of Menefee (2005) and Ramshaw (2006), adds to and embellishes the cultural mosaic that makes tourism destinations unique. However, in terms of the landscapes of sport, it is noteworthy that built sports resources including retro parks can be readily transported (see Chapter 13, *Sport and place competition*). As Mason notes, given that built resources can be recreated (*see* Case study 11.1) it is the social experience of sport (as a composite of activity, people and place) that should be developed as a unique competitive advantage for tourism destinations (see Chapter 6, *Spectatorship and spectator experiences*).

LANDSCAPES OF SPORT AND SOCIETY

Globalization of the media and increased personal and information mobility have given rise to widespread concern for the safety and sustainability of sportscapes. Stadiums have in the past been synonymous with a range of social impacts such as litter, traffic congestion and lack of parking but most particularly perhaps antisocial behaviour. The stadium is a hotbed of parochialism and identity formation. It is also a highly gendered setting that offers intensity and potential for confrontation and aggression. The links between crowd conflict at stadiums, fighting between groups of rival fans and riot police are not new.

Jones (2001) points out that the social impacts of stadium developments more generally accrue unevenly across different sections of society. It is typical that women gain less benefit from the construction of a stadium given that stadiums are generally venues for male-dominated sports. Thus, opportunity costs associated with stadium development arise from the commitment of resources from facilities that may have benefited other groups within the community (Lee, 2002). The negative social costs associated with a stadium facility are borne locally. While providing top-class sports events and 'propagating a consumerist vision of international culture' may satisfy many stadium users, Jones (2001:853) argues that this may or may not constitute a substantial contribution to the local community. Local residents may also perceive anti-social behaviours associated with large recurrent gatherings of event goers to be a negative impact on the community. This may be felt particularly in cases where stadiums are located in residential areas.

Lee (2002:863) reports on a community workshop held to discuss resident views on Vancouver's BC Place stadium in which the facility was described as a 'rather unfriendly, under-utilised, monolithic structure, isolated from adjoining areas'. In order to combat this image it is argued that stadiums need to be 'socialized' for multiple, wider and inclusive community use rather than an exclusive and male-dominated domain. Developing sustainable stadium–community partnerships has in recent years extended to local health improvement strategies (Ratinckx & Crabb, 2005). This has emerged as one means by which to ensure that a stadium makes a positive contribution at the local community level. Thus, the term 'healthy stadium' has entered the vernacular to describe a stadium that promotes the health of visitors, sports fans and the local community, where people can engage in positive, healthy experiences playing or watching sport or a range of other cultural activities. The concept of the 'healthy stadium' is based on creating supportive and healthy working and living environments, integrating health promotion into the daily activities of the setting and integrating healthy living initiatives of the stadium with the wider community.

A range of 'healthy stadium' initiatives that have become part of stadium experience and/or the community outreach programmes include healthy eating, responsible alcohol consumption, physical exercise and activity, sustainable travel, healthy lifestyles (including anti-smoking), environmental awareness and widening community access to stadiums. The development of stadiums in association with tertiary education institutions, including in some cases sports and health science disciplines such as physical education (e.g., biomechanics, kinaesiology, sports psychology), sports medicine (e.g., epidemiology, injury prevention, sports physiotherapy) and public health (e.g., human nutrition, diabetes research, public education and awareness), has emerged as a recent development in integrated stadium design. Such initiatives provide a synergy that serves healthy stadium and community integration programmes that are intended to achieve positive rather than negative stadium impacts at the local community level.

CONCLUSION

Discourses on globalization raise a number of fundamental debates (see Chapter 2, *Sport and tourism in a global world*). One relates to whether globalization leads to a creeping standardization of the landscapes of sport. Bale (1993) argues that the forces in sport to create 'level playing fields' have given rise to sportscapes that are barely differentiated between different parts of the world. Simultaneously, it is evident that local resistance and the negotiation of global forces can safeguard differences between places (Bale, 2000; Silk, 2004), perhaps extending to a globalization counter trend that will see elements of local uniqueness and heritage fostered to entrench differences between places. Indeed, the coexistence of opposing forces for homogeneity and diversification is now widely acknowledged (Washington & Karen, 2001; Harvey & Houle, 1994).

This chapter recognizes evidence of growing local diversification in sport, set within the wider context of globalization. However, replication and imitation will remain a threat to the uniqueness of tourism places and tourist experiences in a global world in which many sports resources are highly transportable. The widespread replication of retro parks following the Oriole Park (1992) model is clear evidence of the systematic erosion of local uniqueness through imitation. The competitiveness of tourism destinations is to a degree determined by unique local initiatives relating to the landscapes of sport, both natural and built. That said, it is apparent that the unique experiences of sports places, for both local communities and visitors alike, remain a critical element of the competitiveness of tourism destinations.

CHAPTER 12

Place Attachment

Tourism is about places. It is about the difference between places and the flow of travellers who seek out these differences. In the case of sport tourism, it involves the search for places that provide sporting opportunities and experiences that cannot be obtained by staying at home. This chapter emphasizes the relevance of sport places to place attachment. Despite its relevance to sport and tourism, place has received relatively little attention in the sport tourism literature. Here we explore the concept of place as it relates to sports, arguing that sport may be an important place maker.

PLACE AND PLACE ATTACHMENT

Place is a complex concept that is not easily analysed and broken down into component parts. It is holistic in nature and while there may be shared interpretations of a place (Eisenhauer, Krannich & Blahna, 2000), at its core, place meaning resides in the minds of individuals. Despite these challenges, and the multiple perspectives from which place is examined, there is widespread agreement that place is space that is infused with meaning. 'What begins as undifferentiated space becomes a place as we get to know it better and endow it with value' (Tuan, 1974:6). Crouch (2000:64) distinguishes place from space in a tourism context by suggesting:

> ... [s]pace can be a background, a context, a 'given' objective component of leisure and tourism. In that way it is seen as a location, a National Park or a site where particular leisure/tourism happens, a distance between things. Place can be a physical image that can be rendered metaphorical as the content of brochures, 'landscape' as a foil for what people might imagine they do… In this way it may be

*that place is understood to be a cultural text that people read and
recognize directed by the particular intentions of a producer or
promoter.*

Under this conceptualization, there is no inherent 'true' meaning associated with place (Davis, 2005). Meanings are negotiated and may be influenced by cultural, political and economic interests. Given the dynamics of
globalization, this process of negotiation is one of the few constants.

The construct of place attachment is a useful way of studying place
(Williams, Patterson & Roggenbuck, 1992; Kyle, Graefe & Manning, 2005).
In the context of leisure and recreation, Williams et al. (1992) argue that
place is not just an economic commodity but encompasses emotional as
well as functional ties between people and environmental settings. It is
articulated as being a blend of place dependence and place identity. Williams
et al. (1992) developed a survey instrument to measure place attachment,
thereby enabling considerable empirical insight to be gained in this area. In
terms of its component parts, place dependence is concerned with 'how well
a setting serves goal achievement given an existing range of alternatives'
(Jorgensen & Stedman, 2001:234). It measures function and the subject's
willingness to substitute other sites for their particular activities (Kyle,
Absher & Graefe, 2003). In contrast, place identity involves

*... those dimensions of self that define the individual's personal
identity in relation to the physical environment by means of
a complex pattern of conscious and unconscious ideas, beliefs,
preferences, feelings, values, goals, and behavioral tendencies and
skills relevant to this environment.* (Proshansky, 1978:155)

Place identity is emotional/symbolic in nature rather than functional and
reflects the importance of a setting to an individual's perception of self (see
Chapter 4, *Culture and identity*).

The subfield of leisure and recreation has been dominated by place-based
research related to outdoor recreation (e.g., Kyle, Graefe & Manning, 2005).
With the exception of Bale's (e.g., 1989, 1993) work, there has been relatively
little examination of place, let alone place attachment, in the realm of sport.
This lack of attention is surprising given the potential of sport to influence
place identity and given sport's unique dependence on specific types of
settings. It is also surprising given the challenges and opportunities that sport
faces in an increasingly globalized world as suggested by Williams and Kal-
ternborn (1999:215).

*With circulation and movement more the rule than the exception an
important geographic dimension of leisure [sport] practices is to*

understand how people in differing cultural contexts use leisure and travel to establish identity, give meaning to their lives, and connect to place.

Sport settings and place attachment

Tuan (1974, 1975) argued that the development of sense of place normally requires long residence and deep involvement with an emphasis on home. Relph (1976) adopted a similar position with his suggestion that sense of place was most applicable in the local environment, where individuals are in a position to develop deep attachments rather than the superficial connections commonly associated with tourism. In fact, he used the 'disneyfied' landscapes of tourism as an example of one of the least likely settings for sense of place to develop.

Clearly, home environments foster place attachment but this does not negate the significance of other settings. One of Tuan's (1975:164) central points was that '[h]ome is place because it encloses space and thereby creates an "inside" and an "outside"'. Competitive sport offers a similar potential with its distinction between home and away. Spectators cheering the home side may feel closely connected to a stadium even if they travelled a great distance to get there. Similarly, recreational sport subcultures present their own unique determination of who 'insiders' are relative to 'outsiders', with these insiders having the potential of forming strong attachments to the places where they engage in their sport. Tuan (1975:165) argued that

> *[t]o remain a place it has to be lived in. This is a platitude unless we examine what 'lived in' means. To live in a place is to experience it, to be aware of it in the bones as well as with the head.*

In many ways, engagement in sport is the epitome of 'living in' a setting given the potential depth of sporting engagements and emotions. The kinaesthetic nature of sport very literally fosters a connection between the participants' 'bones' (skeletal, muscular and nervous system) and the setting.

Crouch's (2000:68) discussion of embodiment through sport is consistent with this view.

> *'Embodiment' is a process of experiencing, making sense, knowing through practice as a sensual human subject in the world. The subject engages space and space becomes embodied in three ways. First, the person grasps the world multi-sensually. Second, the body is 'surrounded' by space and encounters it multi-dimensionally. Third,*

*through the body the individual expresses him/herself through the
surrounding space and thereby changes its meaning.*

Athletes involved in extreme sports in natural settings exemplify
embodiment and the likelihood of it leading to place attachment, but this
argument can be extended even to the realm of sport spectatorship. Spectators experience the event multi-sensually as they watch the competition,
listen to the players, announcers and crowd noises, smell and taste the food
prepared in the stadium and feel the ebb and flow of the game albeit on the
'seat of their pants'. As stadiums grow larger, emerging technologies like the
live broadcast of referee comments mitigate the space boundaries between
players and spectators. In conjunction with these connections to place, the
fact that sporting competitions are characterized by unpredictable outcomes
serves to engage spectators emotionally. Crouch (2000) captures the essence
of this embodiment argument by suggesting that, 'Leisure/tourism [and
sport] are moments of expression through the body that activate places'
(Crouch, 2000:69). Such activation is one of the key ways that sport fosters
place attachment.

At another level, but closely related to the embodiment argument, the
unique type of physical movement associated with a particular sporting
activity provides a specific and often powerful link to a place. For example,
Crang (2004:82) suggests that

*the mode of perceiving the landscape and our bodily relationship may
well change, as where we think of a shift from the physical exertion of
slowly climbing a peak to the stomach-churning thrill of hurtling from
a bridge on a bungee line…from an appreciation of the individual and
sublime nature we have an accelerated body and an inverted sublime
or a body pitted against the rocks and rapids in whitewater rafting…*

Others, such as Warzecha and Lime (2001), express a similar view by noting
that passive activities normally are less place dependent than active sport
activities such as white-water rafting. In the latter activities, the recreationist
is not only in much more direct contact with the setting, but is in fact
dependent on this setting.

PLACE DEPENDENCE

There has been a surprising lack of attention directed toward the concept of
place dependence in the literature. While it has been widely incorporated as
a dimension of place attachment in empirical research (e.g., Williams et al.,

1992; Kyle et al., 2005), it is seldom discussed in detail within these studies. One exception is Jacob and Schreyer's (1980:373) reference to 'the importance an individual attaches to the use of a particular recreation resource'. More commonly, however, researchers defer to the theorizing of Stokols and Shumaker (1981:457) who defined this functional dimension of place attachment as 'an occupant's perceived strength of association between him- or her-self and specific places'. This association is based on the potential of a place to meet the specific needs of the user and how well it compares to other places in terms of this potential.

A place dependence framework

Stokols and Shumaker's (1981) framework of place dependence is divided into two main parts (also see Shumaker & Taylor, 1983). First, occupants of settings assess their dependence on a particular setting in terms of its quality relative to their activity needs. Second, they compare the potential of this setting to meet their needs against the potential of alternative places. In both cases, an occupant's assessment of place dependence tends to be subjective.

At a site level, individuals make subjective assessments by comparing the outcomes of their site-based sport activities with their expectations. The difference between these comparative points determines their level of satisfaction. Key factors in this determination include: 1) the level of previous experience that these occupants have had in terms of the sporting activity and in terms of other sites; 2) the amount, calibre and utility of the resources for a given sporting activity; and 3) the value or salience of each goal associated with the resource needs of the activity. Sport tourists also assess the ability of a setting to meet specific activity goals by comparing it against other settings. Key factors in this comparison include: 1) the level of awareness that an individual has of other settings; 2) how familiar or how much experience the individual has at these sites; 3) how mobile the individual is; and 4) the degree of resource specificity associated with the activity.

More generally, an assessment of place dependence is tied to its character. The greater the number of specific needs that a place is able to meet relative to a particular sport activity, the more embedded and extensive place attachment is likely to be. If the setting meets higher-order needs such as self-actualization as well as basic needs related to survival and belonging, it is likely to be more valued than if it is only meeting the lower-level needs. Finally, place dependence is influenced by temporal factors such as an appreciation of decreasing setting options over time. An awareness of the loss of natural sites due to urban sprawl is one example of this. Similarly, an individual who has been forced to abandon an activity site that was highly valued may be nostalgic for the former site and, therefore, be harsher in the assessment of the ability of the new site to meet his or her goals.

Sport and place dependence

While Stokols and Shumaker (1981) used a variety of sport examples (e.g., surfing and downhill skiing) to illustrate their framework, there are several unique features of sport that bear additional emphasis. First, one of the distinctive dimensions of sport is that it is usually rule bound, with many of these rules articulated in terms of space and time (Hinch & Higham, 2004). The specific regulations of individual sports may, therefore, contain activity goals that are more objective than those found in other types of activities. Second, sport settings can also be divided into those that are built and, as a result, are relatively transportable versus those that are based on natural resources and are, therefore, dependent on natural resource characteristics on site (see Chapter 3, *Sport and contemporary mobility*). Typically, participants have more choice in terms of built facilities although the high costs associated with the development and operation of facilities such as swimming pools and stadiums tend to limit their location to urban areas of sufficient population to meet threshold use levels (Bale, 1989; Hinch & Higham, 2004). Sports, such as white-water kayaking or downhill skiing, that require a specific combination of natural resources are often found in peripheral areas. Their successful development depends not only on these resources but also on transportation access and supporting infrastructure. Third, assessments of place tend to be made in the context of performance objectives. It is not just a matter of experience but also a matter of skill. The types of terrain that provide a novice snowboarder or kayaker with an enjoyable experience are much different from those required by advanced or elite participants in these sports. Finally, the range of flexibility in terms of resource calibre narrows considerably as the competitive nature of the sport increases.

The example of downhill skiing helps to illustrate the utility of Stokols and Shumaker's (1981) framework. In assessing a specific downhill resort in terms of place dependence, a skier or snowboarder makes subjective decisions about how well the resort meets his/her activity objectives. He or she compares resource qualities such as snow conditions, terrain, quality of trails and perhaps ungroomed terrain as well as a multitude of service aspects, access, social interactions and other qualities. Such qualities are assessed in terms of the number of these characteristics that are present, the quality of these resources and their overall capacity to facilitate the desired skiing experience. Given the different expectations of skiers in terms of their previous experience, skills and competitiveness, levels of place dependence vary from one individual to the next.

Skiers and snowboarders also compare their experience at a given resort to their experience at other resorts. Such comparisons are influenced by their exposure to broadcasts of skiing and snowboarding events at other sites, word-of-mouth, promotional material and other sources of information to which they have been exposed. Their ability and willingness to travel are also factors. The resorts that they feel are inaccessible are then excluded from their comparison group. Resource specificity is a major element in the assessment of skiing/snowboarding resorts. For example, advanced skiers are unlikely to rate resorts highly that have terrain dominated by beginner or intermediate trails. In terms of the general character of the place, while it may be true that a recreational skier may value the place more highly if it meets a large number of his/her needs, an expert skier/snowboarder is more likely to weight a characteristic like snow conditions higher than a bundle of lesser-valued aspects. Skiers/snowboarders who identify strongly with the skiing/snowboarding subcultures are likely to be more dependent on specific sites than casual participants. Finally, as urban sprawl and development encroach on what would formally have been considered a potential downhill skiing/snowboarding site, skiers/snowboarders are likely to have a greater appreciation of their dependence on existing sites.

PLACE IDENTITY

The second major component of place attachment is place identity or the emotional/symbolic bond between an individual or group and a setting. As in the case of place dependence, sport and tourism play a significant role in the determination of place identity. Case study 12.1 explores one intriguing aspect of place identity construction as it relates to sport and tourism, specifically how global flows of sport tourists may prompt mediation (and be mediated in ways) that is directed in terms of selected place identities. This section then expands on the basic concept of place and its link to identity.

Case Study 12.1

Sport, tourism and cultural encounter: The 2005 Lions tour and the 'Barmy Army' in Aotearoa New Zealand
Mark Falcous (University of Otago)
The 2005 British and Irish Lions (hereafter, the Lions) rugby tour of New Zealand was a significant tourist event with economic, social and cultural dimensions. For the purposes of this brief case study, it provides insights into the ways a sports tourist influx was significant in informing the mediated identity politics which are a constituent part of global interdependence. Specifically, the Lions tour revealed ways in which cultural 'encounters' associated with the global

flows of sports tourism were mediated in ways that evoked and re-energized particular, selective, place-based national identities.

Whilst there has been a wealth of research revealing how media constructions of international sports events are active in evocations of nationalism of various kinds (Maguire & Poulton, 1999; Maguire & Tuck, 1998; Garland & Rowe, 1999; Bishop & Jawaorski, 2003), little has been said to connect them with the mobilities of sports tourists which increasingly surround these events. Yet what was evident in research surrounding both the New Zealand press coverage (Falcous & West, 2008) and advertising (Falcous, 2007) associated with the 2005 Lions tour was the way the travelling British and Irish fans were significant in informing media constructions surrounding the tour. This case study points to how the 'Barmy Army' (the epithet by which Lions fans came to be known) provided a stimulus for nationalist discourse in particular, selective ways.

Contextualizing the Lions Tour and mediated nationalisms

Historically, men's rugby union has been a central pillar of dominant narratives of New Zealand nationhood (Crawford, 1985; Fougere, 1989; Phillips, 1987; MacLean, 1999; Hope, 2002; Ryan, 2005; Hokowhitu, 2005). *Imagined* as egalitarian and inclusive, rugby was promoted to embody all that was distinct in the colonial outpost, yet simultaneously, was inherently connected to European heritage and values. Yet, recently the longstanding connection between nationalism and rugby has entered a state of flux metonymical with the ongoing challenges to the former settler colony's hegemonic relations, rendering a post-colonial *crisis* of New Zealand nationhood (see During, 1985; Flearas & Spoonley, 1999; Pearson, 2000). Specifically, post-World War II demographic shifts and ongoing immigration; the continued weakening of attachments to Britain; the assertive politics of previously marginal cultural interests – especially Māori and strategies of state minimalization and neo-liberalization have complicated the political, economic and social certainties of the past, thus challenging the hegemonic settler national imaginary.

In line with these broader shifts, rugby's structure, ethos and organization have been fundamentally realigned with global corporate media economies. The subsequent 'crisis' of the national game has several interconnected dimensions: professionalization; heightened player mobility; the growing power of non-local corporate and media brokers; changing demographics on the field and fears of economic vulnerability compared to traditional rivals. The media narratives which have historically asserted men's rugby as the key custodian of the national character have both constituted and reflected this 'crisis' discourse. Central to the 'crisis' is the failure of the national team to exert the playing dominance of the pre-professional era, most notably in the rugby world cup. For the Lions tour of 2005 the 'threat' was further heightened by the presence of an English coach and players who had won the preceding World Cup in 2003. In this sense, the event was widely billed as a pivotal test of the national game – and hence the nation writ large. What was perhaps less anticipated was how the influx of Lions fans informed these ongoing narratives.

Mediating New Zealand's encounter with the 'Barmy Army'

Within the six national and regional newspapers we sampled (see Falcous & West, in press) the influx of Lions fans provided a significant thread informing the narrative of the tour as a nationally unifying event. Anticipation surrounding the incoming tourist influx was a prominent feature of pre-tour coverage. An evocative *New Zealand Listener* (4–10 June 2005) front cover, for example, headlined 'Pom Bomb The Barmy Army Invades NZ'. In large feature articles the *Sunday Star-Times* headlined: 'Stopping the Barmy Army in its tracks' (15 May 2005, B20), the *New Zealand Herald:* 'Barmy Army ready to storm NZ' and the *Otago Daily Times:* 'Barmy but we mean no harmy' 14–15 May 2995:48). Such coverage speculated on the likely size, nature and economic impact of the tourist presence.

Specifically, the travelling Lions supporters were envisioned as threatening to 'out-support' local fans thus calling into question the patriotic fervour of New Zealanders. In conjunction with the national Rugby Union's appeals, the press sought to rouse pre-tour patriotism urging every citizen to mobilize in a show of nationalism to counter the 'threat' of the tourist influx.. For example, in an emotive tabloid style *The Sunday News* published a full front-page image depicting All Black Captain Tana Umaga mimicking the infamous British World War I recruitment poster that compelled citizens: 'your country needs you'. The accompanying text read:

> *Cometh the hour, cometh the fan. That's the message to kiwi rugby supporters as the country braces itself for an invasion by the Barmy Army. Union bosses have been joined by All Blacks coach Graham Henry and skipper Tana Umaga in calling for New Zealand to be united – on and off the field* (The Sunday News, *10 July:1*)

The key undercurrent of this evocative construction was the fear that New Zealanders were 'cashing-in' by selling their tickets to wealthy Lions fans who, benefiting from favourable exchange rates, would dominate the crowds at games. Responding to this, Henry was quoted as saying that if there were less All Black than Lions fans 'it would send a message to the world that our nationalism is questionable' (*The Sunday News,* 17 April 2005, 6–7). Henry further appealed to the public by claiming that 'pride in being New Zealanders is the paramount reason' that players play for the All Blacks. In these constructions the fear of imbalanced global economies threatening loyalties exercised around rugby, and a reactionary re-trenchment to nationalism to counter them, is writ large.

The high-profile nature of the Lions tour and the saturation levels of media interest saw numerous advertising campaigns from both local and global corporations. As has been argued elsewhere (Falcous, 2007), these adverts were consistent with a quest to reconcile the ongoing historical reassessment of colonialism and its legacy that challenges nationalist unity. In conjunction with the foregrounding of Māori culture, advertising distanced settlers – Pākehā – from British ethno-cultural heritage and loyalties, allowing them to claim a cultural identity connected to Aotearoa and distinct from an imperial past. Akin to press coverage, the tourist influx featured in these mediations

that surrounded the event. For example, New Zealand Telecom's 'Blackout' advertising campaign centred upon the tourist 'invasion' – urging locals to 'Unite for Victory'. Featuring television, print advertising and billboards, the promotions drew upon the genre of World War II British propaganda films and urged New Zealanders to unite – aided by Telecom technology – to repel the 'invading' Lions. Most specifically, this centred upon the presence of Lions fans. One television advertisement script read as follows:

> *Invasion is imminent!*
>
> *25,000 Barmy army Light infantry have reached our shores*
>
> *But don't worry we'll be ready for them. Use your push to talk mobile to outsmart the enemy*
>
> *Join the resistance - Get behind the All Blacks with Telecom and unite for victory*

Thus, as with press coverage, the tourist influx was mediated as something to be countered with displays of nationalism (and consumption) within such advertising. Furthermore, Lions fans were constructed through caricatured stereotypes of the English specifically: wearing sandals, socks and knotted handkerchiefs on their heads and talking in upper class accents. Such constructions, humorously constructed or otherwise, both reflect back idealizations of the national self and assert distinctions from 'the British'. As During (1985) notes, historically such themes have been pivotal in generating a colonial nationalism distinctive from the imperial centre. The obvious historical inversion here is the revision of the World War II service of New Zealanders to the then fading British Empire, thus obscuring a history of loyal allegiance and, subsequently, contemporary ethno-cultural ties to the former imperial centre. Confronting the Lions – including their fans – afforded opportunities for assertions of a distinctive decolonized sense of settler – Pākehā – New Zealand.

The 2005 Lions rugby tour provided useful insights into the ways sports tourist flows are constituent to the mediated identity politics that are a part of global processes. In a moment of uncertainty for New Zealand nationhood's key custodian – men's rugby – the presence (and threat) of the Lions fans provided impetus for mediated reassertions of dominant nationalisms in a variety of ways briefly noted above. The way in which these media narratives surrounding sports tourist flows inform identity politics requires further exploration. Indeed, as a brief closing point, it is worth illustrating how the simplicities of such mediations are problematic at numerous levels. Hence, although the New Zealand media deployed the catch-all 'Barmy Army' label to refer to Lions fans, as Morgan (2007) notes, it was resisted by many fans on the grounds that its specifically cricketing and English connotations were entirely inaccurate in capturing the diverse national affiliations, interests and identities of travelling Lions fans.

Selected references

During, S. (1985). Postmodernism or postcolonialism? *Landfall*. 39, 366–380.

Falcous, M. (2007). The decolonising national imaginary: Promotional media constructions during the 2005 Lions Tour of Aotearoa New Zealand. *Journal of Sport and Social Issues*. 31 (3), 374–393.

Falcous, M. and West, A. (2008). Press narratives of nation during the 2005 Lions Tour of Aotearoa New Zealand. *Sport in Society*. 12 (2), 155–171.

Place Identity and Self-Identity

'Place provides a fundamental means by which we make sense of the world and through which we act' (Sack, 1988:642). It serves as both a reference point and a context in which we live our lives. It connects us and helps us to address the question of 'who we are' by answering the question of 'where we are' (Dixon & Durrheim, 2000; Hull, Lam & Vigo, 1994). The meanings that we attach to places and our understanding of the bonds that accompany these meanings are referred to as place identity (see Chapter 4, *Culture and identity*). Kneafsey (2000:36–37) emphasizes the broad range of place identities that exist by suggesting that different meanings 'are attached to particular places by different groups of people who experience places in different ways – as residents, business people, policymakers and tourists, for example'. This claim also holds true for the full range of groups involved in sport. While this multiplicity of meanings makes it difficult to define place identity, the ideas presented by Korpela (1989) and Proshansky, Favian and Kaminoff (1983) build on the idea that place identity is an emotional bond between people and places. Korpela (1989:245) emphasizes the connection between place and self-identity by describing place identity in terms of the 'cognitions of those physical settings and parts of the physical environment, in or with which an individual – consciously or unconsciously – regulates his experiences of maintaining his sense of self'. Proshansky et al. (1983:59) are even more direct in their view that place identity is a *sub-structure of the self-identity of the person consisting of, broadly conceived, cognitions about the physical world in which the individual lives. These cognitions represent memories, ideas, feelings, attitudes, values, preferences, meanings, and conceptions of behaviour and experience which relate to the variety and complexity of physical settings that define the day-to-day existence of every human being.*

As such, it is apparent that place identity goes beyond an emotional bond between people and places. Sport encompasses and is a leading example of an activity that lends itself to place making.

Breakwell (1986, 1992) identified four principles as part of a model for the development of identity: distinctiveness, continuity, self-esteem and self-efficacy. While their work was rooted firmly in the realm of self-identity, Twigger-Ross and Uzzell (1996) note the similarity of these principles to those raised by Korpela (1989) in the context of place. Twigger-Ross and Uzzell have successfully applied this framework in the realm of place identity (Table 12.1). Their research focused on home environments and their findings supported the four principles of their model.

Arguably, tourism and sport environments also represent fertile realms for processes of place development. Much of this promise rests on the fact that as subsets of leisure tourism and sport offer considerable scope for the exercise of choice, thereby enabling individuals and groups greater control than may be available in their place of residence. For example, sport tourists can travel to places that are distinct from the destinations of other travellers. They may, in fact, identify with a 'home team' or a 'recreational area' that they feel distinguishes them from their residential neighbours. Continuity may be pursued by returning to the same activity site such as a surf beach or the same season ticket seats in the stadium of their

Table 12.1 Place Identity Process Theory	
Distinctiveness	**Personal Distinctiveness Through Places Frequented**
Continuity	Continuity of identity through place
a. Place-referent	**a.** Specific places as referents to past selves
b. Place-congruent	**b.** Similar place types as referents to past selves
Self-esteem	Association with preferred places
Self-efficacy	Ability to manage personal lifestyle within a place

(Source: Twigger-Ross and Uzzell, 1996)

favourite team. If this is not possible, they can seek out similar beaches or similar seats in other stadiums. Self-esteem and prestige have long been recognized as important factors in the selection of travel destinations. From a sport tourism perspective, self-esteem may be enhanced by involvement in a wide range of activities such as golfing at the home of golf in St. Andrews, Scotland or visiting a host city to watch a Fédération Internationale de Football Association (FIFA) World Cup football match. Self-efficacy could be found by an outdoor enthusiast who is able to participate in his or her preferred activities while visiting a national park. Similarly, a western visitor to the 2008 Beijing Olympics, who was able to negotiate what may have been a very foreign environment, is likely to have gained a sense of self-efficacy and developed his or her place identity of Beijing as a result. While there has been little empirical research on this subject to date, there is considerable potential to advance the understanding of place identity related to sport tourism.

Place identity in tourism and sport

'Tourism is essentially a place-based phenomenon involving the production of destination identity at different scales' (Dredge & Jenkins, 2003:383). Whatever the scale of the destination marketing organization, its primary objective is to influence destination image so that it is attractive to visitors. In many ways, destination image is the flip side of place identity. Although the terms are not used consistently in the literature, destination image is generally articulated from the perspective of potential visitors while place identity is articulated from the perspective of parties that have direct experience in the place. Ideally, there is consistency in these two perspectives but many of the critiques of tourism reflect a presumed or sometimes real difference in terms of the interpretation of place. One of the most serious criticisms in this area concerns the commodification of culture and its perceived negative impact (Kneafsey, 2000). Boissevain (1996:114) has suggested that the commodification of culture through tourism is 'neither as crude nor as spectacular as the critics of cultural commoditization have suggested'. In their examination of attraction-based identity related to the Māori of New Zealand, McIntosh, Hinch and Ingram (2002) found that cultural identity could be commodified through tourism in a way that indigenous hosts felt was sustainable. Nevertheless, the commodification of culture is a tricky business which may create unsustainable tensions between the place identity of locals and the place identity and destination image of tourists. Sport, in contrast to other types of manifestations of culture, offers considerable advantages in terms of the maintenance of cultural authenticity (see Chapter 8, *Authentic experiences*) and sustainable levels of variation in terms of place identity (see Chapter 4, *Culture and identity*).

When examined as independent phenomena, sport is as much, if not more, a place maker as tourism. Nauright's (1996:69) assertion that sport 'is one of the most significant shapers of collective or group identity in the contemporary world' can be extended to the realm of place identity. Not only does sport provide insight into the identity of a group but it can also provide accessible insight into the identity of a place. McGuirk and Rowe's (2001) study of the Newcastle Knights and the Australian Rugby League Grand Final provided evidence of repositioning of place identity in Newcastle based on the success of their rugby league team. While the success of the Newcastle Knights was consciously used as a place making strategy in this case, even in the absence of a conscious place making strategy, sporting success would have influenced place identity.

SPORT, PLACE AND THE CRISIS OF IDENTITY

Proshansky et al. (1983:66) theorize that 'extreme variations in the physical environment experienced by a person may indeed threaten the self-identity of the individual'. They go on to suggest that self-identity 'depends on the development of a meaningful place-identity; and where the latter is distorted because of a lack of consistency and continuity in home and school experiences, the integration of self-identity will also suffer' (Proshansky et al., 1983:67). While these disruptions related to place can be problematic at an individual level, they are also problematic at a global level and have been referred to as a 'crisis of identity' (Maguire, 1993).

In Chapters 2 (*Sport and tourism in a global world*) and 4 (*Culture and identity*), two arguments were presented that help to explain the basis for this crisis. Firstly, globalization is eroding differences between self and 'other' thereby making it impossible to define oneself in terms of what one is not. Secondly, deterritorialization and, more specifically, the declining influence of the nation-state are leaving a void that was once filled by national identity. In rendering problematic both space and time, globalization has confused one of our traditional bases for identity (Miller et al., 2001). In his examination of place, identity and Futbol Club Barcelona, Shrobe (2005) found that the increasing globalization of sport is, in fact, straining the bonds between the Futbol Club and its traditional place identity in Barcelona. Other examples can be found throughout the sporting world as teams are deterritorialized in an attempt to tap into larger global markets.

Another contributor to this crisis is the emergence of a culture of consumption as a principle characteristic of globalization. This culture of consumption has a direct impact on how we view place. Sack (1988:643) makes this point by arguing:

> Other activities allow us to create places and instil them with meaning, but the actions of mass consumption are among the most powerful and pervasive place-building process in the modern world. By purchasing or consuming products, people participate in the construction of their everyday environment, and advertisements' depiction of the contexts that products are supposed to create provides idealized pictures of what these places or contexts should be like.

Glocalization and the pursuit of place identity through sporting communities

Giddens (1991) has suggested that as globalization continues to advance, local areas will strive to differentiate themselves for two reasons. The first is an economic response in which local areas seek to distinguish themselves from their competitors while the second is more of a social-psychological response through which the locals seek to enhance their self-identity. The economic response has been termed glocalization, which is the 'global-local dialectic wherein local identity is reinforced by global processes' (Dredge & Jenkins, 2003:386). Its economic logic is illustrated by Sack's description of the sequence of events when a place enters the global market.

> A place is often thought of as a unique set of attributes at a unique location. This is especially so before a place becomes 'commercialized'. Therefore we can expect that when a place 'enters the market,' so to speak, it must advertise itself as having generic qualities such as being accessible and having this type of service or that. As places become 'consumed,' they lose much of their former uniqueness. Commercialization makes them appear more like other places. At this point they (like other generic mass-produced products) must differentiate themselves from competing places. (Sack, 1988:661)

Glocalization is a primary strategy of the tourism industry (e.g., Dredge & Jenkins, 2003; Santos & Buzinde, 2007) as this industry is at the forefront of trying to distinguish a given destination from its global competitors. Sport is increasingly being used as a strategy to distinguish local places from their global competition. The fierce competition to host major international sporting events such as the Olympics is a good illustration of this approach (Whitson & Macintosh, 1996).

Sport involves shared meanings and experiences that can provide the foundation for community building. In a world characterized by increased mobility, a wide variety of communities have emerged including those that are focused on specialized sporting activities. Such communities tend to associate with particular places or types of places. While these associations may be driven by place dependence, for individuals who feel increasingly alienated in a globalized and mobile world, such settings also promote place identity thereby contributing to an individual's sense of self. Sport is, therefore, a place maker even as it is being commodified as part of the globalization process. Managers of sport landscapes and facilities need to recognize this dimension of their settings (Kruger, 2006).

Sport tourism places and the construction of identity

The pursuit of tourists and the benefits they provide serve as a strong rationale for place making. Place identities are constantly being (re)constructed in order to meet tourist desires for particular characteristics such as authenticity and tradition (Kneafsey, 2000). In their manipulation of destination image, tourism marketers are also influencing the way that locals understand the places in which they live and, indeed, their own identities. While sport has long been one of the characteristics that make up place identity from the perspective of the locals, glocalization processes have brought it to the forefront of place marketers. Three ways that sport has been used to (re)structure place identity based on its authentic connection to place are presented below. These strategies include: 1) the promotion of sport festivals as windows into local culture; 2) the shaping and articulation of sporting character inclusive of performance, heritage and the general ethic of sport in a community; and 3) capitalization on the kinaesthetic nature of sport activity.

Sport festivals

Festivals have long been an important part of local communities throughout the world. They are often tied to religious practices, major historical events such as past military victories or to seasonal events like spring planting or fall harvest. Under globalization, many festivals have been commodified. The distinction between culture as art and culture as a way of life has become blurred (Jeong & Santos, 2004). What was once seen as a celebration of local community is now presented as a manifestation of local culture for consumption on a global stage. While such festivals present opportunities to highlight local culture, their commodification as tourism attractions presents unique challenges. The key to addressing these challenges lies in the maintenance of the 'local celebration' (Hinch & Delamere, 1993). If this sense of local celebration is lost and the festival becomes a performance for outsiders (Greenwood, 1989), then it will have lost much of its power as a place maker.

Sport festivals represent a unique type of cultural celebration. Host cities of multi-sport festivals are not only judged in terms of their physical setting but also in terms of hospitality shown to participating athletes and other visitors as well as their general ambiance. Sporting festivals which feature local sports and athletes can provide a powerful cultural experience for visitors. A good example of this is the Ulaanbaatar Naadam festival in Mongolia (O'Gorman & Thompson, 2007), which features the traditional Mongolian sports of horse racing, archery and wrestling. It is produced for consumption by the locals as well as by visiting tourists. A similar example is the Arctic Winter Games, which feature a traditional games component drawn from Inuit and Dene culture (Hinch & de la Barre, 2005). The core attraction of both of these events is the local celebration of sporting culture. While these events provide the opportunity for visitors to gain insight into an authentic dimension of local culture, and while spectatorship is an accepted part of these festivals, the challenge that promoters face is to avoid overwhelming the locals with visitors. To do so puts place identity at risk.

Sporting character

In their study of the influence of the Newcastle Knights rugby team as an agent of the (re)negotiation of place identity in Newcastle, McGuirk and Rowe (2001:54) observed that

> The social institution of sport and local sporting 'character' are part of the fabric of place identity and the fortunes of sporting performances are frequently invoked in various dimensions of place representation. In particular, sport often draws on and provides an acute sense of territoriality both within and between cities... Sporting performance and sporting identity are thus deeply territorialized and are significant contributors to the material and symbolic process through which place identity is formulated.

McGuirk and Rowe (2001) demonstrate that the success of the Newcastle Knights in the 1997 Australian Rugby League Grand Final was used by local media and politicians in an attempt to reposition their city as a champion in the face of 'deindustrialization'. Similar strategies have been used by an assortment of cities throughout the world including Edmonton, Canada, which at one point was promoting itself as the 'City of Champions'. Sporting successes do provide extensive and generally positive exposure for a city that can elevate its reputation and transcend the particular sport in which success has been achieved. The downside of this strategy is that the cyclical nature of sport performance almost guarantees that sporting success will be of a limited duration, making this strategy of place identity vulnerable to sudden but predicable reversals.

One way that cities have avoided this dependence on contemporary sporting successes is to promote a broader sport ethic. This is one of the strategies that Glasgow has used to change its place identity from a city in the depths of decline to a city seen as being vibrant and healthy (Porteous, 2000; Hooper, 1998). Cities like Boulder, Colorado and Queenstown, New Zealand, have also benefited from this image that sees them as being characterized by a population of active outdoor enthusiasts. Alternatively, place identity can be tied to sporting heritage. Ramshaw and Hinch (2006:401) suggest that by re-creating sporting pasts for a tourist audience, a destination can present nostalgic images that contribute to a positive place identity. They suggest that

> … *manifestations of sporting culture combine with an assortment of other symbols of culture to produce place identities. A nostalgic perspective of sport allows places to construct a favourable identity, with which its residents are comfortable and which provides an anchor in a turbulent and constantly changing world.*

Kinaesthetic nature of sport

A third way that sport tourism can be used to construct place identity is through the provision of tourism experiences that capitalize on the kinaesthetic nature of sport. In his commentary on place identity, Sarbin (1983:339) states that in answering the 'who am I' question in the search for self-identity 'the motoric conduct of the child' who is exploring his/her world is the functional equivalent of an older adult asking 'where am I'. Sarbin is an environmental psychologist of considerable repute, so his reference to the motoric conduct of the child is particularly interesting given the kinaesthetic nature of sport. It is the contention of the authors that the kinaesthetic character of sport during later stages of a life cycle is an extension of the 'motoric conduct of a child' in the sense in which Sarbin has used it. People use the kinaesthetic nature of sport to help explore and make sense of their worlds. The sensory feedback that competitive or recreational athletes receive in response to their kinaesthetic sporting activity provides them with physical insight into the environment in which they are engaged. Even spectators are able to gain insight into a place, albeit primarily vicariously, by observing the kinaesthetic dynamic of sporting activities in particular settings. Such insight, especially for the athletes themselves, provides an authentic experience of place and serves to shape the identity associated with these settings.

CONCLUSION

In this chapter, we argued that place lies at the heart of tourism and that sport involvement is one of the ways that place attachments are formed. Globalization has brought increased mobility and rapidly changing under-standings of home. Where earlier understandings of home suggested that place-based identities were likely to be relatively static and tied to home, increased mobility has challenged these forms of identity. The bonds between places and people are now recognized as going beyond the home environment.

One of the more fertile grounds for the establishment of place attachment in a global world is found in the realm of sport. Place attachment is fostered through the dependence of individual sports on certain types of environ-ments given their unique rule sets and requirements. This is especially true in terms of sports that depend on unique features in the natural environ-ment. Consistent with other globalization trends, however, many sports that have traditionally been housed in these natural settings are being modified in ways that adapt them to much more transportable built facilities (see Chapter 3, *Sport and contemporary mobility*). Rock climbing provides a good example, with its origins firmly established in outdoor areas of mountains, canyons and the like. Increasingly, however, variations of rock climbing are being offered in popular indoor climbing facilities under much more controlled conditions. The supply and variation of climbing sites are, therefore, very dynamic suggesting that current views of sport place depen-dence are also being challenged.

We also argue that sport fosters place identity. A very tangible form of this is evident in the competitive bidding processes that characterize major sporting events like the Olympics and FIFA World Cup football. This may be described in terms of glocalization processes in which cities attempt to establish their global relevance as well as their local identity by hosting these events. Sport continues to serve as a basis for nation-based place identity although this form of collective identity has been complicated by the rise of professional sport and sport subcultures. Sport mobility, as manifest in sport tourism, often means that these place identities do not necessarily correspond with traditional place identities of home. Finally, Sarbin's (1983) argument that the motoric activity of a child is in fact an exploration of identity suggests that the kinaesthetic nature of sport tourism is also a form identity building, albeit at a later stage of development. This aspect of personal and place identity making merits further enquiry.

CHAPTER 13

Sport and Place Competition

Rapid development of telecommunications and transportation technologies, in association with privatization and deregulation (Silk, 2004), have given rise to new relationships between cities, regions and states in terms of international trade, business development, capital investment and job growth. This has seen the rise of what Castell (1996) refers to as the 'transnational network society'. 'Advances in telecommunications, flexible manufacturing, and new transportation technologies emerging from the use of computers and new materials have created the material infrastructure for the world economy, much like the construction of railways in the nineteenth century' (Silk, 2004:352) Thus, places have come to compete in new ways. The economic dominance of once powerful industrialized cities has been supplanted by the accelerating industrialization of developing economies and intense competition to attract high-technology industries.

Sports resources (Bale, 1994) and elite sports talent (Maguire, 2005) are some of the 'raw materials' to which Silk (2004) refers. The 'brawn drain' describes the draining of athletic talent from periphery to core areas, a phenomenon that takes place at various levels of spatial analysis. Increasingly, athletic talent is being displaced from teams of representation and, indeed, codes of sport altogether, on the basis of economic disparity. For example, the Indian Cricket League (inaugurated in 2007) has witnessed players retire from international cricket to take up lucrative contracts to play Twenty-20 cricket for domestic Indian teams. The sport economies of England and France have benefited by the defection of elite southern hemisphere rugby league players whose salaries are more limited in the southern hemisphere under salary caps. Players, coaches and team managers move freely between countries, taking 'intellectual property' to rival national teams, in the search for lucrative contracts. Sports teams, competition

CONTENTS

leagues, sports stadiums and other constructed sports resources are also mobile 'raw materials' of the new transnational world economy. They are also prominent in the construction of place identity (Cornelissen, 2004). Investment in sport is now seen as a component of economic development and regeneration strategies, particularly as they relate to the visitor industry and the hospitality service sector (Silk, 2004).

PLACE AND PLACE COMPETITION

Place refers to the meanings that are attached to space (Tuan, 1974), which may be understood as a cultural text that people recognize and interpret (Crouch, 2000) (see Chapter 12, *Place attachment*). Place identity is constructed through awareness and understanding of what places represent and may be shaped or influenced by the deliberate efforts of individuals, companies, corporations, media, marketing agencies and tourism destination management organizations. Constructions of place are highly subjective. People, both individually and collectively, are constantly defining, refining and redefining the meanings that they attach to space. Place meanings are renegotiated as aspects of people's lives change (Hinch & Higham, 2004). The assumption that place meanings can be actively constructed, negotiated and refined is fundamental to principles of place promotion and place marketing.

It is widely acknowledged that the influences of globalization, in terms of commerce, business location and investment patterns, have brought places, however distant, into direct competition. The manifestations of these forms of competition, according to Hall and Page (2003), include commerce, human capital, investment, travel flows and leisure tourism. As a consequence local, regional and national economies face increasing competition from other places whether they be close or distant (Hall, 1998). Kolter *et al.* (1993:346) argue that we are living in a time of 'place wars', a term that is built on the notion that places must compete to survive (Hall, 1998, Page & Hall, 2003). The globalization of the world's economy and the accelerating pace of technological change are two forces that require places to learn to compete. Hall (1998) has argued that places must learn to think more like businesses – developing products, markets and customers. Page and Hall (2003:309) highlight the need to commodify particular aspects of place in the process of place marketing. 'In the case of urban [or regional] re-imaging, marketing practices, such as branding, rely on the commodification of particular aspects of place, exploiting, reinventing or creating place images in order to sell the place as a destination product for tourists or investment'.

Heightened attention to place marketing and place promotion has been one consequence. Sport and tourism have figured prominently in efforts to influence place identity and place promotion (Chalip, Green & Hill, 2003; Harrison-Hill & Chalip, 2005).

SPORT AND PLACE IDENTITY

Silk (2004) notes that space is imbued with power relations that are, certainly in the case of sports spaces, linked to the politics of identity. Within the wider context of place wars and place competition, it is noteworthy that sport exerts a significant influence on the meanings that people attach to space. The cultural dimensions of sport are readily harnessed by sports organizations, destination management organizations and media to represent and disseminate the lifestyles and ways of living associated with specific places. These meanings may be significant in terms of the decision-making processes of tourists. They are also central to the experience of tourists and have become increasingly prominent in terms of the strategies used by sport and tourism destination managers to build place identity and to position tourism destinations in terms of being interesting, attractive or unique.

There are many ways in which sport can be harnessed to serve interests in building or enhancing place identity (Hinch & Higham, 2004). At a general level the development of major sports facilities can serve as anchor projects for urban renewal (Hall, 2001), but they may also become symbols of place identity and vehicles for place promotion when developed in close association with dedicated sports precincts (e.g., Melbourne, Australia), leisure spaces (e.g., Cardiff, Wales), inner city attractions and activities (e.g., Camden Yards, Baltimore), educational facilities (e.g., Goodison Park, Liverpool), iconic land or cityscapes (e.g., Newlands, Cape Town) or elements of environmental design (e.g., Olympiastadion, Berlin).

In association with major sports facilities, mega sports events may be deployed in the pursuit of stated social, cultural, environmental and economic goals, many of which bear relevance to the construction or dissemination of place identity. Sports events may be coordinated with cultural performance, business network, media and tourism marketing initiatives as well as strategies aimed at promoting the environment, culture, leisure and lifestyle values of specific places (Hall, 1998; Brown, 2001). Such ambitions are increasingly justified by, and specifically linked to, tourism marketing and visitor growth opportunities (Brown, 2001). Once the exclusive domain of industrialized western countries, these ambitions are now being pursued by developing world and non-Western cities and states. Indeed the very act of bidding for the rights to host global sports mega-events, let alone success in the competitive bidding process, has become a prominent stage upon which elements of place competition are actively played out. Cornelissen (2004) illustrates these points in critical detail in exploring in the case of South Africa the extent to which sports mega-events may be taken up as the mechanism to serve interests in economic investment and growth, as well as the construction of place identity and interests in place-based promotion (see Case study 13.1).

Case Study 13.1

Aspirant politics: Place, positioning and sport mega-events in South Africa

Scarlett Cornelissen (Department of Political Science, University of Stellenbosch)

On one level the selection of South Africa as host of the nineteenth World Cup finals of the Fédération Internationale de Football Association (FIFA) in 2010 may be seen as the culmination of a long-standing campaign by which the holding or attempted hosting of high-profile sport events has become a steady component of post-apartheid rule. On another level, South Africa's active involvement in international competitions to host such events is exemplary of the extent to which sport mega-events – and all of the economic, investment and growth contingents which have come to be associated with them – are regarded as pursuable alternative development instruments for industrializing and developed countries alike. In this, sport mega-events represent instances by which the international politics of place competition centres on the generation of spectacle through sport.

Sport mega-events may be defined as major sport competitions of limited duration and often thrilling appeal and are held on a regular, rotating basis across the world. South Africa, notably excluded from partaking in many of these competitions for the better part of the twentieth century, has become an active participant since the end of apartheid. The city of Cape Town's bid – officially launched in 1992 – for the 2004 Summer Olympics inaugurated a continuous and ever more aspirant sport event campaign. In 1995 South

Africa hosted the world championship of the International Rugby Board (IRB), and in 1996 the country provided the venue for the biennial continental football championship, known as the Africa Cup of Nations. The national teams' serendipitous victory of the tournament trophies – and the racial unity this temporarily fostered – provided an additional rationale for South Africa's subsequent pursuits around major international sport competitions. The country hosted the All Africa Games in 1999 and two further world championships in 2003 – the International Cricket Council's World Cup and the Women's World Cup of Golf. However, securing the rights in 2004 to host the FIFA World Cup represented a particular victory to South Africa's bid campaigners, who, having made an initial unsuccessful submission for the 2006 FIFA tournament, extended their campaign for the 2010 finals.

The present-day importance of sport mega-events stems in part from the healthy growth in the commercial significance of sport over the past three decades, represented by the increase in value of aspects such as sport sponsorships and merchandizing and the growing commoditization of sport fandom and loyalty. The contingent commercialization of flagship competitions by some of the major international sport federations has given momentum to sport's commoditization. It has, however, been the growing search for 'alternative' development opportunities in the context of a perceived more competitive and risky international environment by political authorities, and their increased regard for sport-event-driven growth as a viable policy option, which has lent sport events a wider significance in the contemporary era. The proliferation in the number of international sport competitions today – ranging in levels of spectatorship from small to large scale and in elite to amateur participation – bears testimony to this.

The processes which underpin sport events' developmental significances for political authorities are numerous and interwoven with other aspects related to the changing nature of international capital. First, place-based promotion is a major rationale for urban or national authorities to host large-scale events. This can be explained by the degree to which sport and events provide useful anchors around which place promotion activities can be designed; sport's easy appeal and values that are universally applied to it, such as amiability, goodwill and also competitiveness, allow for the creation of destination imaging which can readily be disseminated. Second, and in a related fashion, sport events can be used to provide particular material, cultural and spatial representations of hosts, in the design, for example, of event-related infrastructure (such as stadia) or in the discursive use of event sloganeering, which can be aimed at showing facets of distinctiveness or allure of the host. Third, attempts are often made to use sport events to stimulate or bolster economic sectors that are regarded as close ancillaries to sport – most notably tourism. In this exercise, efforts are made to exploit the synergies that exist between tourism and sport, particularly in terms of the degree to which both involve mobility and consumption.

All of these aspects feature prominently in post-apartheid South Africa. The country's campaign around sport mega-events is one pillar in a three-pronged approach adopted by the national government, which also emphasizes the development of tourism as a priority economic sector and the drawing of foreign direct investment as a macro-economic strategy. Two key national agencies carry primary responsibility for this – the International Marketing Council, which has the task of carrying through sustained promotion campaigns to potential investor markets, and South African Tourism, the national tourism promotion body. The country's success in hosting some tournaments, such as the 2003 Cricket World Cup and, more significantly, the tasks around preparing and planning for the 2010 FIFA finals, have led to

a belated policy reorientation by which the generation of a sport event economy is seen to be an objective which straddles the goals of tourism and investment enhancement.

Tourism is one of the sectors which has seen most meaningful growth in South Africa after 1994. Its significance lies in the way in which economic outputs have flowed from the continuous rise in tourist arrivals (to a current market of about eight million tourist arrivals, of whom two-quarters are from Western Europe and the greater number are from other parts of Africa). Its importance also lies in the extent to which activities around foreign investment promotion have tended to hinge on the accomplishments of tourist branding and imaging in primary international source markets. The country's continued tourist success is, however, heavily dependent on positive international media exposure. The tourism sector is anticipated to draw greater benefit from the 2010 tournament, with expectations that the event will draw close to 500,000 foreign visitors and that it will generate tourism revenue of approximately US$1.6 billion. However, as is the case with other events of this nature, providing reliable forecasts of tourism impacts is very difficult.

In one regard the 2010 World Cup represents an international marketing campaign for South Africa of an unprecedented scale, albeit until now of an overwhelmingly negative nature. The years leading up to the finals have been marked by a great deal of international publicity and speculation over South Africa's ability to complete all infrastructural preparations; on the potential effects of crime and the possibility that political instability may jeopardize the tournament. Amid this, South Africa's authorities have sought to use the 2010 event, which has been named 'the African World Cup' to represent the continent in a more favourable light. This is mostly aimed at countering the effects of Afro-pessimism on tourist arrivals and investments to the continent. The 2010 Local Organising Committee has notably defined their aim, 'to strengthen the African and South African image, (to) promote new partnerships with the world as we stage a unique and memorable event … (and to) be significant global players in all fields of human endeavour'. Clearly, aspirations around the 2010 tournament not only extend well beyond the development of South

Africa but also aim at uplifting the wider African continent. This may be an ambition which is difficult to realise.

Selected references

Alegi (2001). 'Feel the pull in your soul': Local agency and global trends in South Africa's 2006 World Cup Bid, *Soccer and Society*, 2, 3:1–21.

Roche, M. (2000). *Mega-Events and Modernity: Olympics and Expos in the Growth of Global Culture*. London: Routledge.

Tomlinson, A. and Young, C. (Eds.) (2006). *National Identity and Global Sports Events: Culture, Politics and Spectacle in the Olympics and the Football World Cup.* Albany: State University of New York Press.

Sports offer the potential to build strong associations between specific people – participants and spectators – and particular places. Sportspeople, be they motivated by recreational engagement or competitive achievement, may engage in sports that are strongly associated with specific places (Bourdeau & Corneloup, 2002). Elite athletes may build elements of place identity based on the fortunes of competitions that are played out in particular competition settings. Spectators and fans may become passionate and partisan in their support for particular sports teams and the places where they compete. Bale (1993) uses religious metaphors to describe sport places, including the playing field as sacred turf, spectator gatherings and movement as pilgrimage and the stadium as cathedral or place of worship. In this way the team colours become ceremonial regalia providing a sense of unity as well as personal, social and place identity. The religious metaphor has also been adopted and applied by tourism scholars. MacCannell (1973) argues that tourism is analogous to a pilgrimage and that tourists are motivated by the search for the authentic. Given that tourism may be viewed as a search for sacred sites, the growing prominence of sport in terms of place identity (Hinch & Higham, 2004) and the potential for sports to offer authentic cultural experiences of place are noteworthy (see Chapter 8, *Authentic experiences*).

Further to this end, sport may give pervading meaning to space by allowing onlookers, however distant, to develop home-like ties to specific sites and places of competition as well as allegiances to collections of people. Sport gives meaning to place when spectators watch competition matches, championship finals and/or sports events. Broadcast and reporting media contribute to building a sense of place associated with a sport team, stadiums and other places of competition. Some sports venues may develop home-like qualities as team allegiance builds. A Newcastle United FC fan who has never visited Newcastle (e.g., someone who lives outside the United Kingdom) may build a strong allegiance with their team and affinity for

St. James' Park (Newcastle) through insignia or symbols of loyalty (e.g., wearing the team shirt), watching their team on television, following competition results with interest and perhaps joining the team's fan club.

Clearly, building such allegiances is not conditional upon actually visiting a particular city, stadium or site of competition. This idea of 'home' in a sporting context stands in stark contrast to the notion of home as place of permanent residence. It is, perhaps, analogous to the concept of 'multiple homes' as discussed in Chapter 3 (*Sport and contemporary mobility*), although that analogy fails to capture the home-like qualities that may be built in association with a place that one has never visited. Yet such sentiments, and the allegiances that they may create, offer the potential to build place identity, which may serve as a foundation for the construction of destination branding strategies that build upon fan loyalties. To return to the aforementioned example, a long-standing supporter of Newcastle United FC who finally manages to visit England's north-east is likely to feel immediately at home on the streets of Newcastle and at St. James' Park and, furthermore, is likely to be welcomed by local fans.

Beyond local clubs with regional, national or global supporter catchments, this aspect of sport and identity has similar application at higher levels of representative sport. It is noteworthy that at regional, national or international levels of representation sport, the area that a sports team represents may in fact require 'home' supporters to travel considerable distances to support their team (Gibson et al., 2002). A national team performing in international competition may attract 'home' supporters from throughout the country that it represents, many of whom travel as domestic tourists. Indeed expatriates (players and supporters alike) may also return to their country of origin to support or compete in sports teams. The spatial area that a sport team or club actually represents may vary considerably from the spatial extent of the team supporter and player catchments. This raises the prospect of spectators travelling as domestic or international tourists, without feeling that they are leaving 'home' or indeed feeling that they are going 'home', which may have interesting implications for the visitor experience (Gibson et al., 2002; Hinch & Higham, 2004), and it may also give new meaning to place attachment.

In addition, sport may contribute to place identity through aesthetics and sporting heritage. In terms of the former, place identity can be constructed through both natural and built elements of the sports landscape (Bale, 1993). While surf lifesaving events on Australia's Gold Coast speak volumes of the environment, society and lifestyles of a particular place (Chalip, 2002), so too do constructed facilities such as Wimbledon and Wembley, and heavily modified sports spaces such as St. Andrews and Henley. At such venues iconic elements of design can come to symbolize a sporting venue in ways that contribute in powerful ways to place identity and place promotion. Wimbledon's lawn playing surface and Wembley's arch stand as good examples. The aesthetics of sports places may over time merge with successive chapters of sporting heritage (Gammon & Ramshaw, 2007) that also influence the ways in which sports sites become endowed with meaning (Bale, 1993). As new rivalries in sport emerge over time, and as new champions eclipse the records of old, layers of sports heritage are established and auras of tradition enriched (Gammon & Ramshaw, 2007). Such processes act to embellish unique manifestations of place identity in ways that are broadly disseminated by broadcast and popular media.

Sport and place marketing

Marketing is central to the success of many tourism destinations. Tourism marketing commodifies places in an attempt to construct place images, create associations between places and brand images and differentiate between competing places (Hudson, 2008). Such actions may also be harnessed to actively influence the re-imaging of places (Hall, 2002). The creation of fresh, distinct, unique and appealing imagery as well as the transplanting of vague or negative images are outcomes that may be sought through place marketing. These efforts are, in many cases, aimed specifically at target tourist markets. However, it has become increasingly common for civic marketing campaigns to try to influence the perceptions, imagery and actions of local residents, regional and wider domestic visitor markets and business communities as well as potential visitors (Page & Hall, 2003). Indeed in light of the forces of globalization and mobility, the spectrum of target audiences for such activities has continued to expand. They now might include potential second home owners, commercial or residential property investors and tertiary education markets as well as those for whom a change in lifestyle values may be an attractive proposition. Clearly, then, the actions of those who engage in place marketing are aimed at actively and consciously influencing the meanings that are attached to a particular place (Baloglu & McClearly, 1999) so as to appeal to the personal factors held by a targeted or general audience (Gallarza, Saura & Garcia, 2002).

While place meanings may be actively renegotiated and engineered, it is noteworthy that such processes may be highly contested. Silk (2004:352) examines the 'new cultural politics of belonging and difference, the categories of inclusion and exclusion, in the powerful symbolic spaces of representation of the contemporary North American cityscape'. He uses the case of Memphis, which he describes as a city that has 'recentered itself around a spectacular space of sporting consumption ...' (Silk, 2004:349). This was an important part of a wider strategy to attract corporate headquarters and target industries (e.g., information technology and biomedical research) and foster tourism and hospitality development through investment in sport and place marketing. The process has resulted in the symbolic commodification of place (Whitson & Macintosh, 1996) in order to create positive place meanings and destination image. The creation of spectacular sites of consumption, the manufacturing of heritage and tradition and the sanitizing of places of play have been central to the Memphis strategy. Through these strategic efforts the city of Memphis has ascended the global urban hierarchy. However, the process has simultaneously divided the city and 'created new lines of inequality and exclusion' (Silk, 2004:366).

IMAGING AND RE-IMAGING PLACES

Sport can be a powerful agent in the imaging, re-imaging and branding of tourism places. Historically, a prominent strategy serving this field of endeavour has been the hosting of hallmark sports events (Getz, 1997; Hall, 1992a), which has led to accusations of corruption and bribery in event bidding and decision-making processes (Jennings, 1996). High-profile sports events are associated with considerable public attention including visiting media programmes, television broadcasting and sports media reporting. This can be harnessed to increase the prominence and standing of places as well as serve as an agent of change in terms of imagery and place meaning. Branding, place awareness and destination positioning may also be served through these avenues (Chalip & Costa, 2005). While some sports events receive global coverage, others are easily linked to specific national or regional television spectator audiences. As such sports broadcasts can be used strategically to access specific public audiences.

The Olympic Games has long been used to serve the imaging or re-imaging of places, often quite cynically, to serve political ends (Weed, 2008). The cities of Los Angeles (1984), Seoul (1988), Barcelona (1992) and Atlanta (1996) all used the hosting of the Olympic Games as a mechanism to build place imagery. However, Australia was the first Olympic host nation to take advantage of the Olympic Games to vigorously pursue tourism for the benefit of the whole country (Brown, Chalip, Jago & Mules, 2002). The Australian Tourist Commission undertook the re-imaging of Australia as an international tourism destination in association with the Sydney 2000 Olympic Games (Morse, 2001). These ends were served principally through the development of promotions with Olympic sponsors, conference, convention and incentive travel initiatives associated with the Olympic Games, visiting media programmes and close consultation with television broadcasters.

Of course in the scheme of things relatively few sporting events command global media and public attention. However, second tier sports of national or regional market range may also offer value in constructing place imagery within more modest spatial scales of analysis (Gratton et al., 2005). In contrast, the development of sport-related leisure and cultural services is an alternative approach that may be used to construct place images based on sport. This approach goes beyond the support of high-profile professional sports to the development of a sporting ethic through such things as parkland and shorefront development, which encourages active sporting pursuits such as jogging, cycling and sailing. Increasingly, the development legacies associated with hosting sports events in specific cities may be aimed at local communities in a deliberate bid to promote healthy living and, in doing so, build local place identity that is desirable and attractive. Glasgow has used this approach to reposition itself as an active healthy community both in terms of self-identity and destination image (Porteous, 2000; Hooper, 1998). Questions, of course, remain as to the extent to which sports may serve such interests in developing world, peripheral and indigenous nations (Cornelissen, 2004).

Sports events aside, the re-imaging of places for tourism, as well as dedicated tourism marketing efforts, may exploit strong and in some cases unique associations between sport and place. The distinctive images associated with some sports subcultures have been harnessed in association with places where specific landscapes and associated sports are prominent. The lifestyle values associated with many marine and mountain-based sports, such as surfing and kite boarding on one hand, and X-Games snowboarding and extreme skiing on the other, may be effectively linked to brand values. These are sports that are associated with values such as freedom, spontaneity, escape from authority, risk and personal autonomy, as expressed through clothing, lifestyle, employment (often casual, seasonal or short term) and personal mobility. These brand values may be harnessed in the interests of place promotion by tourism destinations that have grown in association with specific sports and the subculture values with which they co-exist.

SPORT AND TOURISM PLACE COMPETITION

This discussion of sport and place offers food for thought in terms of tourism places. This is particularly the case if one accepts Relph's (1976) argument that while local residents exist as existential insiders, tourists by contrast are poorly placed to achieve a meaningful 'sense of place' at the destinations they visit. Relph justifies this argument based on his perception of the superficial nature of many tourist experiences and the tendency of the tourism industry to present 'disneyfied' landscapes devoid of deeper meaning. Such views of tourism contrast markedly from the position that tourism involves a serious pursuit of meaning and authenticity (MacCannell, 1973). More specifically, it has been persuasively argued by Cuthbertson, Heine and Whitson (1997) that many types of travellers are likely to form strong attachments to the place, an example being the strong attachment that nomadic people have to the places they travel through.

Travelling for pleasure beyond the boundaries of one's life-space implies that there is some experience available at the destination that cannot be found at home and which compensates for the costs of the trip (Cohen, 1996). Standeven and De Knop (1999) build on this line of argument by discussing sport tourism as an interplay of the cultural experiences of physical activity in association with the cultural experiences of place.

DESTINATION IMAGE AND REGIONAL TOURISM DIFFERENTIATION

The challenge facing tourists, perhaps increasingly so in a world subject to the forces of globalization, is to achieve experiences at a destination that have meaning (Williams, Patterson, Roggenbuck & Watson, 1992; Morgan, 2007). Elements of uniqueness become an important means of differentiating between places. It has been noted elsewhere (see Chapter 2, *Sport and tourism in a global world*, Chapter 11, *Modern landscapes and retro parks*) that sports environments are subject to widespread forces of standardization and homogenization. Hinch and Higham (2004) argue that standardized sportscapes compromise efforts to differentiate places, to the potential disadvantage of tourism and visitor experiences. Interestingly, some elite competitors themselves have argued that such developments alter the sport experience. The retractable roof of the Rod Laver Arena (Melbourne), home of the Australian Open tennis grand slam, is on occasions closed not due to the threat of rain but rather to offer players relief from direct sun and summer heat. Some players, most notably Australia's own Leyton Hewitt, have argued that players should endure the heat, which is a fundamental part of competing in the Australian Open. No doubt for many spectators, sitting in the heat of the Australian summer is also a defining element of the sport spectatorship experience. There is an argument, clearly, that the standardization of sports venues and the imposition of technology has at the very least diluted, and for some fundamentally altered, the sport experience for both competitors and spectators.

The uniqueness of destinations lies the heart of tourism (Williams & Shaw, 1988). Mitchell and Murphy (1991) argue that the search for regional diversity in the landscape is an important travel stimulus. The strategic use of distinctive and recognizable elements of the natural landscape, as they relate to the branding of tourism destinations, has become an important aspect of sport, event and tourism management (Xing & Chalip, 2006). Interests relating to destination image and place marketing, as well as the regional differentiation of destinations, may be well served by efforts to communicate brand values that consumers associate with well-defined attributes and positive benefits (Chalip, 2005).

The branding of professional rugby teams competing in the Super 12 in 1996 was established based on elements of the physical environment and cultural setting that are regionally unique (see Table 13.1). The Blues franchise based in Auckland (New Zealand), for example, was branded to evoke images of a harbour city with immediate proximity to island parks, marine reserves and a range of marine sports and recreational pursuits, images that clearly build upon the 'Auckland, city of sails' brand. The neighbouring Chiefs franchise based in Hamilton was branded to reflect the position of the wider region as a prominent centre of indigenous Māori culture. Rotorua, a prominent destination where attractions such as the Whakarewarewa thermal reserves, Māori villages, cultural performances and the Māori Arts and Craft Institute are present, is the cultural tourism centrepiece of this region.

Equally, in the South African context, the Lions (Johannesburg) rugby franchise induces images of African landscapes, big game reserves and the viewing of iconic African megafauna. By contrast the Sharks franchise based in Durban, and extending to the provinces of Natal, Kwa-Zulu, Eastern Province and Border (situated on South Africa's Indian Ocean coastline), is branded to bring to mind images of climate, beaches, surfing and marine activities, including viewing sharks in the wild. Table 13.1 lists the original Super 12 franchises that were created in 1996 and the logos and brand images associated with those franchises. These elements of regional distinctiveness serve the branding of prominent professional sports teams and in doing so also serve interests in building place images that are regionally differentiated.

Table 13.1	Rugby Super 12 franchise regions and brand images		
Franchise (base)	**Regional representation**	**Brand images**	**Visitor attractions**
Blues (Auckland)	Auckland, Northland and North Harbour	'City of sails' brand Harbour city Blue water harbours Maritime lifestyle values	Sailing (Waitemata harbour) Hauraki Gulf Marine Parks Diving in marine parks Windsurfing Gulf Harbour golf course Harbour cruises
Chiefs (Hamilton)	Waikato, King Country, Counties-Manukau, Thames Valley, Bay of Plenty	Centre of indigenous Māori culture	Thermal reserves Rotorua Māori villages Māori cultural performances Māori Arts and Craft Institute
Hurricanes (Wellington)	Taranaki, East Coast, Hawke's Bay, Poverty Bay, Manawatu, Horowhenua, Waiarapa, Wellington	Windy Wellington Harbour city Capital city National/political centre	Te Papa (National Museum) Houses of Parliament National monuments Cook Strait
Crusaders (Christchurch)	Nelson Bays, Marlborough, West Coast, Canterbury, Mid-Canterbury, South Canterbury	English city English heritage Garden city	English architecture Punting on the River Avon Canterbury Museum Farming settlements Antarctic exploration
Highlanders (Dunedin)	North Otago, Otago, Southland	'Edinburgh of the South' Scottish heritage Gold mining heritage Southern Lakes	Scottish heritage Scottish place names Gold mining attractions Highland (alpine) landscapes Queenstown ochs and burns (lakes and rivers)

Continued

Table 13.1	Rugby Super 12 franchise regions and brand images—*continued*		
Franchise (base)	**Regional representation**	**Brand images**	**Visitor attractions**
Reds (Brisbane)	Queensland	Great Red KangarooRed continentTropical northTropical climate	Native wildlifeTropical climateCoastlinesBeach and surf cultureDesert interior, national parks
Waratahs (Sydney)	New South Wales	Summer climate Blue mountains Coastal scenery	Sydney harbour Sydney beaches National Parks
Brumbies (Canberra)	Australian Capital Territory	Rural landscapes Rural lifestyles Mountains	Rural activities Wine and food Mountain recreation Mountain sports
Lions (Johannesburg)	Mpumalanga and Gauteng	Iconic Africa Games reserves Wildlife African landscapes	Game reserves Wildlife viewing African megafauna Hunting
Bulls (Pretoria)	Free State, North West, Northern Free State, Northern Gauteng and Griqualand.	National capital Farming communities Rural lifestyle High veldt Climate	Outdoors activities Rural landscapes National Parks

Table 13.1	Rugby Super 12 franchise regions and brand images—*continued*		
Franchise (base)	**Regional representation**	**Brand images**	**Visitor attractions**
THE SHARKS Sharks (Durban)	Natal, Eastern Province and Border	Coastal setting Beaches	Beach lifestyle Climate Marine activities (e.g., surfing) Marine wildlife viewing
STORMERS vodacom Stormers (Cape Town)	Western Province, Boland and South Western Districts.	Maritime climate Iconic landscapes Heritage	Table Mountain Coastal wildlife Heritage

* The provinces that comprise these franchise regions have changed periodically since the inception of Super 12 in 1996 (and the addition of two franchises, the Western Force and Cheetahs in 2006).

An investigation of the branding of professional sports teams was undertaken by Higham and Hinch (2003) following the professionalization of rugby union and the inception of the Super 12. In conducting a series of interviews with relevant sports management, sports marketing, regional tourism organization (RTO) and destination marketing representatives in the Highlanders (New Zealand) franchise region, their work specifically addresses the contribution of the franchise, and its branding, to place promotion and tourism. They found a general view that the Highlanders brand serves as a vehicle for regional differentiation in both domestic and international travel markets. As the marketing manager of the Otago Rugby Football Union explained 'The Highlanders brand reflects the terrain, the Scottish heritage and the values of the region: honesty, integrity and hard work … it is very much reflective of what we are all about'. Thus the strong Protestant work ethic and Presbyterian values of the first Scottish settlers who migrated to Aotearoa/New Zealand, and who settled in the southern city of Dunedin in 1848, remain evident in the brand images associated with the Highlanders rugby team. This, according to the manager of the Dunedin Council's Economic Development Unit, 'translates into actual value for tourism'. The branding of the Highlanders represents a vehicle for regional tourism differentiation and the promotion of a regional tourism product (Higham & Hinch, 2003:249).

COMPETITION BETWEEN LOCATIONS

Globalization and high personal mobility have combined to create an environment of intense competition between places. Political boundaries and nationalisms that may previously have negated competition between places have been swept aside. Spatial constraints and geographical proximity no longer underpin sports competition leagues in the way that they did in the past. Sports leagues, formerly based on local or regional competition catchments, are more commonly formulated based on new non-spatial criteria. Access to financial markets, time zones (including the time zones of television audiences) and spectator demand are considerations in the formulation of sports leagues and the designation of venues to host sports competitions. Traditional spatial criteria demarcating franchise boundaries are being challenged. This is certainly the case in terms of competition leagues that now typically span countries and continents. The 2008 European Championship league final between Chelsea and Manchester United was played in Moscow (Russia). In the ultimate contrast to the circumstances under the former State Socialist regime, and as a response to the anticipated influx of English football fans for the final, spectators were able to use valid tickets for the game as temporary visas to allow entry into Russia for the weekend of the final.

Standard distance and home venue criteria have also been eroded in terms of where games take place. It is no longer uncommon for 'home' games to be taken 'on the road' in order to introduce live team sports to new and existing groups of fans who may exist in large numbers in cities and countries far removed from the team itself. It has been acknowledged by the Australian Rugby Union (ARU) and New Zealand Rugby Union (NZRU) that the hosting of Bledisloe Cup rugby tests in Hong Kong in 2008 was a vehicle to access the spectator and tourism markets of Asia. This was the first time the rivalry has been contested outside New Zealand or Australia. It is also seen as a stepping stone towards regular rugby games in Asian cities and perhaps the entry of an Asian team into the Super 14 if that competition continues to expand. This move is based on interests that focus on unlocking latent demand for the sport of Rugby Union among the populations, including expatriates, of Asian cities.

Modern sports exist in a continual state of change. The dynamics of change are often driven by economic processes that bear upon the structure of competitive sports (e.g., the development of new league competitions), the location of sport facilities and the rise and fall of sport attractions. Bale (1989:77) refers to 'the growth and decline in importance of different sport locations', which parallels Butler's (1980) tourist area lifecycle theory. Sports attractions exist within a hierarchy in a similar fashion to other types of tourist attractions (Leiper, 1990). This hierarchy reflects the fact that some sports centres primarily draw upon a local catchment, while others situated higher in the sports hierarchy draw upon district, regional, national or international catchments. Previously, as Bale (1989:79) explains, sports facilities were situated in central locations 'as close to potential users as possible in order to maximise pleasure from the sport experience and to minimise travel, and hence cost'. Latterly, this formula has changed as new factors have emerged that influence the status of sports locations. These factors include facility sharing, changing access to infrastructure and travel nodes, proximity to tourism and service developments and associations with media markets (Stevens, 2001). Bale (1989) uses the term 'spheres of influence' to describe the power of attraction of sports teams. The way in which spheres of influence now exist has been transformed by globalization and contemporary mobility.

The potential for place competition is perhaps greatest in cases where sports can be either reproduced or transported (Hinch & Higham, 2004). Green sports are those that are dependant on the integration of a physical activity with specific environmental attributes (Bale, 1989). Sports such as surfing, cross-country skiing, windsurfing, sailing, mountain climbing and orienteering are examples of green sports, as they are built around specific features of the natural environment as sources of pleasure, challenge and competition. The experiential value of these sports is largely dependent upon the mood of the landscapes where they are performed. These landscapes are inherently non-transportable. Claims of the 'original' or 'spiritual' home of sports may also be emphasized to counter transportability and promote authentic experiences. English sports administrators claim priority in many modern sports (e.g., tennis, rugby, cricket) that have been globalized through the forces of migration and mobility. These strategies may counter transportability and have utility in terms of place competition.

However, other sports are readily transported. Sports that are traditionally played in outdoor settings can also be transported and performed in indoor sports centres and arenas. Examples include tennis, netball, athletics and even equestrian activities. These sports demonstrate what Bale (1989:171) refers to as the 'industrialisation of the sport environment', which relates closely to the concept of transportability.

The application of technology to the modern stadium demonstrates the height of sport transportability. Stadium sports such as football are transportable and this offers opportunities for building new markets and generating revenue. End-of-season tours by Manchester United FC to Dubai and Japan, tours that place much greater emphasis on promotional and media outcomes than on field performance, are a deliberate attempt to build fan support and merchandise revenue. Some sports facilities may be built, permanently or temporarily, at locations designed to maximize market access. Such developments offer the potential to enhance the status of sports, such as snowboarding and beach volleyball, through increased public awareness and spectatorship. However, the transportability of sports also presents the threat of the displacement of a sporting activity from its original location. Retaining and enhancing the idiosyncrasies and elements of uniqueness associated with tourism places are important strategies to mitigate this threat (Bale, 1989:171).

Tour circuits, as well as one-off sporting contests, are also highly mobile. Tour circuits incorporating a sequence of different places where competition occurs are a hotbed of place competition. Tour circuits have two noteworthy implications for sport tourism. First, they transform the athlete or contestant into a sports traveller as the tour circuit moves from one venue, city, country or continent to the next. Secondly, they create intense competition between places for inclusion on tour schedule. Examples of highly mobile sports tours abound. The IRB International Sevens circuit, most notably the annual tournament that is hosted in Hong Kong (China), has been developed and promoted as a sports festival, often in association with other urban tourist activities. Coastal cities across the various continents compete to 'host' ocean yacht races as ports of call. Formula One (F1), which currently involves seventeen races in the annual Grand Prix circuit, is another example of a seasonal professional sport circuit. A recent addition to the F1 circuit is the new Dubai Grand Prix, which is built upon commercial interests and place competition (see Case study 13.2). Indeed, the emergence of the rival A1 Grand Prix (A1GP) circuit, which signals a return to moderated financial and technological parameters and competition based on national representation, signals a reaction to the overbearing commercial interests of F1.

Case Study 13.2

Dubai, sport and peak oil

In recent years Dubai has built through sport and tourism an image of futuristic development, economic power and luxury. Transportable sports such as F1, Super Cars, golf, ocean yachting and horse racing, among others, have been developed as mechanisms to build an image of affluence and elitism. Sport is the cornerstone of a multi-billion dollar strategy to build the image of the Gulf region, drive tourism and alleviate economic dependency on oil and natural gas. Under peak oil scenarios the need to invest in the future of the Gulf economies has been recognized. Oil revenues are being actively invested in the development of a commercial hub in a region that is strategically located between Europe and the increasingly powerful economies of the east, particularly India and China. Sport and sport-related tourism form a prominent part of this strategy.

In mid-November 2007 the European professional golf tour was extended, not for the first time, to an annual tournament that takes place far beyond the European continent. Four European golf tour tournaments now take place in the Gulf; the same number that takes place in the United Kingdom (Gillis et al., 2007). The Dubai Desert Classic is the richest golf tournament in the world with prize money alone (excluding appearance payments) of US$20 million. Similar courses of investment and domination are taking place in sports as diverse as racing, football, cricket, tennis, rugby sevens, motor sport, athletics and ocean racing. The Gulf states of Saudi Arabia, Qatar, Oman, Kuwait, Bahrain and the United Arab Emirates have all pursued tourism, luxury holiday homes and sport as key development initiatives, none more so than Dubai. Gillis et al. (2007 np) cite Ken Schofield, former chief executive of the European Tour (golf), who oversaw the development of the 'Beyond our Boundaries' strategy:

> It is 25 years since the European Tour played an event outside the borders of Europe, the 1982 Tunisian Open. The Tunisian Tourist Board offered £60,000 provided we would make it an official event. The Tour's decision to expand helped put the emirate Dubai and other parts of the Gulf on the sporting map ... The boundaries of golf have gone way, way beyond Europe and the European Tour as we know it will eventually cease to exist.

Similar developments have been directed towards other sports. Bahrain was the first Gulf state to claim an F1 Grand Prix in 2004. Dubai money is behind the new A1GP series, an alternative to F1. Abu Dhabi, which has the greatest oil reserves in the Gulf, is due to host its F1 Grand Prix in 2009. This was facilitated by the government's purchase of a five percent stake in Ferrari. The race will take place on an island in the shadow of a new Ferrari theme park. Qatar has hosted a round of the MotoGP championship since

2004, a race that in March 2009 will take place under lights to suit European television audiences. In terms of international cricket Sharjah holds the record for staging the most one-day internationals at a single venue. In 2005 the International Cricket Council (ICC) moved from Lord's to take up residence in Dubai's Sports City. A new ground is being built to house the ICC Academy. Recently Manchester United FC was paid $50 million to set up a football skills academy in Dubai (Gillis et al., 2007).

In Qatar, the state-owned Qatar Investment Authority (QIA) has a fund of US $50 billion, which has been invested in hosting the end-of-season women's tennis championship (held previously in Madrid, Spain) from 2008 to 2010. The capital, Doha, hosted the Asian Games (athletics) in 2006 and will host the Asia Cup (football) in 2011. An underground football stadium is being purpose built for the Asian Cup. It is bidding to host the World Indoor Athletics Championships in 2010 and recently announced its intention to bid for the Olympic Games in 2016. This intention in itself signals the ambition that Doha be seen to sit alongside iconic world cities that seek to contest the hosting rights for the Olympic Games. The importance of the value of these sports in terms of place position is evident in the words of Hasan Ali bin Ali (Chairman of the Doha 2016 Games bid committee) who states that 'We hope people will come to Qatar and see a different Arab world than they perceive it to be' (cited by Gillis et al., 2007 np).

Economic development and place promotion that is anchored by sport and tourism are not without their critics. Gillis et al. (2007) describe this as an investment of petrodollars that is distorting world sport. The Gulf states covet the FIFA World Cup and Qatar has developed academies for young African footballers, which has been criticized as the trafficking of African football talent. Qatari wealth has also been invested in Kenyan athletes and Bulgarian weightlifters who have been lured to Qatar by 'passports of convenience' and salaries to train in and ultimately represent Qatar. Gillis et al. (2007) also highlight concerns that interests in sport development exclude the nationals of the Gulf States and are instead directed towards the interests of tourists and expatriates.

Source: Gillis, R., Oliver, B. and Briggs, N. (2007). The political economy of sport. *The Observer*. 11 November 2007

CONCLUSION

Globalization and contemporary mobility have brought places into intense competition. Cities have engaged competitively in the development of constructed infrastructures and facilities to attract investment and transnational businesses (e.g., financial services, technology, telecommunications) as well as tourism and hospitality development. Sport and tourism have figured prominently in terms of place competition as cities compete for prominence and standing in a global urban hierarchy. International sports events, professional sports franchises and new stadia are 'powerful and effective vehicles for the showcasing of place and the creation of destination image' (Silk, 2004:355). The prominence of sport celebrities in global media markets may also serve interests in enhancing the prominence of places they represent. The development of tourism and hospitality services have, alongside efforts to compete in the global sports marketplace (Wilcox & Andrews, 2003), been a prominent aspect of global place competition. Convention centres and hotels that provide conference and meeting facilities and support services are part of this trend. The creation of sport, tourism and entertainment precincts, extending to casinos, megaplexes and cinemas, in sanitized and physically bounded inner city zones, is described by Bélanger (2000) as the 'spectacularization of spaces'.

Such efforts to augment the global standing of places may, however, lead to undesirable side effects. The development of clean, safe and sanitized consumption spaces may result in the creation of sterile tourist bubbles of inner city entertainment. Such spaces of consumption are inevitably based on selective interpretations of cultural meaning that create alienation and exclusion based on race, gender, income and class (Silk, 2004). Furthermore, as Silk (2004:372) notes, 'the urban core begins to look exactly like every other city; multinational stores replace local shops, unsubtle signs of Disneyfication emerge, gentrification removes long-term residential populations and destroys the older urban fabric, and the city loses some of its marks of history tradition, and distinction'. This standardization of cityscapes as a by-product of attempts to climb the global urban hierarchy is an example of globalization processes that erode the uniqueness of places. Clearly, the renegotiation of place and deliberate strategic efforts to enhance the competitiveness of places require the careful negotiation of local and global interests.

PART 6

Conclusion

Globalization, Mobility and Identity: Building Theoretically Informed Insights into the Study of Sport and Tourism

CONTENTS

Weed's (2005) paper on sports tourism theory and method used the analogy of bricks in the brickyard to decry the lack of theoretically informed research serving the study of sport and tourism. He argues against the need for isolated and descriptive studies in the field of sport and tourism, which add random bricks (i.e., scholarly papers) to the stockpile of accumulated knowledge. Rather, he calls for the arrangement of bricks into an edifice or theoretical structure that provides a foundation for advancing research serving the field. Gibson (2006:2) echoes this concern with her call for the study of sport and tourism to 'move beyond description to explanation' by grounding investigations in theory. This book responds by attempting a critical discussion of sport and tourism in a way that is situated within the overarching themes and the theories and concepts underpinning the study of globalization, mobility and identity.

In doing so we have sought to achieve the benefits of interdisciplinary perspectives; an aim that has been greatly supported by the insights provided by a number of scholars who have contributed case studies that are anchored in a range of disciplinary fields (i.e., physical education, sports psychology, political science, the sociology of sport, tourism studies, leisure studies and economic geography). Within the broad context of globalization, mobility and identity, the heuristic of activity, people and place, as drawn from the work of Weed and Bull (2004), has provided the structure for the chapters presented in Parts 3–5. This, we hope, has allowed a critical and theoretically informed examination of these core elements of sport and tourism phenomena. This chapter concludes by providing a brief integrated discussion of the foregoing chapters in a manner that explicitly addresses the overarching themes that have informed our writing.

GLOBALIZATION

Processes associated with globalization have driven the compression of time and space, growing interdependencies across spatial and non-spatial boundaries, the emergence of more flexible forms of production and the uneven distribution of impacts arising from new forms of production. In Chapter 2 (*Sport and tourism in a global world*), we argued that sport and tourism have featured prominently in these processes both as agents of the acceleration of global processes and in terms of the manifestation of consequential impacts. The confluence of sport and tourism has proven to be a fertile ground for the study of globalization. Two key issues related to globalization in the context of sport tourism have emerged. The first is the question of whether globalization leads to homogenization. While some scholars in the realm of sport disagree with this thesis, many tourism scholars see homogenization as a real threat. The second issue is the concern that globalization is leading to (de)territorialization, a situation in which traditional territorial boundaries lose their relevance as they are bypassed by new interdependencies at various levels of spatial scale. In the context of sport, (de)territorialization is reflected in the erosion of 'patriot games' as the dominant form of sport in favour of more cosmopolitan forms of professional sport and the emergence of worldwide sporting subcultures. Similarly, global business networks are breaking down many of the former territorial boundaries that dominated the tourism trade. The irony of this is that tourism is driven by perceived differences between places, yet the travel trade itself is characterized by (de)territorialization processes that tend to moderate these differences.

The theme of globalization lies at the core of all of the discussions presented in Chapters 5–13. There are, however, particularly salient points that bear emphasis. Sport tourism activities are clearly being impacted by globalization. Chapters 5, 6 and 7 (Part 3) demonstrate this in the context of elite competition, spectatorship and serious recreational sports. At a fundamental level, all of these realms are characterized by the compression of space and time and growing interdependencies. Elite athletes must travel the globe to compete, spectators are now able to stay connected with elite athletes and teams regardless of where they are competing and serious non-elite athletes have become part of sporting worlds which are no longer constrained by local or national boundaries. These chapters demonstrate that sporting activities are a manifestation of culture and that the culture of consumption that has accompanied globalization is a major characteristic of elite sport, spectatorship and serious recreational sport. Globalization processes do, however, present a sometimes contradictory array of opportunities and threats. One of the best examples of this has been the introduction of live big screen broadcasts of sporting events in satellite locations both adjacent to and removed from the actual event. This development has the potential to dramatically alter the current relationship between activity, people and place for better or worse. Further theorizing and empirical research in the field are required to develop a level of understanding that captures the potential benefits of this trend and obvious threats that it may present.

Globalization processes and impacts also permeate the 'people' dimensions of sport tourism (Chapters 8–10, Part 4). We argue that the search for authenticity remains strong in a globalized world where the consumption of sport experiences is one of the ways in which individuals and collectives of people can articulate their place in the world. Rather than searching for authenticity of the object, it is posited in Chapter 8 (*Authentic experiences*) that under globalization, the search has turned toward the authenticity of the experience in which sport and travel offer unique experiential opportunities. With its focus on temporary sport migrants, Chapter 9 (*Temporary sport migrants*) demonstrated that globalization has been characterized by a change in migration motivations from those that are centred on production (e.g., employment, career development and livelihood) to consumption (e.g., leisure lifestyle) or, more commonly, a combination of production and consumption. Chapter 10 (*Transnationalism, migration and diaspora*) explores aspects of transnationalism both in terms of elite athletes engaged in sport labour migrations and recreational participants in sports. These discussions also highlight the diminishing distinctions between production and consumption and work and leisure among mobile transnational communities of sport participants.

Globalization processes have also informed the 'place' related chapters (Chapters 11–13) presented in Part 5. Chapter 11 (*Modern landscapes and retro parks*) highlights the growing local distinctiveness of some sports, which is critical to the competitiveness of tourism destinations. In doing so it also draws attention to the potential for replication and imitation in a global world of transportable sports resources. These discussions emphasize the need to foster unique sports experiences that are place dependent. Anchoring sport experiences in terms of distinctive elements of culture, heritage and nostalgia may be a strategy that counters the high transportability of global sports and nurtures local competitiveness. A fundamental proposition of Chapter 12 (*Place attachment*) is that globalization has been accompanied by a change in the way we understand 'home' as a result of increased mobility. It is argued that it is no longer primarily the home environment that is the subject of place attachment but that these bonds have become increasingly relevant in the context of sport tourism places. Chapter 13 (*Sport and place competition*) highlights the growing competition between places, however distant, and the complexities of adopting sport-based strategies to renegotiate place meaning and enhance place competitiveness.

MOBILITY

Contemporary mobility is the second of our three overarching themes and is closely associated with processes of globalization. A broad range of mobilities is discussed in Chapter 3 (*Sport and contemporary mobility*), including personal and professional, commercial and political and environmental and amenity mobilities. The traditional practice of viewing tourism as short-term leisure travel restricts the study and understanding of sport and tourism phenomena. Viewing sport and tourism through the broader lens of mobility provides a richer vein of analysis and inquiry. Dramatic changes in sport and tourism mobility have challenged the historical connections between sports and places. Researchers, therefore, need to consider these new linkages and their implications. Particular attention should be given to those sports that are becoming detached from place and those that are place dependent. Insight into these areas can be gained by studying mobility – the various flows of resources, activities and people across sporting places.

Chapter 5 (*Globalization and the mobility of elite competitors*) highlights the dramatic growth in the mobility of elite athletes and their activities over the past quarter of a century. New forms of sport mobility have challenged performance and given rise to new directions in countering 'home team advantages' in sport competition. Chapter 6 (*Spectatorship and spectator experiences*) addresses not only the increased mobility of spectators but also the mobility of sites of consumption, in the form of alternative broadcast venues. Chapter 7 (*Recreational sport and serious leisure*) recognizes that while the motivations of recreational participants are strikingly different from those of elite athletes, these sport tourists are just as serious about negotiating the constraints of travel in order to pursue their sporting interests and ambitions. This is especially true in the case of recreational athletes who treat sport as serious leisure. However, just as their motivations to travel differ from those of elite athletes and the spectators who follow elite athletes, their behaviours and experiences of destinations are also likely to be different.

The mobility theme is also highlighted throughout the 'people' dimension of sport tourism. Although little direct reference to mobility is made in Chapter 8 (*Authentic experiences*), the search for authenticity and its importance to sport travellers presents one of the more powerful motives to negotiate the constraints of travel. This incentive is one of the keys to mobility. In contrast, mobility is an explicit theme in Chapter 9 (*Temporary sport migrants*) as mobility perspectives encourage the study of diverse manifestations of temporary migration. Chapter 10 (*Transnationalism, migration and diaspora*) emphasizes the high mobility of sports, both in historical and contemporary times, as well as the mobilities of sports participants. These mobilities extend from recreational participants including second home owners to competitive (non-elite) and elite sport labour migrants who exist in highly mobile transnational communities. The manifestations of such diverse sport-related mobilities, including migration, return migration and visiting friends and relatives (VFR) (on a range of spatial and temporal scales), and the consequences of generating and receiving regions certainly warrant further academic attention.

Our discussions of modern landscapes and retro parks in Chapter 11 (*Modern landscapes and retro parks*) highlight the mobility of sports resources, both natural and built, and sports participants. Such mobilities figure prominently in discourses relating to global environmental change, biodiversity loss and climate change. Sport has been a driving force of change in both natural landscapes and urban design. It is critical that manifestations of such change are not only sustainable but also that they build distinctive rather than replicated elements of place. The concept of mobility lies at the heart of place attachment. For many of the early scholars in this area (e.g., Relph, 1976; Tuan, 1975), mobility was seen as a barrier to forming strong bonds to place. Their focus was on the sense of place related to home. Chapter 12 (*Place attachment*) not only argued that it is possible to become attached to places away from one's original home but that sport has several qualities that help to foster this attachment. In this respect, Chapter 13 (*Sport and place competition*) addresses the mobility of sports at various competitive levels. The relevance of global, national and regional sports to tourism places is featured through such diverse mediums as the hosting and staging of global sports events and the use of sport team brands to advance interests in regional differentiation and place promotion.

IDENTITY

The third of the three themes that underpinned this book is identity. Like mobility, identity is intimately related to the processes of globalization. In fact, globalization has resulted in a crisis of identity as traditional reference points have been eroded or lost altogether. Sport and tourism are fertile grounds on which to respond to this crisis, with the tourism industry in particular being in the business of providing travel experiences that enable leisure travellers to build personal narratives away from the constraints of work. The confluence of sport and tourism is especially attractive in terms of the development of these identity narratives. Cultural discourses around sport play important roles in the formation of individual and collective identities. While the hegemony of the dominant class still exerts substantial influence, the emergence of the Gay Games, Paralympics and various counter cultural-oriented extreme sports is evidence of sport's ability to forge more contemporary and more fluid identities. In addition to this discursive approach to identity formation, the 'corporeal realities of the lived sporting body' (Hockey & Collinson, 2007) make sport a unique and, increasingly, an important identity maker in a globalized world. Tourism's ability to package these sporting experiences and to sell them in the global marketplace underscores the relevance of sport tourism as a powerful identity maker.

Identity themes were firmly embedded in the activity-based chapters (Chapters 5–7). While the thematic emphasis in Chapter 5 (*Globalization and the mobility of elite competitors*) is mobility, it is clear that the individual and collective identities of these athletes help to determine how well they perform while travelling away from home. The placement of New Zealand artefacts and symbols of indigenous identity in the New Zealand quarters of the Olympic Village (Beijing) reflects an attempt to reinforce national identity and to provide some familiar reference points in what could be an alien environment. Chapter 6 (*Spectatorship and spectator experiences*) raises questions related, for example, to identity and diasporas, in particular, the question of whether migrants see themselves as hosts or guests when they attend a competition between a team from their place of birth and one from their current place of residence. Identity themes are central in Chapter 7 (*Recreational sport and serious leisure*), with one of the key arguments being that travel in the pursuit of serious leisure is motivated in large part by the need to construct one's identity. Sport travel experiences provide a form of social capital that can be used to build personal narratives and to position oneself in a collective.

The 'people' based chapters are also infused with identity themes. Chapter 8 (*Authentic experiences*) suggests that the pursuit of existential authenticity is a form of self-making. The fact that sport tourism experiences are a form of commodification does not negate the potential to function as diacritical marks of identity, thereby contributing to the identity of both the guests and the hosts. The identity theme is also explicitly addressed in Chapter 9 (*Temporary sport migrants*) with identity building being the primary consideration of 'seekers'. Such temporary sport migrants build their identities around their leisure experiences rather than through material possessions and traditional working careers. Identity is also central to the discussions presented in Chapter 10 (*Transnationalism, migration and diaspora*), which considers some of the elements of collective and/or personal identity that are derived from sports in a global and mobile world. These linkages extend to the sport-related identities of transnational and diasporic communities as well as the national identities that may be built on some sports much more than others.

In terms of 'place', given the high mobility of sports resources (Chapter 11, *Modern landscapes and retro parks*) it is argued that the unique historic and nostalgic associations between sports places and contemporary sport experiences are critical to the uniqueness and competitiveness of tourism places. Such associations cement the importance of place in the 'activity, people and place' tripartite as it becomes fundamental to the sport experience and the building of personal or collective identity through sport experiences. The concept of place identity is central to Chapter 12 (*Place attachment*). It is argued that sport tourism offers a variety of unique features that serve to foster place dependence and place identity. In forming attachments to sport places, individuals are able to address the crisis of identity that has accompanied globalization. They are also able to build personal and group narratives that become integral parts of their identity. Place identity is a central element of the discussions presented in Chapter 13 (*Sport and place competition*), which considers the ways in which place identity can be both constructed and destroyed within the wider context of place competition as the politics of identity are played out.

MEETING THE CHALLENGE

In response to Weed (2005) and Gibson (2006), we have sought to situate our discussions of sport and tourism within the overarching themes of globalization, mobility and identity. In doing so we have attempted to engage with theoretical perspectives relating to globalization (e.g., Harvey, 1989), mobility (e.g., Hall, 2004) and identity (e.g., Maguire, 1999) and related conceptual frameworks, including leisure constraint theory (e.g., Jackson, Crawford & Godbey, 1993), serious leisure (e.g., Stebbins, 1982, 1993), authenticity (e.g., Cohen, 1988; Wang, 1999) and place identity (e.g., Slack, 1988). These concepts have withstood the test of scholarly critique in other realms of the social sciences but are only beginning to be used in the context of sport tourism.

Globalization is an influential focus of theorizing in the social sciences. While work in the field of globalization has lost some of its emotional edge in recent years, it has matured as deeper and broader insights have been achieved. Progress has also been made in terms of the development of interdisciplinary perspectives and understandings, which are valuable in informing the study of sport and tourism. The mobility and identity themes fit nicely alongside globalization. The emergence of mobility perspectives in the tourism literature (Hall, 2004; Burns & Novelli, 2008) opens new lines of inquiry, which are obscured when tourism is narrowly defined (e.g., Chapter 9, *Temporary sport migrants*). Sport and tourism have, in turn, become a focal point for identity construction and certainly merit continued attention in this regard.

The heuristic of activity, people and place that serves as the framework for chapters 5–13 is drawn from Weed and Bull's (2004:37) conceptualization of sports tourism as 'a social, economic and cultural phenomenon arising from the unique interaction of activity, people and place'. This heuristic emphasizes that in sport and tourism activity (i.e., sport), people (e.g., athletes and spectators) and place (e.g., tourism destinations) are inextricably integrated and, as such, makes a significant contribution to this book far beyond providing the structure for the chapters presented in Parts 3–5. For example, it has allowed us to appreciate that the professionalization of a sport activity has a direct bearing on the mobility of athletes and spectators, which in turn has a bearing on the meanings attached to the places where sports are played. As new place identities affect global processes, they continue to have far-reaching consequences for the component elements of activity, people and place.

Globalization, mobility and identity are major social science themes. Their interplay through activity, people and place in a sport tourism context is substantial, complex and dynamic. As such, this is a rich area for continuing academic enquiry in which empirical studies that are consciously integrated with existing literature contribute to theorizing sport tourism.

References

Abbott, A. and Smith, D.R. (1984). Governmental Constraints and Labour Market Mobility: Turnover among College Athletic Personnel. *Work and Occupations*, 11, 1, 29–53.

Adams, P. (1995). A Reconsiderati'on of Personal Boundaries in Space-Time. *Annals of the Association of American Geographers*, 85, 2, 267–285.

Adams, P. (1999). Bringing Globalization Home: A Homemaker in the Information Age. *Urban Geography*, 20, 4, 356–376.

Adler, P.A. and Adler, P. (1999a). Resort Workers: Adaptations in the Leisure-Work Nexus. *Sociological Perspectives*, 42, 3, 369–402.

Adler, P.A. and Adler, P. (1999b). Transience and the Postmodern Self: The Geographic Mobility of Resort Workers. *The Sociological Quarterly*, 40, 1, 31–58.

Adler, P.A. and Adler, P. (2001). Off-time labor in resorts: The social construction of commercial time. *American Behavioral Scientist*, 44, 7, 1096–1114.

Aitken, C. and Hall, C.M. (2000). Migrant and Foreign Skills and Their Relevance to the Tourism Industry. *Tourism Geographies*, 2, 1, 66–86.

Allison, M. (1982). Sport, Culture and Socialization. *International Review for the Sociology of Sport*, 17, 4, 11–37.

Amin, A. and Thrift, N. (1997). Globalisation, Socio-Economics, Territoriality. In Geographies of Economies, (R. Lee and J. Wills ed.) pp.147–157, London: Arnold.

Andrews, D. (2006). Sports-Commerce-Culture: Essays on Sport in Late Capitalist America. New York: Peter Lang.

Arbena, J.L. (1994). Dimensions of International Talent Migration in Latin American Sports. In The Global Sports Arena: Athletic Talent Migration in an Interdependent World, (J. Maguire and J. Bale ed.) pp.99–111, London: Frank Cass & Co. Ltd.

Archer, E.G. (2003). Imperial Influences: Gibraltarians, Cultural Bonding and Sport. *Sport in Society*, 6, 1, 43–60.

Ateljevic, I. and Doorne, S. (2000). 'Staying within the Fence': Lifestyle Entrepreneurship in Tourism. *Journal of Sustainable Tourism*, 8, 5, 378–392.

Baade, R.A. (1996). Professional Sports as Catalysts for Metropolitan Economic Development. *Journal of Urban Affairs*, 18, 1, 1–17.

Baker, J., Cote, J. and Abernathy, B. (2003). Sport-Specific Practice and the Development of Expertise Decision-Making in Team Ball Sports. *Journal of Applied Sport Psychology*, 15, 1, 12–25.

Bale, J. (1982). Sport and Place: A Geography of Sport in England, Scotland and Wales. London: C. Hurst & Co. Ltd.

Bale, J. (1986). Sport and National Identity: A Geographical View. *The British Journal of Sociology*, 3, 1, 18–41.

Bale, J. (1989). Sports Geography. London: E & FN Spon.

Bale, J. (1993). Sport, Space and the City. London: Routledge.

Bale, J. (1994). Landscapes of Modern Sport. Leicester: Leicester University Press.

Bale, J. (2003). Sports Geographies. London: Routledge.

Bale, J. and Sang, J. (1994). Out of Africa: The 'Development' of Kenyan Athletics, Talent Migration and the Global Sports System. In The Global Sports Arena: Athletic Talent Migration in an Interdependent World, (J. Maguire and J. Bale ed.) pp.206–225, London: Frank Cass & Co. Ltd.

Balmer, N.J., Nevill, A.M. and Williams, A.M. (2001). Home Advantage in the Winter Olympics (1908–1998). *Journal of Sports Sciences*, 19, 2, 129–139.

Bass, D., Wells, F. and Ridgeway, R. (1986). Seven Summits. New York: Warner Books.

Baudrillard, J. (1983). Simulations. New York: Semiotext.

BBC Sport. (2002). IRB to Debate Players' Welfare http://news.bbc.co.uk/sport1/hi/rugby_union/international/2139083.stm (Retrieved July 19 2002).

BBC Sport. (2005). Dallaglio: Players' Careers under Threat http://news.bbc.co.uk/sport1/hi/rugby_union/4390867.stm (Retrieved 31 March 2005).

Beal, B. (1995). Disqualifying the Official: An Exploration of Social Science Resistance through the Subculture of Skateboarding. *Sociology of Sport Journal*, 12, 3, 252–267.

Bearns, M. (2003). Adding Some International Flavor. Ski Area Management, 42, 5, 40–41 & 58.

Beauchamp, P. (2008). Event Horizons Expanding. Sunday Herald, September 17, pp. 73.

Becken, S. (2007). Tourists' Perception of International Air Travel's Impact on the Global Climate and Potential Climate Change Policies. *Journal of Sustainable Tourism*, 15, 4, 351–368.

Belhassen, Y. and Caton, K. (2006). Authenticity Matters. *Annals of Tourism Research*, 33, 3, 853–856.

Bell, M. and Ward, G. (2000). Comparing Temporary Mobility with Permanent Migration. *Tourism Geographies*, 2, 1, 87–107.

Bellan, G.L. and Bellan-Santini, D.R. (2001). A Review of Littoral Tourism, Sport and Leisure Activities: Consequences on Marine Flora and Fauna. Aquatic Conservation: *Marine and Freshwater Ecosystems*, 11, 4, 325–333.

Bender, C. (2000). Snowmaking Survey. *Ski Area Management*, 39, 6, 52.

Ben-Porat, G. and Ben-Porat, A. (2004). (Un)Bounded Soccer: Globalization and Localization of the Game in Israel. *International Review for the Sociology of Sport*, 39, 4, 421–436.

Bianchi, R.V. (2000). Migrant Tourist-Workers: Exploring the 'Contact Zones' of Post-Industrial Tourism. *Current Issues in Tourism*, 3, 2, 107–137.

Biosecurity Zealand (2007). Pests and Diseases: Didymo http://www.biosecurity. govt.nz/didymo (Retrieved 14 August 2007).

Blumen, O. (1994). Gender Differences in the Journey to Work. *Urban Geography*, 15, 3, 223–245.

Boniface, B.G. and Cooper, C. (1994). The Geography of Travel and Tourism. Oxford: Butterworth Heinemann.

Boniface, P. and Fowler, P. (1993). Heritage and Tourism in the 'Global Village'. London: Routledge.

Boon, B. (2006). When Leisure and Work Are Allies: The Case of Skiers and Tourist Resort Hotels. *Career Development International*, 11, 7, 594–608.

Boorstin, D.J. (1964). The Image: A Guide to Pseudo-Events in America. New York: Atheneum.

Booth, D. (2000). Modern Sport: Emergence and Experiences. In Sport in New Zealand Society, (C. Collins ed.) pp. 45–63. Palmerston North: Dunmore Press.

Booth, D. and Loy, J.W. (1999). Sport, Status, and Style. *Sport History Review*, 30, 1–26.

Bosscher, V.D., Knop, P.D., Bottenburg, M.V. and Shibli, S. (2006). A Conceptual Framework for Analysing Sports Policy Factors Leading to International Sporting Success. *European Sports Management Quarterly*, 6, 2, 185–215.

Bossevain, J. (1996). Ritual, Tourism and Cultural Commoditization in Malta: Culture by the Pound? In *The Tourst Image: Myths and Myth-Making in Tourism* (T. Selwyn ed.) pp. 105–119. Chichester: Wiley Press.

Bourdeau, P., Corneloup, J. and Mao, P. (2002). Adventure Sports and Tourism in the French Mountains: Dynamics of Change and Challenges for Sustainable Development. *Current Issues in Tourism*, 5, 1, 22–32.

Bourdeau, P., Corneloup, J. and Mao, P. (2004). Adventure Sports and Tourism in the French Mountains: Dynamics of Change and Challenges for Sustainable Development. In Sport Tourism: Interrelationships, Impacts and Issues, (B.W. Ritchie and D. Adair eds.) pp. 101–116, Clevedon: Channel View Publications.

Bourdieu, P. (1978). Sport and Social Class. *Social Science Information*, 17, 6, 819–840.

Bourke, A. (2003). The Dream of Being a Professional Soccer Player: Insights on Career Development Options of Young Irish Players. *Journal of Sport and Social Issues*, 27, 4, 399–419.

Boyle, P., Halfacree, K. and Robinson, V. (1998). Exploring Contemporary Migration. Harlow: Addison Wesley Longman Limited.

Boyle, R. and Haynes, R. (2000). Power Play: Sport, the Media and Popular Culture. London: Pearson Education.

Bray, S.R. and Carron, A.V. (1993). The Home Advantage in Alpine Skiing. *Australian Journal of Science and Medicine in Sport*, 25, 76–81.

Breakwell, G.M. (1986). Coping with Threatened Identity. London: Methuen.

Breakwell, G.M. (1992). Social Psychology of Identity and the Self Concept. Guildford: Surrey University Press.

Bromberger, C. (1994). Foreign Footballers, Cultural Dreams and Community Identity in Some Northwestern Mediterranean Cities. In *The Global Sports Arena: Athletic Talent Migration in an Interdependent World*, (J. Bale and J. Maguire ed.) pp. 171–182. London: Frank Cass & Co Ltd.

Brown, B. (2004). Village People Play for the Boomers. The Australian, pp. 8–10.

Brown, D. (2001). Modern Sport, Modernism and the Cultural Manifesto: De Coubertin's Revue Olympique. *International Journal of the History of Sport*, 18, 2, 78–109.

Brown, G., Chalip, L., Jago, L. and Mules, T. (2002). The Sydney Olympics and Brand Australia. In Destination Branding: Creating the Unique Destination Proposition, (M. Morgan, A. Pritchard and R. Pride ed.) pp.163–185, Oxford: Butterworth-Heinemann.

Brown, R.M. (1935). The Business of Recreation. *Geographical Review*, 25, 3, 467–475.

Buckley, R.C. ed. (2004). *Environmental impacts of ecotourism*. Oxford: CAB International.

Bull, C. and Weed, M. (1999). Niche Markets and Small Island Tourism: The Development of Sports Tourism in Malta. *Managing Leisure*, 4, 3, 142–155.

Burns, P.M. and Novelli, M. eds. (2008). Tourism and Mobilities: Local-Global Connections. Wallingford: CABI.

Butler, R. and Hinch, T.D. (2007). Tourism and Indigenous Peoples: Issues and Implications. Oxford: Butterworth-Heinemann.

Butler, R.W. (1990). Alternative Tourism: Pious Hope or Trojan Horse. *Journal of Travel Research*, 28, 3, 40–45.

Butler, R.W. (1996). The Role of Tourism in Cultural Transformation in Developing Countries. In Tourism and Culture: Global Civilisation in Change, (Y. Nuryanti ed.) pp. 91–112, Yogyakarta: Gadjah Mada University Press.

Butler, R.W. (2005). The Influence of Sport on Destination Development: The Case of Golf at St. Andrews, Scotland. In Sport Tourism Destinations, (J.E.S. Higham ed.) pp.274–282, Oxford: Elsevier Butterworth Heinemann.

Bywater, M. (1993). The Youth and Student Travel Market. *Travel and Tourism Analyst*, 3, 35–50.

Cachay, K. (1993). Sports and Environment, Sports for Everyone-Room for Everyone? *International Review for the Sociology of Sport*, 28, 311–323.

Carmichael, B. and Murphy, P.E. (1996). Tourism Economic Impact of a Rotating Sports Event: The Case of the British Columbia Games. *Festival Management and Event Tourism*, 4, 3/4. 127–138.

Carmichael, B. and Murphy, P.E. (1997). Tourism Economic Impact of a Rotating Sports Event: The Case of the British Columbia Games. *Festival Management and Event Tourism*, 4, 127–138.

Carr, N. (1998). The Young Tourist: A Case of Neglected Research. *Progress in Tourism and Hospitality Research*, 4, 4, 307–318.

Carr, N. (1999). A Study of Gender Differences: Young Tourist Behaviour in a UK Coastal Resort. *Tourism Management*, 20, 2, 223–228.

Carter, S. (1997). Who Wants to Be a Peelie Wally? Glaswegian Tourists' Attitudes to Suntans and Sun Exposure. In Tourism and Health: Risks, Research and Responses, (S. Clift and P. Grabowski ed.) pp. 130–150, London: Pinter.

Cartwright, R. (1996). Tourists' Diarrhoea. In Health and the International Tourist, (S. Clift and S.J. Page ed.) pp. 44–66, London: Routledge.

Cater, C. and Cater, E. (2007). Marine Ecotourism. Oxford: CABI Publishing.

Chadee, D.D. and Cutler, J. (1996). Insights into International Travel by Students. *Journal of Travel Research*, 35, 2, 75–80.

Chalip, L. (2001). Sport Tourism: Capitalising on the Linkage. In Perspectives: The Business of Sport, (D. Kluka and G. Schilling ed.) pp.77–89, Oxford: Meyer and Meyer.

Chalip, L. (2004). Case Study 3.1: Olympic Teams as Market Segments. In Sport Tourism Development, (T.D. Hinch and J.E.S. Higham ed.) pp.52–54, Clevedon: Channel View Publications.

Chalip, L. (2005). Marketing, Media, and Place Promotion. In Sport Tourism Destinations: Issues, Opportunities and Analysis, (J.E.S. Higham ed.) pp.162–176, Oxford: Elsevier Butterworth-Heinemann.

Chalip, L. (2006). The Big Buzz of Big Events: Is It Worth Bottling? Geelong: Deakin University.

Chalip, L. (2006). Towards Social Leverage of Sports Events. *Journal of Sport & Tourism*, 11, 2, 109–127.

Chalip, L. (2008). Leveraging benefits from Sport Tourism. Unpublished keynote address, First Commonwealth Conference on Sport Tourism, Kota Kinabalu, Malaysia, May 13–15, 2008.

Chalip, L. and Costa, C. (2005). Building Sport Event Tourism into the Destination Brand: Foundations for a General Theory. In Sport Tourism: Theory and Concepts, (H. Gibson ed.) pp.86–105, London: Routledge.

Chalip, L. and Costa, C.A. (2006). Building Sport Event Tourism into the Destination Brand: Foundations for a General Theory. In Sport Tourism: Concepts and Theories, (H. Gibson ed.) pp. 86–105, London: Routledge.

Chalip, L., Green, B.C. and Hill, B. (2003). Effects of Sport Event Media on Destination Image and Intention to Visit. *Journal of Sport Management*, 17, 214–234.

Chalip, L. and Leyns, A. (2002). Local Business Leveraging of a Sport Event: Managing an Event for Economic Benefit. *Journal of Sport Management*, 16, 2, 132–158.

Chalip, L. and Mcguirty, J. (2004). Bundling Sport Events with the Host Destination. *Journal of Sport & Tourism*, 9, 3, 267–282.

Charnofsky, H. (1968). The Major League Professional Baseball Player: Self-Conception Versus the Popular Image. *International Review for the Sociology of Sport*, 3, 39–55.

Chiba, N. (2004). Pacific Professional Baseball Leagues and Migratory Patterns and Trends: 1995–1999. *Journal of Sport and Social Issues*, 28, 2, 193–211.

Chiba, N., Ebihara, O. and Morino, S. (2001). Globalization, Naturalisation and Identity: The Case of Borderless Elite Athletes in Japan. *International Review for the Sociology of Sport*, 36, 2, 203–221.

Clarke, J. and Salt, J. (2001). Foreign Labour in the United Kingdom: Patterns and Trends. *Labour Market Trends*, 109, 10, 473–484.

Clarke, J. and Salt, J. (2003). Work Permits and Foreign Labour in the UK: A Statistical Review. *Labour Market Trends*, 111, 11, 563–565.

Clarke, N. (2005). Detailing Transnational Lives of the Middle: British Working Holiday Makers in Australia. *Journal of Ethnic and Migration Studies*, 31, 2, 307–322.

Clarke, S.R. and Allsopp, P. (2001). Fair Measures of Performance: The World Cup of Cricket. *Journal of the Operational Research Society*, 52, 4, 471–479.

Clarke, S.R. and Norman, J.M. (1995). Home Ground Advantage of Individual Clubs in English Soccer. *The Statistician*, 44, 509–521.

Clawson, M. and Knetsch, J. (1966). The Economics of Outdoor Recreation. Baltimore: John Hopkins Press.

Club, E.F. (2008). Hope University http://www.evertonfc.com/club/hope-university.html (Retrieved 01 February 2007).

Coakley, J. (2004). Sports in Society: Issues and Controversies. Boston: McGraw Hill Higher Education.

Coakley, J. (2007). Sports in Society: Issues and Controversies. Boston: McGraw Hill.

Coalter, F., Allison, M. and Taylor, J. (2000). The Role of Sport in Regenerating Deprived Urban Areas. Edinburgh: Center for Leisure Research, University of Edinburgh.

Cohen, E. (1974). Who Is a Tourist? A Conceptual Classification. *Sociological Review*, 22, 4, 527–555.

Cohen, E. (1988). Authenticity and the Commoditization of Tourism. *Annals of Tourism Research*, 15, 3, 371–386.

Cohen, E. (1995). Contemporary Tourism - Trends and Challenges: Sustainable Authenticity or Contrived Post-Modernity. In Tourism: People, Places, Processes, (R. Butler and D. Pearce ed.) pp.12–29, London: Routledge.

Cohen, E. (2002). Authenticity, Equity and Sustainability in Tourism. *Journal of Sustainable Tourism*, 10, 4, 267–276.

Cohen, E. and Taylor, L. (1976). Escape Attempts. London: Pelican.

Coleman, S. and Crang, M. eds. (2002). Tourism: Between Place and Performance. Oxford: Berghahn Books.

Coles, T., Duval, D.T. and Hall, C.M. (2004). Tourism, Mobility and Global Communities: New Approaches to Theorising Tourism and Tourist Spaces. In Global Tourism, (W.F. Theobold ed.) pp.463–481, Amsterdam: Elsevier Inc.

Coles, T. and Hall, C.M. eds. (2008). International Business and Tourism: Global Issues, Contemporary Interactions. London: Taylor & Francis Group.

Coles, T.E. and Timothy, D.J. eds. (2004). Tourism, Diasporas and Space. London: Routledge.

Conradson, D. and Latham, A. (2005). Transnational Urbanism: Attending to Everyday Practices and Mobilities. *Journal of Ethnic and Migration Studies*, 31, 2, 227–233.

Cooper, C. and Jackson, S. (1989). Destination Life Cycle: The Isle of Man Case Study. *Annals of Tourism Research*, 16, 3, 377–398.

Cooper, C. and Wahab, S. (2001). Conclusion. In *Tourism in the Age of Globalisation*, (C. Cooper and S. Wahab ed.) pp. 319–334. London: Routledge.

Cornelissen, S. (2004). Sport Mega-Events in Africa: Processes, Impacts and Prospects. *Tourism & Hospitality: Planning & Development*, 1, 1, 39–55.

Cornelissen, S. (2005). The Global Tourism System: Governance, Development and Lessons from South Africa. Aldershot: Ashgate Publishing.

Cornelissen, S. and Solberg, E. (2007). Sport Mobility and Circuits of Power: The Dynamics of Football Migration in Africa and the 2010 World Cup. *Politikon*, 34, 3, 295–314.

Cossar, J.H. (1996). Travellers' Health: A Medical Perspective. In Health and the International Tourist, (S. Clift and S.J. Page ed.) pp. 23–43. London: Routledge.

Costa, C. and Chalip, L. (2005). Adventure Sport Tourism in Rural Revitalization: An Ethnographic Evaluation. *European Sport Management Quarterly*, 5, 3, 257–279.

Craik, J. (1997). The Culture of Tourism. In *Touring Cultures - Transformations of Travel and Theory*, (C. Rojek and J. Urry ed.) pp. 113–137. London: Routledge.

Crang, M. (2004). Cultural Geographies of Tourism. In *A Companion to Tourism*, (A.S. Lew, C.M. Hall and A.M. Williams ed.) pp. 74–82. Oxford: Blackwell Publishing.

Crawford, S. (1985). The Game of Glory and Hard Knocks: A Study of the Interpenetration of Rugby and New Zealand Society. *Journal of Popular Culture*, 19, 2, 77–91.

Cresswell, S.L. and Eklund, R.C. (2005). Motivation and Burnout among Top Amateur Rugby Players. *Medicine & Science in Sport & Exercise*, 3, 469–477.

Cresswell, S.L. and Eklund, R.C. (2006). Athlete Burnout: Conceptual Confusion, Current Research, and Future Research Directions. In *Literature Reviews in Sport Psychology*, (S. Hanton and S. Mellalieu ed.) pp. 91–126. New York: Nova.

Crolley, L., Levermore, R. and Pear, G. (2002). For Business or Pleasure? A Discussion of the Impact of the European Law on the Economic Aspects of Football. *European Sports Management Quarterly*, 2, 4, 276–295.

Crompton, J.L. (1995). Economic Impact Analysis of Sports Facilities and Events: Eleven Sources of Misapplication. *Journal of Sport Management*, 9, 1, 14–35.

Crosset, T. and Beal, B. (1997). The Use Of "Subculture" And "Subworld" In Ethnographic Works on Sport: A Discussion of Definitional Distinctions. *Sociology of Sport Journal*, 14, 1, 73–85.

Crouch, D. (2000). Places around Us: Embodied Lay Geographies in Leisure and Tourism. *Leisure Studies*, 19, 2, 63–76.

Crowther, N. (2001). Visiting the Olympic Games in Ancient Greece: Travel and Conditions for Athletes and Spectators. *The International Journal of the History of Sport*, 18, 4, 37–52.

Csikszentmihalyi, M. (1975). Beyond Boredom and Anxiety. San Fancisco: Jossey-Bass.

Csikszentmihalyi, M. (1992). Flow: The Classic Work on How to Achieve Happiness. London: Rider Paperbacks.

Darcy, S. (2003). The Politics of Disability and Access: The Sydney 2000 Games Experience. *Disability and Society*, 18, 6, 737–757.

Daily Telegraph (2007). Britons Flying More Than Ever. The Daily Telegraph, pp. T4.

Davis, F. (1979). Yearning for Yesterday: A Sociology of Nostalgia. New York: Free Press.

Davis, J.S. (2005). Representing Places: "Deserted Isles" And the Reproduction of Bikini Atoll. *Annals of the Association of American Geographers*, 95, 3, 607–635.

Dawood, R. (1989). Tourists' Health: Could the Travel Industry Do More? Tourism Management. *December*, 285–287.

De Bres, K. and Davis, J. (2001). Celebrating Group and Place Identity: A Case Study of a New Regional Festival. *Tourism Geographies*, 3, 3, 326–337.

de Villers, D.J. (2001). Sport and Tourism to Stimulate Development. *Olympic Review*, 27, 38, 11–13.

Denham, D. (2004). Global and Local Influences on English Rugby League. *Sociology of Sport Journal*, 21, 2, 206–219.

Devine, A. and Devine, F. (2004). The Politics of Sports Tourism in Northern Ireland. *Journal of Sport Tourism*, 9, 2, 171–182.

Dietvorst, A.G.J. and Ashworth, G.J. (1995). Tourism Transformations: An Introduction. In Tourism and Spatial Transformations. Implications for Policy Planning, (G.J. Ashworth and A.G.J. Dietvorst ed.) pp.1–13, Wallingford: CAB International.

Dixon, J. and Durrheim, K. (2000). Displacing Place-Identity: A Discursive Approach to Locating Self and Other. *British Journal of Social Psychology*, 39, 1, 27–44.

Donaldson, E.A. (1986). The Scottish Highland Games in America. Louisiana: Pelican Publishing Company, Inc.

Donaldson, M. (2006). Behind the Scenes: The Art of Managing Downtime www.sundaystar-times.co.nz (Retrieved 26 November 2006).

Donaldson, M. (2008). World Cup Review: What a Super Idea. Sunday Star Times, pp. B6.

Donnelly, M. (2006). Studying Extreme Sports: Beyond the Core Participants. *Journal of Sport & Social Issues*, 30, 2, 219–224.

Donnelly, M. and Young, K. (1988). The Construction and Confirmation of Identity in Sport Subcultures. *Sociology of Sport Journal*, 5, 3, 223–240.

Donnelly, P. (1996). The Local and the Global: *Globalization in the Sociology of Sport. Journal of Sport & Social Issues*, 20, 3, 239–257.

Dredge, D. and Jenkins, J. (2003). Destination Place Identity and Regional Tourism Policy. *Tourism Geographies*, 5, 4, 383–407.

Duda, J. and Nicholls, J. (1992). Dimensions of Achievement Motivation in Schoolwork and Sport. *Journal of Educational Psychology*, 84, 3, 290–299.

Duke, V. (1994). The Flood from the East? Perestroika and the Migration of Sports Talent Fom Eastern Europe. In *The Global Sports Arena: Athletic Talent Migration in an Interdependent World* (J. Maguire and J. Bale ed.) pp. 153–170, London: Frank Cass & Co. Ltd.

Duncan, T. (2007). Working Tourists Identity Formation in a Leisure Space, Doctor of Philosophy. University College London: London.

Dunning, E.G., Maguire, J. and Pearton, R.E. (1993). Postscript: Sociology and the Sociology of Sport in a Rapidly Changing World. In *The Sports Process: A Comparative and Developmental Approach*, (E.G. Dunning, J. Maguire and R.E. Pearton ed.) pp. 311–312. Champaign, IL, USA: Human Kinetics Publishers.

During, S. (1985). Postmodernism or Postcolonialism? *Landfall*, 39, 366–380.

Duval, D.T. (2002). The Return Visit-Return Migration Connection. In Tourism and Migration: New Relationships between Production and Consumption, (C.M. Hall and A.M. Williams ed.) pp.257–276, Dordrecht: Kluwer Academic Publishers.

Duval, D.T. (2003). When Hosts Become Guests: Return Visits and Diasporic Identities in a Commonwealth Eastern Caribbean Community. *Current Issues in Tourism*, 6, 4, 267–308.

Duval, D.T. (2004a). Linking Return Visits and Return Migration among Commonwealth Eastern Caribbean Migrants in Toronto, Canada. *Global Networks: a Journal of Transnational Affairs*, 4, 1, 51–68.

Duval, D.T. (2004b). Conceptualising Return Visits: A Transnational Perspective. In Tourism, Diasporas and Space: Travels to Promised Lands, (T. Coles and D.J. Timothy ed.) pp.50–61, London: Routledge.

Duval, D.T. (2004c). Cultural Tourism in Post-Colonial Environments. In Tourism and Postcolonialism: Contested Discourses, Identities and Repre-sentations, (C.M. Hall and H. Tucker ed.) pp.57–75, London: Routledge.

Duval, D.T. and Hall, C.M. (2004). Linking Diasporas and Tourism: Trans-national Mobilities of Pacific Islanders Resident in New Zealand. In Tourism, Diasporas and Space: Travels to Promised Lands, (T. Coles and D.J. Timothy ed.) pp.78–94, London: Routledge.

Duval, D.T. and Hall, C.M. (2004). Transnational Mobilities of Pacific Islanders Resident in New Zealand. In Tourism, Diasporas and Space, (T. Coles and D.J. Timothy ed.) pp.78–94, London: Routledge.

Dwyer, L., Mellor, R., Mistilis, N. and Mules, T. (2000). A Framework for Assessing "Tangible" And "Intangible" Impacts of Events and Conventions. *Event Management*, 6, 3, 175–189.

Eco, U. (1986). Travels in Hyperreality. London: Picador.

Eichberg, H. (1994). Travelling, Comparing, Emigrating: Configurations of Sport Mobility. In The Global Sports Arena: Athletic Talent Migration in an Interdependent World, (J. Maguire and J. Bale ed.) pp.256–280, London: Frank Cass & Co. Ltd.

Eisenhauer, B.W., Krannich, R.S. and Blahna, D.J. (2000). Attachments to Special Places on Public Lands: An Analysis of Activities, Reason for Attachments, and Community Connections. *Society & Natural Resources*, 13, 5, 421–441.

Elias, N. (1991). The Society of Individuals. Oxford: Blackwell.

Euchner, C.C. (1993). Playing the Field: Why Sports Teams Move and Cities Fight to Keep Them. Baltimore: The Johns Hopkins University Press.

Fainstein, S.S. and Campbell, S. (2002). Readings in Urban Theory. Malden: Blackwell.

Fairley, S. (2003). Search of Relived Social Experience: Group-Based Nostalgia Sport Tourism. *Journal of Sport Management*, 17, 3, 284–304.

Fairley, S. and Gammon, S. (2005). Something Lived, Something Learned: Nostalgia's Expanding Role in Sport Tourism. *Sport in Society*, 8, 2, 182–197.

Falcous, M. (2007). The Decolonising National Imaginary: Promotional Media Constructions During the 2005 Lions Tour of Aotearoa New Zealand. *Journal of Sport & Social Issues*, 31, 3, 374–393.

Falcous, M. and Maguire, J. (2005). Globetrotters and Local Heroes? Labour Migration, Basketball, and Local Identities. *Sociology of Sport Journal*, 21, 2, 137–157.

Falcous, M. and West, A. (2008). Press Narratives of Nation During the 2005 Lions Tour of Aotearoa New Zealand. *Sport in Society*, 12, 2, 155–171.

Farrell, B.H. and Twining-Ward, L. (2004). Reconceptualizing Tourism. *Annals of Tourism Research*, 31, 2, 274–295.

Featherstone, M. (1991). Consumer Culture and Postmodernism. London: Sage Publications.

Featherstone, M. (1995). Undoing Culture: Globalisation. Postmodernism and Identity. London: Sage.

Fernquist, R.M. (2001). Geographical Relocation, Suicide, and Homicide: An Exploratory Analysis of the Geographic Relocation of Professional Sports Teams in Three U.S. Areas and the Impact on Suicide and Homicide Rates. Sociology of Sport Online, 4, 2,

Field, A.M. (1999). The College Student Market Segment: A Comparative Study of Travel Behaviours of International and Domestic Students at a Southeastern University. *Journal of Travel Research*, 37, May, 375–381.

FIFA (2004). Green Goal: The Environmental Concept for the 2006 Fifa World Cup http://www.oeko.de/oekodoc/292/2006-011-en.pdf (Retrieved 21 October 2008).

Filion, P., Hoernig, H., Bunting, H. and Sands, G. (2004). The Successful Few: Healthy Downtowns of Small Metropolitan Regions. *Journal of the American Planning Association*, 70, 3, 328–343.

Flearas, A. and Spoonley, P. (1999). Recalling Aotearoa: Indigenous Politics and Ethnic Relations in New Zealand. London: Oxford University Press.

Foldesi, G.S. (2004). Social Status and Mobility of Hungarian Elite Athletes. *The International Journal of the History of Sport*, 21, 5, 710–726.

Ford, N. and Eiserm, J.R. (1996). Risk and Liminality: The HIV-Related Socio-Sexual Interaction of Young Tourists. In *Health and the International Tourist*, (S. Clift and S.J. Page ed.) pp. 152–157. , London: Routledge.

Fougere, G. (1989). Sport, Culture and Identity: The Case of Rugby Football. In *Cultural Identity in New Zealand*, (D. Novitz and B. Willmortt ed.) pp. 110–122. Wellington: GP Books.

Francis, S. and Murphy, P.E. (2005). Sport Tourism Destinations: The Active Sport Tourist Perspective. In Sport Tourism Destinations: Issues, Opportunities and Analysis, (J.E.S. Higham ed.) pp.73–92, Oxford: Elsevier.

Frandberg, L. and Vilhelmson, B. (2003). Personal Mobility: A Corporeal Dimension of Transnationalisation. The Case of Long-Distance Travel from Sweden. Environment and Planning A, 35, 10, 1751–1768.

Fredline, L. (2004). Host Community Reactions to Motorsport Events. In Sport Tourism: Interrelationships, Impacts and Issues, (B. Ritchie and D. Adair ed.) pp.155–173, Clevedon: Channel View Publications.

Fredline, L. (2006). Host and Guest Relations and Sport Tourism. In Sports Tourism: Concepts and Theories, (H. Gibson ed.) pp.131–147, London: Routledge.

Frey, J.H. (1982). Boosterism, Scarce Resources and Institutional Control: The Future of American Intercollegiate Athletics. *International Review for the Sociology of Sport*, 17, 53–70.

Friedman, M.T., Andrews, D.L. and Silk, M.L. (2004). Sport and the Facade of Redevelopment in the Postindustrial City. *Sociology of Sport Journal*, 21, 119–139.

Galily, K. and Sheard, Y. (2002). Cultural Imperialism and Sport: The Americanisation of Israeli Basketball. *Sport in Society*, 5, 2, 55–78.

Galtung, J. (1982). Sport as a Carrier of Deep Culture and Structure. *Current Research on Peace and Violence*, 5, 133–143.

Gammon, S. and Ramshaw, G. (2007). Heritage, Sport and Tourism: Sporting Pasts - Tourist Futures. Abington: Taylor & Francis.

Gammon, S. and Robinson, T. (1997). Sport Tourism: A Conceptual Framework. *Journal of Sport Tourism*, 4, 3, 11–18.

Gayton, W.F., Matthews, G.R. and Nickless, C.J. (1987). The Home Field Disadvantage in Sports Championships: Does It Exist in Hockey? *Journal of Sports Psychology*, 9, 183–185.

Geller, J.B. and Carlton, J.T. (1993). Ecological Roulette: The Global Transport of Nonindigenous Marine Organisms. *Science*, 261, 5117, 78–82.

Genest, S. (1994). Skating on Thin Ice? The International Migration of Canadian Ice Hockey Players. In The Global Sports Arena: Athletic Talent Migration in an Interdependent World, (J. Maguire and J. Bale ed.) pp.112–125, London: Frank Cass & Co. Ltd.

Getz, D. (1997). Event Management and Event Tourism. New York: Cognizant Communications Corporation.

Gibson, H. (2005). Towards an Understanding of Why Sport Tourists Do What They Do. In Sport Tourism: Theory and Concepts, (H. Gibson ed.) pp.66–85, London: Routledge.

Gibson, H., Willming, C. and Holdnak, A. (2002). Small-Scale Event Sport Tourism: College Sport as a Tourist Attraction. In Sport Tourism: Principles and Practice, (S. Gammon and J. Kurtzman ed.) pp.3–19, Eastbourne: Leisure Studies Association.

Gibson, H.J. (1998). Sport Tourism: A Critical Analysis of Research. *Sport Management Review*, 1, 1, 45–76.

Gibson, H.J. (2002). Sport Tourism at a Crossroad? Considerations for the Future. In Sport Tourism: Principles and Practice, (S. Gammon and J. Kurtzman ed.) pp.111–128, Eastbourne: Leisure Studies Association.

Gibson, H.J., Willming, C. and Holdnak, A. (2002). Small-Scale Event Sport Tourism: College Sport as a Tourist Attraction. In Sport Tourism: Principles and Practice, (S. Gammon and J. Kurtzman ed.) pp. 3–18, Eastbourne: Leisure Studies Association.

Giddens, A. (1991). Modernity and Self-Identity: Self and Society in the Late Modern Age. Cambridge: Polity Press.

Gillespie, D.L., Leffler, A. and Lerner, E. (2002). If It Weren't for My Hobby, I'd Have a Life: Dog Sports, Serious Leisure, and Boundary Negotiations. Leisure Studies, 21. 3 & 4, 285–304.

Gillies, P. and Slack, R. (1996). Context and Culture in HIV Prevention: The Importance of Holidays. In Health and the International Tourist, (S. Clift and S.J. Page ed.) pp. 134–151, London: Routledge.

Gilmore, B. and Pine, H. (2007). Authenticity: What Consumers Really Want. Boston: Harvard Business School Press.

Giulianotti, R. (1991). Scotland's Tartan Army in Italy: The Case for the Carnivalesques. *Sociological Review*, 39, 3, 503–527.

Giulianotti, R. (1995). Football and the Politics of Carnival: An Ethnographic Study of Scottish Fans in Sweden. *International Review for the Sociology of Sport*, 30, 2, 191–220.

Giulianotti, R. (1996). Back to the Future: An Anthropology of Ireland's Football Fans at the 1994 World Cup Finals in the USA. *International Review for the Sociology of Sport*, 31, 3, 323–347.

Giulianotti, R. and Robertson, R, eds. (2007). Globalization and sport. Oxford: Blackwell Publishing.

Glyptis, S.A. (1982). Sport and Tourism in Western Europe. London: British Travel Education Trust.

Glyptis, S.A. (1989). *Leisure and patterns of time use*. Paper presented at the Leisure Studies Association Annual Conference, Bournemouth, England, 24–26 April 1987. Eastbourne: Leisure Studies Association.

Glyptis, S.A. (1991). Sport and Tourism. In *Progress in Tourism, Recreation and Hospitality Management*, (C.P. Cooper ed.) pp. 165–187. , London: Belhaven Press.

Go, F.M. (2004). Tourism in the Context of Globalisation. In *Tourism: Critical Concepts in the Social Sciences*, (S. Williams ed.) pp. 49–80. London: Routledge.

Goffman, E. (1959). The Presentation of Self in Everyday Life. Harmondsworth: Penguin.

Gore, D.H. (2004). Factors That Contribute to Talent Development in Elite Female Track and Field Athletes, Master of Science, Graduate Faculty of North Carolina State University, North Carolina State University: Raleigh.

Gössling, S. (2001). Tourism, Economic Transition and Ecosystem Degradation: Interacting Processes in a Tanzanian Coastal Community. *Tourism Geographies*, 3, 4, 430–453.

Gössling, S. (2002). Global Environmental Consequences of Tourism. *Global Environmental Change*, 12, 4, 283–302.

Gössling, S. (2007). Ecotourism and Global Environmental Change. In *Critical Issues in Ecotourism: Understanding a Complex Tourism Phenomenon*, (J.E.S. Higham ed.) pp. 70–84. Oxford: Elsevier Butterworth Heinemann.

Gössling, S. and Hall, C.M. (2005). *Tourism and Environmental Change: Ecological, Economic, Social and Political Interrelationships*. Oxon: Routledge.

Graburn, N. (1989). Tourism: The Sacred Journey. In Hosts and Guests: The Anthropology of Tourism, (V. Smith ed.) pp.21–36, Philadelphia: University of Pennsylvania Press.

Grainger, A. (2006). From Immigrant to Overstayer: Samoan Identity, Rugby, and Cultural Politics of Race and Nation in Aotearoa/New Zealand. *Journal of Sport and Social Issues*, 30, 1, 45–61.

Gratton, C. and Shibli, S. and Coleman, R. (2004). The Economics of Sport Tourism at Major Sports Events. In Sport Tourism Destinations: Issues, Opportunities and Analysis, (J.E.S. Higham ed.) pp.233–247, Oxford: Elsevier.

Gratton, C., Shibli, S. and Coleman, R. (2005). The Economics of Sport Tourism at Major Sports Events. In Sport Tourism Destinations: Issues, Opportunities and Analysis (J.E.S. Higham ed.) pp.233–247, Oxford: Elsevier Butterworth-Heinemann.

Graves, P.E. (1980). Migration and Climate. *Journal of Regional Science*, 20, 2, 227–237.

Graves, P.E. and Regulska, J. (1982). Amenities and Migration over the Life-Cycle. In *The Economics of Urban Amenities*, (D. Diamond and G. Trolley ed.) pp. 211–221. New York: Academic Press.

Green, B.C. (2001). Leveraging Subculture and Identity to Promote Sport Events. *Sport Management Review*, 4, 1, 1–19.

Green, B.C. and Chalip, L. (1998). Sport Tourism as the Celebration of Subculture. *Annals of Tourism Research*, 23, 2, 275–291.

Greenwood, D.J. (1989). Culture by the Pound: An Anthropoligical Perspective on Tourism and Cultural Commodification. In *Hosts and Guests: The Anthropology of Tourism*, (V.L. Smith ed.) pp. 17–31. Philadelphia: University of Pennsylvania Press.

Grossberg, L. (1996). Identity and Cultural Studies: Is That All There Is? In Questions of Cultural Identity, (S. Hall and P. Du Gay ed.) pp.87–107, London: Sage.

Groves, D., Obenour, W. and Lengfelder, J. (2003). Colas and Globalization: Models for Sports and Event Management. *Journal of Sport Tourism*, 8, 4, 320–334.

Gruneau, R.S. and Whitson, D. (1993). Sport, Identities and Cultural Politics. Hockey Night in Canada. Toronto: Garamond Press.

Guerrier, Y. and Adib, A. (2003). Work at Leisure and Leisure at Work: A Study of the Emotional Labour of Tour Reps. *Human Relations*, 56, 11, 1399–1417.

Gustafson, P. (2001). Roots and Routes: Exploring the Relationship between Place Attachment and Mobility. *Environment and Behaviour*, 33, 5, 667–686.

Guttmann, A. (1993). The Diffusion of Sports and the Problem of Cultural Imperialism. In *The Sports Process: A Comparative and Departmental Approach*, (E.G. Dunning, J.A. Maguire and R.E. Pearton ed.) pp. 125–138. Champaign, IL, USA: Human Kinetics Publishers.

Haas, W.H. and Serow, W.J. (1993). Amenity Retirement Migration Process: A Model and Preliminary Evidence. *The Gerontologist*, 33, 2, 212–220.

Halbertsam, D. (1999). Playing for Keeps: Michael Jordan and the World He Made. New York: Random House.

Hall, C.M. (1992a). Hallmark Tourist Events: Impacts, Management and Planning. London: Belhaven Press.

Hall, C.M. (1992b). Review: Adventure, Sport and Health Tourism. In Special Interest Tourism, (B. Weiler and C.M. Hall ed.) pp.186–210, London: Belhaven Press.

Hall, C.M. (1997). Mega-Events and Their Legacies. In *Quality Management in Urban Tourism*, (P. Murphy ed.) pp. 75–87. Chichester: John Wiley & Sons.

Hall, C.M. (1998). Imaging Tourism and Sports Event Fever: The Sydney Olympics and the Need for a Social Charter for Mega-Events. In *Sport in the City: The Role of Sport in Economic and Social Regeneration*, (C. Gratton and I.P. Henry ed.) pp. 166–183. London: Routledge.

Hall, C.M. (2001a). Imaging, Tourism and Sports Event Fever: The Sydney Olympics and the Need for a Social Charter for Mega-Events. In *Sport in the City: The Role of Sport in Economic and Social Regeneration*, (C. Gratton and I.P. Henry ed.) pp. 166–183. London: Routledge.

Hall, C.M. (2001b). Territorial Economic Integration and Globalisation. In *Tourism in the Age of Globalisation*, (C. Cooper and S. Wahab ed.) pp. 22–44. London: Routledge.

Hall, C.M. (2004a). Sport Tourism and Urban Regeneration. In Sport Tourism: Interrelationships, Impacts and Issues, (B. Ritchie and D. Adair ed.) pp.192–205, Clevedon: Channel View Publications.

Hall, C.M. (2004b). Tourism and Mobility. Paper presented at the CAUTHE Conference, Brisbane, Australia. February 2004. Retrieved from http://eprints. otago.ac.nz/159/1/Mobility_CAUTHE.pdf (17 September 2008).

Hall, C.M. (2005). Space-Time Accessibility and the TALC: The Role of Geographies of Spatial Interaction and Mobility in Contributing to an Improved Understanding of Tourism. In The Tourism Area Life Cycle: Conceptual and Theoretical Issues, (R. Butler ed.) pp.83–100, Clevedon: Channel View Publications.

Hall, C.M. (2008). Of Time and Space and Other Things: Laws of Tourism and the Geographies of Contemporary Mobility. In Tourism and Mobilities: Local-Global Connections, (P.M. Burns and M. Novelli ed.) pp.15–32, Wallingford: CABI.

Hall, C.M. and Butler, R.W. (1995). Search of Common Ground: Reflections on Sustainability, Complexity and Process in the Tourism System. *Journal of Sustainable Tourism*, 3, 2, 99–105.

Hall, C.M. and Coles, T. (2006). Editorial: The Geography of Tourism Is Dead. Long Live the Geographies of Tourism and Mobility. *Current Issues in Tourism*, 9 4&5, 289–292.

Hall, C.M. and Higham, J.E.S. eds. (2005). Tourism, Recreation and Climate Change: International Perspectives. Clevedon: Channel View Publications.

Hall, C.M. and Hodges, J. (1996). The Party's Great but What About the Hangover?: The Housing and Social Impacts of Mega-Events with Special Reference to the 2000 Sydney Olympics. *Festival Management and Event Tourism*, 4, 1/2. 13–20.

Hall, C.M. and Müller, D.K. (2004). Tourism, Mobility, and Second Homes. Clevedon: Channel View Publications.

Hall, C.M. and Page, S.J. (2002). The Geography of Tourism and Recreation. London: Routledge.

Hall, C.M. and Williams, A.M. (2002). Conclusions: Tourism-Migration Relationships. In Tourism and Migration: New Relationships between Production and Consumption, (C.M. Hall and A.M. Williams ed.) pp.277–289, Dordrecht: Kluwer.

Hammitt, W.E., Backlund, E.A. and Bixler, R.D. (2004). Experience Use History, Place Bonding and Resource Substitution of Trout Anglers During Recreation Engagements. *Journal of Leisure Sciences*, 36, 3, 356–378.

Hammitt, W.E., Backlund, E.A. and Bixler, R.D. (2006). Place Bonding for Recreational Places: Conceptual and Empirical Development. *Leisure Studies*, 25, 1, 17–41.

Hannigan, J. (1998). Fantasy City: Pleasure and Profit in the Postmodern Metropolis. London: Routledge.

Hargreaves, J. (1982). Sport, Culture and Ideology. In Sport, Culture and Ideology, (J. Hargreaves ed.) pp.30–61, London: Routledge & Kegan Paul Ltd.

Hargreaves, J. (1982). Theorizing Sport: An Introduction. In Sport, Culture and Ideology, (J. Hargreaves ed.) pp.1–29, London: Routledge & Kegan Paul Ltd.

Harrison-Hill, T. and Chalip, L. (2005). Marketing Sport Tourism: Creating Synergy between Sport and Destination. *Sport in Society*, 8, 312–320.

Harvey, D. (1989). The Condition of Postmodernity: An Enquiry into the Origins of Cultural Change. New York: Blackwell.

Harvey, D. (1990). The Condition of Postmodernity. Oxford: Blackwell.

Harvey, J. and Houle, F. (1994). Sport, World Economy, Global Culture, and New Social Movements. *Sociology of Sport Journal*, 11, 4, 337–355.

Hede, A. and Alomes, S. (2007). Big Screens: Exploring Their Future for the Special Event Sector. 4th International Event Research Conference. Melbourne: Australia.

Heinemann, K. (1993). Sport in Developing Countries. In The Sports Process: A Comparative and Developmental Approach, (E.G. Dunning, J. Maguire and R.E. Pearton ed.) pp.139–150, Champaign, IL, USA: Human Kinetics Publishers.

Heino, R. (2000). What Is So Punk About Snowboarding? *Journal of Sport and Social Issues*, 24, 1, 176–191.

Henderson, J.C. (2003). Tourism Promotion and Identity in Malaysia. Tourism. *Culture & Communication*, 4, 2, 71–81.

Hewison, R. (1987). The Heritage Industry: Britain in a Climate of Decline. London: Methuen.

Heywood, I. (1994). Urgent Dreams: Climbing, Rationalization and Ambivalence. *Leisure Studies*, 13, 3, 179–194.

Higham, J.E.S. ed. (2005). Sport Tourism Destinations: Issues, Opportunities and Analysis. Oxford: Elsevier Butterworth-Heinemann.

Higham, J.E.S. and Hall, C.M. (2003). Editorial: Sport Tourism in Australia and New Zealand: Responding to a Dynamic Interface. *Journal of Sport Tourism*, 8, 3, 131–143.

Higham, J.E.S. and Hinch, T.D. (2003). Sport, Space and Time: Effects of the Otago Highlanders Franchise on Tourism. *Journal of Sports Management*, 17, 3, 235–257.

Higham, J.E.S. and Hinch, T.D. (2006). Sport and Tourism Research: A Geographic Approach. *Journal of Sport & Tourism*, 11, 1, 31–49.

Hill, J. (1994). Cricket and the Imperial Connection: Overseas Players in Lancashire in the Inter-War Years. In *The Global Sports Arena: Athletic Talent Migration in an Interdependent World*, (J. Maguire and J. Bale ed.) pp. 49–62. London: Frank Cass & Co. Ltd.

Hill, J. (2002). Sport, Leisure and Culture in Twentieth-Century Britain. Basingstoke: Palgrave.

Hiller, H.H. (1998). Assessing the Impacts of Mega-Events: A Linkage Model. *Current Issues in Tourism*, 1, 1, 47–57.

Hiltunen, M.J. (2007). Environmental Impacts of Rural Second Home Tourism - Case Lake District in Finland. *Scandinavian Journal of Hospitality and Tourism*, 7, 3, 243–265.

Hinch, T.D. (1998). Ecotourists and Indigenous Hosts: Diverging Views on Their Relationship with Nature. *Current Issues in Tourism*, 1, 1, 120–124.

Hinch, T.D. (2006). Canadian Sport and Culture in the Tourism Marketplace. *Tourism Geographies*, 8, 1, 15–30.

Hinch, T.D. and De La Barre, S. (2005). Culture, Sport and Tourism: The Case of the Arctic Winter Games. In Sport Tourism Destinations: Issues,

Opportunities and Analysis, (J.E.S. Higham ed.) pp.260–273, Oxford: Butterworth-Heinemann.

Hinch, T.D. and Delamere, T.A. (1993). Native Festivals as Tourist Attractions: Community Celebration or Community Sell-Out? In 7th Canadian Congress on Leisure Research. Winnipeg, Manitoba: University of Manitoba. 30–33.

Hinch, T.D. and Higham, J.E.S. (2004). Sport Tourism Development. Clevedon: Channel View Publications.

Hinch, T.D. and Higham, J.E.S. (2005). Sport, Tourism and Authenticity. *European Sports Management Quarterly*, 5, 3, 245–258.

Hinch, T.D. and Jackson, E.L. (2000). Leisure Constraints Research: Its Value as a Framework for Understanding Tourism Seasonality. *Current Issues in Tourism*, 3, 2, 87–106.

Hinch, T.D., Jackson, E.L., Hudson, S. and Walker, G. (2005). Leisure Constraint Theory and Sport Tourism. *Sport in Society*, 8, 2, 142–163.

Hinch, T.D., Jackson, E.L., Hudson, S. and Walker, G.J. (2006). Leisure Constraint Theory and Sport Tourism. In Sport Tourism: Concepts and Theories, (H. Gibson ed.) pp.10–31, London: Routledge.

Hockey, J. and Collinson, J.A. (2007). Grasping the Phenomenology of Sporting Bodies. *International Review for the Sociology of Sport*, 42, 2, 115–131.

Hodge, K. and Hermansson, G. (2007). Psychological preparation of athletes for the Olympic context: The New Zealand Summer and Winter Olympic Teams. *Athletic Insight: The Online Journal of Sport Psychology*, 9, 4. http://www.athleticinsight.com/

Hodge, K., Lonsdale, C. and Ng, J. (2008). Burnout in Elite Rugby: Relationships with Basic Psychological Needs Fulfilment. *Journal of Sports Sciences*, 26, 835–844.

Hoffer, R. (1995). Down and Out: On Land, Sea, Air, Facing Questions About Their Sanity. *Sports Illustrated*, 83, 1, 42–49.

Hokowhitu, B. (2005). Early Māori Rugby and the Formation of 'Traditional' Māori Masculinity. *Sporting Traditions*, 21, 2, 75–95.

Hooper, I. (1998). The Value of Sport in Urban Regeneration: A Case Study of Glasgow. Sport in the City Conference, Sheffield, U.K., 2–4 July.

Hope, W. (2002). Whose All Blacks? Media. *Culture & Society*, 24, 2, 235–253.

Hudson, S. (1999). Snow Business: A Study of the International Ski Industry. London: Cassell.

Hudson, S. (2000). Snow Business: A Study of the International Ski Industry. London: Cassell.

Hudson, S. (2003). Sport and Adventure Tourism. In *Binghamton*.: The Haworth Press.

Hudson, S. (2003). Winter Sport Tourism. In *Sport and Adventure Tourism*, (S. Hudson ed.) pp. 89–123, New York: The Haworth Hospitality Press.

Huizinga, J. (1938). Homo Ludens: Versuch Einer Bestimmung Des Spielelementes Der Kultur. Amsterdam: Pantheon.

Hull, R.B., Lan, M. and Vigo, G. (1994). Place Identity: Symbols of Self in the Urban Fabric. *Landscape and Urban Planning*, 28, 2–3, 108–120.

Humphreys, D. (1997). 'Shreadheads Go Mainstream'? Snowboarding and Alternative Youth. *International Review for the Sociology of Sport*, 32, 2, 147–160.

Inalhan, G. and Finch, E. (2004). Place Attachment and Sense of Belonging. *Facilities*, 22, 5–6. 120–128.

International Association of Antarctic Tour Operators (IAATO) (2002). Managing the Impacts of Tourism on Antarctic Wildlife. *Scott Polar Research Institute Thirteenth General Meeting Conference*, Cambridge, U.K., 1–4, July.

Drake International (n.d.). Generation Y: Attracting, Engaging and Leading a New Generation at Work. Auckland: Drake International.

Iveco (2007). Iveco and the Māori Haka Dance During Rome's All-Night Events http://www.iveco.com/enus/PressRoom/PressRelease/Pages/1073760557.aspx (Retrieved April 1 2008).

Jaakson, R. (1986). Second-Home Domestic Tourism. *Annals of Tourism Research*, 13, 367–391.

Jack, G. and Phipps, A. (2005). Tourism and Intercultural Exchange. Clevedon: Channel View Publications.

Jackson, E.L. (2000). Will Research on Leisure Constraints Still Be Relevant in the Twenty-First Century? *Journal of Leisure Research*, 32, 1, 62.

Jackson, E.L., Crawford, D.W. and Godbey, G. (1993). Negotiation of. *Leisure Constraints. Leisure Sciences*, 15, 1, 1–11.

Jackson, S.J. (1994). Gretzky, Crisis and Canadian Identity in 1988: Rearticulating the Americanization of Culture Debate. *Sociology of Sport Journal*, 11, 4, 428–446.

Jackson, S.J. (1998a). A Twist of Race: Ben Johnson and the Canadian Crisis of Racial and National Identity. *Sociology of Sport Journal*, 15, 1, 21–40.

Jackson, S.J. (1998b). Life in the (Mediated) Faust Lane: Ben Johnson, National Affect and the 1988 Crisis of Canadian Identity. *International Review for the Sociology of Sport*, 33, 3, 227–238.

Jackson, S.J. and Andrews, D.L. (1999). Between and Beyond the Global and the Local: American Popular Sporting Culture in New Zealand. *International Review for the Sociology of Sport*, 34, 1, 31–42.

Jackson, S.J. and Hokowhitu, B. (2002). Sport, Tribes and Technology. *Journal of Sport and Social Issues*, 26, 2, 125–139.

Jacob, G.R. and Schreyer, R. (1980). Conflict in Outdoor Recreation: A Theoretical Perspective. *Journal of Leisure Research*, 12, 4, 368–380.

Jacobson, D. (1997). New Frontiers: Territory, Social Spaces, and the State. *Sociological Forum*, 12, 1, 121–133.

Jamieson, J.W. (1999). Migration as an Economic and Political Weapon. Journal of Social. *Political and Economic Studies*, 24, 3, 330–348.

Jamieson, K. (1996). Been There, Done That: Identity and the Overseas Experiences of Young Pakeha New Zealanders, Master of Arts, Social Anthropology, Massey University: Palmerston North.

Janelle, D.G. (1968). Central Place Development in a Time-Space Framework. *Professional Geographer*, 20, 1, 5–10.

Janelle, D.G. (1969). Spatial Reorganisation: A Model and Concept. *Annals of the Association of American Geographers*, 59, 2, 348–364.

Janelle, D.G. (1974). Transportation Innovation and the Reinforcement of Urban Hierarchies. *High Speed Ground Transportation Journal*, 8, 3, 261–269.

Janelle, D.G. and Goodchild, M. (1983). Diurnal Patterns of Social Group Distribution in a Canadian City. *Economic Geography*, 59, 4, 403–425.

Jansson, B. and Müller, D.K. (2003). Fritidsboende I Kvarken. Umea: Kvarkenradet.

Jarvie, G. (1989). Culture, Social Development, and the Scottish Highland Gatherings. In *The Making of Scotland: Nation, Culture and Social Change*, (D. Mccrone, S. Kendrick and P. Straw ed.) pp. 189–206. Edinburgh: Edinburgh University Press.

Jarvie, G. (1991). Highland Games: The Making of the Myth. Edinburgh: Edinburgh University Press.

Jarvie, G. (2006). Sport, Culture and Society: An Introduction. London: Routledge.

Jennings, A. (1996). The New Lords of the Rings: Olympic Corruption & How to Buy Gold Medals. London: Simon & Schuster/Pocket Books.

Jeong, S. and Santos, C.A. (2004). Cultural Politics and Contested Place Identity. *Annals of Tourism Research*, 31, 3, 640–656.

Jinxia, D. (2001). Cultural Changes: Mobility, Stratification and Sportswomen in the New China. *Sport in Society*, 4, 3, 1–26.

Johnson, A.T. (1993). Minor League Baseball and Local Economic Development. Chicago: University of Illinois Press.

Johnson, A.T. (2000). Minor League Baseball: Risks and Potential Benefits for Communities Large and Small. In *The Economics and Politics of Sports Facilities*, (W.C. Rich ed.) pp. 141–151. Westport: Quorum Books.

Johnson, D.M. (1981). Disney World as Structure and Symbol: Recreation of the American Experience. *Journal of Popular Culture*, 15, 1, 157–165.

Jones, C. (2001). A Level Playing Field? Sports Stadium Infrastructure and Urban Development in the United Kingdom. *Environment and Planning*, 33, 5, 845–861.

Jones, I. (2000). A Model of Serious Leisure Identification: The Case of Football Fandom. *Leisure Studies*, 19, 4, 283–298.

Jones, I. and Green, B.C. (2005). Serious Leisure, Social Identity and Sport Tourism. *Sport in Society*, 8, 2, 164–181.

Jones, I. and Green, B.C. (2006). Serious Leisure, Social Identity and Sport Tourism. In Sport Tourism: Concepts and Theories, (H. Gibson ed.) pp.32–49, London: Routledge.

Jorgensen, B.S. and Stedman, R.C. (2001). Sense of Place as an Attitude: Lakeshore Owners Attitudes Towards Their Properties. *Journal of Environmental Management*, 21, 233–248.

Jorgensen, B.S. and Stedman, R.C. (2006). A Comparative Analysis of Predictors of Sense of Place Dimensions: Attachment to, Dependence on, and Identification with Lakeshore Properties. *Journal of Environmental Management*, 79, 3, 316–327.

Jutel, A. (2002). Olympic Road Cycling and National Identity: Where Is Germany? *Journal of Sport and Social Issues*, 26, 2, 195–208.

Kaltennborn, B.P. (1997). Nature of Place Attachment: A Study among Recreation Homeowners in Southern Norway. *Leisure Studies*, 19, 175–189.

Kane, M.J. and Zink, R. (2004). Package Adventure Tours: Markers in Serious Leisure Careers. *Leisure Studies*, 23, 4, 329–345.

Kearns, R. and Collins, D. (2006). 'On the Rocks': New Zealand's Coastal Bach Landscape and the Case of Rangitoto Island. *New Zealand Geographer*, 62, 227–235.

Keller, P. (2001). Sport and Tourism: Introductory Report. World Conference on Sport and Tourism, Conference. Barcelona, Spain, 22–23. February.

Kenyon, S., Lyons, G. and Rafferty, J. (2002). Transport and Social Exclusion: Investigating the Possibility of Promoting Inclusion through Virtual Mobility. *Journal of Transport Geography*, 10, 3, 207–219.

Kenz, I. (2005). Attachment and Identity as Related to Place and Its Perceived Climate. *Journal of Environmental Psychology*, 25, 2, 207–215.

Kim, H., Gursoy, D. and Lee, S. (2006). The Impact of the 2002 World Cup in South Korea: Comparisons of Pre- and Post-Games. *Tourism Management*, 27, 1, 86–96.

Kivinen, O., Mesikammen, J. and Metsa-Tokila, T. (2001). A Case Study in Cultural Diffusion: British Ice Hockey and American Influences in Europe. *Sport in Society*, 4, 1, 49–62.

Klausner, M. and Hoch, D. (1997). 'X' Equals 'Team Chemistry'. *Coach and Athletic Director*, 66, 8, 6–7.

Klein, A. (1991). Sugarball: The American Game, the Dominican Dream. Yale: Yale University Press.

Klein, A.M. (1994). Trans-Nationalism, Labour Migration and Latin American Baseball. In *The Global Sports Arena: Athletic Talent Migration in an Interdependent World*, (J. Maguire and J. Bale ed.) pp. 183–205. London: Frank Cass & Co. Ltd.

Kneafsey, M. (1998). Tourism and Place Identity: A Case-Study in Rural Ireland. *Irish Geography*, 31, 2, 111–123.

Kneafsey, M. (2000). Tourism, Place Identities and Social Relations in the European Rural Periphery. *European Urban and Regional Studies*, 7, 1, 35–50.

Korpela, K.M. (1989). Place-Identity as a Product of Environmental Self-Regulation. *Journal of Environmental Psychology*, 9, 3, 241–256.

Kotler, P., Haider, D. and Rein, I. (1993). Marketing Places: Attracting Investment, Industry and Tourism to Cities and Nations. New York: Free Press.

Kraus, R. (1994). Tomorrow's Leisure: Meeting the Challenges. Journal of Physical Education. *Recreation and Dance*, 65, 4, 42–47.

Krippendorf, J. (1995). Towards New Tourism Policies. In Managing Tourism, (S. Medlik ed.) pp.307–317, Oxford: Butterworth Heinemann.

Kruger, L.E. (2006). Recreation as a Path for Place Making and Community Building. *Leisure/Loisir*, 30, 2, 383–392.

Kulczycki, C. and C. Hyatt (2005). Expanding the conceptualization of nostalgia sport tourism. Heritage, sport and tourism: Sporting pasts - Tourist futures. S.G.G. Ramshaw. London, Routledge: 53–73.

Kusaka, Y. (2006). The Emergence and Development of Japanese School Sport. In *Japan, Sport and Society: Tradition and Change in a Globalising World*, (J. Maguire and M. Nakayama ed.) pp. 19–34. New York: Routledge.

Kwan, M.P. (1999). Gender and Individual Access to Urban Opportunities: A Study Using Space-Time Measures. *Professional Geographer*, 51, 2, 210–227.

Kyle, G.T., Absher, J.D. and Graefe, A.R. (2003). The Moderating Role of Place Attachment on the Relationship between Attitudes toward Fees and Spending Preferences. *Leisure Sciences*, 25, 1, 33–50.

Kyle, G.T., Graefe, A.R. and Manning, R. (2005). Testing the Dimensionality of Place Attachment in Recreational Settings. *Environment and Behaviour*, 37, 2, 153–177.

Lai, F.Y. (1999). Floorball's Penetration of Australia: Rethinking the Nexus of Globalisation and Marketing. *Sports Management Review*, 2, 2, 133–149.

Lanfranchi, P. (1994). The Migration of Footballers: The Case of France, 1932–1982. In The Global Sports Arena: Athletic Talent Migration in an

Interdependent World, (J. Maguire and J. Bale ed.) pp.63–77, London: Frank Cass & Co. Ltd.

Larsen, J. (2001). Tourism Mobilities and the Travel Glance: Experiences of Being on the Move. *Scandinavian Journal of Hospitality and Tourism*, 1, 2, 80–98.

Lash, S. and Urry, J. (1974). Economics of Signs and Space. London: Sage.

Lazendorf, M. (2000). Social Change and Leisure Mobility. *World Transport Policy and Practice*, 6, 3, 21–25.

Lee, H.M. (2003). Tongans Overseas: Between Two Shores. Honolulu: University of Hawaii Press.

Lee, P. (2002). The Economic and Social Justification for Publicly Financed Stadia: The Case of Vancouver's BC Place Stadium. *European Planning Studies*, 10, 7, 861–873.

Lefebvre, H. (1991). The Production of Space. Oxford: Blackwell.

Leidner, R. (1991). Serving Hamburgers and Selling Insurance: Gender, Work and Identity in Interactive Service Jobs. *Gender and Society*, 5, 2, 154–177.

Leiper, N. (1990). Tourist Attraction Systems. *Annals of Tourism Research*, 17, 3, 367–384.

Leiper, N. (2000). Are Destinations 'the Heart of Tourism'? The Advantages of an Alternative Description. *Current Issues in Tourism*, 3, 4, 364–368.

Lett, J.W. (1983). Ludic and Liminoid Aspects of Charter Yacht Tourism in the Caribbean. *Annals of Tourism Research*, 10, 1, 35–56.

Ley, D. and Mercer, J. (1980). Locational Conflict and the Politics of Consumption. *Economic Geography*, 56, 2, 89–109.

Leyshon, A. (1997). True Stories? Global Dreams, Global Nightmares, and Writing Globalisation. In Geographies of Economies, (R. Lee and J. Wills ed.) pp.133–146, London: Arnold.

Lindberg, K. and Johnson, R. (1997). Modeling Resident Attitudes toward Tourism. *Annals of Tourism Research*, 24, 2, 402–424.

Low, S.M. and Altman, I. (1992). Place Attachment: A Conceptual Inquiry. In Place Attachment, (I. Altman and S.M. Low ed.) pp.1–12, New York: Plenum Press.

Loy, J.W., McPherson, B.D. and Kenyon, G. (1978). Sport and Social Systems: A Guide to the Analysis of Problems and Literature. Reading: Addison Wesley.

Loy, J.W. and Sage, G.H. (1978). Athletic Personnel in the Academic Marketplace: A Study of the Interorganizational Mobility Patterns of College Coaches. *Sociology of Work and Occupations*, 5, 4, 446–469.

Lundmark, L. (2006). Mobility, Migration and Seasonal Tourism Employment: Evidence from Swedish Mountain Municipalities. *Scandinavian Journal of Hospitality and Tourism*, 6, 3, 197–213.

Lundmark, L. and Marjavaara, R. (2005). Second Home Localizations in the Swedish Mountain Range. *Tourism (Zagreb)*, 53, 1, 3–16.

Maccormick, N. (1996). Liberalism, Nationalism and the Post-Sovereign State. *Political Studies*, 44, 4, 553–567.

Macdonald, F. (1996). The Game of Our Lives. Auckland: Penguin Books (NZ) Ltd.

Maclean, M. (1999). Of Warriors and Blokes: The Problem of Māori Rugby for Pakeha Masculinity in New Zealand. In Making the Rugby World: Race, Gender, Commerce, (J. Nauright and T. Chandler ed.) pp.1–26, London: Frank Cass & Co. Ltd.

Magee, J. and Sugden, J. (2002). "The World at Their Feet": Professional Football and International Labour Migration. Journal of Sport and Social Issues, 26, 4, 421–437.

Magnusson, G.K. (2001). The Internationalization of Sports. *International Review for the Sociology of Sport*, 36, 1, 59–69.

Maguire, J. (1993). American Football, British Society, and Global Sport Development. In *The Sports Process: A Comparative and Developmental Approach*, (E.G. Dunning, J. Maguire and R.E. Pearton ed.) pp. 207–230. Champaign, IL, USA: Human Kinetics Publishers.

Maguire, J. (1993). Globalization, Sport and National Identities: "The Empires Strike Back"? *Loisir et societe/Society and Leisure*, 16, 2, 293–322.

Maguire, J. (1994). American Labour Migrants, Globalisation and the Making of English Basketball. In *The Global Sports Arena: Athletic Talent Migration in an Interdependent World*, (J. Maguire and J. Bale ed.) pp. 226–255. London: Frank Cass & Co. Ltd.

Maguire, J. (1994). Sport, Identity, Politics, and Globalization: Diminishing Contrasts and Increasing Varieties. *Sociology of Sport Journal*, 11, 4, 398–427.

Maguire, J. (1996). Blade Runners: Canadian Migrants, Ice Hockey, and the Global Sports Process. *Journal of Sport and Social Issues*, 20, 3, 335–360.

Maguire, J. (1999). Global Sport: Identities, Societies, Civilisations. Malden, MA: Polity Press.

Maguire, J. (2002). Sport Worlds: A Sociological Perspective. Champaign: Human Kinetics.

Maguire, J. (2004). Sport Labour Migration: Research Revisited. *Journal of Sport and Social Issues*, 28, 4, 477–472.

Maguire, J. and Bale, J. eds. (1994). The Global Sports Arena: Athletic Talent Migration in an Interdependent World. London: Frank Cass & Co. Ltd.

Maguire, J. and Bale, J. (1994). Postscript: An Agenda for Research on Sports Labour Migration. In *The Global Sports Arena: Athletic Talent Migration in an*

Interdependent World, (J. Maguire and J. Bale ed.) pp. 281–284. London: Frank Cass & Co. Ltd.

Maguire, J. and Bale, J. (1994). Sports Labour Migration in the Global Arena. In *The Global Sports Arena: Athletic Talent Migration in an Interdependent World*, (J. Maguire and J. Bale ed.) pp. 1–24. London: Frank Cass & Co Ltd.

Maguire, J., Jarvie, G., Mansfield, L. and Bradley, J. (2002). Sport Worlds: A Sociological Perspective. Champaign, IL, USA: Human Kinetics.

Maguire, J. and Pourlton, E. (1999). European Identity Politics in Euro 1996. *International Review for the Sociology of Sport*, 34, 1, 17–29.

Maguire, J. and Stead, D. (1996). "Far Pavilions"?: Cricket Migrants, Foreign Sojourn and Contested Identities. International Review for the Sociology of Sport, 31, 1, 1–25.

Maguire, J. and Stead, D. (1998). Border Crossings: Soccer and Labour Migration and the European Union. *International Review for the Sociology of Sport*, 33, 1, 59–73.

Maier, J. and Weber, W. (1993). Sport Tourism in Local and Regional Planning. *Tourism Recreation Research*, 18, 2, 33–43.

Majendie, M. (2005). Rugby in Danger of Player Burnout http://news.bbc.co.uk/sport1/hi/rugby_union/4332535.stm (Retrieved May 30 2005).

Manfredini, R., Manfredini, F. and Conconi, F. (2000). Standard Melatonin Intake and Circadian Rhythms of Elite Athletes after a Transmeridian Flight. *The Journal of International Medical Research*, 28, 182–186.

Manrai, L.A. and Manrai, A.K. (1995). Effects of Cultural-Context, Gender, and Acculturation on Perceptions of Work Versus Social/Leisure Time Usage. *Journal of Business Research*, 32, 2, 115–128.

Martin, B. and Mason, S. (1991). Current Trends in Leisure: The Leisure Industry and the Single European Market. *Leisure Studies*, 10, 1, 1–6.

Martin, H.W., Hoppe, S.K., Larson, C.L. and Leon, R.L. (1987). Texas Snowbirds. *Research on Aging*, 9, 1, 134–147.

Mason, D.S., Duquette, G.H. and Scherer, J. (2005). Heritage, Sport Tourism and Canadian Junior Hockey: Nostalgia for Social Experience or Sport Place? *Journal of Sport Tourism*, 10, 4, 253–271.

Mason, P. (2002). The 'Big OE': New Zealanders Overseas Experiences in Britain. In *Tourism and Migration: New Relationships between Production and Consumption*, (C.M. Hall and A.M. Williams ed.) pp. 87–101. Dordrecht: Kluwer.

Mason, T. (1994). The Bogota Affair. In The Global Sports Arena: Athletic Talent Migration in an Interdependent World, (J. Maguire and J. Bale ed.) pp.39–48, London: Frank Cass & Co. Ltd.

May, J.V. (1989). Tourist Health-Taking Action. Tourism Management, December, 341–347.

McCabe, S. and Stokoe, E.H. (2004). Place and Identity in Tourists' Accounts. *Annals of Tourism Research*, 31, 3, 601–622.

McCannell, D. (1973). Staged Authenticity - Arrangement of Social Space in Tourist Settings. *American Journal of Sociology*, 79, 3, 589–603.

McCannell, D. (1976). The Tourist: New Theory of the Leisure Class. New York: Schoken.

McConnell, R. and Edwards, M. (2000). Sport and Identity in New Zealand. In Sport and Society in New Zealand, (C. Collins ed.) pp.115–129, Palmerston North: Dunmore Press.

McCutcheon, J.P. (2002). Free Movement in European Sport. *European Sports Management Quarterly*, 2, 4, 308–320.

McDowell, L.M. (1997). A Tale of Two Cities: Embedded Organisations and Embodied Workers. In Geographies of Economies, (R. Lee and J. Wills ed.) pp.118–129, London: Arnold.

McGuirk, P.M. and Rowe, D. (2001). 'Defining Moments' and Refining Myths in the Making of Place Identity: The Newcastle Knights and the Australian Rugby League Grand Final. *Australian Geographical Studies*, 39, 1, 52–66.

McHugh, K.E. (1990). Seasonal Migration as a Substitute for, or Precursor to, Permanent Migration. *Research on Aging*, 12, 2, 229–245.

McHugh, K.E. (2000). Inside, Outside, Upside Down, Backward, Forward, Round and Round: A Case for Ethnographic Studies in Migration. *Progress in Human Geography*, 24, 1, 71–89.

McHugh, K.E., Hogan, T.D. and Happel, S.K. (1995). Multiple Residence and Cyclical Migration: A Life Course Perspective. *Professional Geographer*, 47, 3, 251–267.

McHugh, K.E. and Mings, R.C. (1996). The Circle of Migration: Attachment to Place in Aging. *Annals of the Association of American Geographers*, 86, 3, 530–550.

McIntosh, A., Hinch, T.D. and Ingram, T. (2002). Cultural Identity and Tourism. *International Journal of Arts Management*, 4, 2, 39–49.

McKay, J. and Kirk, D. (1992). Ronald McDonald Meets Baron De Coubertin: Prime Time Sport and Commodification. Sport and the Media: The ACHPER National Journal, 136, Winter, 10–13.

McKercher, B. and Lew, A. (2003). Distance Decay and the Impact of Effective Tourism Exclusion Zones on International Travel Flows. *Journal of Travel Research*, 42, 2, 159–165.

McLean, F. and Cooke, S. (2003). Constructing the Identity of a Nation: The Tourist Gaze at the Museum of Scotland. Tourism,. *Culture & Communication*, 4, 3, 153–162.

McMurran, A. (2008). Highlanders Will Be Dangerous, Lions Coach Says. Otago Daily Times, pp. 19.

McPherson, B.D., Curtis, J.E. and Loy, J.W. (1989). The Social Significance of Sport: An Introduction to the Sociology of Sport. Champaign: Human Kinetics Books.

Melnick, M.J. and Jackson, S.J. (2002). Globalization American-Style and Reference Idol Selection: The Importance of Athlete Celebrity Others among New Zealand Youth. *International Review for the Sociology of Sport*, 37, 3–4. 429–448.

Miller, F. and Redhead, S. (1994). Do Markets Make Footballers Free? In The Global Sports Arena: Athletic Talent Migration in an Interdependent World, (J. Maguire and J. Bale ed.) pp.141–152, London: Frank Cass & Co. Ltd.

Miller, T., Lawerence, G.A., Mckay, J. and Rowe, D. (2001). Globalization and Sport: Playing the World. London: Sage Publications Ltd.

Milne, S. and Ateljevic, I. (2004). Tourism Economic Development and the Global-Local Nexus. In *Tourism: Critical Concepts in the Social Sciences*, (S. Williams ed.) pp. 81–103. New York: Routledge.

Mings, R. (1997). Tracking 'Snowbirds' in Australia: Winter Sun Seekers in Far North Queensland. *Australian Geographical Studies*, 35, 2, 168–182.

Monbiot, G. (2007). Heat: How Can We Stop the Planet Burning? London: Penguin Books.

Moorhouse, H.F. (1994). Blue Bonnets over the Border: Scotland and the Migration of Footballers. In *The Global Sports Arena: Athletic Talent Migration in an Interdependent World*, (J. Maguire and J. Bale ed.) pp. 78–98. London: Frank Cass & Co. Ltd.

Morgan, M. (2006). Making Space for Experiences. *Journal of Retail and Leisure Property*, 5, 4, 305–313.

Morgan, M. (2007). 'We're Not the Barmy Army!': Reflections on the Sport Tourist Experience. *International Journal of Tourism Research*, 9, 5, 361–372.

Morley, D. and Robins, K. (1995). Spaces of Identity: Global Media, Electronic Landscapes and Cultural Boundaries. London: Routledge.

Mourie, G. and Palenski, R. (1982). Graham Mourie: Captain. Auckland: Moa Beckett.

Mowforth, M. (2002). Tourism and Sustainability. London: Routledge.

Mowforth, M. and Munt, I. (1998). Tourism and Sustainability: New Tourism in the Third World. London: Routledge.

Mules, T. and Faulkner, B. (1996). An Economic Perspective on Special Events. *Tourism Economics*, 2, 14, 314–329.

Müller, D.K. (2005). Second Home Tourism in the Swedish Mountain Range. In Nature-Based Tourism in Peripheral Areas: Development or Disaster?, (C.M. Hall and S.W. Boyd ed.) pp.133–148, Clevedon: Channel View Publications.

Müller, D.K. (2006). Amenity Migration and Tourism Development in the Tärna Mountains, Sweden. In Amenity Migrants: Seeking and Sustaining Mountains and Their Cultures, (L.A.G. Moss ed.) pp.245–248, Wallingford: CAB International.

Müller, D.K. (2007). Second Homes in the Nordic Countries: Between Common Heritage and Exclusive Commodity: Introduction. *Scandinavian Journal of Hospitality and Tourism*, 7, 3, 193–201.

Munasinghe, L., O'flaherty, B. and Danninger, S. (2001). Globalization and the Rate of Technological Progress: What Track and Field Records Show. *Journal of Political Economy*, 109, 5, 1132–1149.

Murphy, P.E. (1985). Tourism: A Community Approach. New York: Methuen.

Murray, D. and Dixon, L. (2000). Investigating the Growth of 'Instant' Sports: Practical Implications for Community Leisure Service Providers. *The ACHPER Healthy Lifestyles Journal*, 47, 3–4. 27–31.

Musa, G., Hall, C.M. and Higham, J.E.S. (2004). Tourism and Health: The Case of Sagamartha National Park (SNP). *Journal of Sustainable Tourism*, 12, 4, 306–331.

Nauright, J. (1996). "A Besieged Tribe"?: Nostalgia, White Cultural Identity and the Role of Rugby in a Changing South Africa. International Review for the Sociology of Sport, 31, 1, 69–85

Nauright, J. (1997). Sport, Culture and Identities in South Africa. London: Leicester University Press.

Newell, K. (2003). You Can Get Here from There. *Coach and Athletic Director*, 73, 5, 34–38.

Nogawa, H., Yamaguchi, Y. and Hagi, Y. (1996). An Empirical Research Study on Japanese Sport Tourism in Sport-for-All Events. *Journal of Travel Research*, 35, 2, 46–54.

O'Brien, D. (2006). Event Business Leveraging: The Sydney 2000 Olympic Games. *Annals of Tourism Research*, 33, 1, 240–261.

Obsequio-Go, M.E. and Duval, D. (2003). Return Visits among Filipino Migrants in Dunedin, New Zealand. *Tourism Review International*, 7, 51–55.

O'Gorman, K. and Thompson, K. (2007). Tourism and Culture in Mongolia: The Case of the Ulaanbaatar Naadam. In Tourism and Indigenous Peoples: Issues and Implications, (R. Butler and T.D. Hinch ed.) pp.161-175, London: Elsevier Butterworth Heinemann.

Olds, K. (1998). Urban Mega-Events, Evictions and Housing Rights: The Canadian Case. *Current Issues in Tourism*, 1, 1, 2–46.

Olin, K. and Penttila, M. (1994). Professional Sports Migration to Finland During the 1980's. In *The Global Sports Arena: Athletic Talent Migration in an Interdependent World*, (J. Maguire and J. Bale ed.) pp. 126–140. London: Frank Cass & Co. Ltd.

Ormrod, J. (2005). Endless Summer (1964): Consuming Waves and Surfing the Frontier. *Film & History*, 35, 1, 39–51.

Osella, F. and Gardner, K. eds. (2004). Migration, Modernity and Social Transformation in South Asia. New Delhi: Sage Publications.

Otago Daily Times. (2005). French Season Too Long: Laporte. Otago Daily Times, July 2–3, pp. 43.

Page, S.J. and Hall, C.M. (2003). Managing Urban Tourism. Harlow: Pearson Education Ltd.

Palmer, C. (1999). Tourism and the Symbols of Identity. *Tourism Management*, 20, 3, 313–321.

Parrish, R. and Mcardle, D. (2004). Beyond Bosman: The European Union's Influence Upon Professional Athletes' Freedom of Movement. *Sport in Society*, 7, 3, 403–419.

Patterson, M.E. and Williams, D.R. (2005). Maintaining Research Traditions on Place: Diversity of Thought and Scientific Progress. *Journal of Environmental Psychology*, 25, 4, 361–380.

Pearce, D.G. (1989). Tourism Development. Harlow: Longman Scientific and Technical.

Pearson, D. (2000). The Ties That Unwind: Civic and Ethnic Imaginings in New Zealand. *Nations and Nationalism*, 6, 1, 91–110.

Perdue, R. (2004). Stakeholder Analysis in Colorado Ski Resort Communities. *Tourism Analysis*, 8, 233–236.

Petty, R. (1989). Health Limits to Tourism Development. Tourism Management. *September*, 209–212.

Phillips, J. (1998). The Hard Man: Rugby and the Formation of Male Identity in New Zealand. In Making Men: Rugby and Masculine Identity, (J. Nauright and T. Chandler ed.) pp.70–90, London: Frank Cass & Co. Ltd.

Piaget, J. (1965). The Moral Judgment of the Child. New York: The Free Press.

Pizam, A. and Mansfield, Y. (1996). Tourism, Crime and International Security. London: John Wiley and Sons.

Porteous, B. (2000). Sports Development: Glasgow. *Leisure Manager*, 18, 11, 18–21.

Preuss, H. (2005). The Economic Impact of Visitors at Major Multi-Sport Events. *European Sport Management Quarterly*, 5, 3, 281–302.

Priestley, G.K. (1995). Sports Tourism: The Case of Golf. In Tourism and Spatial Transformations: Implications for Policy Planning, (G.J. Ashworth and A.G.J. Dietvorst ed.) pp. 205–223, Wallingford: CAB International.

Proshansky, H.M., Favian, A.K. and Kaminoff, R. (1993). Place-Identity: Physical World Socialization of the Self. *Journal of Environmental Psychology*, 3, 1, 57–83.

Raisborough, J. (1999). Research Note: The Concept of Serious Leisure and Women's Experiences of the Sea Cadet Corps. *Leisure Studies*, 18, 1, 67–71.

Ramshaw, G. and Hinch, T.D. (2006). Place Identity and Sport Tourism: The Case of the Heritage Classic Ice Hockey Event. *Current Issues in Tourism*, 9, 4–5. 399–418.

Ratinckx, L. and Crabb, J. (nd). The Healthy Stadia Toolkit: Developing Sustainable Partnerships for Local Health Improvement Strategies. Healthy Settings Development Unit, University of Central Lancashire, Preston:

Reeves, M.R. (2000). Title. Loughborough University: Unpublished PhD thesis.

Reid, D.G. (1989). Changing Patterns of Work and Leisure and the Health Community. *Plan Canada*, 29, 4, 45–50.

Reid, D.G. (2003). Tourism, Globalization and Development: Responsible Tourism Planning. London: Pluto Press.

Reisinger, Y. and Steiner, C.J. (2006). Reconceptualizing Object Authenticity. *Annals of Tourism Research*, 33, 1, 65–86.

Relph, E.C. (1976). Place and Placelessness. London: Pion Limited.

Richards, G. (1996). Skilled Consumption and UK Ski Holidays. *Tourism Management*, 17, 1, 25–34.

Richmond, P. (1995). Ballpark: Camden Yards and the Building of an American Dream. New York: Fireside.

Ringer, G. (1998). Destinations: Cultural Landscapes of Tourism. London: Routledge.

Riordan, J. (1993). Sport in Capitalist and Socialist Countries: A Western Perspective. In The Sports Process: A Comparative and Developmental Approach, (E.G. Dunning, J. Maguire and R.E. Pearton ed.) pp.245–264, Champaign, IL, USA: Human Kinetics Publishers.

Ritchie, J.B.R. (1984). Assessing the Impact of Hallmark Events: Conceptual and Research Issues. *Journal of Travel Research*, 13, 1, 2–11.

Ritzer, G. and Stillman, T. (2001). The Postmodern Ballpark as a Leisure Setting: Enchantment and Simulated De-Mcdonaldization. *Leisure Sciences*, 23, 2, 99–113.

Rivenburgh, N.K. (2002). The Olympic Games: Twenty-First Century Challenges as a Global Media Event. Culture, Sport,. *Society*, 5, 3, 31–50.

Roberts, J. (2004). Going Back to Their Roots. Panstadia. *November*, 52–55,.

Robertson, K.A. (1999). Can Small-City Downtowns Remain Viable? A National Study of Development Issues Strategies. *Journal of the American Planning Association*, 65, 3, 270–283.

Robinson, M. and Smith, M. (2006). Politics, Power and Play: The Shifting Contexts of Cultural Tourism. In Cultural Tourism in a Changing World, (M. Smith and M. Robinson ed.) pp. 1–17, Clevedon: Channel View Publications.

Roche, M. (1992). Mega-Events and Micro-Modernization: On the Sociology of the New Urban Tourism. *The British Journal of Sociology*, 43, 4, 563–600.

Roche, M. (1994). Mega-Events and Urban Policy. *Annals of Tourism Research*, 21, 1, 1–19.

Roche, M. (2000). Mega-Events and Modernity: Olympics and Expos in the Growth of Global Culture. London: Routledge.

Roderick, M. (2006). A Very Precarious Profession: Uncertainty in the Working Lives of Professional Footballers. *Work Employment and Society*, 20, 2, 245–265.

Rosensweig, D. (2005). Retro Ball Parks: Instant History, Baseball, and the New American City. Knoxville: The University of Tennessee Press.

Rosentraub, M.S. (1997). Major League Losers: The Real Cost of Sports and Who's Paying for It. New York: Basic Books.

Rossingh, C. and Bras, K. (2003). Garifuna Settlement Day: Tourism Attraction, National Celebration Day, or Manifestation of Ethnic Identity. Tourism. *Culture & Communication*, 4, 3, 163–172.

Rudkin, B. and Hall, C.M. (1996). Off the Beaten Track. In Health and the International Tourist, (S. Clift and S.J. Page ed.) pp. 89–107, London: Routledge.

Rudolf K. Haerle, J. (1975). Education, Athletic Scholarships, and the Occupational Career of the Professional Athlete. Sociology of Work and Occupations, 2, 4, 373–403.

Ryan, C. (1996). Linkages between Holiday Travel Risk and Insurance Claims: Evidence from New Zealand. *Tourism Management*, 17, 8, 593–601.

Ryan, C. (1997). Similar Motivations - Diverse Behaviours. In The Tourist Experience: A New Introduction, (C. Ryan ed.) pp.27–47, London: Cassell.

Ryan, C. and Lockyer, T. (2002). Masters Games: The Nature of Competitors' Involvement and Requirements. *Event Management*, 7, 4, 259–271.

Ryan, G. ed. (2005). Tackling Rugby Myths: Rugby and New Zealand Society 1854–2004. Dunedin: University of Otago Press.

Sack, R. (1988). The Consumer's World: Place as Context. *Annals of the Association of American Geographers*, 78, 4, 642–664.

Salt, J. (1992). The Future of International Labour Migration. *International Migration Review*, 26, 4, 1077–1102.

Sanderson, A.R. and Siegfried, J.J. (2006). Simon Rottenberg and Baseball, Then and Now: A Fiftieth Anniversary Retrospective. *Journal of Political Economy*, 114, 3, 594–605.

Santos, C.A. and Buzinde, C. (2007). Politics of Identity and Space: Representational Dynamics. *Journal of Travel Research*, 45, 3, 322–332.

Sarbin, T.R. (1983). Place Identity as a Component of Self: An Addendum. *Journal of Environmental Psychology*, 3, 4, 337–342.

Schafer, A. and Victor, D. (2000). The Future Mobility of the World Population. *Transportation Research A*, 34, 3, 171–205.

Scherer, J., Falcous, M. and Jackson, S. (2008). The Media Sports Cultural Complex: Local-Global Disjuncture in New Zealand/Aotearoa. *Journal of Sport & Social Issues*, 32, 1, 48–71.

Schwartz, D.R. (1991). Tourists under Fire - Tourists in the Tibetan Uprising. *Annals of Tourism Research*, 18, 588–604.

Sharpley, R. and Craven, B. (2001). The 2001 Foot and Mouth Crisis - Rural Economy and Tourism Policy Implications. *Current Issues in Tourism*, 4, 6, 527–537.

Shaw, G. and Agarwal, S. (2007). Introduction: The Development and Management of Coastal Resorts: A Global Perspective. In Managing Coastal Tourism Resorts: A Global Perspective, (S. Agarwal and G. Shaw ed.) pp.1–20, Clevedon: Channel View Publications.

Shilbury, D., Quick, S. and Westerbeek, S. (1999). Strategic Sport Marketing. Crows Nest: Allen and Unwin.

Short, J.R., Breitbach, C., Buckman, S. and Essex, J. (2000). From World Cities to Gateway Cities: Extending the Boundaries of Globalization Theory. *City*, 4, 3, 317–338.

Shrobe, H.W. (2005). Place, Identity and Futbol Club Barcelona: A Critical Geography of Sport, Doctor of Philosophy, Department of Geography and the Graduate School, University of Oregon:

Shroder, J.F. (2008). In: Mount Everest, In: *Microsoft Encarta Online Encyclopedia*, 2008, http://encarta.msn.com.

Shumaker, S.A. and Taylor, R.B. (1983). Toward a Clarification of People-Place Relationships. In Environmental Psychology: Direction and Perspectives, (N.R. Feimer and E.S. Geller ed.) pp.219–251, New York: Praeger Publishers.

Silk, M.L. (2002). 'Bangsa Malaysia': Global Sport, the City and the Mediated Refurbishment of Local Identities. Media. *Culture & Society*, 24, 6, 775–794.

Silk, M.L. (2004). A Tale of Two Cities: The Social Production of Sterile Sporting Space. *Journal of Sport & Social Issues*, 28, 4, 349–378.

Silk, M.L. and Andrews, D.L. (2001). Beyond a Boundary? Sport, Transnational Advertising, and the Reimaging of National Culture. *Journal of Sport & Social Issues*, 25, 2, 180–201.

Silk, M.L. and Jackson, S.J. (2000). Globalisation and Sport in New Zealand. In Sport in New Zealand Society, (C. Collins ed.) pp.99–113, Palmerston North: Dunmore Press.

Smaldone, D., Harris, C.C., Sanyal, N. and Lind, D. (2005). Place Attachment and Management of Critical Park Issues in Grand Teton National Park. *Journal of Park and Recreation Administration*, 23, 1, 90–114.

Smart, B. (2007). Not Playing Around: Global Capital, Modern Sport and Consumer Culture. In Globalization and Sport, (R. Giulianotti and R. Robertson ed.) pp.6–27, Oxford: Blackwell Publishing.

Smith, A. (2000). The Impact of Professionalism on Rugby Union, 1995–1999. In *Amateurs and Professionals in Post-War British Sport*, (A. Smith and D. Porter ed.) pp. 146–188. London: Frank Cass Publishers.

Smith, D.R., Ciacciarelli, A., Serzan, J. and Lambert, D. (2000). Travel and the Home Advantage in Professional Sports. *Sociology of Sport Journal*, 17, 4, 364–385.

Smith, V. ed. (1989). Hosts and Guests: The Anthropology of Tourism. Philadelphia: University of Pennsylvania Press.

Sofield, T.H.B. and Sivan, A. (2003). From Cultural Festival to International Sport - the Hong Kong Dragon Boat Races. *Journal of Sport Tourism*, 8, 1, 9–20.

Solomon, M. (2007). A Long Wait for Justice. In *Resistance: An Indigenous Response to Neoliberalism*, (M. Bargh ed.) pp. 75–84. Wellington: Huia Publishers.

Sparvero, E. and Chalip, L. (2007). Professional Teams as Leverageable Assets: Strategic Creation of Community Value. *Sport Management Review*, 10, 1, 1–30.

Standeven, J. and De Knop, P. (1999). Sport Tourism. Champaign: Human Kinetics.

Stebbins, R.A. (1982). Serious Leisure: A Conceptual Statement. *The Pacific Sociological Review*, 25, 2, 251–272.

Stebbins, R.A. (1992). Amateurs, Professionals and Serious Leisure. Montreal: McGill-Queens University.

Stebbins, R.A. (1996a). Cultural Tourism as Serious Leisure. *Annals of Tourism Research*, 23, 4, 948–950.

Stebbins, R.A. (1996b). Volunteering: A Serious Leisure Perspective. *Nonprofit and Voluntary Sector Quarterly*, 25, 2, 211–224.

Stebbins, R.A. (1997). Identity and Cultural Tourism. *Annals of Tourism Research*, 24, 2, 450–452.

Stebbins, R.A. (2005). Challenging Mountain Nature: Risk, Motive, and Lifestyle in Three Hobbyist Sports. Calgary: Detselig.

Stebbins, R.A. (2007). Serious Leisure. London: Transaction Publishers.

Stefani, R.T. and Clarke, S.R. (1992). Predictions and Home Advantage for Australian Rules Football. *Journal of Applied Statistics*, 19, 251–261.

Steinbeck, J. (1963). Travels with Charley. In *Search of America*. New York: Bantam Books.

Stevens, T. (2005). Sport and Urban Tourism Destinations: The Evolving Sport, Tourism and Leisure Functions in the Modern Stadium. In Sport Tourism Destinations: Issues, Opportunities and Analysis, (J.E.S. Higham ed.) pp.205–220, Oxford: Elsevier.

Stewart, B. and Smith, A. (2000). Australian Sport in a Postmodern Age. *International Journal of the History of Sport*, 13, 2–3. 278–304.

Stewart, J.J. (1987). The Commodification of Sport. *International Review for the Sociology of Sport*, 22, 3, 171–190.

Stiegenhaler, K.L. and Gonzalez, G.L. (1997). Youth Sports as Serious Leisure: A Critique. *Journal of Sport & Social Issues*, 21, 3, 298–314.

Stokols, D. and Shumaker, S.A. (1981) People in Places: A Transnational View of Settings. In *Cognition, Social Behavior, and the Environment*, (J.H. Harvey ed.) pp. 441–488. New York: Lawrence Erlbaum Associates Inc.

Stokowski, P.A. (2002). Languages of Place and Discourses of Power: Constructing New Senses of Place. *Journal of Leisure Research*, 34, 3, 368–382.

Stokvis, R. (2000). Globalization, Commercialization and Individualization: Conflicts and Changes in Elite Athletics. Culture, Sport. *Society*, 3, 1, 22–34.

Szivas, E., Riley, M. and Airey, D. (2003). Labour Mobility into Tourism: Attraction and Satisfaction. *Annals of Tourism Research*, 30, 1, 64–76.

Szymanski, S. (2000). A Market Test for Discrimination in the English Professional Soccer Leagues. *Journal of Political Economy*, 108, 3, 590–603.

Szymanski, S. and Smith, R. (1997). The English Football Industry: Profits, Performance and Industrial Structure. *International Review of Applied Economics*, 11, 1, 135–154.

Takahashi, H. (2006). Voluntary Associations Formed through Sport Spectatorship: A Case Study of Professional Baseball Fan Clubs. In *Japan, Sport and Society: Tradition and Change in a Globalising World*, (J. Maguire and M. Nakayama ed.) pp. 98–112. New York: Routledge.

Talaga, J. (1971). An Attempt to Define the Social Position of Football Instructors and Coaches in Poland. *International Review for the Sociology of Sport*, 6, 125–152.

Taylor, J.P. (2001). Authenticity and Sincerity in Tourism. *Annals of Tourism Research*, 28, 1, 7–26.

Taylor Report, Inquiry by the Rt Hon Lord Justice Taylor: Final Report. Presented to Parliament by the Secretary of State for the Home Department, 1990. London: HMSO.

Theberge, N. (1980). The System of Rewards in Women's Professional Golf. *International Review for the Sociology of Sport*, 15, 2, 27–41.

Thomson, R. (2000). Physical Activity through Sport and Leisure: Traditional Versus Non-Competitive Activities. *Journal of Physical Education New Zealand*, 33, 1, 34–39.

Timothy, D.J. and Boyd, S.W. (2003). Heritage Tourism. Harlow: Prentice Hall.

Trauer, B. and Ryan, C. (2005). Destination Image, Romance and Place Experience - an Application of Intimacy Theory in Tourism. *Tourism Management*, 26, 4, 481–491.

Travel, S. (2007). FIVB World Tour Beach Volleyball Championships http://www.stavangertravel.com/event/stavanger-beach-volleyball.cfm (Retrieved July 4 2007).

Tress, G. (2007). Seasonality of Second-Home Use in Denmark. In Seasonal Landscapes, (H. Plang, H. Soovali and A. Prinstsman ed.) pp.151–179, Dordrecht: Springer.

Tuan, Y. (1974). Topophilia: A Study of Environmental Perception Attitudes and Values. Englewood Cliffs: Prentice Hall.

Tuan, Y. (1975). Place: An Experiential Perspective. *Geographical Review*, 65, 2, 151–165.

Tuan, Y. (1977). Space and Place: The Perspective of Experience. Minneapolis: University of Minnesota Press.

Tuan, Y. (1991). Language and the Making of Place: A Narrative-Descriptive Approach. *Annals of the Association of American Geographers*, 81, 4, 684–696.

Tuck, J. (2003). Making Sense of Emerald Commotion: Rugby Union, National Identity and Ireland. *Identities: Global Studies in Culture and Power*, 10, 4, 495–515.

Turner, V. (1974). Dramas. Fields and Metaphors. New York: Cornell University Press.

Twigger-Ross, C.L. and Uzzell, D.L. (1996). Place and Identity Processes. *Journal of Environmental Psychology*, 16, 3, 205–220.

Unruh, D. (1983). Invisible Lives: Social Worlds of the Aged. Beverly Hills: Sage Publications.

Uriely, N. (2001). 'Travelling Workers' and 'Working Tourists': Variations across the Interaction between Work and Tourism. *International Journal of Tourism Research*, 3, 1, 1–8.

Uriely, N. and Reichel, A. (2000). Working Tourists and Their Attitudes to Hosts. *Annals of Tourism Research*, 27, 2, 276–283.

Urry, J. (1990). The Tourist Gaze: Leisure and Travel in the Contemporary Society. London: Sage Publications.

Urry, J. (1995). Consuming Places. London: Routledge.

Urry, J. (2002). The Tourist Gaze: Leisure and Travel in Contemporary Societies. London: Sage Publications.

Van Ham, P. (2001). The Rise of the Brand State: The Postmodern Politics of Image and Reputation. *Foreign Affairs*, 80, 5, 2.

Vaske, J.J. and Kobrin, K.C. (2001). Place Attachment and Environmentally Responsible Behaviour. *The Journal of Environmental Education*, 32, 4, 16–21.

Vellas, F. and Becherel (1995). International Tourism Policies and Public Health. New York: St Martin's Press.

Vikander, N.O. and Solbakken, T. (n.d.). Edged by the Russians: Should Thwarted Norwegian Skiers Look to Psychology. IT Training, 7, 6.

Viken, A. (2006). Tourism and Sami Identity - an Analysis of the Tourism-Identity Nexus in a Sami Community. *Scandinavian Journal of Hospitality and Tourism*, 6, 1, 7–24.

Wang, N. (1999). Rethinking Authenticity in Tourism Experiences. *Annals of Tourism Research*, 26, 2, 349–370.

Wang, N. (2000). Tourism and Modernity: A Sociological Analysis. Amsterdam: Pergamon.

Warzecha, C.A. and Lime, D.W. (2001). Place Attachment in Canyonlands National Park: Visitors' Assessment of Setting Attributes on the Colorado and Green Rivers. *Journal of Park and Recreation Administration*, 19, 1, 59–78.

Washington, R.E. and Karen, D. (2001). Sport and Society. *Annual Review of Sociology*, 27, 187–212.

Waterhouse, J., Reilly, T. and Edwards, B. (2004). The Stress of Travel. *Journal of Sports Sciences*, 22, 946–966.

Webster, D. (1973). Scottish Highland Games. Edinburgh: Macdonald Printers (Edinburgh) Limited.

Weed, M.E. (2002). Football Hooligans as Undesirable Sports Tourists: Some Meta-Analytical Speculations. In Sport Tourism: Principles and Practice, (S. Gammon and J. Kurtzman ed.) pp.35–52, Eastbourne: Leisure Studies Association.

Weed, M.E. (2005). Sports Tourism Theory and Method - Concepts, Issues and Epistemologies. *Sport Management Quarterly*, 5, 3, 229–242.

Weed, M.E. (2007). The Pub as a Virtual Football Fandom Venue: An Alternative to Being There. *Soccer and Society*, 8, 2, 399–414.

Weed, M.E. (2008). Olympic Tourism. Oxford: Elsevier.

Weed, M.E. and Bull, C.J. (1997). Influences on Sport Tourism Relations in Britain: The Effects of Government Policy. *Tourism Recreation Research*, 22, 2, 5–12.

Weed, M.E. and Bull, C.J. (2004). Sport Tourism: Participants. Policy and Providers. Oxford: Butterworth Heinemann.

Weston, R. (1996). Have Fun in the Sun: Protect Yourself from Skin Damage. In Health and the International Tourist, (S. Clift and S.J. Page ed.) pp. 235–259, London: Routledge.

Wheaton, B. (2000). "Just Do It": Consumption, Commitment and Identity in the Windsurfing Subculture. Sociology of Sport Journal, 17, 3, 254–274.

Wheaton, B. (2007). After Sport Culture: Rethinking Sport and Post-Subcultural Theory. *Journal of Sport & Social Issues*, 31, 3, 283–307.

Wheaton, B. and Beal, B. (2003). 'Keeping It Real': Subcultural Media and the Discourses of Authenticity in Alternative Sport. *International Review for the Sociology of Sport*, 38, 2, 155–176.

Whitson, D. and Macintosh, D. (1996). The Global Circus: International Sport, Tourism and the Marketing of Cities. *Journal of Sport & Social Issues*, 20, 3, 239–257.

Wieting, S.G. and Polumbaum, J. (2001). Epilogue: The Future of Exchange between Local Culture and Global Tourism Trends. In *Sport and Memory in North America*, (S.G. Wieting ed.) pp. 237–254. London: Frank Class & Co Ltd.

Wieting, S.G. and Polumbaum, J. (2001). Epilogue: The Future of Exchange between Local Culture and Global Trends. Culture, Sport,. *Society*, 4, 2, 237–254.

Wilcox, R. and Andrews, D. (2003). Sport in the City: Cultural, Economic and Political Portraits. In Sporting Dystopias: The Making and Meanings of Urban Sport Cultures, (R. Wilcox, D. Andrews, R. Pitter and R. Irwin ed.) pp.1–16, New York: SUNY Press.

Williams, A.M. (2006). Community Charged. Panstadia. *Autumn/Fall*, 88–93.

Williams, A.M. and Hall, C.M. (2000). Tourism and Migration: New Relationships between Production and Consumption. *Tourism Geographies*, 2, 1, 5–27.

Williams, A.M. and Hall, C.M. (2002). Tourism, Migrations, Circulation and Mobility: The Contingencies of Time and Place. In *Tourism and Migration: New Relationships between Production and Consumption*, (C.M. Hall and A.M. Williams ed.) pp. 1–60. , Dordrecht: Kluwer Academic Press.

Williams, A.M., King, R., Warnes, A. and Patterson, G. (2000). Tourism and International Retirement Migration: New Forms of an Old Relationship in Southern Europe. *Tourism Geographies*, 2, 1, 28–49.

Williams, A.M., King, R. and Warnes, T. (1997). A Place in the Sun: International Retirement Migration from Northern to Southern Europe. *European Urban and Regional Studies*, 4, 2, 115–134.

Williams, D.R. and Kalterborn, B.P. (1999). Leisure Places and Modernity: The Use and Meaning of Recreation Cottages in Norway and the USA. In Leisure/ Tourism Geographies, (D. Crouch ed.) pp.214–229, London: Routledge.

Williams, D.R., Patterson, M.E., Roggenbuck, J.W. and Watson, A.E. (1992). Beyond the Commodity Metaphor: Examining Emotional and Symbolic Attachment to Place. *Leisure Sciences*, 14, 1, 29–46.

Williams, G. (1994). The Road to Wigan Pier Revisited: The Migrations of Welsh Rugby Talent since 1918. In *The Global Sports Arena: Athletic Talent Migration in an Interdependent World*, (J. Maguire and J. Bale ed.) pp. 25–38. London: Frank Cass & Co. Ltd.

Wong, L.L. and Trumper, R. (2002). Global Celebrity Athletes and Nationalism: Futbol, Hockey and the Representation of Nation. *Journal of Sport and Social Issues*, 26, 2, 168–194.

Woodman, T. and Hardy, L. (2001). A Case Study of Organizational Stress in Elite Sport. *Journal of Applied Sport Psychology*, 13, 2, 207–238.

Wright, R., Higham, J.E.S. and Mitchell, R.D. (2007). Sport, Nostalgia and Tourism Planning: The Case of the 2005 British and Irish Lions Tour of New Zealand. In Sport, Tourism and Nostalgia, (S. Gammon and G. Ramshaw ed.) pp.123–140, London: Routledge.

Wyn, J. and Willis, E. (2001). International Labour and Education Markets for Youth: The Case of Young Australians at Whistler. *Western Research Network on Education and Training*.

Xing, X. and Chalip, L. (2006). Effects of Hosting a Sport Event on Destination Brand: A Test of Co-Branding and Match-up Models. *Sport Management Review*, 9, 49–78.

Yoder, D. (1997). A Model for Commodity Intensive Serious Leisure. *Journal of Leisure Research*, 29, 4, 407–429.

Young, M., Fricker, P., Maughan, R. and Macauley, D. (1998). The Travelling Athlete: Issues Relating to the Commonwealth Games, Malaysia, 1998. *British Journal of Sports Medicine*, 32, 77–81.

Zuefle, D.M. (2004). Differences in Tourist and Host Perceptions of Appalachia: Elasticity in Place Identity. *ERTR: Review of Tourism Research*, 2, 6, 115–120.

Index